Will to Freedom

Modern Jewish History
Henry L. Feingold, *Series Editor*

Other titles in Modern Jewish History

Bondage to the Dead: Poland and the Memory of the Holocaust
Michael C. Steinlauf

The Golden Tradition: Jewish Life and Thought in Eastern Europe
Lucy S. Dawidowicz

The Grandees: The Story of America's Sephardic Elite
Stephen Birmingham

Lest Memory Cease: Finding Meaning in the American Jewish Past
Henry L. Feingold

Our Crowd: The Great Jewish Families of New York
Stephen Birmingham

Torah and Constitution: Essays in American Jewish Thought
Milton R. Konvitz

Will to Freedom

A Perilous Journey
Through Fascism
and Communism

• • • • • •

Egon Balas

SYRACUSE UNIVERSITY PRESS

Library of Congress Cataloging-in-Publication Data

Balas, Egon.
Will to freedom : a perilous journey through fascism and communism/Egon Balas.—
1st ed.
p. cm — (Modern Jewish history)
Includes index.
ISBN 0-8156-0603-6 (alk. paper)
1. Balas, Egon. 2. Jews—Romania—Biography. 3. Jews—Hungary—Biography.
4. Holocaust, Jewish (1939–1945)—Hungary—Personal narratives. 5. Political
prisoners—Romania—Biography. 6. Romania—Biography. 7. Hungary—Biography.
I. Title. II. Series.
DS135.R73 B35 1999
947'004924'0092—dc21
[B]   99-037873

Manufactured in the United States of America

To Edith

Egon Balas is University Professor and Thomas Lord Professor of Operations Research at the Graduate School of Industrial Administration of Carnegie Mellon University. He has published more than 180 papers in technical journals, many with coauthors from around the world. In 1995, Balas was awarded the John von Neumann Theory Prize, the highest honor in his profession.

Contents

Illustrations

Preface

This book tells the story of my life before I came to America. It is an unusual story for the Western reader; much of it may seem to be fiction. But only to those who have not yet learned that life is more improbable than any fiction.

Ever since my family and I immigrated to the United States in the spring of 1967, friends would periodically urge me to write a book like this one. Whenever I would relate some episode of my earlier life, be it from the Hungarian communist underground during the war; or from my arrest, jailing, and escape during the nazi regime; or from my early postwar life as a Romanian diplomat in London; or from my years of solitary confinement in a Romanian Communist prison; somebody invariably would ask, "But why don't you write this down?" Bill Cooper, my colleague at Carnegie Mellon University at the time, was the first one to urge me to do it. Others followed him, and soon my wife, Edith, joined them.

For many years I resisted these calls. I felt that I had more important things to do; my research took precedence. I felt that as long as I was able to discover and prove new theorems, that is what I ought to do. But Edith would disagree; she would argue that the universal human experience embodied in my life before coming to the United States was more important to communicate than the new mathematical results I might still be able to find. Finally, last year I gave in: Here is the outcome.

xi

But what about my life in America? Is the story of the last thirty years not worth telling? Oh yes, it is. But it is a story of a very different nature.

Pittsburgh, Pennsylvania   Egon Balas
August 19, 1997

Acknowledgments

The first version of this book, substantially longer than the last one, was written between the fall of 1996 and the summer of 1997. Edith, my wife, played a major role in persuading me to embark upon this enterprise. Once I started, she became the main sounding board for my recollections; and, of course, she was my first reader. Her insightful comments had a strong impact on my work. My daughters, Anna Balas Waldron and Vera Koutsoyannis, were my next readers. Both of them, as well as my son-in-law, Sherwood (Woody) Waldron, helped improve my writing. A number of friends, colleagues and others interested in my story gave me useful feedback: Susan Mates, Judith Lave, Allan Meltzer, Rina and Julius Youngner, Gissa Weingartner, Karl Weber, and Eileen Kiley. Experts on Eastern European history, politics or economics, like István Deák, Robert Levy, and Michael Montias, as well as two anonymous readers, helped improve the accuracy of my account and gave me valuable comments. Additional editorial improvements came from Kenneth Neal and Carol Sowell. Barbara Carlson helped me with the indexing. Needless to say, I am solely responsible for the statements and views expressed in the book.

Introduction

This is the story of the first forty-four years of my life. As it unfolds, the reader may occasionally wonder, how could so many extraordinary things happen to a single individual? To this I offer three tentative answers. First, all or at least most of the things that happened to me also happened to others who were at the same time in the same place; what is unusual is the combination of events, the fact that all these things happened to the same person. Second, the life of an individual has always been more or less unpredictable, but especially so in times of war or revolution; and the times that I lived through encompassed both. Third, some of my experiences were undoubtedly triggered by my attitude toward life, by the fact that under most circumstances I preferred the role of active participant to that of bystander. If I were a believer in astrology, I would have to consider myself born under a very lucky constellation, not because of the things that have happened to me—which were often horrible—but for having somehow managed to overcome them.

Although my story could undoubtedly serve as a basis for a literary venture, I am not a novelist and this book is not a work of fiction. In writing it, I have done my best to tell the facts as they are, to describe the events as they happened, without embellishments or deviations from reality. Almost all the episodes of my story have witnesses who are still alive, and where it seemed useful I contacted them to corroborate my recollections. When I am not sure of some of the details, I say so.

But if literary accomplishment was not my motivation in writing this memoir, then what was it? To put it simply, to bear witness. Witness to what happened, to how it happened, in the hope of throwing some light onto why it happened. Although in a sense my story is unique, in another sense it is the combination of many typical stories. The thirty years of my life between the mid-thirties and the mid-sixties in a way epitomize the fate of a certain group of people. This group became politically active during World War II in order to resist the nazis, continued to be politically active after the war under the communists in an attempt to build a better society, then discovered to their horror that the system they were involved in was becoming ever more nightmarish. They collided with it and, with very few exceptions, were crushed, marginalized, destroyed as individuals. I count myself among the lucky exceptions whose life took a different turn.

While the story of those years is a compelling one, full of rapid and fascinating turns of events, the first pages of my memoir are devoted to my childhood and some background information that lacks the excitement of the later chapters. Some friends have suggested that the book should open on a note that grabs the reader by foreshadowing the fascinating events that follow, with the childhood brought in later, as a recollection. I thought about this. Indeed, my memoir could start in my cell at the Malmezon, the hellish interrogation center in Bucharest where I spent 745 days in solitary confinement in 1952–1954 and had plenty of opportunity to remember and rethink my entire life. It could then describe my childhood, along with later events, as a sequence of those exercises in recollection, interrupted occasionally by an aside about how I was coping with my loneliness and organizing my time in the cell. Or the story could start with my first arrest by the Hungarian gendarmerie in 1944, when for several months involving interrogation under torture, sentencing, jail, escape, and hiding, the sword of Damocles was constantly hanging over my head, thus providing ample reason for recalling my life—including my not-so-distant childhood.

I have seen some first-rate films and read some excellent books—even an autobiographical novel of outstanding quality—whose story unfolds in flashes of pictures from the past as remembered at a later date, interspersed with the events of that later date. I must say, though, that while I greatly enjoyed some of those movies and books, this was not because of the jumping back and forth in time, but in spite of it. While I fully recognize the artistic merits of such techniques and am aware of the fact that for many viewers or readers they provide a more attractive way to ingest a story, I feel that I should lay out the story of my life according to my own taste, not that of somebody else; and my preference is for telling things more or less in the order in which they happened.

And now let's get on with the story.

PART ONE ▪ June 1922–April 1945

CHAPTER 1

Childhood and Adolescence

I came into this world on June 7, 1922, the firstborn son of Ignác (Ignatius) Blatt and Boriska (Barbara) Blatt, née Hirsch. The Blatts were a middle-class family of Hungarian Jews in Transylvania, which became the north-western province of Romania in 1918. I spent the first two decades of my life in the provincial capital, called Cluj (pronounced Cloozh) in Romanian and Kolozsvár (pronounced Kolozhvaar) in Hungarian.

Transylvania is known in the West mainly through Bram Stoker's *Dracula.* Although the Carpathian Mountains surrounding the province on the north, east, and south provide a suitably formidable setting for a vampire story (they are often called the Eastern Alps), Stoker's novel has no basis in the local folklore—vampires are unknown there. The name Transylvania is of Latin origin and means "the region beyond the forests." At the beginning of the Christian era it formed part of Dacia, the kingdom on both sides of the Carpathians whose conquest by the Romans early in the second century is so vividly portrayed in the bas-reliefs of the Column of Trajan in Rome. In my hometown, whose Roman name was Napoca, there are extensive ruins of a fortress from those times. The Romans withdrew from Dacia after 170 years, never to return again. But they left behind a gift of enormous portent for the local population: Centuries later, the tribes of Vlachs living in the area were speaking a language of undeniably Latin origin, later called Romanian. Its grammar and vocabulary are as close, if not closer, to Latin as those of French, Italian, Spanish, and Portuguese.

Little is known about the history of my native region between the withdrawal of the Romans and the end of the first millennium, when the Hungarians arrived from central Asia and settled in the plains of the former Roman province of Pannonia, west of Transylvania. Their king, Stephen (made a Christian saint because he baptized his people), is the founder of what became known as Hungary, whose borders also included Transylvania. As Hungary became a major European power in the fifteenth century under King Matthias the Just, with Budapest an important center of world culture, Transylvania and its capital, Kolozsvár, flourished. Matthias himself was Transylvanian, born in my hometown, in a house that I remember well, as it had been turned into a small museum that I often visited. The Brothers from Kolozsvár, sculptors of the famous early fifteenth-century statue of Saint George in Prague (a copy of which is displayed in a public square in my hometown), were world-famous artists.

Between the time of King Matthias and the late nineteenth century, Transylvania had a stormy history. For about 170 years it was independent, after which it was reincorporated into Hungary as part of the Hapsburg Empire, although with a special status. During this time it underwent considerable development, including some industrialization toward the end of the nineteenth and the beginning of the twentieth centuries. It also flourished culturally. My hometown boasts some world-renowned scientists, among them the two famous mathematicians Bólyai (father and son). The son, János (John) Bólyai, created the first noneuclidean geometry around 1820. Around 1900 the mathematician Gyula (Julius) Farkas of Kolozsvár discovered a famous theorem of the alternative for systems of linear equations and inequalities, which after World War II helped lay the foundations of linear programming.

The Romania that emerged from World War I inherited Transylavania, Banat, and Bucovina from the Austro-Hungarian Empire, Bessarabia from Russia, and southern Dobrogea (Dobruja) from Bulgaria. Its population more than doubled, reaching over seventeen million. There were sizable minorities, among them close to two million ethnic Hungarians, nine hundred thousand Jews, about eight hundred thousand Germans, plus Gypsies, Greeks, Turks, Bulgarians, and Ukrainians.

At the time of my childhood Cluj-Kolozsvár was a city of about 110,000 people, roughly half of them Hungarian and about a third Romanian. Jews made up a little more than a tenth of the population, and there were several thousand Germans and Gypsies. It was a rather picturesque central European type of city, in the valley of the River Someş (Szamos in Hungarian), partly built on hills with impressive views. It had a beautiful thirteenth-century Catholic church, Saint Michael's, in the main square, a fairly new Greek Orthodox cathedral, several Protestant churches, and at least three synagogues. It had a good opera, a ballet, a symphony, and two theaters, Romanian and Hungarian. Its university was well known for its mathematics and science faculties, as well as for its medical school and clinics. There was a beautiful city park with a lake that had white swans, where people could row in the summer and skate in the winter. The city had a richly endowed, magnificent botanical garden. There was a large open-air swimming facility with two pools and a swimmable portion of the canal traversing the area. There were two soccer stadiums and three complexes of tennis courts. The city was also an industrial center, with the largest shoe factory in southeastern Europe, some smaller textile plants, a medium-sized steel mill, several metallurgical plants, and a tobacco factory. Public transportation was by bus—a car was a luxury that very few people could afford. You could also ride in horse-driven cabs.

Because my parents, grandparents, uncles, and aunts had all died before I became interested in my family history, my knowledge of them is limited to my early memories and what I could learn from conversations around the family table—when it still existed. My grandparents on my father's side—Mór (Morris) Blatt and Fanny née Farkas—lived in a village called Şintereag (Somkerék in Hungarian), not far from Bistriţa (Beszterce) where Bram Stoker placed Count Dracula's castle. My grandfather was the largest among several small landowners of the village, with an estate of about fifty acres, mostly farmland, but also including a vineyard and a grove of fruit trees. He had about fifteen to eighteen cattle and maybe a hundred sheep. He employed quite a few farmhands, a shepherd, and several servants around the house. He got up every morning from mid-March till mid-November at half past three or four o'clock and personally supervised all the work done on the farm. We used to spend every Passover at the estate, and I also spent a couple of summer vacations there. I remember my grandfather as a strong man, ferocious-looking when angry (which he often was), with his eyes gleaming. He was a hunter and liked to walk around with his gun. My grandmother was a very serious woman with an inquisitive mind, who would always question me about what I was learning at school. Unlike most of the urban Jews of Transylvania, my grandparents had not become assimilated into Hungarian culture. They spoke Yiddish to each other, to their children, and to the other Jews of the village, although they used Hungarian (before 1918) or Romanian (after 1918) in their contacts with the authorities, and both languages with the local peasants. They were Orthodox Jews, and religion was central to their way of life. While for my grandfather religion was a complex of rituals and rules whose deeper meaning did not seem to preoccupy him, my grandmother had an interest in and some knowledge of the Talmud (the ancient compendium of Jewish law) and was very demanding of herself and everybody else around her concerning religious observance. She was a very strong-willed lady. Family gossip had it that although my grandfather had the gun and would yell atrociously whenever he got angry, it was my grandmother whose will and wisdom would usually prevail in important matters.

My father had two younger brothers, David and Elek (Alec). The youngest, Elek, who was very close to him, was the only one who went to college and was said to be brilliant. He studied law, but judging from the substantial library that he left behind (he died of a blood infection in Budapest when I was six months old), he had broad interests in politics and philosophy. According to family lore, the leading Transylvanian lawyer of the time, Joseph Fischer, described Elek as somebody whom you should never have as an opponent, for his mind was as sharp as a razor blade.

My father did not go to college. As the oldest son, for a while he helped my grandfather manage the estate. But he soon started trading in cattle, which became a rather lucrative business during World War I, and made some money. After the war, in the new environment created by Transylvania's becoming part of Romania, he teamed up with his brother Elek, and together they went into banking. For a few years they were successful, and my father was considered a rich man when he married in 1919. But by the end of 1922, the year in which I was born, Uncle Elek was dead. Left on his own, my father ceased to be successful, and by the time I was six he was bankrupt. He lost everything. From then on, our family lived on a very tight budget.

My mother came from a very different background. Her parents— Vilmos (William) Hirsch and Regina née Grüner—lived in Dej (pronounced Dezh; in Hungarian, Dés), a town of some forty thousand

Boriska around 1919

inhabitants, where my grandfather was manager of the local branch of one of the banks. They were urban, assimilated Jews, who spoke Hungarian, never Yiddish; and their religious observance was more or less perfunctory. I remember my maternal grandfather as a well-dressed, articulate gentleman, pleasant to talk to, known as "good" to everybody. My grandmother was a well-groomed woman, still attractive in her sixties, a former doll-faced beauty.

My mother, Boriska, and her younger sister, Pirike, did not have a very happy childhood and adolescence. Their pretty, flirtatious older sister, Erzsike, and their younger brother, Pali, were my grandmother's favorites, and the two middle sisters felt a little like stepdaughters. After Erzsike had been married off, my father, Ignác, appeared on the scene and started courting Boriska. My mother was about twenty-two and Ignác was close to thirty-five. He soon earned Boriska's respect, but not her

Ignác with Egon around 1926

love. She had intellectual ambitions, loved music, played the piano, was an avid reader, enjoyed discussing contemporary novels, and would have liked to travel. Ignác shared none of these passions, but promised to make them accessible to her. Boriska would have liked to wait for a teenage sweetheart who was away in the army. But, apart from the fact that they had not seen each other for a very long time, this young man was without financial means and in no way ready to start a family. On the other hand, there was very strong pressure from my mother's parents to say yes to my father. After all, Ignác, in spite of his rural background and lack of urbane sophistication, was financially very well off, and in a position to offer a secure and prosperous home. Most importantly, he was obviously in love with Boriska: he declared that he did not

Egon in the summer of 1927

want any dowry, which was a tremendous relief for the family. Thus, like so many other girls of that time and place, Boriska accepted a marriage that on the face of it had many of the desirable ingredients, but lacked on her part the feeling of passionate love.

The young couple moved to Cluj, where my father bought a nice house on a quiet street in a pleasant quarter of the town, near the city park with the lake. This is the house where I, Egon Blatt, was born and raised. I have relatively few memories of my early childhood. When I was three and a half, my parents had a second son, Robert. I must have been less than enthusiastic about my brother's arrival, since one of my earliest recollections is of being locked in a dark basement laundry room as a punishment for not letting my mother breast-feed Bobby. But later we had much fun together, especially since he was very good at all kinds of ball games.

When I was seven my parents sent me to Elementary School number 7, one of the better Romanian public schools. They could have sent me to a Hungarian parochial school—Hungarian, after all, was my mother tongue—or to the Jewish elementary school, where the teachers spoke a very rudimentary, Hungarian-accented Romanian that they had learned as adults, and where my ignorance of that language would have been inconspicuous. However, my parents wanted me to learn the official language properly, and felt that I would get a better education at a public school. They were right: the public school was far better. To prepare me for the shock of suddenly entering a Romanian-speaking environment, my parents hired a young girl to teach me the language during the summer preceding the start of school. This helped some, but for the first three years I definitely did not excel in my studies. The teacher, Mrs. Wild, was a very strict elderly woman for whom discipline was paramount. Once, when she caught me talking to another student while she was lecturing, she left the rostrum, came to my bench, and hit me several times over my neck and shoulders. Not surprisingly, my report cards contained more criticism than praise. This was doubly unpleasant, both in itself and because I was also doing very poorly with the private teachers whom my father hired to instruct me in religion.

My parents were sharply divided in their religious beliefs: Whereas my father grew up in an Orthodox environment, my mother grew up in an assimilated family and had absorbed through her reading the values of the Enlightenment, the eighteenth-century European philosophy of rationalism. As a concession to my father she followed the ritual rules that he demanded, but did so reluctantly, as she did not believe in them. As far as I was concerned, my father wanted me to do a lot of praying— reading that consisted of Hebrew texts whose meaning I did not understand—to lay on prayer straps every morning, and to go to the synagogue on holidays and pray for hours alongside him, while the other children were playing outside in the courtyard. I disliked it from the first, then came to resent it as foolish and pointless. Finally I came to hate it. My mother tried to temper my opposition by arguing that, no matter what I believed, I should do these things for my father's sake, since they were so important to him, and he cared for me so much. I grudgingly went along, but hated it all deep in my guts. So the reports from my religion teachers—there were several, since none lasted more than a few weeks— were uniformly damning. The school reports now seemed to corroborate their opinion of me: I was either incapable or unwilling to learn anything or follow any discipline. My father was very upset, of course, and my mother needed all her diplomatic skills to save me from a thorough drubbing. Relief came in the fourth grade, my last at the elementary school. We got a new teacher, Mrs. Zimberiu, the headmaster's wife. She was an articulate and discerning woman whose interests went beyond mere discipline, and whose chief ambition was to teach us useful things. Suddenly, I was treated completely differently. I brought home excellent reports and my parents were told something to the effect that they had an unusually intelligent child. I finally earned some respect.

During my first few years at school our household underwent a radical change. As I mentioned earlier, my father declared bankruptcy and our family lost everything except for the house in which we were living. These were the early years of the worldwide Great Depression, and the times were adverse to any new business venture, let alone one without capital. My father could have looked for a job, and maybe he did, but he did not find one. Instead, my parents undertook a massive retrenchment. My brother and I had a nanny who was dismissed. The cook was dismissed. Our family ensconced itself in two rooms (the bedroom and the children's room) and a bathroom; we rented out the rest of the house by the month. This included several rooms on the main floor, as well as servants' quarters and utility rooms in the basement. Some of the tenants' children became my first playmates. A young carpenter who rented one of the rooms in the basement taught me how to ride a bicycle. A half-Hungarian, half-German shoemaker who rented another room in the basement later turned out to be a formidable chess player and would beat me at the game for many years, even after I had become one of the best players of my class.

These arrangements were meant to be temporary, but as the French say, *c'est le provisoire qui dure* (temporary arrangements last longest), and we continued to live with them for eleven years. The only change came when I finished junior high school at fifteen and was given a room to myself, which from then on was no longer rented. For all those years, the rent from those rooms was our family's main income. But it was not enough, and in the late thirties my father had to sell the house.

In the meantime, my father made several attempts at finding some gainful occupation. For a while he undertook to manage my grandfather's estate, living most of the time in Somkerék and coming home every other weekend. He apparently did a good job: he developed a dairy farm, purchased modern equipment for manufacturing butter and cheese, and sold the product—which was of excellent quality—throughout the region. But he did not always get along with my grandfather, and the old man preferred the company of his younger son, David, who was much easier to handle. Besides, David had six children and was living in deep poverty, doing only menial jobs. After about a year it was decided that David should take over managing the farm, since his need was greater. My father then turned to other ventures. For a while, he teamed up with a chemist and started a small margarine factory in our home, with the two of them as the only workers; but after a year or so the thing just fizzled away. Then my father teamed up with two brothers who, like himself, had some expertise in farm products and opened a wholesale egg business, buying eggs from the peasants and delivering them to retailers. I do not think this venture lasted much longer than a year either.

My mother managed to find a job as a cashier at the local steel plant when I was eight or nine. It was a hard, unpleasant job, and my mother worked very long hours. She was always exhausted when she got home, but our family badly needed the income. Her job lasted two or three years, and losing it was such a blow to her that she attempted suicide. This was incomprehensible to me at the time, but later I understood that losing the job was just a trigger for a desperate act that was rooted in a more general unhappiness. It happened one afternoon when my brother and I were invited to a birthday party. My mother looked us over before we left, then took me aside and asked me to promise that I would take care of Bobby and protect him. I did not understand what she meant. I said that we were going to visit friends; there would be no fighting there and Bobby would not need my protection. She said that she did not mean it only for that afternoon; that I was the bigger, stronger brother and that Bobby needed my protection. I was still confused, but naturally promised to protect Bobby. When we came home in the evening, there were strange comings and goings in the house. My mother was ill and could not be disturbed. From the expressions on the faces of those present I immediately sensed that something serious had occurred. I listened in on the many furtive conversations going on, and finally understood what had happened. My mother had taken a lethal dose of drugs and would certainly have died if her mother, who at that time lived in Cluj, had not come to visit unexpectedly. She called the ambulance and my mother was saved.

■ ■ ■

At age eleven, after finishing the four years of elementary school, I went to the Liceul Gheorghe Barițiu, one of the two large Romanian public boys' schools in town. The Romanian word *liceu* (the *l* at the end is the article) is the same as *lycée* in French; the Romanian educational system was modeled strictly after the French one. High school lasted eight years, with a "small baccalaureate" after the fourth year. Those who passed this exam had a choice between two tracks for the next four years: a science track and a humanities track. At the end of eight years there was a tough general exam much like the French baccalaureate, and bearing the same name. The Liceul Gheorghe Barițiu was by far the more demanding of the two public boy's schools in terms of admissions standards, graduation criteria, and discipline. The discipline did not attract me, but the high standards (albeit with an accompanying high failure rate) that the school was known for seemed to outweigh the disadvantages of the disciplinarian spirit. There was a third possibility, a semiprivate school affiliated with the university, where all the rich kids went. My parents offered to pay the tuition if I wished to go there, but I knew it would have been hard for them and I did not think the school was better, just less strict. At the school that I attended, we had to wear uniforms all the time (not only at school) and had a number sewn onto the sleeve of the uniform. Since that number remained the same throughout the seven years that I attended the school, I still remember it: I was student number 173, out of about nine hundred. There were three parallel classes of unequal quality. There was a tough written admissions test and I managed to get into one of the stronger classes. Entering the *liceu* brought major changes to my life. Along with the many new vistas opened by the varied material that I now became exposed to and had to absorb, there was also a sense of responsibility. I had to prove myself for the first time under challenging, often difficult, circumstances.

Although I was only eleven, my parents considered me mature for my age. I had demonstrated my maturity a year earlier, when I fell ill with scarlet fever—a contagious disease which at that time required six weeks of isolation—and was faced with the choice of being treated at home or in a hospital. My parents were ready to do everything necessary to have me treated at home. The family doctor sent them out of the room and told me that, though he was willing to treat me at home, this might be hard on my parents, since the tenants with children would probably leave out of fear of contagion, and their rent would be lost. Moreover, the hospital, a section of the university clinic, was a good one that specialized in this kind of disease. He said that in his opinion it would be better for both me and my parents if I went to the hospital and suggested that I tell my parents I wanted to go there. I took his suggestion, much to my father's relief, and the next day, in spite of my mother's reluctance, I was sent to the hospital for six weeks. I did not enjoy it, but I felt proud of having made a responsible decision like a grown-up.

Thanks to this precedent, I had my parents' full confidence when the school year opened, and I was given money to buy the books and tools that I needed. This required several trips to stationers and bookstores, and I was proud of being allowed to go alone when most of my classmates were with their parents. On one of these trips, I was walking down a quiet, out-of-the-way street when I noticed a small gathering and stopped to see what was going on. A group of about ten peasants had gathered round a man in his early twenties. In his left hand he held a small wooden board (probably the cover of a cigar box) on which there were two identical thimbles and a little gray ball, perhaps two-and-a-half or three millimeters in diameter. The young man was moving the thimbles with his right hand without lifting them from the board, but in such a way that he repeatedly covered and uncovered the little ball with one or the other of the thimbles. The people around him were following every move of his hand and trying to guess where the ball was at every moment. After a few minutes I understood that this was a kind of betting game: once the amount of the bet had been agreed upon (he set the minimum at twenty lei, the equivalent of the price of a schoolbook) and the money "deposited" onto the plate by both parties in full view of everyone, he would move the thimbles around for a while, covering the ball now with one, now with the other; then he would stop and the person who made the bet would try to guess which of the thimbles the ball was under. If the guess was correct, the person would win the bet; otherwise he would lose his money.

As I was following the movements of the thimbles, it seemed to me quite clear where the ball was at any moment; and I could not understand why there were no takers for what seemed to me an easy wager. That made me suspicious. I thought that maybe, once a bet was made, the man would perform some undetectable trick to ensure his winning.

On the other hand, I reasoned that he would have to allow somebody to win the *first* bet in order to encourage others to try their luck. I rapidly convinced myself that this was the case, and decided that it would not hurt me to benefit from the situation. I had in my pocket about sixty or seventy lei for books and stationery. I took out twenty lei and bravely put them onto the board, and the young man matched my bet. Then he started moving the thimbles around, just as slowly and transparently as before, so that I could easily follow the ball's location. This confirmed my suspicion that it was part of the man's game plan to let the first player win. Finally, he stopped and asked me where the ball was. Without the slightest hesitation, I pointed to the thimble where I knew it to be. Slowly he lifted the thimble—and there was nothing under it. "No," he said, "it is here," and there it was beneath the other thimble! I felt as though I had been bitten by a snake.

The surprise was so devastating that I lost my head. "Again!" I said, and pulled out another twenty lei, although one of the people watching us was pulling my sleeve as if to warn me not to continue. The man with the board reciprocated, repeated his previous performance, then stopped and asked for my guess. I pointed to one of the thimbles; he lifted it— and again there was nothing under it. At this point several things happened in quick succession. I suddenly lifted the other thimble, and the ball was not there either. Outraged at this deception, I started shouting, "Swindler! Thief! Give me back my money!" Some bystanders took my side and demanded he return my money. In a split second the man collected his things and the money, and started running toward the end of the street. I took off after him, followed by a few others, yelling all the time, "Thief! Help, thief! Stop him!" The street opened into a busy thoroughfare, and I probably would have lost track of the man there had my cries not attracted the owners of the stationery store on the corner, three young brothers who had come to know me the day before when I bought supplies from them. They stopped the man, beat him up, took back the money, and chased him away, warning him never to return to the quarter. I got back my money, but I never forgot the experience.

The subjects I liked most at school were mathematics, French, Latin, ancient history, and geography. I did not like botany and zoology, but in the third year we learned physics, and that subject at once became my favorite and remained so, along with mathematics, to the end of high school. The most time-consuming subject was Romanian, and it was taught in such a narrowly and offensively nationalistic manner that I loathed every minute of it. Remember, this was 1933–1935, the period when Hitler came to power in Germany, and fascism was on the rise in all of central and eastern Europe.

An episode that happened in my hometown in 1933 or 1934 typifies the atmosphere. A Jew called Mór (Maurice) Tischler, owner of several large forests, went to court to seek redress against his neighbors, a group of mountain people who had stolen vast amounts of wood from his property by brazenly cutting it down and hauling it away. The trial received considerable publicity, as the Iron Guard, the Romanian Nazi Party, had a large following among the mountaineers who perpetrated the theft, and the pro-Nazi press described the event as a trial of a rich, greedy Jew against the poor, exploited Romanian peasants. On the day Tischler was called to testify, an army captain who belonged to the Iron Guard shot and killed him in the courtroom. Part of the press was shocked by the murder, but another part celebrated the captain as a folk hero. The murderer walked away without ever being called to answer for his deed. There were some judicial proceedings, but somehow they never reached the stage of a trial.

The *liceu* and its teachers reflected the general political mood of the country, which was sharply divided. But it so happened that the teachers of Romanian language and literature always landed on the right of the political spectrum, being mostly driven by a narrow, aggressive nationalism and by prejudice against "foreigners"—that is, Hungarians and Jews.

I remember all of my high school teachers by name. The one whom I respected most was the French teacher, Voiculescu. He was a strong advocate of the ideology of the Enlightenment. With his help I came to read fragments of the works of Rousseau and Voltaire. I literally memorized the map of Paris; I knew where all the major monuments were and what they looked like. In the midst of the increasingly anti-Semitic, nationalistic political atmosphere, my breast swelled with enthusiasm at the ideas of *"égalité, liberté, fraternité."* I knew almost nothing about world politics, nor was I interested in the subject at that age, yet when I somehow learned in 1935 that a Jew (the socialist Léon Blum) had become the prime minister of France, I was overwhelmed with joy that such a thing was possible. The ideas of the French Enlightenment also helped crystallize my early opposition to religion. I vividly remember how deeply I was affected by Voltaire's saying, *"Si Dieu n'existait pas, il faudrait l'inventer"* ("If God did not exist, one would have to invent him"). Although I liked mathematics and later physics, the strongest character-forming influences came from my studies of French, Latin, and ancient history, in which I was introduced to classical literature and philosophy. I did well at the *liceu* from the beginning, finishing the first year (which corresponds to the American fifth grade) first in my class. I was second in my class the next year, and first again in the third year, with the best report card in the school. This was in 1935, and it was unusual for somebody with a name like Egon Blatt to be allowed to accomplish something like this. I gained the respect of my classmates, including those who did not like Jews, by achieving what I did without ever being a teacher's pet or breaking the students' solidarity in the many "disciplinary" standoffs between the class and some of the more rigid teachers.

In the summer of 1935, I started earning money by tutoring classmates and other students, an activity that I continued throughout my high school career. My first student was a classmate who received a failing grade in French and had to either retake the exam in the fall or repeat the year. I tutored him throughout the summer and in the fall he passed his exam easily. I was less successful with my next student, another classmate, Otto, whom I tutored for about three years in all subjects. Although he was neither bright nor hard-working, and in addition he was Jewish, nevertheless Otto and I somehow managed to get him a low pass in every subject; but there was one episode in which I felt rather awkward. While Otto did not excel in any subject, he was particularly poor at mathematics. Our math teacher in the fourth grade of the *liceu*, Sverca, was an unusually enthusiastic and gifted pedagogue who went out of his way to make everybody understand what he was teaching. One day, after repeated but futile attempts to help Otto work out a problem at the blackboard, Sverca burst out with, "Jesus, here's something I've never seen in my life—a stupid Jew!" Needless to say, Otto was demoralized. I had to work hard to convince him that a person can be bad at mathematics without being stupid.

An important formative influence came from my private reading. I owe this entirely to my mother. Around the age of ten I was an avid reader of a well-known series of short adventure stories that came out every week in a fifteen- to twenty-page booklet, and I did not want to read anything longer or less immediately exciting. After several unsuccessful attempts at persuading me to try something else, my mother adopted the strategy of bringing home many books from the library and leaving them around our rooms. I gradually began reading Karl May, and for a while fell in love with his novels. He was a German writer of Westerns similar to James Fenimore Cooper's but (in my opinion) much better. I identified with May's main character, Old Shatterhand, the noble-hearted and indomitable fighter who never panicked even in the most dangerous and seemingly insuperable situations, a man who could always be counted on by his friends, and was ready to risk his life for justice and fairness. In retrospect, I think May's novels helped me form a value system—one not generally shared by the boys in my circle—that put character, fairness, courage, and endurance on a footing at least equal to, if not higher than, intellectual ability. I was thirteen when I read May's *Winnetou,* whose hero was a noble-hearted American Indian of that name. I remember finishing the book in the bathtub at two in the morning, and crying when Winnetou died at the end.

However, my mother had a greater ambition: she wanted to lure me away from pure adventure stories to higher literature. I remember well how the breakthrough occurred. I must have been twelve or thirteen when I fell ill with a flu, and my mother decided that now was the time to act: she went to town and brought home a juvenile edition of *The Count of Monte Christo* by Alexandre Dumas. I wanted none of it. The title was repellent, the book was thick, and I figured that I would have to read many pages before anything exciting would happen. "No, thanks," I said. "Maybe I'll read this some other time, but now I want to continue with my adventure stories." We bargained for a while, and then my mother offered the following deal: since I had a temperature and it was not good for me to read much, she would read aloud to me from the new book for about half an hour. That would be it; I would not have to read the rest. Happy to get away with a short period of listening, I went along. She read the first chapter, stopping at the point where Dantès was arrested at his wedding and brutally dragged away from the side of his charming fiancée, Mercedes. She then closed the book and said, "Good night, dear. You don't have to read any more of this." But of course I was already hooked. By the way, the story of the Count of Monte Cristo—the juvenile edition and later the full version—for some reason made an unusually strong impression on me, as if I had somehow sensed that it foreshadowed crucial episodes of my future life.

Once I started reading real literature, there was an abundance to choose from. Throughout history, writers and poets have played a crucial role in Hungarian society, and the average quality of writing among literary people in Hungary (I am referring to things like style, richness, and sophistication of language and imagery, irrespective of content) was uniformly high. Hungarian translations from the classics and world literature were thus usually excellent. This was unfortunately not true of the Romanian translations that I had access to through my school. I remember starting to read Jules Verne's *Five Weeks in a Balloon* in Romanian, then putting it aside and reading the Hungarian version instead. The lending library of which my mother was a member, called Libro, had a catalog of about twenty thousand books carefully selected to provide a good representative sample of classical and contemporary world literature. From Balzac, Victor Hugo, and Zola to Romain Rolland; from Goethe to Thomas Mann, Franz Werfel, Stefan Zweig, and Jakob Wassermann; from Tolstoy, Turgenyev, and Dostoyevsky to Shalom Aleichem and Isaac Babel; from Pirandello to Ignazio Silone; all the well-known nineteenth- and twentieth-century writers of continental Europe were richly represented in fine Hungarian translations. English and American literature were represented by Charles Dickens, Bernard Shaw, H. G. Wells, Rudyard Kipling, Mark Twain, and Jack London, as well as Hemingway, Faulkner, Dreiser, Steinbeck, Maugham, and others. Most of these books made the rounds of our house—my mother would bring them home one or two at a time, for a few days to a few weeks. I started reading them around the age of twelve and they probably influenced my outlook on life at least as much if not more than the philosophical writings that I read a few years later.

When I was twelve or thirteen, my mother disclosed to me a secret side of her life. She had already explained her feelings toward my father, whom she greatly respected but with whom she had never been in love. Now she told me that soon after she married Ignác, she fell madly in love with his brother Elek. It was apparently one of those irresistible mutual attractions which are the stuff of great novels, and they soon began a passionate love affair that ended only with Elek's death at the age of thirty-two, when I was six months old. Upon my hesitant question as to what the implications were for me, she was silent for a while, then said, "I don't mind if you consider yourself the son of Elek." As the question seemed to make her uncomfortable, I never asked for a more definite answer, but I soon convinced myself that there was no need for one: looking at Elek's enlarged photograph hanging on our wall I gradually discovered many of the traits of my own face. On another occasion, when I complained about the religious bigotry and narrowness of my father, she told me that although he was narrow and could often be overbearing, he also had some very noble qualities. As an example, she said that less than a year after Elek's death, at a dinner party at which several other members of my mother's family were present, her bitchy sister Erzsike remarked, "You know, Ignác, some people are badmouthing you, saying that Egon is Elek's son." To which my father replied "I don't care what those people say, Erzsike. Besides, in the village where I come from, there is a saying: It doesn't matter whose cock made it, if my hen laid it, it's my egg." My mother said she was forever grateful for his generous attitude, and sometimes reminded me of it when I complained about him.

My mother was a straightforward person who could not suffer pretentiousness. She also despised sneaky, treacherous behavior. We would occasionally play chess together, and I remember an episode when she grabbed one of her bishops with the intention of knocking out my knight, but was hesitating with her hand on the bishop. This was a bad move and to induce her to make it, I feigned an expression of displeasure. She made the move, I took her bishop, and then she burst out: "This was an ugly, sneaky, despicable gesture on your part; never do that to anybody!" I must have been about twelve when this happened, a seemingly insignificant incident, but it made a deep impression on me. To this day I remember it, and the shame I felt, perfectly well.

In the summer of 1935 I had my bar mitzvah, which I remember more as a burden than a happy celebration. To satisfy my father's wishes I learned a lot of ceremonial stuff that I had to perform on that day, including some singing in the synagogue that I would have rather skipped (I had a terrible voice). However, something that happened on that day had a significant influence on my life during the next four years: My maternal grandmother, who had come to live in Cluj after my grandfather passed away a year or two earlier, gave me a Ping-Pong table as a birthday present. A few months earlier I had started playing Ping-Pong with some friends and my grandmother knew about this passion of mine. With the new table in our courtyard, I was now able to play much more and soon became good at the game.

Ping-Pong, or table tennis, was at the time a sport widely practiced throughout Europe. In Ping-Pong as in tennis, there is an offensive and a defensive style of game, and traditionally the champions were the best of the attackers, those whose strokes had the force and the spin that made them hardest to return. But around 1936 a revolution occurred in the game of Ping-Pong. At the world championship the Romanian team, made up of three players from Cluj—Goldberger, Paneth, and Vladone—won second place with a completely new, exclusively defensive game style: They would return every ball and win by driving the attacker to exhaustion. Their unexpected strategy so upset the international Ping-Pong community that in the following year the World Federation of Ping-Pong decided to change the rules of the game, lowering the net by about three-quarters of an inch in order to favor offense over defense. The reason invoked for this decision was the alleged need to prevent the game from becoming boring. Obviously, winning second place in the world was a big thing, and many youngsters in Cluj became interested in the game.

I received my Ping-Pong table in June, and by the end of September I was beating all the neighborhood kids who used to beat me before. With the advent of fall I normally would have had to stop playing, but one of the older boys (older meaning fifteen), who was the best player in my neighborhood, belonged to an indoor Ping-Pong club and offered to introduce me there so I could continue playing through the winter. There was some opposition from my parents, as the Ping-Pong training sessions ran from eight to ten in the evening and I was getting home around ten-thirty or eleven o'clock; nevertheless, they went along in the end. My mother persuaded my father that, as long as I continued to be at the top of my school class, and even earned money tutoring classmates, there was no reason to prevent me from doing what I wished.

I learned to play Ping-Pong at a competitive level and during 1936 through 1938 participated in many citywide, regional, and national tournaments. Because competing in tournaments was forbidden for students of my school—a prohibition not taken too seriously as long as one's name did not appear in the press—I had to compete under an alias. I chose the name Balázs, a common Hungarian family name beginning with the same letter as mine. Thus I won several second and third prizes for which I was listed in the newspapers as E. Balázs. Besides Ping-Pong, I occasionally practiced skating, swimming, and tennis. I started playing tennis at twelve and continued to play every spring and summer, but there was no such thing as indoor tennis in my hometown, so Ping-Pong remained my main sporting passion until the age of seventeen. Was I a talented Ping-Pong player? In retrospect, not really, but I was certainly an ambitious one. A strong drive carries you a long way. My brother, Robert, three and a half years younger than I, whom I introduced to the game, was more talented. He did not quite catch up to me, but he came close.

Once in 1937 or 1938 I had a chance to play a match with the most talented Ping-Pong player I have ever known, Ernest Diamantstein. He was a man of around thirty who played Ping-Pong for his own enjoyment and did not rigorously train for tournaments as the other players did. But when he did train for three or four months, he became the national champion. Then he stopped playing regularly, but he would still visit the club occasionally and play with whoever happened to be on hand. His game was completely one-sided: he was always on the offensive, irrespective of his opponent's game. Thus the only points he would lose were his own unforced errors. This was very different from the defensive game that was prevalent in Cluj and that had brought the Romanians glory at the world championship. Besides being an extremely talented sportsman, Diamantstein had a certain wisdom about life. At the time when we played, my main strength was in defense (after all, that was the Cluj specialty) but I was making strenuous efforts to develop a strong offense. Also, my best stroke was a forehand spin, and I was trying to strengthen my backhand. We played a match—which, of course, he won without any great difficulty—and then we sat down to talk. He said to me, "Egon, you have a well-balanced game and I have no particular criticism of any of your strokes. However, I want to say this to you: It is one thing to be a good Ping-Pong player and something else again to be a great player, a champion. For the latter, you need to have something—forehand or backhand, offense or defense, whatever—something that you do better than anybody else; something at which you are clearly and unequivocally the best." I remembered this piece of wisdom for the rest of my life, well beyond its meaning in the context of the conversation.

My interest in Ping-Pong did not ruin my performance at school. I continued to alternate between the first and second ranks in my class, expanded my tutoring activities from French to mathematics and Latin, and even came to appreciate Romanian poetry, especially the works of Mihail Eminescu. As a member of the school's literary circle, I ventured to publicly recite a well-known poem by Gheorghe Cosbuc. (This was not a success: I stumbled in the middle of the poem and was relieved when I finally managed to finish it.) In the fifth grade of the *liceu* (American ninth grade) we started studying English. I decided to learn this language beyond the level offered at school, so I used my earnings from tutoring to take private English lessons for the rest of my high school years. It was around this time, when I was fifteen, that I first became acquainted with classical music, and came to love Beethoven's Fifth and Ninth symphonies. Several years earlier I had studied piano playing. I was not bad at it and moderately enjoyed it, but I felt that the effort of hour-long daily practice was not worth making unless one had a stronger interest and more talent than I felt I had, so I stopped studying piano after a couple of years. During and after those years, I was exposed to piano music played occasionally by my mother, but mostly by my Aunt Pirike in Dej, where I spent many summer vacations. She played Chopin for the most part—concertos, waltzes, mazurkas—but also Grieg, Liszt, and others. I enjoyed many of these, but Chopin was my favorite. Also, from the age of twelve I regularly visited the Opera House of Cluj. I would go with one or two friends and instead of buying tickets—that was far too expensive for us—we would tip a few lei to the ushers, who would let us in at curtain time and allow us either to stand or sit wherever we found a free seat. I liked several of the classical operas, but the one that made the strongest impression on me was Gounod's *Faust*. This must have been at least partly for its philosophical content. The message of Mephistopheles, the rebel and eternal critic who calls the ugly reality by its name, struck a chord in me. I seem to have been receptive to romantic settings, and was fascinated by stories involving fate, fatality, a higher calling, and so forth.

Although as a young teenager I had no inkling about and no interest in political issues, I certainly knew about social conflict, and my mother consciously cultivated in me a sense of social justice. In 1939 my father had to sell the house where we were living. The new owners gave us the right to live there for a certain length of time (maybe another year) as principal tenants, and to sublet much of the house to the same tenants that we had before. One day there was a torrential rain. The sewage system of the street got clogged up, and the water on our street rose to a height of almost two feet. My family lived upstairs and did not suffer any damage, but the basement rooms were flooded and the tenants' furniture and belongings were destroyed. There was no flood insurance and the tenants, needless to say, were angry and distraught. The atmosphere in the house was tense. My mother turned to me and said it would be nice if I took a bucket and went down to the basement to help the people get rid of the water. Of course I did so, and felt ashamed of not having thought of it myself. At first I was received with icy looks, but after I had worked steadily for three hours along with the others, the atmosphere toward me became friendlier. The next day, the tenants put together a delegation to see the owner about repairing the floors and the walls in the basement. Even though my family had suffered no damage, my mother suggested that I join the delegation and speak to the owner in support of the tenants' demands. The tenants strongly agreed and I went with them to see the owner. I had never been involved in a situation like this and felt rather nervous; I had no idea of what to say if the owner simply refused to do anything. Fortunately, somewhat surprised to see me among the basement tenants, the owner reacted favorably and the repairs were started immediately.

My relations with the opposite sex during my boyhood were rather complex. I was very sensitive to seduction by feminine beauty, although I would never admit it. From about the age of nine I was periodically in love with girls to whom I would never express my feelings. My brother was the only person in whom I would confide; he always knew who my "sweetheart" was. My first love lasted about two years, till the age of eleven. Another one started in the summer of 1933 and lasted for at least three years. These were girls I knew and occasionally met socially, but I carefully avoided revealing the way I felt about them. Why? I could not explain it then, but my current understanding is that admitting to those feelings would have been tantamount to admitting weakness, vulnerability—and, even worse, exposing myself to possible rejection. My attitude did not change until I had gathered sufficient self-confidence to assess the danger of rejection more optimistically.

As to actual sex, for a while I suppressed my desires—which appeared around the age of twelve or thirteen and became quite strong by the age of fifteen—waiting for some miracle by which I could somehow land a girlfriend. This would indeed have been a miracle, as in those days and in that part of the world decent schoolgirls would not have sex.

My father, with whom I seldom if ever had conversations on anything but casual matters, was obviously prevailed upon to tell me what I needed to know on this subject. Visibly uncomfortable, he broached the topic one day when I was fifteen or sixteen by saying something to the effect that, well, sooner or later I would have to deal with women; and when that happened, I should pay no attention to how pretty the woman's face was, but to how clean she kept herself. In general, I should avoid indecent women and try to find somebody decent. In spite of the awkward tone of this dialogue, I would have appreciated some useful advice as to how to land a lady with the qualities favored by my father, but in that respect he did not have any advice; nor did any of my friends. My sexual initiation finally took place at the age of sixteen or seventeen, in the same manner as it occurred with most of my friends and classmates: I was taken to a bordello. Although I found none of the three or four available girls attractive—they all seemed very vulgar—I did not want to back out of the adventure. I finally chose the one who was the least aggressive, maybe even a little shy. She was obviously pleased by my choice, which she did not seem to expect, and behaved very kindly toward me (my friends told her that I was a virgin). I never saw her again.

■ ■ ■

From my early teenage years, I knew that my professional interests lay in the direction of mathematics, physics, and engineering. During my seventh year in the Liceul Gheorghe Bariţiu, when I was the equivalent of an American high school junior, I developed a strong interest in physics. I was particularly intrigued by such twentieth-century revolutions as relativity theory and quantum mechanics. I went to the library and read extensively about Albert Einstein's special relativity theory; I relived the excitement of the Michelson-Morley experiment,* whose outcome could not be explained in the framework of Newtonian physics, and which served as the trigger point for Einstein's theory. Just as Archimedes asked for a fixed point from which to unhinge the universe, Einstein used the result of this experiment as the fixed point around which a new, revolu-

---

*A famous experiment meant to prove that the speed of light as measured from the earth differs according to whether the direction of the light is parallel to that of the earth's rotation, or perpendicular to it. By contrast, the experiment proved that there is no difference.

tionary theory could be built. I was fascinated by the fact that a single, isolated experiment whose outcome contradicted the accepted wisdom could have such far-reaching repercussions. Savoring the adage that "facts are stubborn things," I was attracted by the iconoclastic daring of Einstein's quest. I was impatient to acquire the mathematical knowledge needed to understand the new physics, not only relativity, but everything about particle physics, Heisenberg's principle of uncertainty, and so on. In order to do so, I even took the decisive step of giving up Ping-Pong. Given the opportunity of pursuing my intellectual interests as they were in 1939, I would have probably become a physicist. But big storms were gathering on the sea that was carrying the boat of my life.

I knew next to nothing about politics until the late thirties, and had no interest in it at all. Of course, I knew about Hitler and fascism and their growing dark influence, but mainly from a distance, not as something affecting me or my world directly. After all, I, a Jew, was still allowed to graduate as first in my class in the spring of 1940. However, from 1938 on, some of the teachers were making openly anti-Semitic remarks in class, and the general trend in the country was not hard to discern. My reaction was a gradually heightened awareness of my Jewishness. Whereas this had not seemed to matter much before, either to me or to others, now it was becoming central to my existence. The more the Jews became objects of hatred and disdain, the more strongly I felt a certain pride in being Jewish, in belonging to the people who gave to mankind Moses, the Ten Commandments, the Bible, Jesus Christ, and, in more recent times, philosophers like Spinoza, statesmen like Disraeli, and scientists like Einstein. This had nothing to do with religion, which I continued to reject, whether Jewish, Catholic, or Greek-Orthodox. I felt I was an ethnic Jew, a son of the Jewish people. I had Jewish blood in my veins. It did not disturb me that this was the nazi definition of who was a Jew; it was also the definition of a good many zionists. At first, I felt some attraction toward zionism. I read about Theodor Herzl's book, *Der Judenstaat (The Jewish State)*, though not the book itself, and its ideas captured my imagination to some extent. But when I took a look at the zionist organizations in Cluj—the main one, to which some of my friends belonged, was Habonim, a Social-Democratic-type of organization—it struck me that they were not offering any remedy against Hitler. They were involved in educational and other similar activities, whereas Hitler and his acolytes were training their mobs in the use of arms. Because of this, I was attracted for a time to the more hawkish zionist ideology of the revisionists, right-wing followers of Jabotinsky, represented in Cluj by the organization called Betar. But when I tried to attend one of their meetings, they would not let me in without a yarmulke, and I refused to put one on my head. That more or less put an end to their attraction for me. It was in this politically unattached state of mind that I faced the two historical events that affected my life at the end of the decade.

In the second half of August 1939 I was engaged in the first courtship of my life. A lady in her late twenties or early thirties came to town for a vacation and was looking for a tennis partner. She was introduced to me; we played once, both enjoyed the game, and started playing daily. Although I was on vacation, playing tennis daily was not my usual life-style. But the lady was very attractive. I knew that she (a Jewish woman) was married to a Romanian judge in another town, but that did not disturb me, as I was not planning to marry her. At first it seemed improbable that a seventeen-year-old boy could have any chance of success with a married woman at least ten years older, but after two weeks the prospects began to look promising. She would agree to meet me in town, and we would have long conversations, along with some petting and kissing. Then suddenly the news broke: Hitler has attacked Poland. The lady talked to her husband on the phone and returned home that very afternoon. That was the last I saw of her.

The outbreak of what very soon became World War II was shocking and frightening, but at the same time electrifying, news: after giving in for several years to every demand of Hitler's, after letting him reoccupy the Saarland and annex Austria through the farce of the Anschluss,* after the letdown and sellout of Czechoslovakia in Munich, Britain and France had finally found the strength to say no, enough is enough. They answered Hitler's latest act of aggression by declaring war on Germany. At last, it seemed, the triumphal march of nazism would be brought to a halt. Little did we expect that Hitler's war machine would finish off Poland in two weeks without major German casualties, and that the following spring Nazi Germany would swallow Norway, Denmark, Belgium, Luxemburg, Holland, and France, each within a few days or weeks, only to emerge from these campaigns stronger than ever. In particular the easy conquest of France was a

*German for "joining," the Nazi term for the annexation of Austria by Germany.

terrible blow to me. The news about the military disarray, the general panic, the lack of will to resist and fight on, was all bitterly disappointing. It seemed as if the Nazi characterization of the Western democracies as weak, corrupt, and decadent—in other words, "rotten"—had been proved accurate.

In September 1940 Hitler decreed that the northern half of Transylvania (almost one-fifth of Romania's territory with a population of more than two million, including Cluj and six or seven other major cities) would be transferred to Hungary. This decision, called the Vienna ruling in the Hungarian press and the Vienna decree *(Diktat)* in the Romanian press, took the form of a de facto ultimatum to the Romanian government, which was given ten days to comply. To nobody's surprise, considering Hitler's easy victories over so many larger, more developed countries, the Romanian government caved in. Less than two years before, in late 1938, after the dismemberment of Czechoslovakia in the wake of Munich, Hitler had ordered through a similar Vienna Diktat the transfer to Hungary of Southern Slovakia, with a population of about one million. Both these acts were shrewd political moves on Hitler's part, since in both cases the territories had largely Hungarian populations (more than half in the case of Northern Transylvania) and their transfer was greeted with enthusiasm by the Hungarian public. Moreover, they could be seen by others who were discontent with the Versailles-Trianon peace agreements as a rectification along more or less ethnic boundary lines of the maps drawn up by those treaties after World War I. Neither in the case of Czechoslovakia, nor in that of Romania, was there any kind of resistance on the part of the governments concerned. The Romanian government did not survive the humiliation. It fell a few days later, only to be replaced with more right-wing forces, eager to cooperate with the Germans.

Hungary's ruler (titled regent) was Miklós (Nicholas) Horthy, admiral of the nonexistent Hungarian navy. (As a result of the treaty of Trianon, Hungary had lost its access to the Adriatic Sea.) Horthy became head of state after the defeat in 1919 of Bela Kun's Hungarian communist regime, which had been in power for several months. Horthy led the right-wing backlash against the short-lived Red government, and gradually consolidated a ruling coalition of the various parties representing the landed aristocracy, the clergy, the industrialists, and the officer corps. Hungary had a parliament with a legal opposition, including the Small Farmers' Party and the Social Democratic Party, but there was a particularly strong emphasis on "law and order." The Communist Party was illegal, and its members, when caught, were sentenced to long jail terms. The police, especially the gendarmerie, were notorious for their brutality. During the thirties, various fascist and semifascist groups became influential among the small bourgeoisie and the peasants, as well as among the officer corps and some of the intellectuals. Their political advances were fueled by discontent over the peace treaty of Trianon, which had despoiled Hungary of more than half of its prewar territory and population and had placed millions of Hungarians under the rule of foreign governments (Romanian, Yougoslav, and Czechoslovak); and by the rapidly spreading poison of anti-Semitism, which, in the wake of Hitler's success in Germany, offered millions of poor or unemployed people the prospect of obtaining jobs and businesses taken away from the Jews.

The Jews of Hungary had long played a leading role in building the country's industry and running its economy. In the twenties and thirties, they played a major role in the professions and in the intellectual life of the nation. More than half the private doctors, almost half the lawyers, and about a third of the journalists were Jewish. But numbers do not tell the whole story. Jewish intellectuals, playwrights, poets, writers, and scientists had played a prominent role in raising Hungary's intellectual and cultural life to a high level recognized worldwide. When, as a result of the increasingly anti-Semitic atmosphere and policies of right-wing governments during the mid- and late thirties, Hungarian Jewish scientists emigrated to the West in droves, their presence in America was marked by such names as those of the mathematician John von Neumann and the physicists Edward Teller, Leo Szilard, and Eugene Wigner, to mention only those who played a leading role in the construction of the nuclear bomb.

In September 1940, when Admiral Horthy entered Kolozsvár (the Hungarian name for Cluj) on his white horse, he was greeted with enthusiasm and patriotic fervor by the Hungarian population. Riding a wave of Hungarian nationalism, Horthy was hailed as the liberator of Southern Slovakia and Northern Transylvania. The fact that he managed to regain these territories without fighting was held in his favor, and few people foresaw the price Hungary would have to pay by joining the German war adventure. As to the Romanian population of Cluj, most of the middle class departed with the Romanian administration, and all the important Romanian institutions were either evacuated or closed down.

My high school was closed, and most of my Romanian classmates left with their parents. Those who were ethnic Hungarians or Germans transferred to one or another of the Hungarian schools. Jews, however, were subject to the rule of *numerus clausus* (Latin for "closed number"), which limited their numbers in any class to 6 percent, roughly the percentage of Jews in the country's population. Also, Jews who had been baptized as Christians and those with only one Jewish parent had priority, and admissions criteria were not based on grades but on connections and social status.

On the other hand, in early October the local Jewish high school teachers obtained the authorities' permission to organize a Jewish school. That is where most of us went, and it turned out to be a wonderful learning experience. A few of the teachers were local, but most of them came from Budapest, bringing with them the aura of a leading European cultural and intellectual center. Some were overqualified for their positions: they had published in professional journals and would have taught at universities had they not happened to be Jewish. The school was secular, religion was taught as one of the subjects. The language was Hungarian, and the curriculum of my class was that of the senior year in all Hungarian high schools. There were considerable differences from the Romanian curriculum; among others, German was the principal foreign language, and we had to learn it in a short time. But the main new thing was Hungarian literature. While many of the compulsory readings were boring, there were some real gems that had a profound influence on me. This was especially true of Imre Madách's play, *The Tragedy of Man*, written in the second half of the nineteenth century, a historico-philosophical drama woven around the basic idea of Goethe's *Faust*. In my opinion, it is in no way inferior to the German masterpiece, and in some respects it is superior. I also enjoyed some of the twentieth-century poetry.

CHAPTER 2

■ ■ ■

The Cause

In October 1940 a decisive event occurred in my life. One day I was approached by Ignác, the older brother of a former classmate of mine, who said he wanted to talk to me. We made an appointment, which resulted in my first exposure to marxism. Ignác was not particularly persuasive, but he gave me brochures and books whose message fell on fertile ground. I avidly read everything I could lay my hands on, and in a few weeks I was more or less converted.

Thus, I learned and internalized the doctrine according to which the history of mankind is a history of class struggles. I found particularly convincing the idea that in the process of earning their daily livelihood, people enter into certain relations with each other, given beforehand and independent of their will, the so called relations of production, which in turn reflect the current state of technology; and that these relations, more than anything else, determine not only people's places in society, but also their thinking, their views, and beliefs. I accepted and absorbed the view of capitalism as a mode of production based on exploitation; as a society ruled by the class of business owners, who wield all the power and control the army and the police as well as the clergy and the educational institutions, whereas the workers and landless peasants are powerless and exploited. I came to believe that capitalism breeds oppression, inequality, greed, exploitation, hatreds of all kinds: nationalism, racism, anti-semitism. I hoped for the day when the exploited workers would become organized politically and start the revolution that would put an end to capitalism and with it to all forms of exploitation. I was enthusiastic about the classless, socialist society that would emerge from the revolution, a paradigm of social justice whose leading principle would be, "From everybody according to his ability, to everybody according to his work." In time, the marxist doctrine envisaged, the fully developed communist society would enjoy an abundance that would make it possible to replace this principle by the more advanced one, "From everybody according to his ability, to everybody according to his needs."

In the Europe of 1940, nazism, fascism in its German incarnation, was in the marxist view just a particularly vicious form of capitalism, its fate closely tied to that of the latter. The Nazi-Soviet Pact was a maneuver allegedly forced upon the Soviet Union in 1939 by the Western powers' refusal to close ranks with it against Hitler, its sole purpose being to gain time for the Soviet Union to prepare for the highly likely if not inevitable war. Communists had to organize themselves and the working class for the coming revolution.

Why was the message of marxism so persuasive to the mind of an eighteen-year-old eastern European Jew in 1940? In the midst of the deep confusion and disorientation produced by the growing strength and success of nazism and the miserable defeat of democracy on the European continent, marxism offered a coherent theory of the development of society and the history of mankind, along with a clear direction in which the solution had to be sought. On an intellectual level, a complete lack of understanding of the present and uncertainty about the future were being replaced with a seemingly scientific, rational explanation of the general trend of evolution as the result of objective forces acting independently of the will of any individual. On an emotional level, the sensations of isolation, abandonment, and desperate hopelessness, were being replaced with a feeling of belonging, of some sort of community with the progressive forces of mankind, whose ultimate victory—in spite of any temporary reversals—was assured by the inexorable forward march of history. In particular, for a youngster who craved some action against the forces of darkness, some participation in the worldwide struggle against those forces, and also an opportunity to prove himself and to perform some act of courage, marxism offered the option of actively joining the Cause.

My involvement in the movement, triggered by one personal encounter, started with a couple of conversations and a lot of reading, then soon snowballed. A few weeks after my first exposure to marxism I had read enough and felt confident enough to present a paper before the literary circle at my school. The paper dealt with the fate of Jewry and essentially summarized the marxist point of view, according to which the Jewish question was just one of the social problems of capitalism, and anti-Semitism was one of its ideological manifestations. A solution to the problem within that system based on exploitation was impossible; but the advent of socialism, a system based on the principle of international cooperation between working people everywhere ("Workers of the world, unite!"), would cure this problem along with every other social disease brought about by capitalism. My main source for the paper was *Untergang des Judentums*, a contemporary book by the well-known Austrian marxist Otto Heller, which I had read in the original German. Although in hindsight the view outlined above should not have carried much power of persuasion, apparently it still did at the time. My talk was a great success among my fellow students and some left-leaning teachers, although its message was of course rejected by those in the zionist camp.

As a result of this paper, which I later found out was also circulated outside the school among left-wing circles, I was soon invited to participate in a discussion group of five or six young intellectuals, all upper-level university students five to eight years older than me. This was quite an honor and a terrific boost to my self-confidence, which also turned out to be an exciting intellectual experience. The group was led by Zoltán Király, a very bright communist intellectual, a chemist who had studied at the University of Brno in Czechoslovakia up to the tragic days of Munich. The discussion topics were theoretical rather than political; any group with an openly political agenda would have been quickly suppressed by the authorities. A couple of books on dialectical and historical materialism by the Hungarian marxists Aladár Mód and Erik Jeszenszky, and a book by the British scientist J. B. S. Haldane on marxism and biology, were among the topics discussed by the group. Király would also invite nonmarxist speakers to present contemporary philosophical ideas and submit them to debate. In this latter category I remember a lecture on Heidegger by a well-known young local philosopher.

A few months after I first met Ignác, he told me that he had not approached me entirely on his own initiative. He was in contact with important "others" who were interested in me. He urged me to consider whether I wanted to get involved in some real action as opposed to philosophical debates, and to think about this carefully, because it would involve serious risks. There would be no satisfactions of the type experienced in the debating circle; on the contrary, since this activity would be illegal and of great practical importance, it would have to be kept totally secret and I would have to avoid doing anything that could arouse the suspicions of the authorities. In other words, I would have to gradually reduce my participation in Király's circle and shortly drop out of it. As much as I enjoyed the intellectual excitement of attending the circle and regretted having to leave it, there was not a moment's hesitation in my answer: it was real action that I wanted—deeds, not words—and I was willing to face the risks.

No sooner had I given Ignác my consent than he introduced me to a man in his early thirties whom he described with the utmost respect as a dyed-in-the-wool revolutionary. His name was Jenö (Eugene) Weinmann, and Ignác told me I was particularly lucky to meet him at such an early stage of my career in the movement. Having made the introduction, Ignác let me know that he and I were no longer supposed to meet, and that Weinmann would be my "connection" from then on. With that, Ignác disappeared from my life. He died in 1943 or 1944 in a Hungarian Work Battalion. Király had the same fate.

I was introduced to Weinmann in February or March of 1941, and from then on we had regular meetings once every week or so. Weinmann had a strong intellectual influence on me. He was an accomplished marxist intellectual, but unlike the people in Király's circle, he was primarily interested in, and thoroughly knowledgeable about, the political theory of marxism rather than its philosophical aspects or its economic doctrine. He set out to train me as a professional revolutionary, which by that time had become my great ambition. Together we read the political essays of Marx—*The Communist Manifesto, Class Struggle in France, The Eighteenth Brumaire of Napoleon III*—and discussed them at length. We also analyzed the current international situation. By the winter of 1940–41 Nazi-Soviet relations were rather tense, and the possibility of war in eastern Europe was real. Weinmann instructed me in detail about the internal political situation in Hungary, the constellation of political parties and currents, and various aspects of the political life of the country. At the same time, he gave me assignments meant to test my reliability as much as my understanding of the political processes. I had to read several Hungarian newspapers representing various political trends or parties and prepare oral reports on how they reflected current events, interpreting their differing perspectives on the same issue, and so on.

There was also ample instruction in the nature of clandestine revolutionary activity, and in the organization of the Hungarian police apparatus that would try to apprehend us. The police department itself was the least dangerous arm of this apparatus. Much worse were the gendarmes, who in theory were merely the rural police (as opposed to the regular police, whose duties were confined to the cities), but who also had urban branches that dealt exclusively with political unrest of any kind and were infamous for their cruelty. In matters relating to the communist movement, the gendarmerie acted under the supervision of the office of the military general staff in charge of counterintelligence, called the DEF (abbreviation for Defensive Bureau). For this reason, the branch of the gendarmerie in charge of fighting the communists was also known as the DEF. They were highly efficient, extremely brutal, and well trained in various methods of torture, of which the most often used was systematically beating the soles of the feet to cause extreme pain without killing the prisoner. The movement's rules of behavior in case of arrest were strict: You had to deny everything, refuse to admit to any illegal activity, and, above all, never implicate another person. Any confession that led to the arrest of another person was considered treason.

My meetings with Weinmann usually started by reviewing our cover story in case we were apprehended for any reason—how and where we first met, the purpose of our meeting, what we talked about, and so forth. We prepared detailed answers to these and many other questions, answers from which we were not supposed to deviate under any pressure, no matter how severe. I was warned at the beginning and repeatedly thereafter that I was getting involved in something dangerous, and that if I felt too weak to resist pressure, possibly including torture, I should get out. I do not know what my reaction to such warnings would have been in normal times, but in 1941 I considered myself a proud soldier of a worldwide army fighting the nazis, and I was ready if necessary to die for the cause.

Along with my ideological education along marxist lines, I was also trying—following the "know your enemy" principle—to understand nazism and grasp the secret of its political success. I read Hitler's *Mein Kampf.* I perused copies of *Der Stürmer.* I watched nazi propaganda films, where I saw huge mass rallies under forests of swastika-emblazoned banners. I heard the chanting of *"Ein Land, ein Volk, ein Fuhrer!"* ("One country, one nation, one leader!") I listened to the song of the SA, *"Wann Judenblut vom Messer spritzt . . ."* ("When Jewish blood splashes from the knife . . .") And yes, I went to see the awesomely effective anti-Semitic propaganda film *Jud Süss (The Jew Süss)* when it was opened in Kolozsvár some time in early 1941, even though the movie house was controlled by fascist gangs in the uniforms of the Arrow Cross Party. If somebody in the audience had recognized me, I would have been badly beaten up or worse. Needless to say, the extreme hatefulness of everything associated with the nazis reinforced my determination to fight this abomination.

In the meantime, important political changes were taking place in Hungary. In December 1940, at the initiative of the prime minister, Count Pál Teleki, Hungary concluded a friendship and nonaggression treaty with its southern neighbor, Yugoslavia. Both countries were nonpartici-pants in the war, and the pact was meant to underscore their common nonbelligerent status. Teleki's timing could not have been worse. Hitler, who was busy securing his southern flank before invading the Soviet Union, found the Yugoslav regime uncooperative and decided to elimi-nate it. Less than four months after the signing of the Hungarian-Yugoslav treaty, Germany sent Yugoslavia an ultimatum. Yugoslavia refused to comply, upon which Germany invaded it. Just before this happened, Hitler let the Hungarian government know that he expected Hungary to join Germany in the invasion and would reward its participation by giving it the Bácska, a former region of Hungary that the Trianon peace treaty had transferred to Yugoslavia. Although the Bacska had long been coveted by Hungary, Teleki, an old-fashioned aristocrat who prided him-self on his gentlemanly honor, was disgusted by the German offer re-quiring him to break an agreement on which the ink had not yet dried. But most of the country's ruling elite had no such qualms and rejoiced in the prospect of a new territorial conquest. Isolated and bitterly disap-pointed, Teleki shot himself, and the next day the Hungarian army marched into Yugoslavia alongside Hitler's Wehrmacht. The newly ap-pointed prime minister, Bárdossy, was more strongly pro-German.

In December 1940 I was introduced to Albert Molnár, a marxist intel-lectual who had lived in the Soviet Union for several years and escaped around 1936 to avoid the gathering storm of the Great Purge. He had settled in Kolozsvár where he was working as a modest clerk at a private company, and had a circle of friends and adherents to whom he would lecture on various cultural subjects, mostly art and literature. He displayed an amazingly broad and deep erudition in such matters and was a spellbinding lecturer on any topic from Shakespeare's plays to form and content in art. Told that my main interests lay in the direction of mathematics and physics, he confronted me with a mathematical problem in economics: Given a national economy consisting of five production sectors—agriculture/mining, construction, steel, machinery, and consumer goods—along with specifications of final demand for consumption goods and of how much each sector needs directly from each of the other sectors, find out what is the total (direct and indirect) consumption of each sector's product by each other sector. (Making machinery requires steel, which in turn requires mining products and machinery, as does the mining operation itself; so the total consumption of steel by the machine industry is larger than the direct consumption in the last stage of machine production, and so forth.) I found this problem fascinating and struggled with the system of simultaneous equations that it involved, but as I had not studied matrix algebra I was unable to come up with the proper expression for the required inverse. Some fifteen years later I was to discover that what I was playing with at Molnár's instigation was none other than a miniature version of Leontieff's input-output model, of which Molnár must have become aware while still in the Soviet Union. (Leontieff published his path-breaking study—which later earned him the Nobel Prize—in the West in 1937, but the origins of his system go back to his experience with Soviet planning models in the twenties.)

I was keenly interested in Molnár's experience in the Soviet Union, and kept questioning him about it. His views were those of the marxist critics of Stalin. Although he did not consider himself an adherent of Trotsky, he was sharply critical of Stalin's undemocratic methods and regarded the Moscow trials* as show trials whose victims had incurred

---

*Between 1936 and 1938 a wave of show trials gripped the Soviet Union. Famous leaders of the 1917 revolution and of the Communist Party, like Bucharin, Kamenev, Zinovyev, and many others, were tried as "enemies of the people" for imaginary crimes like treason, sabotage, and espionage. A central political accusation was Trotskyism, sympathy with the views of Trotsky, the exiled leader critical of Stalin and his policies. Most of the defendants at these trials admitted their alleged crimes, were sentenced to death, and were executed.

Egon in June 1941

Stalin's personal wrath for one reason or another. Many years later I often asked myself why Molnár's experiences and views had not opened my eyes to the true nature of the communist system. There is no simple answer to this question, which I will discuss later in a more general context. Suffice it to say at this point that I viewed the communist doctrine as one based on a well-founded theory that could not be invalidated by the discovery of some anomalies in the Soviet implementation of the blueprint. Besides, nothing that I heard could change the fact that the Communist Party was practically the only force in my environment that was actively fighting the Nazis. Molnár also gave me a copy of an unpublished book that he had written. About 150 pages long, it was a deeply pessimistic assessment of the general outlook for freedom and democracy. Its basic argument was that the command economies and regimented societies of Nazi Germany and the Soviet Union were much better suited for war than the free-market economies and democratic societies of the West. Whereas Western societies were weakened by dissent, complacency, and individualism, the command societies could more easily be mobilized and organized to achieve national goals. It drew the conclusion—described as mankind's tragedy—that for the Western democracies to prevail, they would first have to become like their hated enemies. And having done so, if they indeed prevailed, could they ever become free and democratic again? The book was deeply pessimistic and written in a very persuasive manner.

In June 1941, I finished high school and received my baccalaureate. I was best in my class, which consolidated the respect I enjoyed among my classmates. This later helped me to attract some of them into the movement. However, my joy and relief were soon swept away by a cataclysmic event: On June 22, Nazi Germany, aided by Italy, Romania, and Finland, invaded the Soviet Union. On a two-thousand-kilometer front, from the Kola Peninsula in the north to the Black Sea in the south, Hitler unleashed his formidable war machine against the Soviet Union, whose armies seemed surprisingly unprepared for the attack. Hungary joined the assault a few days later, though Horthy took a cautious attitude and initially sent no more than two divisions to the front. By contrast, Romania, whose leaders viewed the war as an opportunity to regain Bessarabia and Bucovina, regions ceded to the Soviet Union in 1940, participated with twenty-two divisions.

I vividly remember those days of anguish when I was glued to the radio, listening to the latest BBC newscast about the situation on the front. The Soviets were suffering enormous losses of airplanes, tanks, troops, and territory. In a few weeks the whole industrial region in the Ukraine was lost and the Germans were in Kiev. In the north, they reached and cut off Leningrad, while in the center they were rapidly approaching Moscow. Armies numbering in the hundreds of thousands were destroyed, their soldiers killed or captured. I learned new meanings for old words. *Kessel* (German for kettle or cauldron) was the term the German news media and their Hungarian satellites used again and again: The Soviet armies were encircled, enclosed into a *Kessel*, and annihilated. Ironically, one of the German generals was named Kesselring. I followed every battle on the map, in anguish, as if I were a participant. Places I had never heard of suddenly became important as they fell under German occupation, marking new defeats in the unfolding tragedy of the Red Army. From July through October the news from the front was terrible. The first ray of hope appeared in late October or early November, when the German advance was halted before Moscow and Leningrad (the latter was surrounded but never taken).

Less than two weeks after the Nazi attack on the Soviet Union, Hungarian authorities began a massive crackdown on the communist movement in Northern Transylvania. At the beginning of July 1941 the DEF set up temporary headquarters in the outskirts of Kolozsvár in a village called Szamosfalva, and rounded up several hundred communists throughout the region. The underground party organization was almost completely destroyed. It had been built under the Romanian regime before September 1940, and the rules of secrecy—we used to call them conspiratorial rules—in the Romanian movement were much more lax than in the Hungarian one, reflecting the difference in the brutality of anticommunist repression in the two countries. Hungary had had a communist revolution in 1919; hence the extra zeal of the repression, and the need for more circumspection in the underground movement. Very few party activists managed to avoid arrest in the spring of 1941. I was not yet an activist, and Weinmann himself, as I was to find out later, was a somewhat peripheral figure in the party. Of the major party leaders, only two or three managed to avoid arrest by going underground, that is, by assuming false identities and living in hiding. Those apprehended were beaten for weeks; many of them broke and gave away the others. Those who were arrested at a time when their secrets were already known were spared the humiliation of becoming traitors to their cause. However, a few resisted and did not break in spite of the terrible beatings. Most of the arrested communists were sentenced to prison terms: fifteen to twenty years for the leaders, three to ten years for the others. There was no such thing as parole.

The arrests slowed down my involvement in party activity. For a few weeks, my contacts with Weinmann were suspended as a general precautionary measure. When they resumed in late July or early August of 1941, the first order of business was to analyze the arrests, the behavior of those arrested, and the methods of their interrogation, and to draw conclusions for the future. I was amazed by the detailed information Weinmann had about everything that had happened at the DEF, although there had been a complete news blackout until after the trials.

Meanwhile, my career as a student came to an end. If it had been possible, I would have liked to study engineering, but Jews were not admitted to the university. To become a physicist or mathematician was at the time an utterly impractical dream that I did not dare indulge in. However, baptized Jews with perfect scores and the right connections were occasionally admitted. A good friend of my mother and her family, a successful, well-connected engineer who lived in Budapest, offered to arrange for my admission to the Technical University in Budapest if I would agree to be baptized. Although I was an atheist and religion meant nothing to me, my Jewishness apparently still had enough meaning to make me reject this offer (with due thanks). Both my parents agreed, and for once my father approved of my position. I viewed getting baptized for material advantage as deeply humiliating.

An assistant professor of mathematics at the University of Kolozsvár, Teofil Vescan, who was an ethnic Romanian and a communist sympathizer, privately offered a short series of lectures on calculus for Jewish would-be students who were excluded from the university. One of those with whom I attended these lectures was György (George) Ligeti, who later became a world-famous composer. Ligeti went to a different high school than I did, but we were on friendly terms and often had long discussions. Although his main passion was music, he had a considerable interest in contemporary physics and mathematics. He was an extremely avid reader, and knew a lot more about modern science than I did.

Kolozsvár had a precollege school of music. The Winds Department was headed by a democratically inclined professor called Török, who accepted Jewish students with a reasonable academic record. This was quite an anomaly. Since being jobless might have triggered a call-up to a Work Battalion, I enrolled in the school as a student of the flute. This did not involve much time beyond attending classes twice a week, and it gave me the official status of a technical school student. Although my status did not last long, it led to an important development in my family. My brother, Bobby, who at the time was fifteen, was interested in music, and since enrollment in the music school required only a junior high school certificate, I asked Török if he would accept a much younger but more serious student of music than myself. Török agreed, and Bobby enrolled as a student of the clarinet. Unlike myself, Bobby did not stop after a few months, but pursued his studies until his deportation in 1944 and learned to play the clarinet well enough to serve in the famous prisoners' orchestra at the Auschwitz extermination camp. This enabled him to survive the camp itself, but it did not save his life: he was killed during the death march following the evacuation of Auschwitz.

Bobby around 1943

My contacts with Weinmann were resumed on a regular basis after the spring interruption, and I conscientiously performed the tasks he assigned to me. Gradually, these shifted toward political-organizational activities. I was supposed to carefully study the people in my environment with a view to selecting candidates worth recruiting into the movement. Here the leading criterion was not the person's political views (those mattered, but could be shaped to some degree through persuasion), but his character, seriousness, and reliability, as well as his standing among his peers and the extent to which he could influence others.

My social contacts, which until this time had consisted mainly of my former classmates, were broadened by my compulsory participation in weekly sessions of Levente training. The Levente corps was a premilitary organization for all Hungarian youngsters between the ages of eighteen and twenty-one (military service started at twenty-one). By 1941 Jews were excluded from the regular Levente service and were organized instead into special Jewish Levente detachments. The detachment that I belonged to comprised all Jewish youngsters in Kolozsvár in the Levente age group. We had to attend weekly "training" or exercise sessions, which consisted of heavy work assignments like digging trenches, cutting wood, and building roads. There were several hundred of us, under the command of a brutal, hostile commander called Bartha. The days we spent there were daunting and intensely disagreeable.

Through my attitude toward the other youngsters and toward the unpredictable commander and his often capricious task assignments, I earned the respect of the group and made a number of new friends. One among these was Mayer Hirsch, an electrician at Dermata, the largest factory in Cluj, which employed about two thousand workers in the manufacture of shoes, boots, and all types of leather goods. As it was the largest factory of its kind in our part of Europe and supplied the army with boots, it had been placed under military control. This made Hirsch an important connection, and I started meeting him outside the Levente exercises. He belonged to the left-wing zionist organization Hashomer Hatzair, and after several long debates I managed to win him over to our cause. Since his ideology was already leftist, the principal argument that I put to him was roughly this: If he could go to Palestine immediately and join the struggle against nazism there, that would be honorable; however, this was not possible, and by dreaming about a future life in Palestine while our world was aflame, he was using a pretext to avoid action here and now because it was dangerous. Hirsch was a courageous fellow, a first-rate electrician, a hard worker who enjoyed the respect of his peers, and therefore a highly desirable acquisition for our movement. Another Dermata worker whom I met at the Levente exercises was Dezsö Nussbächer. He was a very serious, reliable, and honest person, though not so energetic and active as Hirsch. He also had leftist sympathies and was easily persuaded to actively help the communist movement. I met both these Derrmata connections at regular intervals (though not together—neither knew of the other's involvement) and discussed with them the situation at the factory. A third acquisition through the Levente group was a textile worker from the Ady hosiery factory, György (George) László, another serious, responsible young man who was not hard to persuade to work with us. I also recruited two of my former classmates, Willy Holländer and Ede Lebovits, who were to play important roles in my activities over the next couple of years.

The winter of 1941–1942 brought the war's first favorable political and military developments. In November, the German offensive in the east was halted before Moscow. Not only had the Nazi propaganda machine boasted prematurely about having taken the city, but on November 7, the anniversary of the revolution, Stalin reviewed a military parade in Moscow's Red Square under the very noses of the German troops less than twenty miles away. This was a tremendous morale boost not only to the Soviet troops, but to all those rooting for the Allied cause. In December, the United States entered the war, and there was little doubt in our minds that this was a decisive turning point in favor of the democracies. Moreover, the German armies in the east were obviously suffering from the unusually harsh Russian winter, and the Red Army was occasionally taking the offensive.

My contacts with factory workers made me acutely aware of my own undesirable status as an unemployed person (albeit a "music student" on paper). After several discussions with Weinmann, he suggested that I try to become a factory worker myself. It was not easy for someone to forego apprenticeship and get hired, but perhaps it could be pulled off. This would enable me to join a trade union, and would bring me in contact with "the masses" in a natural way, as one of them, and offer me a platform for revolutionary political-organizational activity. I agreed, but my parents, though they needed any money I could earn, were hard to persuade. My father was especially opposed to the prospect of his son, whose future he had contemplated in such glowing terms, becoming a factory worker. My mother understood that there was something more to this than I was letting on. Although she knew nothing about my involvement in the movement, she knew where my sympathies lay and realized that I was up to something. She did not mind, partly because she shared my values (if not my precise political views, which we never discussed), and partly because she trusted my judgment. To persuade my father, I argued that practical experience in a factory would help me become an engineer.

Weinmann knew the chief engineer at the Iron Works, a local factory with two hundred or three hundred workers. He asked the chief engineer to hire me as an on-the-job trainee, which meant low pay for the first six months, and to assign me to different sections of the plant so that

I could learn as much as possible about the entire production process. After a few weeks I was hired, and I started working at the factory on February 1, 1942. My first assignment was to the lathe shop, where I learned the rudiments of a turner's job. I spent about two and a half months in that shop, enough to find out that it played a relatively minor role in the factory's life, the center of activity being the foundry, where the largest number of people were employed. So in April I had myself transferred to the foundry, where I got acquainted with the tough, exhausting job of casting iron. I learned how to place a metal frame around a wooden mold and fill it with sand, then beat the sand with a heavy, flat-ended steel bar until it became hard; how then to remove the mold while leaving a narrow opening in the hardened sand through which to pour the hot iron; and finally, how to secure the frames for the casting process by placing on top of them two forty-five-pound ingots to make sure they were not blown apart by the gas released when the hot iron was poured. Each of us worked individually, preparing as many frames as we could during a three-to-three-and-a-half-hour period (between ten and twenty frames), after which the casting would begin. This pattern was repeated twice during an eight-hour workday. When the hot iron prepared in the melting oven was ready to be used, we all gathered in front of the oven, each of us holding in his hands an empty casting ladle that could hold about a gallon. The foreman, using a long steel rod, would perforate a temporarily frozen opening toward the bottom of the oven, and the hot, reddish-white liquid iron would spurt forth to be caught by our casting ladles. Dexterity and sharp attention were needed to smoothly replace one ladle by the next without allowing the molten iron to spill on the ground. This was necessary not only to avoid waste, but to prevent the drops of hot iron from hitting the cold ground, then popping up and burning our skin. We all got frequent burns on our lower legs, since occasional spills could not be avoided.

Years later I remembered my life as a foundry worker when I heard about the following exchange in the trial of the leaders of the Romanian Railway Yards' strike in 1935. The judge wanted to break the solidarity of the three strike leaders, one of whom was Jewish; he addressed one of the other two by saying, "Don't you find it unworthy of an honest Romanian patriot to be in the dock with a Jew? What kind of company have you gotten yourself into?" Upon which the man replied, "Your Honor, this Jew and I happen to work side by side in the main foundry.

In our work, it often happens that the hot iron spills and burns our legs. Well, I found that my friend's burnt flesh smells exactly the same as mine."

As soon as I became a factory worker, I joined the Iron and Steelworkers' Union and started visiting its offices after work on an almost daily basis. The trade union movement in Hungary was under Social Democratic leadership, and like the Social Democratic Party itself, it was tolerated by officialdom but viewed as unpatriotic and suspect. Union membership had diminished substantially during the last few years; yet attempts to replace the unions with various right-wing workers' organizations remained largely unsuccessful, and the unions could still provide an important springboard for any mass action that we might want to organize. I tried to make friends with the workers who visited the union offices. I discussed professional matters, sports, and other innocent subjects with them, along with politics, being careful not to give myself away.

Life as a factory worker was not easy. I would get up at dawn, eat something for breakfast, then go to the factory by bicycle. My lunch was a sandwich prepared by my mother. The work was exhausting, and I would return home in the late afternoon blackened with soot. I would then take a shower, eat my dinner, and leave either for the union office or for one of my appointments, of which I often had several on the same day, each lasting from three-quarters of an hour to an hour and a half. I had little time for reading. Yet I was never really tired. I felt that I had inexhaustible resources of energy—a sign, no doubt, of my revolutionary enthusiasm.

■ ■ ■

About a month after I went to work at the factory, Weinmann informed me that I had been found worthy of party membership. I already knew that not all communists were party members and that membership was restricted to only the most dedicated and determined communists, those who were leading the struggle. I was now asked to decide whether I wanted to take this important step, which in many ways was similar to enlisting in an army. In particular, I was to reflect upon the possibility of being arrested and to ponder carefully whether I was prepared to resist any pressure and never betray the party or any of my comrades. I certainly felt ready for this; I had felt so for about a year. So at the beginning of March 1942 I became a member of the Communist Party of Hungary.

Shortly thereafter, Weinmann transferred me to a new party connection, saying that, to his regret, we would not be able to see each other
from then on. "Sorry," he said, "these are the party rules." He said that
my new connection was a very experienced revolutionary from whom I
would have the opportunity to learn much. He added that, unlike himself, who in party language was "clean" (that is, not known to the authorities as a communist), my new connection was "black," which meant
that he was known to the authorities as a communist and was working
underground. I would not be told his identity nor would he be told
mine; we would have to conduct our business by meeting in the street
at agreed-upon places and times and talk while walking. The conspiratorial rules were very strict and had to be followed to the letter. An
appointment for half past six meant that you had to be at the *exact* meeting
place *exactly* at 6:30, neither earlier nor later. You could not stand waiting
for your contact; rather, you had to walk by and meet as if by chance.
Under no circumstances were you to wait more than five or six minutes:
if your contact failed to show up, there was always a "control" appointment, usually at the same place and time a week or two later. If you
missed it, or if your contact did not show up again, that was that. When
an appointment was with an individual you had not previously met,
both persons involved were to use specific code words. In discussing
your political work, even with party superiors, you were not supposed
to identify the individuals involved by their real names, but to use a
descriptive phrase like "our friend at this or that plant." The general
principle was that nobody should know more than was needed in order
to function effectively, thereby limiting the damage from an arrest—
nobody could give away information that he or she did not have.

That spring day was the last time I ever saw Weinmann. I later learned
that in late 1942 or 1943 he was called up for service in a Work Battalion.
The party gave him the option of going underground instead, which
meant that he would be provided with false identity papers, but would
have to find a hiding place for himself. Perhaps he considered this too
dangerous for his wife and their infant daughter; or perhaps he was
unable to find a place to hide. He moved mainly in Jewish circles, and
a good hiding place had to involve Gentiles. In any event, he chose to
report at the Work Battalion.

Work Battalions were made up of Jewish males of military age under
the command of an army captain or lieutenant aided by a few sergeants

or corporals. The quality of life varied according to the personality of the commanding officer. Some battalions lost most of their members to hunger, exposure, disease, beatings, and occasional wanton killings. Others fared better. According to a postwar tally, roughly half the members of the Work Battalions survived. After the war a good friend of mine related his adventures in a Work Battalion whose commanding officer was the older Vescan, father of the young mathematician who had organized the private calculus lectures in 1941. He was a very decent man; as a result, most of the members of his battalion survived and returned to Kolozsvár some time in late 1943, only to be deported in 1944. Weinmann and a few others managed to survive until 1944 and met the advancing Soviet army somewhere in the Ukraine. Alas, the encounter with the liberators turned out to be tragic for Weinmann: His group was shot at by the Russians; he was hit and he died. Such incidents were not unusual. Some people ascribed them to anti-Semitism in the Soviet army, since those serving in the Work Battalions wore yellow armbands (which identified them as Jews). Maybe there was some truth to this, but it is equally possible that the advancing Red Army simply viewed the Work Battalions as helpers of the Germans. After all, the Soviet army's code of conduct was rather harsh and categorical in this respect: anybody who aided the enemy or worked for the enemy, for whatever reason, was an enemy too. A Soviet soldier was never supposed to give himself up; even if captured while unconscious, he was not supposed to work for the Germans under any pretext. Being forced was no excuse: he had to resist and die, if necessary, just as his brothers were dying at the battlefront. Weinmann's wife and daughter were deported to Auschwitz in June 1944 and sent directly to the gas chambers upon their arrival.

For my first appointment with my new connection, I was supposed to be at a certain spot in the city park at 7:15 one evening, with a certain weekly paper held visibly in my hand, walking slowly and passing the same spot no more than two or three times. If a man approached me asking whether I had a watch, I was to answer that my watch was not very good, but that I knew the time anyway. If the man went on to say he felt lucky to have met me, then he was my contact. Otherwise, I was to leave and repeat the same routine a week later at the same time and place. That first meeting went smoothly. My new connection was a well-dressed man in his early to mid-thirties, wearing a light coat and a hat.

Since I did not know his name during most of the two-and-a-half years that I remained in contact with him, I will simply call him PC for party connection. PC was impressive in a different way than Weinmann. He was obviously very bright and knowledgeable, but he was also a down-to-earth, no-nonsense fellow. Frighteningly categorical in his opinions, he exuded the authority of somebody who knows perfectly well what he is doing. He was not interested in discussing theoretical questions, but whenever we met we would briefly review the political events since our last encounter. For the most part, our conversation focused on my practical activities: what had happened since our previous meeting, what were my two Dermata connections reporting, whom I had visited privately among my co-workers at the factory, and so forth. He would listen, then give me instructions in a very specific, concrete manner: Tell so-and-so such-and-such, the time has come to ask him to do something; don't pursue this any longer, it doesn't look promising. He was thoroughly familiar with the trade union that I was frequenting, including the personal traits of the people that I was getting in contact with. He would instruct me: Don't waste your time on so-and-so, he has communist opinions but he's a talker not a doer and he'll never lift a finger to help us; so-and-so is a Social Democrat, it's hopeless to try to convert him, but he's an honest worker who may join us in some common actions, and once he commits himself he can be trusted. Or (about the leader of the Social Democrats in the union): he is a scoundrel; for instance, . . . and a short anecdote would follow.

PC thought it was important for me to build personal relationships with some of my fellow workers and those I met at the union by visiting them at their homes and sharing their everyday thoughts and concerns. I did this, carefully choosing men who had not been infected by pro-nazi propaganda and the prevailing nationalism, but it was hard to nudge them beyond a benevolent but wholly passive sympathy for the cause. Mr. Szabó, a middle-aged worker from the Railway Yards whose home I visited several times, was typical of these men. He had no well-formed political views, but he disliked the nazis, favored the unions, and was very interested in my analysis of the current situation. He agreed that the Allies had become economically stronger than the Axis since the United States had entered the war, and that sooner or later this would lead to greater military strength. He also agreed that Hungary should not have allowed Germany to drag it into the war. Nevertheless, despite agreeing with me in principle, he considered it extremely dangerous and ultimately futile to attempt to translate these ideas into action.

PC also thought that some of my former classmates, with whom I had kept in touch and who were ready to work with us, should make themselves useful by becoming factory workers like myself. Willy Holländer was ready to do this, and managed to find employment in a small metal workshop. There, through the wife of one of his co-workers, he came in contact with a group of women working in the Tobacco Factory, a fairly large plant with about six hundred workers, all female. Ede Lebovits was working full time in his father's small grocery and could not quit, so PC decided to assign him some technical (nonpolitical) tasks. In order to do this, I had to send him to meet someone with a code word and suspend my own contacts with him.

After a few weeks PC told me it was time to start rebuilding the party organization in Kolozsvár that had been destroyed in the spring of 1941. Everything had to be rebuilt from scratch: nobody could belong to the new organization who had been involved in the 1941 arrests or was known to the authorities as a communist. We reviewed the list of those whom I had recruited for our cause and decided that three of them—Holländer, Hirsch, and Nussbächer—were ripe to be made party members. However, there was a problem with Hirsch who, despite having been a zionist in 1941, had been arrested on the basis of erroneous information. Although the authorities had discovered their mistake and released him after a few days, they might have kept him on the books as a suspect. For this reason, PC decided that we should not make Hirsch a member, but that I should continue to work with him on an individual basis as before. That left Holländer and Nussbächer. PC wanted to meet them before finalizing our decision, and for this purpose (as well as for similar future needs) I had to arrange a meeting place. I approached György László, the textile worker, who was living by himself in a rented room that seemed suitable to our purpose. He agreed to give me the key on the afternoon before the meeting and not to go home until late evening, when he would find the key in a designated place.

At the meeting, Willy Holländer reported on his contacts at the Tobacco Factory. An interesting incident had occurred there. The women had signed up through the factory to receive potatoes (which, like practically everything else, were rationed at the time) and had paid for them in advance. When they were not delivered as promised, the women went on a spontaneous strike and gathered in the courtyard, loudly demanding their potatoes. The factory administration called in the police, but the otherwise quite brutal police were not used to dealing with women. They tried to break up the crowd by persuasion, but they failed. The women surrounded several of them and roughed them up. The next day, the police officers who had been beaten by the women were publicly humiliated in the main courtyard of police headquarters. Their epaulets were torn off, and they were expelled from the force to punish them for their "softness"; that is, for allowing themselves to be overcome by a bunch of women. Such a thing could never have happened to the gendarmes.

Dezsö Nussbächer reported on the situation at Dermata, which was pretty bleak: the workers, intimidated by the controlling presence of the military, had become thoroughly passive. Still, he had managed to identify a few people with leftist sympathies who at least were not afraid to talk about politics and were receptive to his (our) views. After Willy and Dezsö had finished their reports, we discussed the current situation and PC outlined the goals of the Communist Party.

Following this meeting, PC authorized me to offer both Willy and Dezsö party membership, emphasizing the responsibilities and risks that this implied. To my disappointment, Dezsö declined the offer. He said he was willing to help, but party membership was too big a responsibility for him. I did not insist, and we decided he would continue working with me as before. Willy, however, accepted the offer enthusiastically and declared himself determined to endure any torture rather than betray the party or his comrades. He was a strong, well-built, healthy-looking man, yet when he was arrested a year and a half later, the DEF broke him in a few days and under the beatings he gave away everything he knew. On the other hand, Ede Lebovits, the other former classmate whom I recruited, was hesitant about accepting the risks. He said he was ready for any sacrifice but he did not know how well he would be able to resist torture, having never been exposed to it. Ede was very thin, physically weak, and unhealthy-looking. Yet, when he was later arrested, about the same time as Willy, he behaved wonderfully during several weeks of beating.

The spring of 1942 brought both good and bad news. The good news was that the Allies had agreed to open a second front in western Europe in 1942. This was a standing demand of the Soviets, who had repeatedly and sometimes publicly asserted that they were bearing the brunt of the war effort, and that while the help they were receiving from the West in industrial goods and military equipment was useful, what was really needed was the opening of a second front in western Europe. In his May 1 speech broadcast worldwide, Stalin announced the agreement. As it turned out, the Allies realized in the summer of 1942 that they were in no position to invade western Europe that year, so they scaled back the opening of the second front to a landing that fall in North Africa. Nevertheless, at the beginning of May our hopes were tremendously uplifted by the announcement. Soon after that, however, came devastating news from the eastern front: the Red Army, which had started a spring offensive near Kharkov in the Ukraine, had been stopped by the Germans after some initial success. The Germans seized the initiative, counterattacked with a huge pincer movement, and surrounded the Russian forces (another *Kessel!*), destroying entire armies and seizing hundreds of thousands of prisoners. (The German claim of a million prisoners was exaggerated, but not as much as we believed at the time.) This decisive German victory was a bitter awakening from our premature belief that the war in the east had changed course. The battle of Kharkov was followed by more than two months of uninterrupted German advances on the whole southern front. The coal-mining and industrial region of the Eastern Ukraine up to the bend of the Don river fell into German hands, and the spearhead of the advancing troops reached the oil fields in the Caucasus centered around Grozny.

On the other hand, as the world was soon to find out, in the autumn of 1941 the Soviets had begun a massive translocation of their industrial enterprises from the western parts of their immense country to the regions in and behind the Ural Mountains, an industrial migration the like of which the world had never seen. This transplantation of entire factories, along with an extraordinary concentration of the national effort toward armaments production at whatever sacrifice and whatever cost in shortages of civilian goods were necessary, was to bear its fruit gradually: By the end of 1942, the Soviets' armament output surpassed that of Germany. In the meantime, the Germans managed to impose a substantial increase in the Hungarian war effort. The Hungarian army on the eastern front swelled from the initial two divisions to more than 150,000 soldiers. They were ill equipped, not very well trained, and were suffering high casualties. An image from those days that remains in my memory is the cover photo of an issue of *Signal*, a lavishly illustrated German magazine in the style of, say, *Life*. The photo showed Hungarian soldiers in combat, with a caption that read, "Our brave Hungarian allies are throwing themselves upon the enemy with their famous battle cry 'Nobosmeg!' " The funny thing is that the "famous battle cry" was a German transliteration of the common Hungarian oath, "Na baszd meg!" meaning "Fuck it!" which expresses frustration more than anything else. But since the Germans did not understand it and most Hungarians could not read the German-language *Signal*, there was no scandal.

That same spring of 1942 also brought good and bad news about the struggle inside Hungary. On March 15, the day when Hungarians celebrate the 1848 revolution against Austria, there was a large demonstration in Budapest by unionized workers and some intellectuals at the statue of Petofi, the great poet and patriot who died in that revolution. The demonstration, organized by communists who had infiltrated the leadership of the Social Democratic youth organizations and trade unions, was quite impressive; the crowd shouted anti-German and antiwar slogans until the police dispersed them, making close to a hundred arrests. This happened in the wake of a change of governments: a few days earlier Horthy had appointed a new prime minister, Miklós Kállay, who was expected to be, and later proved, a much less consistent collaborator with the Germans than his predecessor, Bárdossy. Nevertheless, as the events of March 15 revealed, Kállay did not intend to soften the official stand against the Communists.

Within six weeks of the demonstration, a huge wave of arrests swept through the Budapest party organization. Among scores of others, Ferenc Rózsa, one of the party leaders, was apprehended in early June. After about two weeks, as he refused to break under torture, he was beaten to death. Another party activist, Károly Rezi, was also killed during interrogation. A party leaflet informed us of these events shortly after they happened. In October 1942 Zoltán Schönherz, the secretary general of the Hungarian party at the time, was arrested, tortured, tried, and sentenced to death. By then, Hungarian communists were being tried by special tribunals of the chief of staff, which had been created expressly for this purpose. Schönherz was hanged a few days after sentencing. Such were the grim and all-too-likely prospects that my comrades and I now faced.

The summer of 1942 also brought a change in my employment. My job at the Iron Works was not attractive, the pay was miserable, and the political opportunities were limited. It was the best I could do when I first went to work, but now, with six months' experience behind me, I could try to find a better place. One of my former classmates whom I had tutored in math for a while around 1940, was the son of Jenö Vadász, the owner of a metal-working factory called RAVAG, which employed three hundred to four hundred people. I knew the elder Vadász, since he had usually paid me in person for the tutoring in order to get reports on his son's performance. This factory was a much more specialized and modern plant than the Iron Works. Its main unit, where the largest number of people worked, was the lathe shop where iron, steel, copper, and aluminum pieces were processed in large batches. I went to see Vadász and, based on my half-year–long factory experience, applied for a job in the lathe shop. I suspect his experience with me as his son's math tutor gave him a far more favorable idea of my capabilities than my rather poor skills as a turner would have warranted. In any event, he agreed to hire me, and on September 1, 1942, I started working at RAVAG. Soon after, Mayer Hirsch, one of my two contacts at Dermata, ran into a conflict at work and decided to go elsewhere. This was not good news because of the importance of Dermata, but his position had become so exposed that he felt he could do nothing to help us there anyway. Being a well-qualified electrician with an excellent work record, he felt he could find another job. Since he liked what I had told him about RAVAG, he tried there and was hired. Thus there were now two of us at that plant.

My work at RAVAG was much less exhausting than at the Iron Works, but far from pleasant. RAVAG was mass-producing various items on tight delivery schedules, and speed was of essence. Although I knew how to turn a lathe, I was far from proficient at the task; moreover, the Germans had just introduced a new type of ultrahard steel blade and I had to learn how to use new kinds of tools. The foreman, Szöllösi, a politically right-wing, socially nasty, overbearing person, did not like me, and I sincerely reciprocated his feelings. None of this made my days very pleasant, but after a few months I got a little better at my job and Szöllösi became more relaxed—though I don't remember ever having seen him smile at me.

The workers at RAVAG were in roughly the same political disarray as elsewhere in town. A few were unionized but passive; the majority had been enrolled by Mr. Szöllösi into a right-wing "yellow" organization (i.e., a fake union controlled by the authorities). The leader of this group of workers, Kádár, had been on the Russian front as a soldier and brought back stories about the misery he had found there—proof, he claimed, that communism did not work. Although personal experiences are always convincing, it was not too hard for us to point out that war and occupation invariably produce misery wherever they occur. Another influential worker, Gáspár, though also a member of this organization, never frequented its meetings and was at least as interested in hearing our opinions and interpretations of current events as those of the other side. I found him honest and relatively courageous, so I set out to build a relationship with him. I met his wife, visited him at home a couple of times, and succeeded in bringing him somewhat closer to our views.

Some time during the winter of 1942–1943, RAVAG got an urgent military order that had to be delivered in a couple of months. Because the pace of work, already as fast as it could be, could not be speeded up further, the management issued a call for us to work overtime two hours a day, six days a week. This happened during an unsettled wage dispute, in which the workers were demanding a long-promised pay raise that the management was now refusing. At first everybody complied with the call and worked ten hours a day, but there was a lot of grumbling and dissatisfaction. In private discussions with Gáspár and some of the other workers we managed to put across the idea that if there ever was a chance to get the promised raise, this was it: The management now needed us. So Kádár, Gáspár, and a third person led a delegation to the management and asked for the promised raise. Their request was turned down on the grounds that the nation was at war and the economic situation did not permit such a move. After a heated discussion, the workers announced that there would be no more overtime until the wage issue was settled. The next day, and for several days thereafter, Gáspár sounded the siren at the end of eight hours and all work stopped. Szöllösi approached a number of men individually, offering them various bribes to continue working, and he finally won over a single unskilled worker, a certain Rácz, who was miserably poor and therefore open to temptation.

As soon as our partial strike started, my party connection, PC, wanted to meet me every other day to follow developments closely. When Rácz became the first strikebreaker, PC found that this was the psychological moment when something had to be done: the strikebreaking had to be stopped at any cost, or else the bribes would be extended and others would follow Rácz's example. Up to that point, neither Hirsch nor I had played any conspicuous role in the strike. We did not talk in public; we were not vocal at meetings; we remained steadily in the background. Formally, the leaders of the strike were the leaders of the right-wing organization that usually spoke for the workers, and it was important to preserve this situation. Yet something had to be done to deter Rácz from working overtime. PC suggested that an anonymous message, mocking and half-threatening, might well do the trick by making him ashamed of his behavior and fearful of a beating. I put together a short ironic rhyme, addressed to Rácz by name, in which I taunted him for becoming a "coolie" (slang for a strikebreaker) and warned him that the fate of a coolie is to get roughed up. The rhyme was couched in workers' slang, full of grammatical errors, and printed in crude letters such as a half-literate person might write. Unobserved, I pinned it on Rácz's locker shortly before the brief lunch break, when I knew he would go to his locker and be the first to see it. He read it around midday, then went straight to Szöllösi, showed him the rhyme, and told him that under the circumstances he was not going to continue to work overtime.

Szöllösi was furious. He conferred with Vadász; they called the police, showed them the rhyme, and asked for their help in apprehending whoever was using illegal threats to deter the workers from doing their job. Szöllösi must have named me as a suspect, since I was handed a written citation to show up the next morning at the central police station. That afternoon I had a meeting with PC. Although he was pleased by the fact that Rácz had stopped working overtime, the citation worried him. He asked me what I was planning to say to the police. I said I would firmly deny having written the rhyme, or having anything to do with the strike apart from being an ordinary disgruntled worker unwilling to work overtime without the promised increase. And I would stick to this story no matter what they did to me. To my surprise, PC said that this was not what he would recommend. If I were to show up at the police unafraid and with a firm position, unimpressed by their threats, I would immediately give myself away for the communist that I was. The police knew how to recognize our sort by its fighting spirit. The time to be dignified and proud, he said, is when you are arrested as a known communist; but as long as they do not know who you are, you have to

dissimulate and behave like a frightened youngster having his first encounter with a dreaded institution. Plead innocent, by all means, but let
them see that you're afraid and look anything but strong and determined. If they threaten to beat you, act terrified and beg for mercy. In
particular, you should pretend to be worried about your father finding
out that you've been cited by the police. And so on. As surprised as I
was, I nevertheless quickly realized that PC was right and prepared
myself to play the proper role the next morning.

At the police station, I was addressed rudely and taken to task for
daring to threaten an honest worker for doing his duty. I pretended not
to know what they were talking about. They threatened me by pulling
out a rubber club, upon which I acted frightened and kept repeating my
innocence. When they found me sufficiently intimidated, they gave me
a pencil and ordered me to write from dictation. They began reading the
rhyme, and I started to transcribe it in my usual handwriting, with correct grammar. They said no, I should *print* the letters, so I did, but in a
neat, educated style. I was sure there was no visible connection between
what I was writing and the scribbling on the note to Rácz. Apparently
the police detectives felt the same, because after the handwriting test
they no longer insisted on my authorship of the rhyme. They asked a few
questions about who might have done it, to which I naturally replied
that I didn't know; then they sent me away saying that I would be called
again if needed. Back at the plant, I found out that the police were going
to question Hirsch and Gáspár the next day. I told Hirsch about my visit
to the police and instructed him how to behave. Their visit to the police
brought no solution to the case, but the workers were upset about the
police citations, especially in the case of Gáspár, who was a longtime
employee and one of the most respected persons in the plant. Work was
frequently interrupted by discussions and production suffered. In the
end, Vadász told the workers' representatives (Kádár, Gáspár, and a
third person) that he was giving up on overtime work and would hire
some temporary workers instead. He also offered a partial settlement of
the wage dispute in the form of a lesser raise than had been promised.
A lesser raise was still a raise, and the deal was accepted.

In late 1942 or early 1943 PC called a meeting to form the party's Local
Committee for Kolozsvár. He told me that the connection with the Central Committee in Budapest, interrupted at the time of the arrests in 1941,
had been reestablished some time during the fall of the same year, and

a Regional Committee had been formed for Northern Transylvania, which he was representing. The Local Committee was to have three members: myself as secretary, Willy Holländer, and a middle-aged woman whose name I did not know to take charge of technical matters (I will call her the Technical Woman). The term *technical*, standard in party terminology, referred to things needed to produce party materials, such as typewriters and duplicating machines. Like our earlier meeting, the Local Committee meeting was held in György László's room. Besides Holländer, the Technical Woman, PC, and myself, there was a fifth participant, a woman in her early to mid-thirties, whom PC brought along as another representative of the Regional Committee. The three of us reported on our work and the situations at the places we covered, never mentioning names. At the end PC drew conclusions and gave some directives. After this meeting, the woman from the Regional Committee (I will simply call her the Regional Woman) became my regular connection in place of PC, who nevertheless continued to get in touch with me on special occasions.

In February 1943 a major event irrevocably turned the tide of the war in the east: after three months of incredibly heroic Soviet resistance in Stalingrad on the Volga River, with house-to-house fighting involving hundreds of thousands of soldiers, the German advance was not only halted, but the whole Sixth Army of von Paulus, numbering more than two hundred thousand soldiers, was caught in a huge German-style pincer movement (a *Kessel!*) by Soviet troops advancing both north and south of Stalingrad toward the west. Hitler ordered a desperate attempt to cut through the encirclement from the west. It failed miserably, and after several weeks of extremely high casualties the remnants of von Paulus's Sixth Army surrendered. The significance of this event could hardly be exaggerated: the Wehrmacht never recovered from this blow. The long advance toward the east had finally come to a screeching halt, and the retreat toward the west was begun. What's more, the extraordinary Soviet production effort was now paying off: After Stalingrad, the Soviet armies had a constant, increasing quantitative superiority of equipment (tanks, artillery, and airplanes) over the Wehrmacht troops.

By the time of the battle of Stalingrad, Hungary, whose participation in the war had begun with two divisions or about 40,000 soldiers, had nine divisions on the eastern front. The whole Hungarian Second Army was in the bend of the Don River, holding a sector of about 150 kilometers. This army was completely demolished by the Soviets in late January and early February, with a loss of about 150,000 Hungarian soldiers. For a while the government managed to conceal the proportions of this tragedy, but the truth soon leaked out. Thus, far behind the battle lines where I was living, the atmosphere also started changing: thinking persons of every persuasion could not avoid asking themselves hard questions about the future, which now began to appear in a rather different light.

. . .

A few months after the meeting of the Local Committee, some time in July, PC got in touch with me to discuss a letter from the Central Committee addressed to all party members. In order to facilitate building a national independence front that would unite all those willing to resist Nazi Germany, the Communist Party of Hungary was voluntarily dissolving itself. The letter announced the dissolution and urged all communists to continue their struggle with the same dedication as before. A few weeks later a new party, the Peace Party, was formed, its stated goal being to lead Hungary out of the war and snatch it from the grip of Nazi Germany. All former members of the Communist Party became members of the Peace Party. As far as those of us in Northern Transylvania were concerned, there was practically no change in either our work or our goals; but at the top, in Budapest, this move apparently attracted some new noncommunist, antifascist allies. PC was not at all happy about this event, and a couple of years later his doubts were vindicated: after the war, the leadership of the newly constituted Hungarian Communist Party declared that the self-dissolution of the party in 1943 had been a mistake.

In the summer of 1943 the new Peace Party brought out a well-written, highly persuasive manifesto against the war, and I was put in charge of organizing its distribution in Kolozsvár. Since this was the most important action of the small organization that I built during the war, I will describe it in some detail. The manifesto was of course illegal, and anybody caught distributing it would have been immediately arrested and tortured by the DEF. To realize what such a manifesto meant, one must try to imagine the all-pervasive propaganda barrage and disinformation campaign to which the Hungarian public was subjected. Since Hungary's joining the war in June 1941, censorship had become much harsher: no

news from an Allied source could appear in the press, and all Hungarian-language radio broadcasts from Moscow, London, and Washington
were thoroughly jammed. As long as the news from the battlefront was
in Germany's favor, the lack of objective reporting was less noticeable;
but after the German catastrophe at Stalingrad had changed the course
of the war, the discrepancy between propaganda and reality became
more striking, and the public was thirsting for accurate information. The
Peace Party's manifesto painted a broad, suggestive picture of the world
situation. It gave a complete and persuasive description of the magnitude of the German defeat at Stalingrad and its consequences for the
entire war effort, as well as of the Allied successes in North Africa and
the soon-to-follow invasion of western Europe. Hungary's position in all
this was emphasized. Clearly, Hitler was determined to fight to the bitter
end and drag his allies into the abyss with himself, but Hungary's true
interests, it was pointed out, required her to wrest herself from the mortal
grip of Germany and regain her independence. The manifesto then outlined the goals of the Peace Party: independence from German domina-
tion, disengagement from the doomed war effort, and redirection of the
nation's course to save what could still be saved of Hungary's future. It
also appealed to the citizenry to resist the doomed policies of the country's
current leadership and support those forces working for the nation's
independence.

My task was to organize the distribution of this manifesto throughout
Kolozsvár. We decided that we could realistically plan on distributing
about a thousand leaflets. This had to be done in such a way as to ensure
that every copy would be read by at least one person or family. They
could not simply be left in the street and other public places; they had
to be taken from house to house and dropped into individual mailboxes
or slid under apartment doors. I needed five people to distribute two
hundred copies apiece in five different districts of Kolozsvár, a task that
could be carried out in four or five hours on a single evening, allowing
about a minute and a half per leaflet. It had to be done literally overnight, because once the leaflets started appearing the authorities would
be on the alert. For maximum efficiency it was desirable for each male
distributor to have a female companion; a couple walking the streets in
the evening and making frequent stops was less likely to arouse suspicion than an individual doing the same thing. As to the duplication of
the leaflets, that was the task of the Technical Woman and the group

under her direction, one of whose members—as I discovered later—was my former classmate Ede Lebovits, whom I had sent to an appointment with a code word the year before. It was also the task of the technical group to deliver the five batches of two hundred leaflets to the distributors, through five closely scheduled early evening encounters. The person delivering a batch and the person receiving it needed code words, since they were not supposed to know each other.

For this undertaking I divided Kolozsvár into five geographical zones: the center and four quarters. Two of the quarters were working-class neighborhoods (one around Dermata, another around the Railway Yards) and two were mostly middle-class. The center was entirely middle-class. The five batches of two hundred leaflets had to be handed out in five different places not too far from each other nor from the five distribution zones. I determined these places and times, scheduling the encounters at fifteen-minute intervals. Each of the five distributors had to draw up a route covering all the major streets of his zone. At that time the mathematical model known as the Chinese postman problem, invented in the early sixties, was not yet available, so we had to discover for ourselves the routes that involved crossing a minimum number of streets more than once. Two of the five distributors were Mayer Hirsch and Dezső Nussbächer. Mayer had a steady girlfriend who shared his political views, and he had no qualms about involving her. Dezső knew a serious girl with leftist political views whom he managed to talk into joining him. Three positions remained to be filled. For one of these I approached a former classmate of mine, Menyhért Schmidt, whose political views I had shaped in many earlier discussions. He agreed to distribute leaflets but did not have a suitable partner, a problem that we managed to solve after some searching. For the fourth position I chose a chemist in his early thirties, György (George) Havas, whom I had met at Király's discussion group in 1940 and 1941. Although I had not seen him for more than two years, he agreed to help when I explained that I was working for the Peace Party as a communist and had been given the task of organizing the distribution of its antiwar leaflet. He said he would take along his sister, who was reliable and ready to take the risk. For the fifth position I recruited Misi (Michael) Schnittländer, a former student in his late twenties whom I had met only briefly, but of whom I had heard a great deal from my colleagues in Király's circle. He, too, agreed to participate, along with his steady girlfriend. The team was now complete and we were ready for action. I viewed the involvement of Havas and Schnittländer as a great moral success: Both of them were considerably older than I was, and barely knew me (other than through my reputation), yet they were willing to participate in a dangerous action at my request and under my guidance. I felt very proud.

I do not remember the exact date, but it was at the end of July or the beginning of August 1943 that we distributed the Peace Party's manifesto in Kolozsvár. Hirsch, Nussbächer, and Havas received their leaflets on schedule and distributed them in the center of town and the two working-class neighborhoods; but Schmidt and Schnittländer never got theirs. The Technical Woman, who handed out the batches herself, claimed that her fourth rendezvous, Schnittländer, had not shown up. Afraid that something had gone wrong, she decided not to go to the last of the five appointments, and dumped the two remaining batches of leaflets where no one would find them until morning. Schnittländer, however, insisted that he had kept his appointment at the time and place agreed upon, and we could never establish the truth with certainty.

Despite this foul-up, the action as a whole was considered successful. We managed to distribute six hundred copies of the manifesto in downtown Kolozsvár and the main working-class neighborhoods. The next day the leaflets were carried into the workplaces and surreptitiously passed around. Although they were later confiscated by the supervisory personnel, many people had a chance to read them, and they were talked about for many days and weeks thereafter. Soon the DEF descended upon Kolozsvár and launched a thorough investigation that led to arrests later in the fall.

During this same summer two of Dezsö Nussbächer's connections at Dermata matured sufficiently for me to get in direct contact with them. One of these was a leather worker in his mid-forties named Hentz. A former union member, he was sympathetic to our cause and enjoyed considerable respect among his co-workers. The other was a cabinet-maker in his early thirties, Galambos, who had been active as a communist in the past but had lost his party contact at some point. Both men were Gentiles, which was an important advantage at that time. They were willing to meet with me and discuss the situation at the factory with a view to undertaking something when an opportunity arose; however, they were extremely cautious and did not think the situation was ripe for action. I met with each of them regularly on an individual basis (neither was aware of the other) and prepared them for more active involvement in the near future.

It was around this time that PC asked me to meet another member of the Regional Committee, a working-class intellectual whom he called "the writer." This man was in hiding, and I met him through an appointment with a password. He was a somewhat short man, about forty years old, who wore a big black mustache, and was very warm and friendly to me. The purpose of the meeting was for us to get acquainted, possibly to allow him to assess me. We had a long conversation about the political situation, and he showed me something he was writing, a kind of anti-war manifesto with a more local flavor than the one we had distributed. I had no inkling of the horrible fate that awaited him in the very near future.

In the meantime, an important episode occurred in my private life during the late spring and summer of 1943, involving my new acquaintance, the so-called Regional Woman. She was in her early to mid-thirties, good-looking, intelligent, and, judging by the nature of her activities, exceptionally courageous. She was in hiding and had several years of party activity behind her. We would meet about once a week, when I would report my activities to her. She was single and so was I, and although she was thirteen years older than me, I found her very attractive. Around June we became lovers. This was my first relationship, and it filled an important gap in my life. My partner had had several love affairs in the past, at least one of which had left her emotionally scarred. Our relationship lasted for a few months, until she was arrested. Despite our intimacy, I did not know her name and she did not know mine.

During 1943 the course of the war went steadily in favor of the Allies. The economic superiority of the Anglo-American-Soviet bloc was being gradually turned into military superiority and was finally making itself felt on the battlefields. After the Anglo-American landing in Morocco, the tide turned in North Africa: whereas Rommel had scored spectacular victories over the British in the previous year, the joint British and American forces now proceeded to crush his army, and its remnants were hastily evacuated across the Mediterranean. In early July, the Allied forces landed in Sicily, and at the end of the month Mussolini's regime collapsed. The Italian king and some of the military leaders concluded a separate peace with the Allies. The Germans, in a spectacular act of bravado, kidnapped the captive Mussolini and reinstated his rule over the northern part of the country, but this was clearly a rear-guard action and the Allied superiority on the Italian front was obvious to everybody following the events there. In the meantime, the Allies intensified their bombing of German industrial and communication centers, and the German people, for whom the first few years of the war had been a succession of triumphal marches, were now suffering heavy losses on the home front too.

Closer to where I was living, the war on the eastern front had also seen some encouraging developments. In late June and early July an enormous battle developed in the region of Kursk, on the central front, between a huge German army massed for an offensive, and even larger Soviet forces which by now outnumbered the Germans in tanks, airplanes, mobile artillery, and other equipment—most of which, by the way, were of Soviet manufacture. The battle raged for weeks, causing huge losses on both sides, and ended with a German retreat toward the former Polish border. During the following months, the Red Army reconquered most of Western Russia and a good part of the Ukraine. By early 1944 most of the German conquests in the east were lost.

CHAPTER 3

■ ■ ■

In Hiding

In 1943 I turned twenty-one, which was the military age in Hungary, and I was supposed to be drafted in October along with every other male of my age. The Jews were drafted into Work Battalions rather than into military units, but everything else was the same as for the regular army draft. During the summer I underwent the official medical examination, was found fit for service, and was given the name of the enlistment center where I was to show up on October 3. As early as April or May of 1943, however, PC told me that the party had decided to ask me to go underground (that is, into hiding) when I was due for enrollment. This, of course, meant desertion and was a highly risky undertaking, but so was everything else I was doing. The circumstances of going underground involved procuring false identity papers and finding a reasonably safe hiding place with someone willing to serve as host. The party would help with some of the papers and would pay me a monthly allowance sufficient for my living expenses, including rent to be paid to the would-be host. I was supposed to take care of everything else, and had several months to prepare.

I chose to become the student Antal Szilágyi. The name was that of an actual person, a worker roughly my age at RAVAG, whose birthplace and birth date I knew. I managed to obtain a copy of his birth certificate. Besides that important piece of identification, I obtained from PC a student photo identification card (for which I had provided a photograph showing me with a small mustache) made out for Antal Szilágyi, first-year law student. After the war I found out that the person at the

65

university who procured my fake photo identity card was Mihai Pop, a communist medical student and an ethnic Romanian. As a law student, I would have the advantage of rather loose attendance requirements and thus some justification for spending much of the time at home. While these pieces of identification would be useful in case of some problem, the standard ID used at the time in Hungary was the domicile registration certificate issued by the Housing Office. I would have to create a fake one. I received some empty registration forms and a relatively good imitation of the rubber stamp of that office, along with a brief oral instruction by PC in how to make a handwritten text in ink disappear in order to be replaced at one's convenience. He told me what chemicals to buy from the pharmacy and how to mix them in order to obtain a liquid that made ink disappear from a document.

The most difficult problem, however, was to organize a relatively safe hiding place. Since I was going to be wanted as a deserter, I could not possibly take a job, even under a false identity: there were too many hurdles to risk facing with my faked documents, and besides, I could have easily been recognized. In fact, I was supposed to stay most of the time at my hiding place, going out only in the evening and only when I had to. This meant that my host or hosts had to know that I was in hiding. I talked to Zoltán, one of my fellow workers at RAVAG, who was a strong communist sympathizer but did not have the determination to act on his convictions. He was a Gentile, which placed him in a better position to help me, since hiding with Jews was much less safe than hiding with Gentiles. In approaching Zoltán on this issue, I told him that the movement needed a hiding place for a comrade, a single person, and was willing to pay a reasonable amount for his rent and food. There was no need for Zoltán to know that the person was myself, so I did not tell him. I asked him if he knew somebody sympathetic to our cause whom he could approach with such a request. The person would, of course, have to know that his or her tenant was in hiding, and he or she had to live in a place not too exposed to the view of neighbors. Zoltán thought about the problem and after a while came back with the name of an elderly couple that he described as very decent, old-time sympathizers with the movement, who were not politically active or known in any way to the police. They lived in a very modest house in a good neighborhood that seemed to satisfy the requirements I had outlined. The man, Gyula Iszlai, was a bricklayer in his late fifties, who still worked when he could find work; his wife, about the same age, worked occasionally as a laundress and did the cooking. They had a son of nineteen or twenty who lived with them and worked in a tailor shop downtown, and a married daughter who was no longer at home. The situation sounded promising, so I asked Zoltán to raise the matter with the family and, if they were willing to go along, arrange for me to visit them (without giving them my name) in order to work out the details.

After receiving Zoltán's positive answer a week later, I showed up at the house one evening and introduced myself simply as the person in charge of discussing the matter raised by Zoltán. Having had dealings with the movement in the past, they were not surprised that I did not give my name. First, there was a thirty-to-forty-minute confidence-building discussion, in which we talked about the political situation and the inevitable victory of the Allies, and I told them how much we appreciated their willingness to help. Then I outlined our needs in terms of the hiding place. They showed me the house in which they lived, the more modest of two isolated buildings in the same courtyard, seventy or eighty feet apart. It had a main room that served as both kitchen and living room, a bedroom accessible only from the kitchen, and a third room accessible only from the outside. There was no bathroom; there was only an outhouse without running water in the back of the courtyard. For washing themselves, they used water from a faucet in the kitchen, and containers of different shapes and sizes. The couple slept in the bedroom, and their son, Bertalan (Berci for short), slept in the third room. This was the room they were willing to rent, saying that Berci could sleep in the living room–kitchen and would certainly understand, since the family was in need of money. As to food, Mrs. Iszlai shopped and cooked for their family of three, and if the tenant was willing to share in their modest meals, that would be fine. I asked who was living in the other house of the courtyard and found the information satisfactory. On the whole, the circumstances seemed favorable from the point of view of safety, and that was what mattered in the first, second, and third place.

There was one problem, however: while both husband and wife were strongly sympathetic to the movement, as was their married daughter who lived in another part of the city, their son was not only uninterested in politics, but also opposed to any involvement on the part of the family. He would therefore have to be left in the dark about the true nature of our business, for otherwise he could become a nuisance and a source of danger. I expressed some doubt about whether this could be pulled off, since the tenant would have to spend much of his time at home, which might make it difficult to keep Berci in the dark. His mother assured me that Berci left home early every morning and returned just in time for dinner; as long as he saw some advantage from the arrangement, he would be about as interested in how their tenant spent his days as he was in the Chinese alphabet. It came out in the discussion that Berci was contributing part of his income from the tailor shop (too little in the opinion of his father) to the household, so I suggested that in order to make him more cooperative he should have his contribution reduced in exchange for giving up his room, and that the amount in question should be added to the price of room and board. This was accepted, and after agreeing on a price that was well within the means of my monthly allowance, we sealed the deal to begin October 1 and agreed that I would bring the tenant around at that time. At the end of my visit, I asked them not to discuss our arrangement with anybody, not even the daughter who sympathized with the cause, as long as there was no need for it. As if to set an example, I said that, although I fully trusted our friend Zoltán, it was better for everybody, himself included, if he did not know about our arrangement. I was therefore going to tell him that I had had a useful discussion with the Iszlais, but in the end another solution was found for the comrade in need of a hiding place. This I did indeed tell Zoltán, while thanking him for his efforts on our behalf.

When October came, I took my leave from my workplace, letting everybody know that I was going to the Work Battalion. At home, I had a long talk with my mother a few days before I had to leave. I remember this conversation well, since it was the last one we ever had and was emotionally very trying for both of us. I had always felt very close to my mother. I took her to a park where we sat on a bench, and I told her that I was not going to show up at the enlistment center but instead would be leaving town to go into hiding. I told her that I was part of an underground organization that was fighting for the right cause and that had the means to help me hide. Naturally, she was extremely worried that I was putting myself in mortal danger. She quietly wept. I answered that we were all in mortal danger, that the nazis were determined to kill us all, and that there was no telling whether the Work Battalion would be safer than hiding. I even told her that it was not clear who would be safer—I, who was illegally going underground, or she, my father, and my brother, who were legally staying at home. The Germans did not trust the Hungarian government and could occupy Hungary any day, in which case they were likely to subject the Hungarian Jews to the same treatment they had applied to the German Jews, the Polish Jews, and those in the other German-occupied territories—a treatment that we knew was terrible, without knowing the exact dimensions of the catastrophe. I wish these words of mine had not come true, but unfortunately, that is exactly what happened eight months later.

Besides, I told my mother, a worldwide struggle was going on that would decide the fate of mankind, and I wanted to be part of it. I had no intention of dying, and the organization I was part of did not want me to die, but to live and work for our cause. Of course there were risks, but if I had to die, at least I would know that I was not dying without doing something. She tried to master her anguish and pain, and said she was very proud of me. Then I discussed with her what to do when my disappearance would be discovered by the authorities. My father could not be informed beforehand about what I was doing, since he would not have understood and accepted it. On the other hand, I did not want him to simply find out from others that I had not shown up at the enlistment center. So I left home the night before I was supposed to enlist, leaving behind a letter addressed to my parents, in which I pretended I was going across the border to Romania in an attempt to reach Palestine. (The border ran about eight or ten miles from Kolozsvár, and clandestine crossings were risky but still common.) I told my mother that this letter could be shown when the authorities came inquiring. As for my brother, Bobby, I told him the truth just before the day I left. He was scared but said he trusted me to know what I was doing.

The day before I left home, I visited the Iszlai family and told them that I was their new tenant, and that I would be arriving the next evening. I brought along some of my personal belongings, so that I would not have to bring everything at once. I gave them the details of my false identity (my name as shown in my papers and my status as a law student), and they told me that they had spoken to their son Berci and everything was prepared. A few days earlier PC had given me an advance payment equal to my first two months' allowance; so I paid the Iszlais for a month's room and board. The next evening I arrived wearing my best suit, a coat, and a hat, and carrying a single piece of luggage.

I soon got used to my new environment and way of life. The Iszlais' place was toward the upper end of Majális utca, a long street starting close to the center of town and leading up a rather steep hill. The lower half of the street, leading up to the Botanical Garden, was a very nice middle-class residential neighborhood, with many elegant villas surrounded by gardens. Above the Botanical Garden, the houses became more modest and the street gradually turned into a lower-middle-class neighborhood. At the very top there was a working-class cemetery, the Házsongárd. The Iszlais' home was located in the poorer section of the street. I spent most of my days in my room and, weather permitting, in the large, pleasant courtyard garden. I ate by myself or with Mrs. Iszlai at noon, when Iszlai and Berci were at work, and we would all eat together at dinner. I tried to be as friendly as I could to Berci, who did not know about my situation and to whom I had to pretend that I was at the university or elsewhere during the day. My only problem with him was that he loved dancing and sometimes invited me to join him at a dance party. He could not understand why I had to prepare all night for an exam the next day instead of going dancing. I think he thought me rather foolish, with a strange set of priorities; but apart from that we got along well. He even shared with me the secret of his weapon for conquering the girls he danced with: before leaving for the dance, he would stick into his trousers pocket the biggest cucumber he could find in the kitchen. He claimed it had a magical effect on his dance partners.

Mrs. Iszlai also introduced me to the Molnárs, the family living in the other house, which was in fact the main building on the property. The man was a clerk at the post office, his wife worked as a manicurist, and they had a twelve-year-old daughter, Nora, who needed tutoring in mathematics. Although as a law student I was not supposed to be particularly good at math, I nevertheless undertook the required tutoring for a rather modest fee, and this arrangement worked out to everybody's satisfaction. Nora's grades improved, and the tutoring gave me access to the Molnárs' radio (the Iszlais did not have one). When Mrs. Molnár was at home, I would listen to the BBC's German-language news, saying that I was listening to Berlin.

I would go out into the street only in the evening, well dressed, with my hat pulled down as far as custom permitted, and wearing eyeglasses. I would never go through crowded streets, and when somebody who seemed familiar came toward me from the opposite direction, I would take out my handkerchief and wipe my nose to cover my face. The eye-glasses I was wearing had lenses made of plain glass. I had ordered them from an optician to whom I explained that they were for my hypochon-driac grandfather, who thought he needed eyeglasses though the doctor said he did not. At first the optician wanted me to bring in my grandfa-ther so he could talk him out of his illusion, but when I told him that my grandfather could not walk he agreed to help our family by making the glasses. My outings into the city were for the purpose of meeting my connections. These meetings took place in the same way as before, except they were now always in the evening.

Soon after I went underground, the DEF descended upon Kolozsvár and started mopping up our movement. The first news to reach me about this was that the Technical Woman had been arrested. As I found out then, her name was Ilona Grünfeld and she had been given away by one of the people in her group, a man whom I did not know but who was apparently known to the DEF as a communist sympathizer. He had eluded arrest for a while by frequently changing his residence, but in the end he was apprehended; he was then cruelly beaten, and he gave away Ilona Grünfeld. Other arrests followed: Holländer and László were ap-prehended, apparently as a result of Grünfeld's weak behavior; worse, my own party connection at the time, as well as my lover, the Regional Woman, did not show up at our appointment, and I soon found out that she had also been arrested. I learned that her name was Ilona Hovány. The news of her arrest came as a particularly hard shock to me. The other member of the Regional Committee whom I had met a couple of months earlier, the middle-aged "writer," was also arrested. His name, it now turned out, was Béla Józsa. Finally, I learned that the DEF had brought down from Budapest one of the arrested leaders of the Peace Party—and of the Communist Party before its self-dissolution—István Szirmai, who apparently had been the person in charge of the connection with the Regional Committee for Northern Transylvania. My other connections remained at large, and the two most wanted persons were the secretary of the Regional Committee and myself. The secretary of the Regional Committee was none other than my old PC, who I now discovered was called Sándor (Alexander) Jakab. All this I found out from Ede Lebovits, whom I telephoned after Ilona Hovány did not show up at our appoint-ment, and asked to meet me the next evening. Ede was rather scared when I contacted him; he had heard that I had not shown up at the enlistment center and that as a result of the arrests the DEF knew about my activities and was in hot pursuit. He nevertheless showed up at our appointment. Since I had not been his party contact and was not familiar with his activities, I asked him whether anybody among those arrested knew about him. He said that his sole party contact was Ilona Grünfeld, whose name he had only found out after her arrest, and who did not know him by name either. So it seemed that Ede was out of the reach of the DEF. Nevertheless we decided not to meet again until I got in touch with him.

Having lost my contact with the party, I was now on my own. For the reasons mentioned, I could not take a job to earn a living. The two months' allowance I had from the party could be stretched to cover my payments to the Iszlais till the end of the year; then I would be up in the air. I was weighing various more or less risky means of raising funds that I might undertake once the arrests were over, but after the many heavy blows of that fall, I finally ran into luck. One evening in early December, as I was climbing Majalis utca on my return from an outing, I passed a couple immersed in quiet conversation, of which I nevertheless overheard a short fragment. Although it was dark and I could not see their faces, I recognized the man's voice as a familiar one that I very much wanted to hear. I turned around and said loudly, "Good evening, sir." The couple stopped. The man, whose face I could not see because his hat was pulled down, whispered something into the woman's ear, then took two steps toward me, extended his hand and said: "What a pleasant surprise, my young friend." It was Sándor Jakab, my old PC. We quickly agreed on a time and place to meet the next evening, and he left in the company of the woman.

The news I heard when we met was a shock to me. Sándor Jakab (I will simply call him Sanyi) told me that many of those arrested—among them Ilona Grünfeld and Willy Holländer—were broken by the beatings and gave away everything they knew. Béla Józsa, on the other hand, refused to say anything and was beaten to death. As I was to find out later, the precise circumstances were as follows: beaten to a pulp and ready to die rather than betray the cause he was fighting for, Józsa refused to eat. When they tried to force-feed him, he resisted. Apparently the food was forced down into his lungs and that killed him. Sanyi also told me that Ilona Hovány was found to be pregnant and refused to tell the DEF who the father was. The other prisoners did not know either. To

Sanyi's surprise, I gave him the solution to the puzzle: if Ilona was indeed pregnant, then I was the one responsible. I had a terrible feeling as I imagined how much the pregnancy must have aggravated Ilona's suffering under arrest. Later, in the spring, I learned that she had given birth to a son whom she called Attila. Presumably due to Ilona's brutal handling by the DEF and the dire conditions of her subsequent imprisonment, Attila's health was very fragile and he died soon after the liberation of Kolozsvár, some time in early 1945.

Since the DEF was still in town around Christmas 1943, we suspended all our activities except for occasionally seeing each other and a couple of other people to find out what was going on with the investigation. Sanyi gave me the equivalent of my allowance for another four months, just in case. The party funds had been raised from well-to-do sympathizers, and now, with only the two of us still at large, there was no dearth of money.

One evening, around February 1944, Ede, who was my main source of information about the activities of the DEF, did not show up for an appointment. This was very serious and I suspected trouble. Although we had the usual "control" appointment one week later, I decided not to wait until then and called the grocery store where he worked, using a public telephone far from the place where I was living. His father picked up the phone, and when I asked for Ede, he said in an anguished voice that Ede had left town with a friend. The meaning of this was clear: Ede had been taken away. I hung up and left the telephone booth and its surrounding area in a hurry. I could not imagine how the DEF had managed to track down Ede, whose name was not known to any of those arrested. As I found out after the war, the DEF, knowing that I had recruited several of my friends into the movement, showed Ilona Grünfeld pictures of my classmates and friends and asked her to pick out the man who was working with her in the technical section. She identified Ede. I informed Sanyi about Ede's arrest. He in turn had other sources and soon found out that Ede was bravely resisting interrogation: instead of bringing the agents to his appointment with me, he took them to several fictitious appointments where nobody showed up. After each such outing the frustrated agents gave him a terrible beating, and when he was no longer able to bear it, he would invent another fictitious appointment. This gained him a few days' respite, because they had to leave him unharmed enough to be driven to these appointments.

A few weeks later we found out that the DEF had concluded its investigation and its contingent of detectives had returned to Budapest. A trial took place and the detainees were sentenced to prison terms of varying lengths. As well as I can remember, Szirmai got twenty years, Hovány fifteen, and the others between five and ten years. Most of them remained in jail in Kolozsvár until the summer of 1944, when the men were sent to a punitive Work Battalion from which some managed to escape, while others ended up in German concentration camps and were killed. Ilona Hovány, Ede Lebovits, György László, and István Szirmai survived. Willy Holländer was killed.

I resumed my regular meetings with Sanyi and on one occasion he brought along a woman in her late thirties, whom he introduced as another comrade in hiding. She had worked as part of the technical group, and went underground when her contact was arrested by the DEF in early 1944. She struck me as particularly bright and knowledgeable about all human matters. As I found out later, she was a pediatrician named Regina Josepovits, and an exceptionally decent person. After the war we became close friends, but I met her only once while in hiding.

March 19, 1944, was a fateful day in the history of Hungary and for Hungarian Jews in particular. Dissatisfied with his control over Hungary and weary of what he saw as a wavering attitude on the part of the Hungarian regime, Hitler decided to occupy his satellite. He summoned Hungary's regent, Horthy, to a meeting in the middle of March, told him to appoint a more decisively pro-German government, and informed him that he was sending his troops into Hungary to enforce this decision. He proposed a new prime minister in the person of Döme Sztólyai, who until then had been Hungary's ambassador to Berlin. Upon his return on March 19, Horthy found the German troops marching in. He quickly made the change demanded by Hitler and appointed Sztólyai. At the beginning of April, Jews throughout Hungary were ordered to wear a yellow star and subjected to a plethora of other crippling and humiliating restrictions.

At the beginning of May the gendarmerie moved the Jews of Kolozsvár out of their dwellings into a ghetto set up on the territory of the brick factory near the railway station. The ghetto consisted of a group of tentlike structures improvised in a few days. About eighteen thousand Jews—those from Kolozsvár itself and from the villages and small towns within a certain radius of the city—were gathered in the ghetto; in the second half of May and the first week of June, all were loaded into railway cattle cars and taken away to an unknown destination. From my hiding place I could gather only fragmentary information about what was happening, but everything I heard sounded ominous. At first, when the forced move into the ghetto was decreed, a rumor was spread among the victims that they would be taken to a labor camp called Kenyérmezö somewhere in western Hungary. In reality, no such camp existed, and as I was to find out later, the Jews were deported to Auschwitz. My host, the bricklayer Iszlai, came home one day in May visibly upset with the news that a German soldier, when asked by a Hungarian civilian where the Jews were being taken, answered, "Don't worry, you won't see them again." I will describe later what happened to the deportees of Kolozsvár. Although at the time I did not know where they were taken, I had the worst possible premonitions about the fate of my family and friends.

One day toward the end of May I saw, through the glass door of my room, three men enter the courtyard and go into the Molnárs' house. One of them was a German officer. They seemed to be going from house to house; before they entered our courtyard I had seen them cross the street after coming out of another house. I had no idea what they were after, but as the Iszlais were not home I thought I had better not be home either. The window of my room looked back onto the garden, which was about a hundred feet long and ended in a ditch separating the property from the Botanical Garden. I locked my door and jumped out through the window (which was not high), crossed the garden, and took up a position in the ditch from which I could observe the house without being seen from it. In case something threatening developed, I could flee through the Botanical Garden. After spending a few minutes at the Molnárs', the three men came out and left without trying to enter the Iszlais' dwelling. They then moved on to the next house. When the danger had passed, I returned to my room by the same route through which I had left it.

One morning about ten days later, before I had dressed, I heard the front gate open. I jumped to the glass door and saw a police officer coming straight to my room. The Iszlais were not at home; the two men were at work and Mrs. Iszlai had gone to the market. The officer knocked on my door; I said, "Enter," and he did. He looked around and asked for my papers. I gave him the three pieces of identification that I had, one by one, asking what was the problem that brought him to my place. He said he would explain, but in the meantime I should get dressed, for I would have to go with him. I started dressing but insisted he tell me what the problem was. He seemed a little perplexed by the fact that my papers seemed to be in perfect order, and asked questions about my family and who in Kolozsvár knew me. I said that many people knew me—my colleagues at the university, for instance, and my best friend so-and-so who lived not far from us. I gave him a fictitious name and an address a couple of kilometers away from where we were, wrote it down for him, and offered to accompany him there (it seemed unlikely that he would follow up my offer). He then asked me what my religion was. Protestant, I answered, as could easily be seen from my papers. Was anybody in my family Jewish? No, as far as I knew, not even a distant relative. What were my grandparents? On my father's side they were Protestant and on my mother's side Catholic. Then why did I feel the need to hide? I protested energetically that I wasn't hiding at all and had no reason to, that I was taking courses regularly at the university, which could easily be checked. I then repeated my offer to go right away to the friend whose address I had written down. Did I have enemies, he asked, who would want to do me in? That was a possibility, I said, but I wasn't aware of any such person. Well, he said, there was a neighbor who maintained that he saw me jump out of my room through the window and hide in the ditch behind the house. Was there such a ditch? Oh, I said, so *that* was it! My friend and another colleague had visited me a few days earlier; we had played various games, and it was during one of these that I had jumped through my window and gone to the ditch. The neighbor wasn't necessarily my enemy, just a very suspicious person who didn't know young people or understand their games. I was sure that the officer would have more wisdom than to take such a thing seriously. We discussed this at some length, and after a while he seemed persuaded. He told me I did not need to accompany him; he would take along my domicile registration certificate, check with the housing office, and if everything I told him was true, I had no reason to worry. I thanked him for his understanding and he left with my certificate in his pocket.

To say that I felt relieved would be a crude understatement. In fact, I felt that I had just looked death in the face and it had somehow turned away from me. But there was no time for rejoicing; the danger had not completely passed. There was not a moment to lose. I had to leave my hiding place and change my identity; I also had to instruct my hosts as to how to behave when the police came back for me, which could happen at any time, starting later that day. I packed a few indispensable items, locked my door, and left the house. I knew that Mrs. Iszlai was due back from the market around ten-thirty or eleven o'clock, and I wanted to intercept her on her way home. I posted myself at an appropriate observation point on the lower half of the long street and met her there as she was coming home. I told her what had happened and said that, as a consequence, I had to leave. Naturally, she became upset and scared. I tried to calm her down by explaining that the police had no inkling of who I was, that they simply had a malicious report from a neighbor and suspected me of being a Jew. When they came back—which they would—the Iszlais should say that I had gone out of town for a couple of weeks but had left my things there. Should the police ask any further questions about me, they should say that they had posted a room-for-rent sign and I had shown up claiming to be a student interested in renting their room. My papers had been in order and they had no reason to suspect any foul play. Two weeks after the police officer's visit to me, unbeknownst to the Iszlais, I contacted their daughter, Annus, who lived in another part of town and was a Communist sympathizer. She told me that the police had indeed come back and had questioned her parents at length about me. They had stuck to their story and the police finally left, cautioning the Iszlais to let them know when I returned. Annus offered to bring me those of my things from her parents' house that I might need.

I found myself in a precarious situation when I had to leave the Iszlais' house. I had no alternative hiding place and my papers had suddenly become worthless. I had to change my name and assume a new identity. Because the new Hungarian government was canceling military deferments for most student categories, I decided to become a medical student; medical students' deferments were likely to hold up longer than others. I had taken with me the chemicals needed for changing my name in the papers that were still in my possession, and I had a few blank housing office registration forms, along with the fake rubber stamp. I needed a quiet place to work on those changes. I mentally went through the list of my contacts still at large, in order to choose someone who might be of help to me. My choice fell on Galambos, the Dermata worker. Although in the past he had been active for a while as a communist, that had been under the Romanian regime and the Hungarian authorities did not seem to know about him. I knew that he was married without children and lived in a small two-room apartment in one of the better quarters of town. He was of course Gentile. Since my only contacts with him had been walks along the streets of Kolozsvár, he was quite surprised at my unexpected visit. He introduced me to his wife as a friend, and we went into the other room to talk. I explained my situation and asked whether he was willing to take me in under conditions similar to those in which I had lived with the Iszlais. He panicked and said there was no way he could do that: the atmosphere at Dermata was terrible and several workers there knew about his communist sympathies in the past. They might denounce him to the authorities, in which case he could be fired from his job or worse. I saw no use in insisting, so I said I understood and would leave the next morning, but I needed a couple of hours to take care of my personal documents. At first Galambos said he would prefer it if I did not spend the night in their apartment, but I answered that I had no choice: it was too late in the evening for me to go out and look for alternative accommodations. If he still disagreed, he should call the police and hand me over. My sudden change of tone had its effect: he felt ashamed and said he would rather go to jail than do something like that. He went into the other room to discuss the situation with his wife, and when he came back he said it was fine for me to spend the night there and I could sleep in the other room.

I immediately began to doctor my papers. For the sake of having as little ink to erase as possible, the medical student that I was about to become was called Antal Somogyi. Leaving the first name unchanged posed no problem, since Antal (Anthony) was a very common name among Hungarians. The choice of the second name meant that I had only to replace the "zilá" in Szilágyi with the "omo" in Somogyi. This job was soon completed successfully, and I felt substantially relieved: whereas earlier in the day I had felt a constant anguish as I walked the streets of Kolozsvár, now I felt that I could go out and move around more confidently in the possession of my new identity. There was only one problem left. Military papers were increasingly becoming more important than civilian ones, and I had none. The standard military ID for males was a military passport (in Hungarian, military book), a booklet that looked like a passport except that it was somewhat larger in size and thinner, since it did not need pages for visas. Inside the booklet were the personal data of the individual, along with his military status. I asked Galambos about his military booklet and he showed it to me. It would have suited my needs rather well, as few things besides the name re-quired changing. I told Galambos about the technique for doctoring documents and showed him how to do it in case he happened to need it. Then I told him that if he lost his military booklet, he had only to report the loss immediately—there was no penalty or investigation. He would receive a confirmation of his report by return mail, and within six weeks a new military booklet. I suggested that he inquire about this and confirm the information; after which, if he wanted to help me, he could give me his military booklet and report that he had lost it. I would then replace the name. He said he believed me without needing to check, and would like to give me his military booklet right away so he could see how I made his name disappear from it. This was done beautifully on the spot, to our mutual satisfaction, and Galambos said he would report the loss the next day. I now had reasonably good personal identification papers as Antal Somogyi, medical student.

The next morning I set out to find room and board on a standard commercial basis. This meant a much more dangerous way of life than the one I had before, because I had to behave like a medical student all the time instead of hiding in my room all day. I peered over the news-paper ads for room and board, and visited those places whose locations seemed acceptable. I inspected them first from the outside to see how they looked, then, if everything else seemed OK, I went inside. I was still wearing eyeglasses and a hat, and used my handkerchief frequently. I settled for a room in the working-class neighborhood around the railway station, far from the Majalis utca where I had stayed with the Iszlais, and also far from the center of town and from those areas of the city where I had previously lived and worked. The environment seemed all right, though not excellent. The family understood that I was facing exams and therefore needed to study diligently most of the time; nevertheless, I still had to go out and face the danger of being recognized.

■ ■ ■

One of the first things I did after renting the room was buy myself a couple of medical textbooks, so I could display them in my room as the objects of my study. About this same time, I decided to arm myself with a handgun. Of course, guns were not on sale to the public in Hungary, but the area where I was living had many rooms requisitioned for the

Wehrmacht, and I had heard that the German soldiers were short of Hungarian currency and sometimes sold their pistols. I approached one of the German soldiers who was staying in my neighborhood and struck up a conversation with him as if to practice my German. After a while we got into a discussion about the fair price of a pistol, and I ended up buying his, along with a modest supply of bullets (maybe fifteen or twenty). He even taught me how to handle the gun.

In my new environment I could not stay home all the time, so I would go out for several hours each day, trying to find routes and places with as few people as possible. This was, of course, rather risky in my situation, but I had no choice. I soon got used to feeling in constant danger of being recognized and apprehended. A couple of times I went to the city's main cemetery, a beautiful but somewhat desolate place where one could spend time alone without provoking attention. The cemetery was on a hillside overlooking the city, and while I was there one morning around June 1, the sirens went off. People quickly left the cemetery to seek shelter. I acted as if I was doing the same, but in fact I just moved from one part of the cemetery to another until everybody disappeared and I was by myself. Soon I heard, then saw high in the sky above the city, what I knew to be American bombers, small silvery objects glistening in the sunshine; then I heard the bombs fall on the city. I can hardly describe the exhilaration that the sight of the American bombers aroused in me. I felt as if they had brought the message, "You are not alone, we are coming." As I found out a few hours later, the bombs fell mostly on the railway tracks and in the area around the railway station.

While the house where I was staying and its immediate neighborhood suffered no damage in the bombing, my room and board arrangement there did not last more than two weeks. I gradually befriended my hosts and they showed me the family photo album: to my horror, I discovered that one of the uncles who occasionally visited them was a foreman at the Iron Works where I had worked in 1942, who would certainly recognize me if he saw me. I immediately set out to find another place and, using the same method as before, located a room in another quarter called Donáth ut. I left within a day of discovering the dangerous uncle, settling my rent and giving some credible excuse which I no longer remember.

My next hiding place was in a lower-middle-class environment. The rather good-looking house consisted of two apartments: the front one was inhabited by a young divorced woman and her mother and the back one by a widow in her late fifties or early sixties. It was the widow who was offering a room for rent in the back of the house, with a separate entrance from the courtyard. Behind this room, the courtyard extended toward a hill and continued in a garden whose back end was toward an open area. The woman was easily amenable to offering board along with the room. We agreed on the terms—which were much less financially convenient than those of my previous room—and I moved in. Although my room had a separate entrance, my movements could still be observed by the owner, who was at home most of the time. Just as at my previous place, I was forced to spend time away from the house.

On June 6, 1944, the Allies landed in Normandy—an event that, needless to say, marked another decisive turning point in the war: finally, the much-heralded second front in western Europe was opened. I remember the joy I felt upon hearing the news, but it was joy mixed with regret. Too late! Could it not have come a little earlier? Could it not have prevented the roundup and deportation of the Jews? After the air raid in early June there were no others, but there were frequent alarms. On those occasions everybody had to go to the air raid shelter, which was in the cellar of the house and also served the needs of several neighbors. So willy-nilly I had to get acquainted with new people, another high risk that I could not avoid. One of these neighbors was a gendarme colonel. Although he was a regular uniformed officer and not a detective, I was afraid that he might be familiar with my picture, as I had been on the gendarmerie's wanted list for the last eight months. I was now wearing my glasses all the time and had changed the appearance of my hair, but still. . . . I watched his face carefully when we first met and exchanged a few banalities, but he seemed completely indifferent. Another acquaintance who soon caused me headaches was a woman in her forties who lived a few houses down the street but was assigned to our shelter. She expressed a keen interest in talking to me and had many questions about my student career and my feelings about the medical vocation. I soon discovered that her interest had a special reason: she was looking for a husband for her twenty-year-old daughter and figured that a doctor in the family would not be a bad thing. The way I became aware of this was that one Sunday morning she appeared on my doorstep with an air of urgency, telling me that her daughter, Mary, was ill and I had to come immediately to examine her. I explained that I would be pleased to help her or her daughter if I could, but I was only a third-year student, years away from finishing, and had no right to practice as a doctor. I would actually be breaking the law, which I was sure neither she nor her daughter wanted me to do. I urged her to call a doctor, but my protests were to no avail. She had long realized, she said, what a serious person I was, studying all day and speaking competently about everything. Both she and her daughter trusted me and wanted to hear my opinion about her illness. Even if they were to call a doctor later—which they could not do on Sunday anyway—they still attached great importance to my opinion. Naturally, she would pay me for my services, an offer that I turned down immediately. Reluctantly, I went to the house, where Mary was in bed with fever and a sore throat. I examined her as a medical person would (to the best of my knowledge at the time): I looked into her throat after pushing down her tongue with the handle of a spoon, and found it red. I took her temperature with the family's thermometer and found it to be somewhat elevated, but not dangerously so. I then listened to her breathing by applying my ear to her back and to her chest, as I had seen doctors do. Finally, I said that according to all appearances she had a bad cold or a flu, that she should start taking aspirin and pyramidon (an over-the-counter medicine used at the time in central Europe for reducing fever), and that the next morning they should call a doctor to make sure she did not develop pneumonia. I was lucky: the medical visit ended without complications and a couple of days later the mother told me that Mary was better.

During June and July I met Sanyi about once a week, sometimes once every two weeks. At these meetings we exchanged information and planned various actions, such as organizing a small group with my contacts at Dermata that would carry out sabotage acts against the Germans. It was doubtful whether my contacts were willing to go that far toward risking their lives; even if they were, there was the problem of acquiring explosives. Sanyi had lost his contact with Budapest, so we had no indication as to what type of actions the party currently favored; the idea of a sabotage group was our own. It never got beyond the drawing board because subsequent events made it moot before we could master the difficulties.

I remember one of our meetings particularly well because of its emotional content. We met in the city park in late afternoon on July 13, and

I told Sanyi that it was my mother's birthday and that I felt terribly frustrated and impotent because she and the rest of my family had been taken away along with the other Jews of Kolozsvár. To which he answered, "You are not alone," and showed me a photograph of his mother who, he said, had also been taken away. This came to me as a double surprise—first, that he was carrying a photograph that could give him away; second, that he was Jewish, which I had not known. I asked whether he knew where the Jews had been taken. He did not, but he confirmed the suspicion I had, that the destination of the trains carrying the Jews was not Kenyérmező, as had been rumored, but some place outside Hungary. He expressed the opinion that most likely we would never see our loved ones again.

On one occasion toward the end of July, Sanyi told me about an incident that had just taken place in Budapest. One of the leaders of the Peace Party, (and, of course, of the former Communist Party), Endre Ságvári, a man in his early thirties who had gone into hiding, was sitting at a table with a comrade in a coffee shop in Buda when they were suddenly cornered by four agents of the DEF who came to arrest them. Ságvári pulled out a handgun and shot three of his assailants before being shot himself (he died; the agents survived). This episode was of interest because it marked an important departure from the earlier behavior of party members: armed resistance to arrest. I was glad I had acquired my pistol.

Around the middle of July I discovered that Manci, the young divorced woman living in the front apartment with her mother, owned a small summer house on a nearby street, Törökvágás ut, which went up the hill toward the Hólya forest. Large cracks had developed in one of its walls, and it had been uninhabited for some time. I took a look at the house. It stood alone in a sizable courtyard, and in spite of the cracks it seemed habitable. Since it was much better from the point of view of privacy and offered the possibility of moving in and out unobserved by the neighbors, I accepted Manci's offer to rent it to me, with board, for about the same price that I was paying the widow in the courtyard. Thus I moved again. I took my meals at Manci's apartment, where I had a chance to listen to the news on a pretty good radio set. I used the same trick I had used at the Molnárs' house, listening to the German edition of the BBC, and claiming I was listening to Berlin.

Several weeks went by. I managed to get hold of a Russian language manual (in Hungarian) and started learning. I did not find the Cyrillic alphabet too difficult, and managed to learn it in a few days; the grammar was complicated, but no more so than in German, and I memorized a small vocabulary of everyday words. My chief problem was pronunciation, since the Hungarian phonetic transcription of Russian gave only a vague idea about how the words were actually pronounced. In the meantime, I was living the dangerous life of a wanted fugitive with a precarious hiding place. Every time I went out, I might run into an acquaintance. I walked very carefully, keeping my eyes wide open and trying to make sure that whenever somebody approached me I saw the person's face before he or she saw mine. That sometimes made it possible to avoid undesirable encounters, but not always. Late one afternoon I was crossing a long, narrow footbridge that connected the city park to the Donáth quarter where I was living. Before I had reached the middle of the bridge, I saw coming toward me from the opposite end none other than Szöllösi, my former foreman at RAVAG. It was too late to turn around. I pulled out my handkerchief and started blowing my nose, covering my face until I passed him. He gave no sign of having recognized me, but he could have. If he had, and if he reported his discovery, that would have certainly called the gendarmes' attention to the quarter where I was living. It seemed unlikely that I would be able to carry on this way of life for much longer without being discovered, and I considered my chances of survival very slim. And then something happened.

On August 26, a day which I remember very well, I went over to Manci's apartment around eight o'clock in the morning to have breakfast and listen to the news. The morning hours were best for listening to the radio, since Manci was away at work and only her mother was at home. The news that morning was unusually rich in positive content: with the Red Army at the Dnyester River on the old Romanian border, the Romanian military dictator, Marshall Antonescu, had been arrested three days earlier with the cooperation of the king, and a pro-Allied government was formed. Romania promptly turned against the Germans, gave them an ultimatum to leave the country without delay, and joined the Russians in fighting the withdrawing Wehrmacht. In three days the Soviet and Romanian armies liberated most of Romania beyond the Carpathian

Mountains, and Bucharest was firmly in their hands. All this was happening just a few hundred kilometers from where I lived. That same morning, on the western front, the Allied troops were entering liberated Paris. For the first time in many months the news was so heartening and the collapse of the German war machine seemed so near, that I allowed myself to indulge in daydreams about survival and liberation.

It was in this rather heady mood that I left the apartment around nine o'clock and headed back to the house. As I turned the corner of Törökvágás ut, the street leading up the hill, and approached the house, I noticed three men coming toward me from the upper part of the street. One of them was my neighbor, the gendarme colonel, who addressed me with, "Good morning, doctor; these gentlemen from the housing office are looking for you." I said good morning, introduced myself, and the colonel continued down the street, leaving me alone with the two men. One was a tall man in his late forties, on the heavy side and almost completely bald, wearing dark-rimmed eyeglasses; the other was even taller and much younger, a lanky man in his early thirties with a black mustache. Both were well dressed. The heavier man explained that they were from the housing office and that, according to their files, the house at number 12 was empty. They had come to find out whether it was habitable, and were surprised to see that someone was in fact living there. Could I explain the situation? Of course I could, I said: The house had indeed been empty until recently, because it was damaged, but a few weeks ago I had rented it and so currently it was occupied by me. They said they would have to check to see why their office had no evidence of the house being occupied. But as long as they were there, would I permit them to enter the house and inspect the damage? Of course, I said. We crossed the courtyard, I opened the door with my key, and we entered.

Once we were in the living room, my visitors started examining the cracks in the wall. After a couple of minutes the bald man said, "Let me take some notes," and reached into the right pocket of his jacket. But when he pulled out his hand with a swift movement, suddenly turning straight toward me, what he held was not a notebook but a pistol. He grasped it tightly with both hands, his forefingers stretched along both sides of the barrel, pointing it toward my stomach, with his body slightly bent over. "Don't move!" he shouted.

I didn't. My pistol was not in my pocket; it was hidden in the house. But even if I had had it, it is unlikely I would have had a chance to use it.

"Put your hands behind your back," he continued. I had little choice but to obey him. "Tie him up," he said to the other man, who quickly produced a leather strap and tied my hands and lower arms together behind my back. As soon as this happened, the bald man said, "Boss, you can come out." The door of the wardrobe opened and a small, stocky, fiftyish man climbed out. He had an ugly round face and dark, piercing eyes. At the same time, the younger man opened the door of the house and called out, "Laci, you can come in," whereupon a very young man— the fourth member of the team, who apparently had been hiding in the courtyard—came in.

As soon as I met the two "housing officials" I was on my toes, sensing danger; yet I did not expect to be arrested, as this was not how people were usually apprehended. Instead, a car would come before dawn, detectives would surround the house or apartment, and finally the agents would ring the bell or knock on the door, forcing their way in if necessary. This is what I had in mind when I hid my pistol. But apparently, in view of the sharpening of the struggle and the increased likelihood of suspects offering resistance to arrest, the DEF had adopted more sophisticated methods. As I was to find out later, the "boss" belonged to the DEF. His name was András Juhász and he was the head of the DEF's detachment of gendarmes in Kolozsvár.

I was momentarily surprised when the bald man pointed his gun at me, but my shock lasted only a couple of seconds. Then three ideas crossed my mind. One was, "The game is up: goodbye to life and dreams of survival." The second was, "This is your hour of trial: collect yourself, steel yourself, be ready to resist." The third one, irrelevant under the circumstances, lasted only for a fraction of a second: "So this is how you're really supposed to hold a gun."

As soon as the "boss" climbed out of the wardrobe and the fourth man came in from the courtyard, they pushed me down onto a chair and started questioning me. Who was I? Antal Somogyi, medical student. My papers? In my pocket. They held the papers against the light and said that they were fake. No, I said, they were not. Then suddenly the boss held before my eyes my high school graduation photograph, with "Egon Blatt" on the back of it in my own handwriting. "And who is this?" he asked. At that point I decided that it made no sense to continue denying my identity; so I answered simply, "That's me." Then followed an avalanche of questions, of which I answered only the first: How long had I been living at my current address? I gave the correct date. To the next question, where had I lived before I moved there, I simply said, "I'm not answering that question." I gave the same answer to all the subsequent questions, or simply replied with "never," "nobody," etc. They asked questions such as: When did I last meet my comrades? Who was I in contact with? Who gave me money? How did I acquire my false papers?

As the questions kept flying and I kept refusing to answer them, the agents became more and more heated. I, on the other hand, was gradually overcome by a strange feeling of defiance rooted in the sense that I had nothing to lose; they would probably kill me anyway. At one point the boss changed his tone and said quietly, with a menacing expression on his face: "If you don't speak, we have other methods." To which I answered, "I know you have. You can kill me like you killed Béla Józsa, but that won't do you much good." This provoked a mixed reaction. The boss said threateningly, "You think you are ready to die, but there are things worse than death." However, the bald man, who may have been a native of Kolozsvár, said nervously, "Who told you that nonsense about Józsa? We don't kill people; Józsa died because he refused to eat." I registered with satisfaction that my invoking Józsa's death had touched a raw nerve. After all, the Russians were closing in fast on Transylvania. For a while the agents kept asking questions, and I expected to be beaten at any moment, but that did not happen in the house. Instead, after about twenty or thirty minutes, they sent out the youngest member of the team to fetch the car (probably parked around the corner), put me into the back seat squeezed between two of the agents, and drove me to the gendarmerie's Kolozsvár headquarters on Monostori ut. They also put a few of my things, like underwear and handkerchiefs, into a bag, and took my coat and hat along.

How was I discovered? How did the DEF find my hiding place? I have never found the answer to this question. There are many possibilities. The gendarme colonel may, after all, have recognized my face from my photo, which he almost surely had seen at some point. Or Szöllösi may have recognized me on the bridge and reported his discovery, triggering a tight supervision of the main streets and bridges connecting the Donáth quarter to the rest of the city. Ede Lebovits and his family had lived in the Donáth quarter, and the family grocery where Ede had worked was very close to where I was living. I knew that Ede had been arrested and his family deported, but I did not know that the grocery had been taken over by the former assistant, who may have known me from my visits to Ede. This man may have seen and recognized me. Or perhaps somebody else recognized me, and once the DEF had a strong indication of the neighborhood I was living in, they could easily have spotted me on the street when I went out, as I was forced to do almost daily, and followed me.

CHAPTER 4

■ ■ ■

Under Arrest

At the gendarmerie headquarters, I was put into a cell with a wooden plank and a small window protected by iron bars close to the ceiling. I was not left by myself for long; soon I was taken to the boss, who told me with an air of importance that a very high-ranking officer wanted to talk to me. He took me to another office, where a man in his sixties with silvery hair, in an elegant uniform the like of which I had seen only in movies, was seated at a desk. He was a general, the commandant of the gendarmerie for Northern Transylvania. He sized me up from top to bottom with evident curiosity; then said, with no hostility in his voice: "So, finally, here you are. We have been looking for you for almost a year. Where have you been hiding?"

"Sorry, sir, I can't answer that question."

"You are a communist, aren't you?"

"Yes, I am."

"Why are you a communist and what do you communists want?"

I said that I was a communist because I believed in the justice of the communist cause.

Did I know anything about the Soviet Union? the commandant asked. Yes, I did. What is the population of the Soviet Union? About two hundred million. And how many members does the Soviet Communist Party have? About four million.

"Correct," he said, apparently surprised that I knew the figure. "And you call this justice, four million people ruling the two hundred million?"

I said that the party members were a vanguard, that their number did not reflect the support that the regime enjoyed. This support was better reflected in the way their soldiers fought on the battlefield, and they did not do badly in that respect. Further, I said, this issue was beside the point, because the communists' current goal was not to introduce communism in Hungary—that would be up to the Hungarian people to decide when they were free to make a choice—but to help extricate Hungary from the war, reestablish her independence, and prevent Germany from dragging her down into the abyss as it was collapsing.

This line of reasoning was not to the commandant's liking: he became visibly irritated, turned to me with a hostile look on his face, and said, "You are a Jew. Why is it that all the communists are Jews?"

I answered that this was not so, that there were plenty of non-Jewish communists, but that given the treatment the Jews were receiving, it was certainly not surprising that some of them turned to the communist movement in self-defense.

Abruptly, the commandant ended the audience. "Take him away," he said to the boss. I was led out of the office and back to my cell.

I was left alone for about an hour, during which I was given some food. Then the guard (a gendarme) took me to the boss, who started my first official interrogation. I gave my name as Egon Blatt, with my correct birth date and birthplace. He then asked basically the same questions as he had asked at the house when I was arrested, but this time he sat behind a typewriter and typed my answers. Again, he became angry when I refused to answer his questions. Several times he jumped to his feet and made menacing gestures, and once he stepped in front of me and hit me in the stomach with his fist. The blow hurt, of course, but to my surprise it was not followed by a more serious beating, and the interrogation ended with my signing the minutes that simply recorded my refusal to answer the various questions. I was led back to my cell and had the whole evening and night to think about my situation.

I was puzzled by the lack of torture, a mystery that was solved the next morning. I firmly resolved not to turn in anybody, whatever happened to me, even if I had to die. I thought through all the information that the DEF had collected about our actions and organization through the arrests in the fall of 1943, and tried to anticipate the questions that would follow. The detectives certainly would want the names of the people who had distributed the manifesto of the Peace Party in the summer of 1943. They knew that I was the organizer of that action and would surely press me for the identity of the participants, all of whom were still at large. They knew that I had contacts at Dermata and would probably want to know who they were. They had already pressed me for my earlier hiding places, as well as for the source of my money and my papers. Finally, they obviously assumed that I was in contact with Sanyi and would press me hard to lead them to our next meeting place. My first line of defense would be simply not to answer the questions; but I was not sure how long I could stick to that under torture. I wanted to have a second line of defense to fall back on before I completely lost control of myself, so I thought up various fictitious versions of events— basically harmless, more or less believable lies—that I could substitute for the truth and in particular for the names that I knew the DEF would want from me.

The next day, August 27, the younger of the two "housing officials" who had arrested me, the one with the black mustache, came into my cell and informed me that soon we were to leave for the railway station to take the train for Budapest. It suddenly became clear why I had not been beaten: I had to be kept fit for "public transportation"; they would not want to put on display a man who had been "handled" by the DEF. Early in the afternoon the boss and the two "housing officials" drove me to the station. Before we left, they tied my hands again with a leather strap, and when we got out of the car, I had a man on each side holding my arms. I was pushed into a first class train compartment, with the boss and the younger "housing official" sitting on either side of me, while the bald man said goodbye to his colleagues and returned to the car. My hands were still tied, though not behind my back, and my coat was placed in my lap to cover my tied hands. It crossed my mind that if I could somehow free my hands, the agents would not notice it. But I saw no way of doing that, and even if I had, I saw no way of using my hands effectively against the armed agents accompanying me.

We traveled through a beautiful landscape on that mild, sunny, late summer afternoon, and as we crossed the mountains and headed toward the Hungarian plain I said goodbye to Transylvania, to which I now felt attached, and which I would most likely never see again. Toward evening, the agents took turns going to the dining car, and the younger one brought some food for me. He said he would untie my hands to enable me to eat, but showed me the pistol in his pocket in case I tried "something foolish."

Again it crossed my mind to do "something foolish." I tried to imagine what would happen if I suddenly threw myself against the window in order to break it and jump out, but it seemed completely hopeless: the window probably would not break; if it broke, the opening would be too small to let my body through; and if I somehow wriggled through without the agents grabbing my body or my legs, I would fall on my face or head from a train moving at about sixty kilometers an hour. In the best of circumstances this might amount to a successful suicide attempt. After I ate, my hands were tied again. At one point the agents took me to the toilet, but that occasion again offered no opportunity for attempting escape.

We traveled all night and arrived at Budapest's Keleti Pályaudvar (Eastern Railway Station) in the morning. It was a beautiful, sunny morning that started what was to be the most difficult day of my life. An agent was waiting for us and took us to a car. I was seated in the back with my hands tied and the tall agent beside me, while the boss took the front seat near the driver. I was taken to the headquarters of the DEF in Buda, on the west side of the Duna (Danube). On the way I could see the boss's face through the rearview mirror. He and the driver were talking with muffled voices, so I could not hear the conversation; but at one point the driver asked something and pointed with his head toward me. The boss's answer was to strike a dignified pose and twirl his mustache, the latter gesture a typical Hungarian expression of pride. This was the opposite of describing me as frightened and docile, and in my defiant mood I registered the boss's gesture with satisfaction, rather than with apprehension about what this would cost me in the days to come.

The trip to the DEF took half an hour to forty minutes. Budapest is a beautiful city, but, needless to say, under the circumstances I did not appreciate its beauty. As I later found out, the DEF changed its headquarters every year or so (at least that is what had happened for the last three years, either on purpose or by chance), and at the time of my arrest it was on the right bank of the Danube, in a low, spacious building that had been confiscated from the Printers Union. The car was driven into a large courtyard surrounded by a high concrete wall on three sides, with the low building on the fourth. I was led out of the car and into the building. First, I was taken into a small office, where my things were inventoried and my belt and shoelaces taken away. My feet were chained together at the ankles so that I could separate them by a foot at most; that is, I could walk only in small steps. In addition, my right wrist was handcuffed and chained to my left ankle, further restricting my movements. After that, I was told to grab my coat and was led through the hallway to a small door. When it was opened and I crossed its threshold, I was struck by a sight that seemed to be from another planet.

I was at the edge of a large rectangular hall, perhaps thirty by fifty feet, with a tile floor and large windows overlooking the courtyard. Forty or fifty people, mostly men but also some women, were sitting on the floor in equally spaced, neatly arranged rows. There were about two feet between neighbors in the same row, and about six feet between the rows. The prisoners—it was instantly clear that that is what they were—looked miserable. They were dressed in whatever they happened to be wearing at the time of their arrests. They sat on their coats or small bundles of other clothing in a rigid position best described as "at attention": their arms and legs were folded in a uniform, prescribed way; they did not move, turn their heads, or utter as much as a single word. Several uniformed gendarmes, holding rifles with bayonets attached, watched over them, walking up and down in front of and between the rows. Three or four male prisoners were in chains like myself; the rest were not. Their faces were frightening. All had dark circles under their eyes; some had bruises and showed signs of beating. They were pale and their looks reflected pain. Suffering was in the air. My immediate reaction was, "No, impossible, you cannot spend more than a few hours in this subhuman condition." But soon I was to get used to what I was seeing, and to much worse.

I was given a place on the floor between two prisoners and curtly told the rules of the place: I was to fold my coat and sit on it during the day, in the position prescribed by the chief gendarme in charge. The chief would change every eight hours, and the sitting position would be changed every thirty to fifty minutes from, for instance, "arms folded on your chest" to "arms folded behind your back," depending on the chief. Talking, turning around, standing up, or even getting out of the prescribed position was forbidden. The penalty varied from exhausting and humiliating physical exercises to being hit over the head or neck. Food, served three times a day, was to be eaten in the same sitting position, with permission to move one's hands. There was no shower and the only washing facility was a faucet at the toilet. There were three outings to the toilet under the gendarmes' supervision: in the morning, after lunch, and before bedtime. (Whoever needed more was out of luck: a few days later I witnessed a scene in which a prisoner in his sixties asked to go to the toilet, was refused, and asked again, insisting that he had to urinate. To the amusement of the other gendarmes, the guard gave him a short string and advised him to tie up his penis.) For half an hour each day the prisoners had permission to take off their shirts and search themselves for lice, of which there were plenty. All the prisoners slept in place, on the tiled floor, with permission to lie flat after bedtime, using their coats as covers and their shoes, jackets, or pullovers as pillows.

I sat down in the prescribed position and after less than half an hour I learned that, in spite of the strict interdiction, one could actually talk to one's neighbors. This was done by carefully watching the gendarmes' movements and whispering when they were not too close and had their eyes turned elsewhere. "Who are you?" I heard a whisper from my left. Without moving my head, I whispered back my name and the place I was brought in from. The man on my left was Pali (Paul) Schiffer, a leading left-wing Social Democrat in his mid-thirties. On my right was a young blonde woman, Magda Ságvári, the widow of the communist leader killed a few weeks earlier in a failed attempt to arrest him. The first thing I was told in these surreptitious exchanges with Pali was that Magda did not know about her husband's death and should not be told, because that might demoralize her.

Pali asked me about the latest news, and I related the events involving Romania and the liberation of Paris. I asked him in turn what he knew about the Jews of Kolozsvár who had been taken away. He said that all the Hungarian Jews from the provinces had been handed over to the Germans and deported. Nothing beyond that was known about them. They had either been killed or detained in German camps, but the DEF had no access to them; deportation was a one-way street. I asked how long he and the others had been at the DEF. The times varied between a few weeks and four or five months.

Soon the small door on my left opened, and the boss who brought me to Budapest walked down between the rows to where I was sitting. He told me to get up and follow him, and led me through the same door into the hallway, and from there into another room with a thick door and thick, closed windows. Sound insulation, I said to myself. There were three men in the room besides the boss. One of them was the younger agent who had brought me from Kolozsvár. Another man, who seemed to be in charge, was in his forties, strongly built, muscular, medium-sized, with only a little blond hair left. He had a brutish face and a threatening posture. As I was to find out later, his name was Papp and he was the head of the detective squad in charge of my case (among several others). The fourth man was blue-eyed, blond, very tall, and athletic. His name was Ferenc (Frank) Kékköi, but the prisoners referred to him among themselves as Verö Feri, or Feri the Beater, for that was his function and unique vocation.

Detective Papp was sitting behind a typewriter placed on a small table. He motioned me to approach the table and started filling out an interrogation record. He asked for my name, birthplace, and birth date, my father's and mother's names, my domicile, and how long I had lived there. I answered each of those questions correctly, giving my name as Egon Blatt. For my domicile, I gave the address where I had been arrested. Next, he asked where I had been living before June 1944, and I said "I'm not answering that question." He rose from his chair, came close to me, and from about two feet away delivered, with a sudden swing of his right leg, an enormous kick to my testicles. I groaned and my knees gave way; I half-collapsed but did not quite fall. Papp walked back to his seat and resumed the questioning. I stuck to my first line of defense and refused to answer the relevant questions. He came back several times in different forms to the central question about my party contact: Who was it? When did I last see him? When and where was I supposed to meet him? And so on. It was obvious that this was the question that they considered most urgent, and hoped to extract information from me that would enable them to arrest Sanyi. My answer was that I had no party contact.

After a while Papp said, "OK, we'll see how long you'll play the hero." He got up and, together with the tall athletic man, took off my chains, then ordered me to remove my shoes and socks and lie down on my belly. They bent my legs at the knees so that my lower legs were in a perfectly vertical position, side by side, with the soles upward, exposed horizontally, also side by side. Feri the Beater turned on a radio to loud music. It happened to be the overture to *The Barber of Seville,* which made me reflect for a moment on the irony of it all: had it not been for the circumstances, I would have enjoyed that piece. He then got behind me with a huge, heavy, rubber truncheon that he chose from among several hanging from a rack on the wall. What happened next was horrible, but I clearly remember that amidst the horror my overwhelming sensation was one of utter surprise. I expected a painful blow, one that would hurt badly and make me suffer. But what I experienced was entirely different: I felt as though I had been thrown from the tenth floor of a building and landed on my feet. I felt the blow in the marrow of my bones, but I clenched my teeth and did not utter a cry. A second blow followed, then a third. The pain got worse with every blow. Finally I could not withhold a howl. They stopped for a moment and forced my socks into my mouth as a gag. Then they continued.

After twenty blows they ordered me to stand. I was barely able to; my feet were swollen beyond recognition. Detective Papp ordered me to run in place. I could not and did not even want to try. But he took a smaller rubber truncheon, got into a squatting position, and started hitting my toes with it, forcing me to jump. This was how they got me to run in place. At the time I thought it was simply an additional form of torture; later I learned that it was part of a well-studied technique, its purpose being to prevent permanent deformations of the feet. After running in place for several minutes, I was told to stop, and Papp resumed the questioning. As I still felt in control of myself, though I was shaking, dripping with sweat, and felt a bit hazy, I continued to stick to my first line of defense and refused to budge from my earlier answers. I was ordered back on the floor in the same position as before. Inadvertently, I bent my toes and Feri warned me that if I bent them, they would be broken. I got another twenty blows. As my socks had been stuffed into my mouth from the beginning, it made no difference if I shouted or groaned. I tried to refuse to hold up my feet, but I was kicked in the side and beaten with the truncheon on various parts of my body, so in the end I reverted to the prescribed position and continued to absorb the blows to my soles. At the end of this second round of twenty blows, I was again ordered to my feet and forced to run in place by blows to my toes from a small truncheon. The detectives took a short break, ostentatiously drinking water and eating juicy fruit. This was obviously meant to bring psychological pressure to bear, as I was thirstier than I could remember ever having been in my life.

Next the agents tried another form of torture that I had heard about before: I was subjected to electric shocks from a generator that one of the agents held in his lap while he turned its handle. One of the two wires leading from the generator was festooned around my ankle, the other was applied successively to my head, the back of my neck, the inside of my mouth, and my genitals. The faster the handle was turned, the stronger the current that coursed through my body. It made my body shiver and jerk, and amidst the convulsions I understood how easily this "treatment" could throw somebody into a panic and make him or her lose control. But I also realized that this was mainly a psychological weapon, meant to intimidate and frighten rather than to produce pain, for its effect was incomparably milder than the beatings I had suffered.

After about half an hour of electric shocks the questioning resumed, with the same result as before. This was followed by another beating session; but apparently Feri the Beater wanted a rest, because when I was ordered back to the floor the beating was resumed by Papp. He delivered the blows with the same expertise as the Beater, and this third round of twenty was no easier than the first two. The running in place was even tougher than before, and I felt that I might soon lose consciousness. Nevertheless, as the questioning was resumed, I stuck to my earlier answers. Although I had prepared a second line of defense, I was not planning to use it in this first interrogation. I somehow thought that after a while they would stop beating me, as they could not intend to kill me before they had extracted the information they wanted. But after they had rested a little, Feri the Beater resumed his role and I was ordered to the floor a fourth time.

At this point I felt that I could not go on any longer, and decided to switch tactics. But I wanted the change to appear spontaneous, so I took the first few blows, then suddenly turned around and said I was willing to speak. The four agents surrounded me with expectant faces. Yes, I said, I had a party connection whom I was supposed to meet at such-and-such a place at eight o'clock in the evening on August 27 (the day I was taken to Budapest). In case one of us did not show up, we were supposed to meet one month later at the same time and place. This put the next meeting a month into the future. Of course, the time and place I gave were fictitious; my purpose was to gain time. My "admission" was greeted with incredulity. One of the agents said, "You're too young to deceive us." But I insisted that I was telling them the truth. They tested my veracity with questions about who my party connection was. I told them I did not know his name but confirmed their physical description of Sanyi, adding that he had grown a mustache (which was not true). They asked a few questions about the meeting of the Local Party

Committee in the winter of 1942–43, all the participants of which, other than myself, had been arrested in the fall of 1943. I confirmed exactly what I knew was already known to them about that meeting. I reproduced their information accurately and without hesitation, and that must have worked. They then returned to the question of my next meeting with Sanyi, its time and place, and I repeated the September 27 date and the rest of the information I had given. Finally, I was relieved to hear Papp say, "We'll break all your bones if he doesn't show up," since this meant they had accepted my answer.

At this point I was given a glass of water and the interrogation continued. As to where I had lived before June, I was determined not to give away the Iszlais under any circumstances. Instead, I gave the address of a family that had been deported, saying that I had simply rented a room from them and they had had no idea of my being in hiding. A few more questions followed, concerning possible friends, connections, and helpers. I listed as my only contacts (other than Sanyi) the people from whom I had rented the house, the woman from whom I had rented a room before I moved into the house, and my recent acquaintances from the air raid shelter, adding that none of them knew I was in hiding, which happened to be true. What about my other contacts? Who and where were the people who distributed the Peace Party leaflets in the summer of 1943? I knew that the DEF had learned from Grünfeld, who had been arrested and broken in the fall of 1943, that ten people—five couples— had been involved. Although some of the participants had been deported, most of them were serving in Work Battalions. The latter could have been apprehended by the DEF, so it was essential for me not to divulge their names. I took the line that I had indeed organized the distribution of the leaflets, and yes, there were five men involved, some of them possibly with girlfriends; I even remembered the times and places where they met or were supposed to meet Grünfeld to receive their share of leaflets for distribution. However, I maintained that I did not know the names of any of the participants. They had been mobilized by Béla Józsa, who sent them to me for instruction; I met them at specified places through code words and never learned their identities. Since Józsa was dead, this was a harmless admission, and naturally the agents did not like it. But they just said, "You will not get away with this. We will come back to it." Apparently they were not in the mood to reopen the beating session.

I was ordered to put on my socks and shoes. But the shoes would no longer fit and I was unable to put them on. They insisted that I must, but I could not. Then one of them grabbed a shoe and forced my foot into it while another held me down; first one foot, then the other. I felt terrible pain and was convinced that this was just another form of torture, since they could have let me go back with my shoes in my hands, as I would have preferred. I was to learn later, though, that this rule was also an integral part of the recipe for "treatment," since forcing the foot back into the shoe and keeping it there most of the time was thought to prevent the swelling from leading to permanent deformation.

I was again put in chains and led back to my place in the common hall. I was shaking and had the chills; my feet were completely out of shape and every step was torture, which must have shown on my face. I was also nauseated. Soon the first whisper came. "How many blows?"

"About seventy," I said.

"That's quite a lot. But the first day is the toughest. Is anybody coming after you?" The question was a polite way of asking if I had pulled in anybody, betrayed anyone's name. As I was soon to learn, the prisoners' main criterion for judging each other's behavior was how many people were arrested as a result of the prisoner's interrogation, that is, how many people "came after" him or her.

"No," I said. Dinner was served after a while, and I remember that it was red beans. I felt like vomiting rather than eating, but to my surprise not only the guards, but also my neighbors, insisted that I eat. "You must preserve your strength," my neighbor whispered. "You must eat." I forced myself to swallow some of the food.

When toilet time came, I was simply unable to get up. One of the gendarmes approached me threateningly. "Shall I kick you up? Are you a man or what?" Then he turned to my neighbor, who was already standing: "Help this wretched guy stand up." The march to the toilet, which was out in the courtyard, was torture for me that evening, although in the weeks to come it was to be the most pleasant part of the day: in lining up for the slow march (there were only two toilets, so there was a waiting line for maybe fifteen or twenty minutes), it was possible to switch places and get acquainted with other members of the group, as well as to conduct whispered conversations. This was our main daily news channel. Back from the toilet, I was finally allowed to take off my shoes for the night. I made them into a pillow with my jacket, lay down, and covered myself with my coat. I felt chilly and nauseated, my whole body ached, and my feet were huge lumps of pain. Yet I felt a strange sense of satisfaction: I had survived the first day without pulling in anybody.

The following day I was taken to interrogation by the same people, except that the younger agent was not present this time. They started by reopening the issue of my next appointment with Sanyi, saying that I had lied to them. I repeated what I had said before, upon which they unlocked my chains, ordered me to take off my shoes and socks, stuffed the socks into my mouth, and started hitting my soles with the heavy rubber truncheon. This time the blows were even more painful, because the soles were all swollen and blistered. After twenty blows they stopped and forced me to run in place. I was in worse pain than the first day, yet the first shock had passed, and I was saying to myself, They bought my story once, they will have to buy it again. Indeed, as I learned over the next two weeks, there was a ritual to the interrogation: It had to start with a thorough beating to "mollify" the victim, that is, to make him more ready to talk. To initiate the beating, they would reopen one of the questions whose answer seemed least credible or most important to them. Anyway, after twenty blows to my swollen feet, a two-inch blood blister broke and spilled its contents all over the floor. Nonchalantly, Feri the Beater pulled out a first-aid kit and poured iodine over the bleeding blister to disinfect it. Disinfection seemed to be a routine part of the torture: the prisoner had to be kept in shape for further beating. Then my foot was bandaged, only for the bandage to be taken off the next day along with my socks so that the next twenty blows could be administered. It sounds crazy, yet that is what happened.

During the next two and a half weeks I was interrogated almost every day by the same three or four people. Those were very trying days. Typically the small door on my left would open quietly and one of the detectives would appear on the doorstep. He would slowly look over the rows of inmates, taking his time to select his victim, savoring the tense atmosphere of terror that his appearance created in the room. Then he would quietly pronounce a name, often just a first name like "Egon," or would simply motion to a prisoner with a movement of his finger. The victim would then get onto his feet and follow him to the torture chamber. On those days when the choice did not fall on me, I felt a kind of relief hard to describe. When it was me, the routine was more or less the same as the second day's: there would be an opening of, You lied when you said this or that, followed by a beating session of at least twenty blows. As soon as I understood this, it became easier to take the blows. Any pain is easier to take when you can foresee an end to it. The agents also applied the electroshock treatment a couple of times, but I was not very sensitive to it. The real torture was the beating. Regarding the substance of the questioning, I adopted the following strategy: Admit what you know they have already learned from previous arrests; do not give any new facts; do not name any new persons. Of course, the most difficult issue was that of the persons whose existence was known to the DEF but whose identity I did not want to reveal. For these, I had to invent stories explaining why I did not know their names. Each of these stories by itself was more or less credible, but together they amounted to what my torturers would often repeat: "You didn't give us anybody, you bastard."

To start with, they asked who recruited me into the party. I said it was Béla Józsa. For this I had to invent a story about how I came to know Józsa, a story that did not involve anybody else. The actions involving persons arrested earlier—Hovány, Holländer, and Grünfeld—I admitted without any embellishments, except for concealing the identities of people not known to the DEF. I claimed that I did not know them by name, since they had been recruited by Béla Józsa or by one of his connections, and sent to me through appointments with code words. This was not impossible, of course, but the cumulative effect of these stories made them less than credible: they involved the persons who enrolled me into the movement, all the people who distributed the Peace Party's manifesto and had not been arrested in 1943, my connections at Dermata, and others. Nevertheless, in each of these cases, once I told a story, I stuck to it. I realized that if I budged on any of them, even in unimportant details, I would pull the ground from under all of them.

One of the least credible stories I had to defend concerned the military booklet that I had received from Galambos, in which I had replaced his name with that of Antal Somogyi. My story was that I found the booklet by chance under a bench in the city park. I realized the weakness of this claim, but simply could not think of anything better: if I had not found it by accident, then somebody must have given it to me, and this could not be attributed to Józsa, since the booklet was from 1944, after Józsa had died. So I stuck to this barely credible story, and the day they questioned me about it was one of the few when I got far more than twenty blows on my soles. In the end, though, they had to enter my original version into the official protocol, including the specific bench in the park that I named, and the day and time on which it happened. This was followed by an exact description of the procedure whereby I replaced the original name, about which I spoke the truth. Needless to say, this was not the kind of confession a detective of the DEF was proud of extracting, and I was made to pay for having them swallow it. Another issue arose when, a few days after my forced departure from Kolozsvár, the gendarmerie there made a thorough search of the house where I lived, found my pistol, and sent it to Budapest. Who gave me the pistol? This time I told them the truth, namely that I had purchased it from a German soldier. Although I withheld none of the details, they found this story unbelievable and I was beaten again.

Toward the end of the second week, Detective Papp reopened the issue of my rendezvous with Sanyi, and when I repeated that the next meeting was scheduled for September 27, he became quietly threatening and said in an ominous tone: "Look, half the time until September 27 has already passed. If on that day your friend does not show up, I would not like to be in your shoes. This is a last opportunity for you to climb out of the grave you have dug for yourself." Although I shuddered at the thought that what he foresaw was sure to happen, I did not show any hesitation and stuck to my claim.

Around mid-September we heard that fighting was going on close to Kolozsvár, at Turda, which was on the other side of Hungary's border with Romania. There were three ways in which news of this type could get to us. First, it could come through two young female prisoners who were working in the kitchen. There they overheard conversations among the personnel and occasionally had a glimpse at the newspapers. These women would bring in our meals from the kitchen and distribute them, an occasion for some whispered communications. Second, new prisoners were brought in every few days, and they would be quizzed about the news by their neighbors, the same way I had been. Third, some of the gendarmes guarding us occasionally read newspapers while sitting in front of us. The prisoners in the front rows could make out the headlines. Suffice it to say that we knew more or less accurately what was happening in the world, mostly on the nearby eastern front. Shortly after September 20 I got the news that Kolozsvár had become part of the war zone. I felt an enormous relief, for now my appointment with Sanyi, allegedly scheduled for September 27, was no longer verifiable, and Papp's threats became moot. But the impact of this development on my case went well beyond that crucial detail. In a couple of days I felt that my person had become less important. The interrogations were taken over by the two detectives who brought me from Kolozsvár. Papp and Feri the Beater were busy with new people.

I was still beaten at the beginning of each session, but the beatings were much milder. The rule was still twenty blows—maybe the detectives had to report on the amount of beating they administered—but there was simply no comparison between a blow from Feri the Beater or Papp and a blow from the boss. At the time I attributed this to the fact that the boss was a few years older and seemingly not so strong as the other two. But later I found out that this man, András Juhász, whom the prisoners called Pipás (the one with the pipe), was the detective who had beaten Ferenc Rózsa to death in 1943. At least he was in charge of the interrogation on the night when Rózsa, unable to walk back to the large room, had to be carried there and dumped on the floor, where he died during the night. Evidently, with Kolozsvár no longer accessible, the relevance of any information concerning my contacts there had shrunk to minuscule proportions. In fact, the focus of my interrogation shifted from attempts at extracting new admissions, to tying up loose ends and making a consistent story out of the sequence of episodes recorded in the previous sessions. Thus, about four weeks after my arrival in Budapest, my case was closed and the minutes of my interrogations were ready to be handed over to a prosecutor for preparing my trial. Nevertheless, I was to spend another two to three weeks at the DEF, as trials were organized for groups of people rather than single individuals. I became a member of a group of about fifteen to twenty communists for whom a trial was being prepared.

∎ ∎ ∎

This may be a good place to say a few more words about the inferno where I was tortured, along with many others. The group of detectives—gendarme officers in civilian clothing—known to us as the DEF constituted a singularly efficient organization. Cruel and inhumane, but efficient. Most of the communists active during the war years were apprehended after rather short periods of activity. Most of them were quickly broken and sent to trial, then to jail. A few, though never broken, were sentenced based on their comrades' depositions and sent to jail. A few were killed, perhaps sometimes inadvertently. But to say that the torture was not meant to kill, but only to break the individual, does not make it any the less murder when it resulted in a prisoner's death. Few innocent people were ever arrested, and when this happened they were freed within days.

At the time of my arrival, the man in charge of the DEF's operations was a gendarme officer called István (Steven) Juhász (no relative of András Juhász the Pipás, who arrested me; Juhász, meaning "shepherd" is one of the most common Hungarian family names). The DEF worked in very close cooperation with the political branch of the Budapest police, headed at the time by Tibor Wayand. Both István Juhász and Wayand came to see me soon after my arrival; they sized me up in a brief conversation that left no imprint on my memory. The leaders as well as the detectives of the organization held military ranks within the gendarmerie, but wore civilian clothing. The guards, on the other hand, were uniformed gendarmes. The number of detectives was remarkably small, well below a hundred, with perhaps a few score more stationed in the provinces. After the war, many of the detectives, among them András Juhász the Pipás, escaped to the West; but István Juhász, Papp, and Feri the Beater were caught, sentenced to death, and hanged. I do not know what happened to Wayand.

One episode may serve as an illustration of the DEF's efficiency. While I was at the DEF a young man in his twenties escaped. He was not one of the heavily guarded inmates—that is, he was not in chains. One morning, when he was taken to the toilet, he somehow managed to hide behind the small wooden shack, and when the guards returned with the other prisoners, he jumped a fence and ran for freedom. The detainees at the DEF wore no prison garb, so he was dressed like any ordinary civilian, and he was from Budapest, so he knew the city well. Within minutes his absence was discovered, the area near the toilet was searched, and soon everybody knew that he had escaped. Needless to say, we were quietly jubilant. Imagine our distress, then, when he was brought back before the end of the day. As we later found out, the brains of the DEF figured that, as he had no money for a bus or trolley and was from Pest on the left side of the Danube, he would probably cross one of the bridges on foot. They dispatched teams of two detectives to each of the five or six nearest bridges across the Danube, and these took up their positions inconspicuously within minutes. One of the teams apprehended the fugitive a little later as he was crossing their bridge. (He was beaten to pulp but survived the incident.) To put this in perspective, one should weigh the fact that Budapest was at the time a city of two million people.

The gendarmes who guarded us were primitive and extremely brutal, but there were a few exceptions. One of them, called Toth, was sympathetic to the prisoners' suffering to the extent of closing his eyes to the breaking of rules: One could have a conversation under his supervision, one could ask for—and receive—a glass of water, one could occasionally even persuade him to take somebody to the toilet outside the schedule. Once, however, Toth took a message to a prisoner's wife, telling her that her husband had survived his interrogation. He was caught, and disappeared from our midst; later we learned that he was sentenced to twelve years in jail. But he was quite exceptional. The majority of the fifteen or so gendarmes guarding us were the scum of the earth, cruel and often sadistic animals.

As for the prisoners, my comrades: at the beginning they were all from Budapest, and I was the only one who had been brought in from the provinces. Pali Schiffer, my neighbor on the floor of the common hall the day I arrived, was a very bright, knowledgeable, widely read person, broadly cultured and with a unique zest for storytelling, as I was to discover. László Grünwald, a man in his late forties who was a former member of the Central Committee of the Communist Party and a leader of the Textile Workers' Union, had been expelled from the party a year before his arrest because he was suspected of treason in connection with the arrest of another member of the Central Committee. He had a convincing explanation for the events that led to his expulsion, and took the position that, due to the scarcity of information with which the clandestine Central Committee had to work, errors like his expulsion from the party were likely to be committed. He had full confidence that after the war an impartial investigation would rehabilitate him. I liked his attitude and the fact that when arrested and tortured he was not broken, or at least did not pull in anybody after himself, in spite of his long activity and many connections. I found Grünwald wise and practical, with rich experience in many aspects of life. Because of his behavior at the DEF, he was highly respected by the detainees despite his having been expelled from the party. He was one of the four people in chains at the time of my arrival.

The most influential prisoner, especially among the younger inmates, was a man just one year older than me, Jenö Hazai, the head of a communist-led workers' youth organization in Budapest. He had been arrested together with several others about four months before my arrival, and exercised a sort of positive leadership that helped sustain the morale of his group, even though his own behavior under interrogation had not been impeccable; he had been unable to completely avoid pulling in others. He was a very astute, smart youngster, with an excellent sense of orientation and talent for quickly grasping new situations and developments; in a word, he had strong leadership qualities. He was also in chains. His fiancée, Rózsi (Rose), was one of the female prisoners who worked in the kitchen. A third prisoner in chains was Sándor (Alexander) Lichtmann, a man in his thirties, a metal worker (turner), and one of the leaders of the Budapest party organization, who had also been arrested several months before me. Before his arrest he had been the party connection of Hazai and of several other detainees. The fourth inmate in chains was Pityu (Steven) Deutsch, a member of the same youth organization as Hazai. I do not remember why he was in chains.

Ferenc Iliás was a rather special case. He was the (communist) leader of a large noncommunist farmers' organization. He had many connections and was terribly tortured for many weeks. He resisted, and when he felt that he could not take it any more, he grabbed the gun of the gendarme nearest to him and pushed its bayonet into his own neck in an attempt to kill himself. Wounded, he was taken to the hospital and returned a few days later for continued interrogation. Nevertheless, he did not drag anybody in. Károly Fekete was to play an important role in my life, so I will talk about him in detail later. At this point it is enough to mention that he was in his mid-twenties, a goldsmith and silversmith, and a member of the Communist Party, who had been arrested while on active military duty. Revolutionary activity while on active military duty was punishable by death, so he had the cloud of a likely death sentence over his head all the time. Two other prisoners who indirectly played roles in my adventures subsequent to my detention at the DEF were András Hegedüs, a communist engineering student who worked under the direction of Lichtmann and was arrested shortly after me in the first half of September; and István Blahó, a young communist steelworker who had spent a couple of months at the DEF before my arrival.

Among the women, I have already mentioned Magda Ságvári, the widow (unbeknownst to her) of Endre Ságvári, and Rózsi, the fiancée of Hazai, who worked in the kitchen. A third female prisoner, Zsuzsa (Susan) Fehér, was the sister of a well-known communist leader still at large and had been tortured to give him away. She did not.

All these prisoners, especially those who had spent more than three months at the DEF, were in pretty bad physical shape. While I was at the DEF, new prisoners were brought in at the rate of several per week. One of those who was put in chains (so now there were six of us in this condition) was László Fischer, a cabinetmaker in his early thirties, who apparently was involved in some important party action that had occurred in August. He was taken to interrogation soon after his arrival and delivered back several hours later in bad condition. He whispered to his neighbor that he did not know how long he could stand the ordeal and did not want to harm anybody. During the night he took from his jacket a safety pin that somehow had not been discovered during the search after his arrest, and repeatedly stuck it into his wrist until he found a vein, which he then perforated. He bled for several hours, until the big pool of blood that formed near his sleeping place was spotted early in the morning. By that time he was unconscious but still alive. The guards immediately tied his arm above the wrist to stop the bleeding, and tried to revive him by splashing cold water onto his face. When this failed, they took him to the hospital. There he was revived, the wound he made in his wrist was treated, and four or five days later, after it had healed a little, he was returned to the DEF. Perhaps the time was sufficient for his connections to find out about his arrest and hide or not show up at their appointments; perhaps the incident tempered the zeal of his interrogators; but in any event, although he was beaten a few more times, nobody came after him.

Another arrest made by the DEF in late September was that of Márton Schiller, an architect and party leader. He was beaten, but much less harshly than would have been the case just two weeks earlier. For the first time we had the impression that outside events were having some effect on our interrogators.

A group of about forty prisoners was brought in toward the end of September or the beginning of October. They were communist miners from Tatabánya, Hungary's major coal-mining region, who were accused of planning and partly carrying out sabotage actions. Their leaders, Goda and Mannhercz, were in their forties, well built, and physically strong. Goda in particular had a very imposing presence. One curiosity about the miners' group was that several of its members were of German ethnic background; not many ethnic Germans in Hungary were communists. The arrival of this group at the DEF gave us moral reinforcement: it showed that the communist movement had at least some popular roots in Hungary and sent a similar message to our torturers.

In early October the DEF moved to a new location east of the Danube in Pest, into the confiscated building of a former rabbinical seminary on Rökk Szilárd utca. We were all moved into a large room under conditions almost identical to those at the previous place. It was here that the events of October 15 caught us. In early October 1944 the Red Army crossed the pre-1940 Hungarian-Romanian border and conquered the city of Szeged, only 150 kilometers southeast of Budapest. The government of Regent Horthy decided to attempt a turnaround similar to the Romanian coup of August 23, but the Germans got wind of these plans and on October 14 sent heavy reinforcements to Budapest. The next day they kidnapped Horthy's son and gave the regent an ultimatum forcing him to resign under the threat of having his son shot. Ferenc Szálasi, head of the Arrow Cross Party (the Hungarian nazi movement) took over the country as both regent and prime minister.

As we learned about these developments, we found out that several of the gendarmes guarding us were strong sympathizers of the Arrow Cross Party and thought that their time had come. At night, some of the inmates overheard the gendarmes planning to take the patriotic initiative of liquidating us as enemies of the Fatherland. We decided that something had to be done. A delegation of inmates asked for an immediate audience with the leaders of the DEF, informed them about the gendarmes' conversations, and reminded them that they would be held responsible for our fate. We never found out what action was taken with respect to the gendarmes, but a few days later most of the male prisoners were transferred to the military prison on Margit Körut (Margaret Ring), one of the main boulevards of Pest, where we were to stand trial before a special tribunal of the chief of staff. The female detainees were sent to a women's prison in Conti utca and brought to the trial from there.

At the military prison we were all put into a large common cell. Unlike before, we were free to speak to each other and no longer constrained in our movements within the cell. Also, we had bunks with straw-filled mattresses to sleep on, and could wash ourselves every morning. We had a couple of days to prepare for the trial, and we agreed to take a united political stand by not showing repentance for what we had done and maintaining instead that our actions were meant to serve the true interests of the nation. We were assigned a defense lawyer who advised us to show repentance, but we dismissed his advice.

The trial was brief, the whole group of fifteen to twenty people being tried in two long sessions that took a little more than half a day, allowing each of us an average of fifteen or twenty minutes. We did not quite know what to expect in view of the slippery political situation: Horthy had just been forced to resign, and the Arrow Cross Party, a rabid nazi-type organization, had just taken over. But to our considerable relief, we noticed that Horthy's picture was still hanging on the wall of the courtroom where we were being tried. This was a good omen, signifying that the tribunal had not yet been taken over by the Arrow Cross mob. We all stuck to our agreement and answered in the negative when asked whether we regretted what we did. But when Fekete took the stand and gave the same answer, the judge said that because he had engaged in revolutionary activities while under active military duty, the prosecutor was asking for the death penalty in his case. The judge was willing to give him a life sentence, but only if he repented; otherwise, he would be sentenced to execution by firing squad. He gave Fekete fifteen minutes to think the matter over and ordered a break. In view of the exceptional situation, the senior prisoners advised Fekete that he was absolved of his obligation to abide by our agreement and urged him to utter the words the judge was asking for. As important as it was to show a dignified attitude at this political trial, it was not worth his life. He agreed, and after the break changed his position according to the judge's wishes. At the end, Károly Fekete received a life sentence, while the rest of us received sentences of two to fifteen years, specifically, fifteen years for Sándor Lichtmann, fourteen for me, twelve for László Grünwald, ten for Jenö Hazai, and two for András Hegedüs. After the sentencing we were returned to our cells in the Margit Körut prison, and the female convicts were sent back to their own prison. We later found out that this trial was the last act of the special tribunal of the chief of staff: within a few days, a court of the Arrow Cross regime took over all trials.

I was more than relieved. A jail sentence of fourteen years may sound like a terrible thing today, but in October 1944 there was only one question that mattered: was it a death sentence or not? And it could easily have been one. Outside our jail, the terror of the Arrow Cross Party had already started. We were aware that the courtyard of that very jail was the scene of executions. Just a couple of days after we were moved there, we got wind of the execution of a parachuted British spy in the prison courtyard; at least this was the way it was described to us. Only after the war did I discover that this "British spy" was none other than Hanna Szenes, a Hungarian Jewish girl living in Palestine, who as a young zionist volunteered for the mission of being parachuted by the Royal Air Force into Hungary in order to organize a resistance group against the Germans. She was caught, sentenced to death, and executed. Thus, we had no reason for complacency about the trial, and we really did not know what to expect. Had we been tried by a court appointed by Szálasi, the new head of state, instead of one still loyal to Horthy, there would likely have been several death sentences. Luckily for us, the court that tried us was a few days behind events.

After the trial, we set out to organize our life in the prison. The communists were not the only prisoners, but there were two cells in which we were in the majority. It was a great joy to be able to talk to each other. I came to know and befriend several of my comrades, in particular László Grünwald. We had long discussions in which I learned many details about recent Hungarian history, the situation in the trade unions and in the country in general, the successes and failures of the communists. But we discussed many other things, and I broadened my horizons in several directions. In the evenings, after we all "went to bed" on our bunks, somebody would tell a story and everybody else would listen. The most successful storyteller was Pali Schiffer, who remembered many famous novels of world literature in great detail and would recount them in installments. Some of the prisoners were able to recite poems; others knew revolutionary songs, which of course could not be sung very loudly. I had frequently read about prisons being the revolutionaries' universities, and I found that characterization more convincing than when I had read it.

The food was insufficient, and we were all hungry most of the time. But packages started arriving from the outside for some of the prisoners whose relatives lived in Budapest, and these packages were voluntarily handed over for distribution in equal portions to the whole "collective" by a prisoner elected for this purpose. These additions to our daily rations of food were not substantial in quantity, but they seemed delicious, and the solidarity expressed through the process of sharing had a strong effect on the morale of the group. In general, the more experienced prisoners exercised a leadership role whose primary goal was to keep up morale by influencing the conduct of their fellow inmates in the direction of a dignified attitude, maintaining solidarity in things big and small (like the sharing of food packages), refusing to despair in the face of our uncertain fate, and rejecting feelings of doom. Some basic tenets of this morale building were that everybody had to pull himself together, force himself to exercise, strictly respect the rules of hygiene, keep his clothing as clean and well mended as possible, and participate in the life of the collective by performing the tasks assigned to him. Maintaining the cleanliness of our clothing and generally trying to look as civilized as possible were important not just for psychological reasons, but also to prepare for a future attempt at escape. Should we somehow manage to escape from the jail, our survival outside depended crucially on our appearance.

The prison was not heated, and by mid-November it was quite cold. While many of the prisoners, weakened by months of detention, were suffering from colds, flu, chronic diarrhea, and other ailments, I felt perfectly healthy. I had not spent enough time in jail to become physically weakened and was still in reasonably good condition. But I had been arrested in August wearing a light suit and, as the cell was growing ever colder, I felt uncomfortable. Luckily, one of the miners from Tatabánya whom I befriended, Friedmann (an ethnic German), gave me his pullover, as he had two sweaters. This helped keep me warm and enabled me to stop wearing my coat in the cell, keeping it in good shape against the possibility of an escape.

The prison had an inmate from Kolozsvár who was serving the third year of an eight-year sentence. His name was György (George) Nonn, and he had lived in my home town until the spring of 1941, where he had been the leader of a communist group in a youth organization. He then moved to Budapest and was apprehended in the wave of arrests that shook the communist organization of the capital in the spring of 1942. He was sentenced that summer and had spent more than two years in the Margit Körut military prison. Very bright and astute, and a Gentile, he had caught the attention of the prison administration and at the time of our arrival was working as a clerk in the main office. Thus he had access to news, could organize contacts with the outside world, was informed about the decisions of the prison administration, and could even influence the assignment of prisoners to certain jobs within the prison. I had not known him in Kolozsvár—he had left the scene just as I was getting involved in the movement—but made his acquaintance in prison and told him about things that had happened in our town during the last two years.

The most important information that Nonn was able to convey to us was the fact that preparations were being made to evacuate the prison when the Soviet troops came closer to Budapest. We learned that the prisoners would be taken by train to Komárom, a town on both banks of the Danube little more than a hundred kilometers west of Budapest. The leadership of our group, which consisted of three or four people including Lichtmann and Hazai, decided that we should prepare ourselves to escape during the trip. This decision was preceded by discussions in smaller groups, and, though almost unanimous among the members of our group, it was opposed by two communists who had been in prison for more than two years. These two, Miklós (Nicholas) Gergely and György (George) Kondor, argued that an escape would be too risky and unnecessary, because when the Russians caught up with us wherever we happened to be, the guards would let us go. We, on the other hand, took the view that before the Russians could liberate us, the Germans or their Arrow Cross allies would kill us if they had a chance. Our disagreement was to a large extent rooted in the fact that those two had been associated for a long time with the prison guards. They knew the chief guard, a Sergeant Major Csonka, and tended to trust him. The rest of us were more attuned to what was happening on the outside, were more aware of the dangerous situation that had developed after the Arrow Cross Party took control, and had no confidence whatsoever in the benevolence of Csonka and his acolytes. In view of this disagreement, we decided that we would go ahead with our plans without the participation of the two dissenters.

To prepare for the escape, we had to collect tools for cutting a hole in the wall or the floor of the railway car. This was made possible by the fact that several prisoners were assigned to the prison workshop, where they had access to tools. The communists were not the only inmates of the prison; there were common-law criminals of every kind, but Nonn saw to it that as many as possible of the prisoners assigned to the workshops were selected from our group. I also played a role in this assignment game. The manager of the prison warehouse, a certain Lieutenant Retkes, needed a clerk, and I got the job on Nonn's recommendation. Retkes was a man in his late fifties, ferocious-looking and rude; yelling was his favorite activity, and he exercised it with and without reason. But I soon discovered that this was just his way of blowing off steam: he was like a dog that barks but rarely bites. When I put some of his inventories in order, he was satisfied and we got along well. While working for Retkes, I managed to change my jacket for a military tunic, which was much warmer. I also managed to steal a number of sharp tools: I would take them from the warehouse in the evening when I was returned to my cell, then hand them over to Hazai, who was collecting and hiding them. As we were inventorying blankets, I stole quite a number of them and passed them on to a fellow inmate, a young tailor, who cut them up and made them into enough warm waistcoats for ten or fifteen prisoners. Retkes never caught me stealing tools or blankets, for I went about it with great care: every one of these actions was planned in minute detail, with credible cover stories in case something went wrong. But one day I discovered a detailed map of Budapest in the drawer of his desk. I did not want to steal it, for the risk of being discovered was too great (no one other than myself had access to the desk drawer). In order to have some orientation in case of an escape, I began studying the map, absorbing as much information as I could about the layout of the city, its main arteries, boulevards, etc. But while looking at the map I lost my vigilance and was caught as Retkes suddenly entered the room. I thought this was the end of my job, but after yelling at me wildly and cursing me for long minutes, he finally let me explain that I was a provincial guy who had never seen our beautiful capital about which I had heard so much, and I simply could not resist the temptation of looking at it at least on the map. He did not fire me, but from then on he was suspicious of me and never left me alone in his office.

One day the door of our cell was unexpectedly opened and a new, remarkable prisoner was let in. He was a tall, good-looking officer, a first lieutenant in full uniform, but with his epaulets torn off, as was the habit in the military when an officer was downgraded or convicted. He had a very dignified, proud demeanor, and the guards had enormous respect for him; they would address him by his military rank. When we asked him the reason for his being where he was, he answered that he had had political disagreements with the new Arrow Cross Party leadership and that, although he had always considered himself a firm opponent of communism, he nevertheless could not condone ruining the country and its whole army in order to please the Germans. Needless to say, we were very pleased to salute such a distinguished "fellow traveler" in our midst, and expressed our appreciation for his position. Respected both by the guards and the communist prisoners, the first lieutenant rode a wave of popularity in the first days after his arrival. He was also a very sociable, easy-going, pleasant person with a good sense of humor, and an indefatigable, successful storyteller. But a few days later, to our surprise, our group found out from Nonn that the first lieutenant, far from being a political dissident as he pretended, was simply a crook and not even associated with the military. He posed as an officer while carrying out various complicated and rather clever embezzlement schemes. After some deliberation, the leaders of our group decided that it might be in our interest not to deprive the "officer" of his assumed identity, but instead to use his authority with the guards to our advantage. Consequently, he was told that we knew exactly who he was and why he had been sent to jail, but that we would not reveal this information to anybody as long as he agreed to cooperate with us. He readily agreed, and the first task he received was to cement and cultivate his relationship with as many of the guards as possible. To facilitate this, he was put in charge of various activities that required contact with the guards. This decision turned out to be a wise one, as events later proved.

At the end of November or the beginning of December the plan for the prison evacuation was finally put into action. On the last day the prisoners' possessions were returned, including their personal identification papers (though not the fake ones like mine). The papers of prisoners with heavy sentences or Jewish names were worthless; but those of Gentile prisoners with light sentences were quite usable. And since several prisoners in the latter category had more than one piece of identification, some of their papers were distributed among those of us who had none. Thus I was given the birth certificate of András Hegedüs, a Gentile engineering student of my own age, who had received a two-year sentence, while Hegedüs retained some other pieces of identification for himself. This was an extremely helpful development, since Hegedüs's document suited me perfectly and was genuine, not a fake. In the same manner, other prisoners with heavy sentences received personal documents of those with lighter sentences; for instance, Károly Fekete, our comrade with the life sentence, received one of the papers of István Blahó, who had a three-year sentence.

On the day of the evacuation we were taken under military guard to Keleti Pályaudvar, the same railway station where I had arrived in Budapest about three months earlier, and were put into three railway cars. To our regret, we were not able to arrange for our group to stay together. The sorting was, as far as I could ascertain, in alphabetical order, with communists, common criminals, and various types of fugitives all together. I got into the first car, together with Fekete, Grünwald, and others. Most of our comrades, including the group that had the tools, got into the second car, and some into the third. After we got into the railway cars, they were sealed from the outside. The train started late in the afternoon and proceeded very slowly, with frequent stops. Since those of us in the first car did not have any tools, we could not undertake anything, but we rooted for our comrades in the other cars. Around nine in the evening, when it was already dark, the train was still in the vicinity of Budapest. After several more stops, we heard a loud commotion. The door was opened, soldiers came into the car and started searching it. We heard that several of the prisoners had escaped. As there were no tools in our car, the search ended without any result, but the guards were visibly upset and hostile. Finally, after maybe an hour, the train started again and early the next morning we arrived in Komárom.

As we later found out, what had happened was this: Soon after the train started, the men who had the tools in the second car moved into a corner and began making a hole in the floor. They were hindered in their work by the fact that some of the noncommunist prisoners became suspicious and threatened to alert the guards if anybody attempted anything "foolish." But the work went on nevertheless, while the other communist prisoners sang to cover the noise, and blocked the way and the view to the critical corner of the car. As it grew dark, the hole in the car floor was large enough for a person to climb out and get onto the platform between the two cars. Thus, between Kelenföld and Budaörs, still in the outskirts of the capital, one by one, twelve of the communist prisoners climbed out of the car and jumped from the slow-moving train. Among them were Hazai, Lichtmann, Hegedüs, and Schiffer. They managed to walk back to Budapest, got in contact with their comrades, obtained identification papers and hiding places, and resumed their underground party activity. To the best of my knowledge they all survived the war. What exactly led to the discovery of the escape I never found out, but apparently the last person who jumped was seen or somehow aroused the suspicion of the guards, who then stopped the train and started searching the neighboring area as well as the train itself. Nobody was caught.

Once in Komárom, we expected to be taken to a prison. But instead of being led into the city from the railway station, we were ordered to march in the opposite direction, away from the city, toward the south. The guards accompanying us were furious and threatening because of the escape from the train, for which they could be held responsible. We were in a depressed mood, since we had just missed the event for which we had been preparing ourselves for weeks. The landscape we were traversing was becoming more and more desolate. Our attempts to find out where we were being taken foundered on the hostility of the guards. The mood among us was tense and soon turned ominous: if we had suddenly been lined up to be executed, we would not have been very surprised. Finally, after a march that seemed to last forever, we arrived at our destination. It was the notorious Star Fortress, a huge, pentagon-shaped former military fortification that had been transformed into a prison. An enormous iron gate opened and we were led into a spacious inner courtyard. The prison cells were in the fortifications that surrounded this courtyard in a circle. The newly appointed commandant of the Star Fortress was none other than Sergeant Major Csonka, formerly the chief of guards at the Margit Körut military prison in Budapest, which we had just left behind.

Before being sent to our cells, we were lined up in the courtyard to listen to an angrily barked threatening speech by Sergeant Major Csonka, who assured us that he would make us pay for the escape of our comrades. Then he read the list of names of the newly arrived prisoners to learn who was present and who had escaped. As he started reading the list in alphabetical order, I quickly made a decision. When he called my name, I remained silent. He looked up and slowly, loudly repeated the name: Egon Blatt. Several seconds passed, during which my heart beat faster: would somebody speak up to betray me, in order to earn some brownie points in the new place? Luckily for me, nobody did. Finally, Csonka wrote something on the list and then broke the silence by reading the next name. I let out a sigh of relief, but the danger was not yet completely over. Less than halfway down the list, Csonka read out the name of András Hegedüs, the prisoner whose birth certificate I held and who had escaped from the train. At that point I stepped out and yelled Here! Csonka looked me over as he did with all the others, then read the next name. From then on, until my liberation, I lived as András Hegedüs. Little did I suspect at the time that the person whose identity I so readily assumed was to become Hungary's prime minister for several years in the mid-fifties.

A moment of reflection is in order at this point. The group that was lined up in the courtyard of the Komárom fortress contained twenty to thirty people who knew that I was Egon Blatt and not András Hegedüs. Yet none of them betrayed me, either then or later during our stay in Komárom. None of them tried to buy a favor, perhaps even save his skin, by revealing the truth about me. And this was not out of fear of retaliation on my part or the part of my comrades, since a would-be informer could have acted in secret. I have had so many negative experiences with human nature throughout my life that I feel the need to stress this outstanding positive experience. True, the people that I am talking about were not a cross section of the human race: they were committed to a cause, they were communists (the non-communist prisoners did not know my true name). Nevertheless, this was a remarkable show of solidarity between the members of an ethnically diverse group of Hungarian, Jewish, and German individuals, albeit communists.

■　■　■

By the time we were taken there, the Star Fortress of Komárom had become the dumping ground for the prisoners of all the jails of Hungary as these were evacuated one after another under the pressure of the rapidly advancing Soviet armies. The communists were just a small part of the prison population. Besides them and the common criminals, there were all kinds of fugitives, Jehovah's Witnesses, Jews, and Gypsies (some with their families). Many of the prisoners were very weak, and some were ill. The cells were rather crowded. We slept on bunk beds arranged in two layers, one above the other; both layers had straw-filled mattresses. I much preferred the upper layer, as it had more air, and I did not mind the discomfort of having to climb up and down. The food was much poorer than in the Budapest jail we had come from. On the other hand, there was a daily walk in the prison courtyard. There was no sanitation and no access to medical help of any kind. Whoever fell sick with a serious illness would die. A man in his late thirties in our cell died of erysipelas, a skin infection on the face which, if untreated, leads to a general blood infection. Another prisoner, a young communist called Rosenthal, was in the terminal stage of tuberculosis and becoming visibly worse every day. Unlike the others, he was not expected to get up from his bunk. He had a high fever, and we managed to get him some extra blankets. Apart from this, there was no help and there could be no question of taking him to a hospital. In a couple of weeks he died. I was close to his bunk and remember the bitter feeling of helplessness at not being able to do anything about it.

The prison population was large, in the many hundreds, and rapidly changing. New groups were frequently brought in, and once a week a group was put together and handed over to the Germans to be deported. Among those who did not escape from the train bringing our group to Komárom were László Grünwald, Károly Fekete, István Blahó, Miklós Gergely and György Kondor (the two older prisoners who had disagreed with the escape plan); several of the miners who had been with us at the DEF; and the fake first lieutenant who enjoyed such respect among the prison guards. Every few days, perhaps once a week, everybody had to gather in the courtyard, where Sergeant Major Csonka put together a selection of prisoners to be handed over to a group of German soldiers in SS uniforms. Without knowing the exact destination of these prisoners, we knew that deportation meant a very high probability of death. Csonka selected the inmates for the transport according to several criteria: Jews, heavily sentenced communists, and Gypsies were his favorite picks. He called names from a list, looked over the prisoners he called, and chose the deportees on the basis of his instincts. Some of the prisoners he knew by both name and looks. Thus, among the first victims of Csonka's selection were the two older prisoners from Margit Körut,

Gergely and Kondor, who had put their trust in him. Both were communist and Jewish; although their names were rather neutral, Csonka knew them to be Jews and accordingly ordered them into the group to be deported at one of the first selections. I did not know much about Gergely, but I had become quite friendly with Kondor, who was a very talented painter and designer, and a kind man in his late thirties or early forties. He never returned from the deportation.

On another occasion Csonka called out from the list the name of Friedmann, the German miner who had given me his pullover. Friedmann was a big, well-built man with a wide face, flat nose, blue eyes, and blond hair. He looked like a textbook German, and Csonka did not select him. But after calling a few other names, he then called Friedmann's younger brother. The list did not contain the information that they were brothers, and the younger Friedmann, to his misfortune, did not have the Teutonic looks of his brother: He was somewhat slender, not so tall, with reddish hair, a slightly curved nose, and plenty of freckles on his face. So Csonka decided to select him: "Step out, Jew." The younger Friedmann quietly asserted that he was not Jewish, but Csonka remained unimpressed. Several others spoke up and said that Friedmann was not Jewish. Then Csonka got mad at being contradicted and started yelling, "I know who is a Jew. Don't try to teach me!" He ordered the younger Friedmann to join the group of those selected for transport. There was a moment of silence as the young man took his place in the group, after which the older Friedmann stepped out from amongst us and walked over to join his brother. We were seeing them both for the last time. I do not know where there group was taken, but I found out after the war that they both perished.

I survived several such selections by sheer luck. Of course, my change of name played an important role in this: Hegedüs was not a Jewish-sounding name. On one occasion Csonka looked at me at length and asked, with some hesitancy in his voice, "Are you a Jew?" I answered, half laughing, "No, how could I be? I am András Hegedüs," and that was all. Others, both Jews and Gentiles, were selected to some extent at random. István Blahó, the young steelworker who got a sentence of three years, was called out as a Jew, which he was not. Desperately, he showed that he was not circumcised. It did not help: Csonka was not interested in being proved wrong. Blahó was selected; he also perished. A section of the fortress held Gypsies with their families. One morning at dawn we woke up to terrible noises coming from the courtyard: loud yelling, desperate shrieks, screaming women, crying children. The Gypsies were being deported in one large group.

Around mid-December we got the news that Budapest was completely encircled by the Soviet army. German and Hungarian troops in the city continued to fight, however, and Budapest was not liberated until two months later. In the meantime, the Red Army was advancing westward well beyond Budapest, and its advance units were approaching Komárom. As we expected, however, we prisoners were by no means to be abandoned by our captors. As soon as the war zone came close enough, it was decided that we were to be dragged along with the withdrawing administration.

CHAPTER 5

■ ■ ■

Escape and Liberation

Right after Christmas, on December 26 or 27, 1944, the Star Fortress of Komárom was evacuated. Because the railway station and the tracks around it had been severely damaged, an evacuation by train was not possible. We were lined up in the prison courtyard with our belongings, arranged in a marching column, and told that we would proceed by foot to an unspecified destination. "Whoever steps out of the column or tries to escape will be shot on the spot," we were told. I noticed with considerable relief that the guards accompanying us were not German SS soldiers but the prison guards of the Star Fortress.

At the outset, there was a guard on each side of the column for every three or four rows; but as time went by, the placement of the guards became a lot less regular. I was marching with several of my comrades, and talked to László Grünwald about possibly escaping together if an opportunity arose. We all had the personal identification papers we had received in Budapest. The leaders of our group—Grünwald had become one of them at the Komárom fortress—asked the "first lieutenant" to engage the guards in conversation during the march, so they would not pay too much attention to the column of prisoners. He did this quite successfully, pulling several of the guards around him into long conversations.

The convoy started out toward the north, into the city of Komárom, and across the bridge over the Danube. On the northern bank of the river, in the part of the city which today belongs to Slovakia and is called Komarno, we turned left and followed the road in the direction of Pozsony

(Bratislava in Slovakian) and Vienna. In the early evening, as we were passing through the village of Kisaranyos, about twelve kilometers west of Komárom, it became fairly dark and the column loosened up considerably. The rows became irregular and the guards were somewhat dispersed. At one point the road was partially blocked by a truck convoy, and our column was forced partly onto the sidewalk. I felt the urge to act: "This is it," I said to myself. "This is the opportunity we've been waiting for." I looked around: the nearest guard was about twenty feet ahead of me, the next one behind me was further away. I looked for Grünwald, but he had moved up several rows to talk to somebody else. As I was getting ready to act, I suddenly saw in front of me Károly Fekete enter an open gate and run through the courtyard behind it. In a split second I decided to do likewise. I quickly stepped through the same gate and ran through the courtyard. For a moment I thought of running in a different direction from Fekete, so as to make it harder for the guards to follow if they saw us and tried to catch us. But I immediately rejected the idea as I instinctively realized the advantages of a partnership in escape. So I followed in the footsteps of Fekete, jumping a fence, running through another courtyard, then jumping another fence. There we stopped and squatted together, listening and watching carefully in the dark, but nobody seemed to have noticed our disappearance. The vague noise that was coming from the marching column was quickly fading into the distance. We looked at each other: we were free!

That is, for the moment. For nothing could have been more precarious than our situation as young males of military age, without any excuse for not being in the army. The few remaining districts of Hungary were under martial law and swarming with gendarmes and Arrow Cross militias. We quickly agreed to stay together, thereby linking our fates to one another. We exchanged information about our identity papers: I was András Hegedüs, engineering student, while Karcsi (diminutive of Károly) Fekete was István Blahó, steelworker. He would call me Andris (diminutive of András) and I would call him Pista (diminutive of István). We quickly concocted a story to justify our situation: we were members of a Levente (premilitary) formation being evacuated from Budapest to Germany, and we had become separated from our group because Pista was sick with dysentery (widespread at the time) and I was taking care of him. As soon as Pista got better, we were going to continue on our own toward Germany and join our unit, for which we had invented a number and a destination—Stuttgart, if I remember correctly.

The courtyard where we found ourselves belonged to a farmer's house. There was a stable that had some hay in it and we were thinking of spending the night there, but we decided it would be better to contact the farmer rather than risk being discovered by him later. Besides, sooner or later we would have to talk to people and see how they reacted to our demeanor and our story, so why not bite the bullet immediately? We entered the house, introduced ourselves, and asked politely whether it would be possible for us to spend the night there and continue our journey the next morning. The family's reaction was neither friendly nor hostile; it was as if they were used to strangers stopping by. They did not question our story, and told us that when soldiers asked to spend the night they usually let them use the stable. There were no soldiers there at present, so we were welcome to do the same. We thanked the farmer and went out to the stable. We lay down in the hay and put together our first plan of action. Karcsi had an address in Komárom for an aunt of one of our fellow inmates, Emil, who had described her as not quite a communist sympathizer, but favorably disposed toward her nephew whom she knew to have been arrested and jailed as a communist. We decided to try our luck with this aunt; maybe she could hide us or help us to hide until the Russians came. Having made this decision, we went to sleep. We slept very well in the hay, at the end of a day that had been for both of us one of the most tumultuous in our lives.

In the morning we woke up to the sight of German soldiers entering the stable. This was not a pleasant sight, but we were not overly panicked. They were not SS soldiers, and ordinary Wehrmacht soldiers did not usually check the identities of Hungarians. The people we were afraid of encountering were Arrow Cross militias, Hungarian gendarmes, and German SS soldiers. I addressed the soldiers in German and asked whether we could be of any help to them, explaining at the same time who we were and what we were doing in the stable. They were friendly and offered us bread with artificial honey. I might not have liked it in normal times, but on that morning it seemed like the best thing I had eaten in a long time. Later we went inside the house to thank the hosts for the shelter. We offered to help if there was anything to be done around the house, secretly hoping that we might be invited to stay for a few more days, but there was nothing of the sort forthcoming: Farmers are not usually busy around December. So we left the house and the village, and walked toward Komárom, on the same road by which we had come the day before as prisoners in a convoy.

Walking back to Komárom felt like walking on thin ice, because our civilian identity papers and our story were not likely to stand up to the scrutiny of a gendarme or an Arrow Cross militiaman, and we had absolutely no military papers. Whenever possible, we chose side roads parallel to the main road, making detours where necessary. Finally, as darkness fell, we reached the outskirts of the city. We made one or two inquiries to find the address we were looking for, and reached the house without incident in the early evening hours. We saw several patrols on the street stopping people and looking at their papers, but we managed to avoid all of them. Inside the house, Karcsi spoke to Emil's aunt, giving her news about her nephew. About ourselves, we thought it prudent not to tell the truth at once, but instead served up our current story as a starter, adding that we did not like the idea of going to Germany and would prefer to stay behind if we could find shelter. But this was of no avail: the moment Karcsi uttered the name of the nephew, whom the aunt knew to be a convicted communist, she panicked, as we could clearly see from her frightened expression. She said we had to leave immediately; she had not maintained contact with her nephew for quite a while and was not in a position to help us out in any way. At this point I interceded and tried to appeal to her feminine side: "We understand," I said, "and we will leave. But Pista is seriously ill; he has dysentery, and he cannot spend the night in the street." Could we stay until the next morning, sleeping on the floor in any place she could offer us? She called a male member of the family into the room, told him what our discussion was about, and asked for his opinion. He shared her apprehension about letting us spend any time in their apartment, and they repeated the need for us to leave immediately. When I invoked Karcsi's illness again, they said that at the corner of the street there was a civilian hospital where we could ask for Karcsi to be admitted if he was ill. Having no choice, we left the house in the direction indicated and soon reached a building that seemed to be the hospital.

The idea of asking admission to the hospital on the grounds of Karcsi's alleged dysentery seems today, and seemed to us at the time, rather outlandish. But sometimes you have to play the only card that fate deals you. Without any place to go, without the means to buy shelter for the night, with the sword of Damocles over our heads in the form of the numerous patrols in the city streets, we saw no better alternative and no particular danger either in trying this idea. So we climbed the few stairs to the entrance of the building and pressed down the handle on the large gate. As soon as we were inside the gate and let it close behind us, we realized we had been utterly misled. The place did indeed seem to be a hospital, as we saw a couple of people in white robes or with white armbands. But "civilian" it was definitely not: everybody who was not in hospital garb was military, and the door we had just entered was guarded from the inside by two armed soldiers. Naturally, they stopped us and asked what we wanted. Perhaps we could have simply said, "Sorry, this is a mistake" and turned around; but we did not. Were we afraid that they would get suspicious and ask for our papers? Or was it simply that we had nowhere else to go? I can not remember exactly what our reasoning was, but we took the *alea jacta est** approach and said we wanted to talk to the officer in charge of the hospital. We were led before a man in his fifties, a reserve officer, who listened to our story without hostility; but when we reached the point about Karcsi suffering with dysentery and needing medical care, he explained that most of the military hospital (for that is what it was) had been evacuated to the west a few days earlier. He had remained behind with a small sanitary crew to take care of a few last things, and they would also be evacuated in a few days. There were no doctors left; at best Karcsi could get help from a paramedic. When he saw that, in spite of what he had told us, we wanted to stay, he suggested that we could talk to the priest who had been left behind by the theological seminary, to which the building had belonged before being requisitioned for the military hospital, and which would again take possession of it after the evacuation.

Encouraged by the nonhostile, neutral-to-friendly attitude of this reserve officer, we then asked to see the reverend. A man around forty in a black priest's robe, he listened to our story, asked to see our papers, looked at them carefully, then asked how long we thought we needed to stay. We said just a couple of days, long enough for Karcsi to get better; as soon as he was on his feet again we would leave. The priest said we

*Latin for "The die is cast" (Caesar upon crossing the Rubicon).

could stay for a couple of days, but would have to leave before the rest of the hospital personnel were evacuated, which could happen any day. Needless to say, we were very happy with his decision and thanked him heartily. We were given two beds in a large hall, and Karcsi went to bed immediately. We asked for a thermometer and he rubbed it until he managed to raise the temperature beyond thirty-eight degrees Celsius. The next morning a medic came to see Karcsi, gave him some medication against fever and dysentery, and told him to take plenty of liquids. And that was it as far as our alibi was concerned.

The few days we spent in the hospital seemed wonderful. We had our first baths in many months. To a large extent we managed to get rid of our lice, though not completely, since the eggs that we could not see would in time produce new offspring. We did not want to ask for a disinfection of our clothing or at least our underwear because doing so might have aroused suspicion. The food at the hospital was probably bad, but under the circumstances it seemed to us manna from heaven. We had plenty of time to talk and get to know each other better. Karcsi's mood was fundamentally gloomy. When I inquired about the reason for this, after he had not only avoided the death sentence but had also managed to escape, he explained that his fiancée, Edith, was Jewish and had been deported; he would probably never see her again. It was no consolation to him, of course, that my parents and brother had also been deported.

Karcsi told me the story of his party activities in the military, which included stealing weapons and ammunition from the army and giving them to his party comrades. The story of his arrest stuck in my mind. He had deserted the army shortly before in order to avoid being arrested, as he had come under strong suspicion. He was at a clandestine meeting with false identity papers when it was overrun by the DEF and all the participants were arrested. Karcsi was interrogated first, and of course his papers were immediately discovered to be fake. He was badly beaten in an effort to make him reveal his name. He had good reasons to resist doing this because, as a military man engaged in revolutionary activities—including the provision of arms to the enemies of the regime—and a deserter from active duty, he could be sentenced to death. Furthermore, under the Hungarian legal system at the time (the spring of 1944) a person in his situation could be court-martialed, which in his case would have meant the death penalty, but only within seventy-two hours of his arrest. So Karcsi was playing for time and wanted to hide his identity at any cost for at least three days. Thus, when he felt that he would soon lose his self-control under the beating, he suddenly "confessed" to being Béla Schwarcz, a Jew in hiding. This confession was serious enough to be believed, and the DEF agents fell for it. Next, the other participants of the clandestine meeting were interrogated. Some did not know Karcsi by name, but others did; and the next day somebody, who had been badly beaten divulged Karcsi's real name: Károly Fekete. Now Schwarcz was a typical Jewish name in Hungary, whereas Fekete was not (by the way, both names mean "black"; one in German, the other in Hungarian). Who would believe that a Gentile would pretend to be a Jew in the spring of 1944? Of course, the DEF agents did not believe the man who said that Schwarcz was Fekete; they rather believed the "Jew" who had confessed to being Schwarcz. It took several face-to-face confrontations and two additional witnesses to convince them that Karcsi was Fekete rather than Schwarcz; but by the time they got Karcsi to admit who he really was, the deadline for the court martial had expired.

Two days after we entered the military hospital, on December 31, a group of lower-rank Wehrmacht officers came into the building and asked to be housed for a couple of nights while in transit. Their demand was, of course, granted, and they installed themselves in one of the halls. They did not ask for food, and seemed to be reasonably well provided with food, drink, and cigarettes. That evening, the Hungarian reserve officer and a couple of aides organized a modest New Year's Eve party to which they invited everybody, including the German officers and us. As I was among the few Hungarians present who understood German, and the only one who spoke it with tolerable proficiency, I had to play the interpreter much of the evening. The conversation started with a few news items that the Germans brought to the table, mostly about the battle that was raging around the encircled Hungarian capital—the Soviet ring around the city had been closed a week earlier. To my surprise, the Germans did not express the same certainty that the Hungarian radio and newspapers were proclaiming about the soon-to-be redemption of Budapest through a joint German-Hungarian tank offensive. Most of the officers in the group were Austrian, I found out from our conversation during the evening. They were not at all upbeat; they complained about the length of the war and the difficulties everybody was facing. At midnight they did not toast either to victory or to Hitler, and later, when one of them got drunk, he whispered into my ear, "Hitler kaput." This New Year "celebration" was a sad one for me. I could not help thinking all the time about my family, where they might be if they were still alive, and what they might be feeling at that moment.

After a few days in the hospital, during which I tried to talk to as many of the paramedics and nurses (they were all male, by the way) as I could, I discovered that several of them were from Transylvania. Although, as András Hegedüs, I pretended to be from Budapest, I told them that my grandparents were from Transylvania, where I had spent many wonderful vacations; thus we found a pleasant subject of common interest and became friends. Far from Transylvania though we were, these young soldiers were not at all eager to move farther away from what they considered their home, and were not looking forward to the evacuation. In fact, as we talked, it became clear that they were looking for ways to desert the army and return home as soon as the front had "passed." Needless to say, I reinforced these inclinations as much as I could, and as an engineering student and a person more knowledgeable and cultivated than they were, I earned their respect.

I soon found out from my new friends that the hospital's administrative office had a good supply of forms for health recovery certificates, the papers that wounded soldiers received upon their release from the hospital to enable them to spend three to four weeks resting and recovering at home before reporting back to their units. However, the certificates needed two signatures, one by the commanding officer of the hospital, the other by a medical officer. They also required two different rubber stamps: a straight one that served as a letterhead on the certificates, and a round one on or under the signatures. Here my brief but vital experience in forging identity papers came in handy, as did Karcsi's thorough familiarity with military rules and habits. After more exploratory discussions we struck a deal with two of my new friends: we would prepare for them valid-looking health recovery certificates made out for the places they wanted to go in exchange for access to the forms for our own use. I set to work on the certificates aided by Karcsi. The men who gave us the forms knew the names and ranks of the officers whose signatures were required. We had no models, but I produced a credible signature for the commanding officer and Karcsi signed the second name. The straight rubber stamp was available in the office, so we used it to provide a letterhead; but the round rubber stamp, which was actually the more important one since it certified the signatures, was missing. This posed a problem, which we solved as follows. In the place where the round stamp was supposed to be applied, we pressed the straight stamp down twice in the form of a large X. Then we wrote in small handwriting "round stamp lost in bombing," and signed this remark with the name of the commanding officer. The certificates looked very official and we strongly hoped that they would work. Our friends, who were the first to receive them, were very satisfied. We obtained in exchange several certificate forms for ourselves, which we did not fill out at the time, but which we equipped with all the stamps and signatures required and divided equally between the two of us, in case we were separated by some unforeseen event. We then stashed them away in a part of our clothing where they were least likely to be found if we were searched.

As a bonus, both Karcsi and I obtained military caps. Furthermore, I exchanged my good-looking but civilian coat for the military coat of one of the soldiers to whom we had given the certificates. Since we intended to leave the hospital as convalescent soldiers with health recovery certificates, a military coat seemed more useful to me than my civilian one; while the young soldier who was preparing to desert in the hope of getting home was not so much afraid of the Hungarian authorities or the Germans (with whom he had had no quarrel up to that point) as of being caught in military uniform by the approaching Red Army and then either shot or taken prisoner as an enemy. He therefore saw it as a useful part of his desertion strategy to rid himself of everything military, and was happy to exchange his military coat for my civilian one. Such were the differences in perspective between two individuals in apparently similar situations and contemplating similar actions—but with different backgrounds, experiences, and outlooks. I hope the young soldier succeeded; he left the hospital a few days later and I never heard of him again.

Karcsi and I were now ready in principle to leave the hospital with reasonably good military certificates. We put together a detailed story of the battle in which we had been wounded, based on information collected from the soldiers. We provided ourselves with rather serious injuries that, as they were internal, could not be easily checked: I had a brain concussion and Karcsi had pulmonary emphysema. We also knew what our symptoms were and what our treatment at the hospital had been, and, of course, we had the number and exact name of our military unit. Had we been arrested, these things could have been checked, but neither easily nor quickly (fortunately for us, there were no computers yet). All we needed was a place to go for our "convalescence." According to our identity papers we were both from Budapest, which was by then encircled and inaccessible, so we could freely choose the places where we wanted to go. Of course we needed shelter, for we had no money to pay for room and board. Here luck smiled upon us again. A couple of days after we consummated the deal over the certificates, a soldier came to the hospital from a neighboring village, where he had spent a month at home convalescing after having been wounded, treated, and released from the hospital. He came to complain that his wound had been very serious and that the four weeks of convalescence were not nearly sufficient; he was asking for a medical examination and an extension of his health recovery period. Our friends told him to talk to me and ask for my advice; I might be able to help him.

At first I found it a bit dangerous to be cast in such a role. Karcsi and I both regarded our doctoring of the certificates as a necessary but highly risky operation, to be kept absolutely secret outside the circle of the four of us who made the deal. We did everything to persuade the two soldiers (who were not trained in the rules of conspiracy) not to brag to anybody about the nature of their certificates, not even to their families or their best friends, not now and not later during their "convalescence." Otherwise, they would be risking not merely unpleasantness, but death. But after talking to the newly arrived soldier, Feri (Frank), I gradually changed my mind. Feri was a big, well-built, obviously well-fed man in his late thirties, married, and a butcher by trade. He was a law-abiding citizen and not a great hero. He had been called up for military service and sent to the front, where he found life unbearable because of the constant danger; fear was a sensation he simply could not get used to. So his wound, which was serious but not mortal, came to him as a godsend. He had a good time at the hospital and enjoyed the time spent at home in convalescence. Now that his health recovery certificate was about to expire, he was quite desperate at the idea of returning to his unit and being sent back to the front. He literally begged for help and hinted to his willingness to send half a pig—smoked or otherwise—to any officer who would help him.

I showed due understanding for his predicament, briefly told him the story of my own and Karcsi's (that is Pista's) injuries at the front, and then mused about how life makes different people face different problems. Whereas he had a house and a family to go to for his convalescence and only needed an extension of his leave, we on the other hand were just about to start our one month's convalescence, but had nowhere to go because our hometown, Budapest, had been encircled. I introduced him to Karcsi and the three of us chatted for a while to create an atmosphere of trust. In the end we told him that there was no longer any doctor at the hospital to examine him, and besides, even if there had been, it was not clear whether half a pig would be enough to induce him to deprive the Fatherland of such a brave, athletic soldier as Feri seemed to be. We offered a different solution: if he was willing to take the risk of getting a certificate without a medical examination, which was not exactly legal, we could perhaps get him one that had originally been meant for somebody else who, as far as we knew, had never shown up for it. We would fill in Feri's name and specify his village, Szend (today called Szákszend), as the destination, and make it valid for a month, which was the official time limit. In exchange, he would have to allow us to spend our own convalescence at his house, where we would be willing to help with any work he might have for us. We assured him that we needed only modest sleeping accommodations and food; in particular, we promised not to eat more than half a pig during our month there. He gladly accepted and waited until we "clarified the situation" concerning the certificate intended for that other person. When we got the certificate ready for him, he found it in perfect order. He told us he had come to Komárom by horse-drawn carriage, and could take us with him back to his village. We gladly agreed. This was around January 4 or 5.

Before Feri's arrival, we had attempted to arrange to stay behind after the rest of the hospital was evacuated. We had explained to the priest that as young Leventes we would have to go to Germany to find our unit, but that we would prefer to stay behind, as the war was lost anyway and we felt that we belonged here, not in Germany. The priest said he understood our dilemma and that everybody had to follow his conscience; whatever we did, he wished us luck, but he could not offer us shelter in the building, because that would mean putting the integrity of the theological seminary at risk, which he was not willing to do. We thanked him for his hospitality in accepting us when we had come and said we understood his position.

. . .

Upon Feri's invitation, we filled out our health recovery certificates in our respective names, with Szend as our destination for a month, and left the hospital in Feri's carriage. Szend is about forty kilometers south-southeast of Komárom. We first followed the road to Kisbér, twenty-eight kilometers due south of Komárom, then turned east in the direction of Tatabánya until we reached Szend after about thirteen or fourteen kilometers. Riding in the carriage was much less risky than walking on the road. Although Karcsi and I had good identity papers in our pockets, we were still not overly confident. First of all, we were a rather odd-looking couple. I had a military coat over a military tunic, with a military cap, but was wearing civilian pants, belt, and shoes. Karcsi had a military cap; a coat that, although civilian, could be taken for a military one from a distance; military-looking boots and belt; but civilian knee breeches and a blue sock on one foot, a brown sock on the other. We had created an elaborate story about how our uniforms had been partly—in Karcsi's case, almost entirely—destroyed when we were wounded and how the hospital gave us whatever clothing was available when we left, but this did not change the fact that we were strange-looking individuals. Besides, in spite of our relatively good papers, if we had been arrested and searched, the rest of the certificate forms—stamped, signed, but not completed—could have been found on us, thus giving us away. Also, I was circumcised, which in that part of the world was taken as a sure sign of Jewishness. We could have thrown away the uncompleted certificates instead of trying to hide them, but that would have left us without papers after a month; and although we fervently hoped that the Soviets would catch up with us before the end of the month, we could not be sure of this.

The three-to-three-and-a-half-hour carriage ride went smoothly. We arrived in Szend in the evening, without being stopped once on our way. Feri's house, which was on the main street, looked like one of the better dwellings of the village. We spent the first night inside the house, but the next day we were installed in a storage room that was connected to the house by a door, usually locked from the inside. The storage room, which had another door opening into the courtyard, was quite large and rather cold, having three of its walls toward the outside and without insulation. There was no furniture other than a small table and two wooden chairs, but there were several straw-filled mattresses on the floor, two of which we took possession of; the rest of them were meant for other possible visitors. There was a wood-burning iron stove in the room, and Feri let us chop and take as much firewood as we needed. As a result, we did not suffer from cold during the day, when the fire was on, but at night the room cooled down quickly as soon as the fire burned out, and we had only our coats on top of a thin blanket to cover ourselves. Twice a day, in the morning and early afternoon, Feri would come into the storage room from the house and bring us food. We would have preferred three meals a day rather than two, but we kept our wishes to ourselves. We offered to do some work, but the only task we were assigned was to cut firewood for the other rooms in the house. We did not go out into the village at all and spent most of our time inside, some of it in the courtyard.

A few days after we were settled in our new environment, Feri, looking as pale as death, came into the storage room from the outside, followed by two gendarmes with guns on their shoulders. As we later found out, somebody in the village had informed the gendarmes that Feri had not gone back to the army but was at home, and the gendarmes had come to check on him. When they asked him who else was in the house, he told them about us. The gendarmes asked to see our papers. We showed them and explained our situation. They examined the papers, found them in order, and left. We were not just relieved, but jubilant that our health recovery certificates had passed this major test. But Feri could not get over his fright. Three days later he was still trembling and would come into the storage room outside the "regular" mealtimes to discuss "the situation," by which he meant the danger of being discovered. He dropped some hints as to whether we could leave earlier than planned, but we told him we had nowhere else to go and reminded him of our understanding. Last but not least, we argued that his health recovery certificate was by no means better than ours, so all three of us were in the same boat: he was in no greater danger with us around than without us. I cannot say for sure that this calmed him down, but he stopped talking about his worries.

One day, in an episode which at the time seemed unimportant but later acquired some significance, a group of three or four Hungarian soldiers asked Feri whether they could spend the night in his house, and he led them to our room where they could use the straw mattresses to sleep. We spent the evening in friendly conversation, consisting mainly of their telling us about their adventures on the front. We learned a lot of details about life at the front, which would be potentially useful if we ever came under interrogation. We in turn entertained them in other ways. Finally, we described our situation according to our assumed roles, and added that both of us felt too weak for front service and were planning at the end of our recovery period to ask for an extension. However, our problem was that even if we got one, we had nowhere to go to spend the additional weeks of convalescence. One of the soldiers, who was from Szimö, a village north of Komárom, in the part of Hungary that used to belong to Czechoslovakia, told us that we could spend a few weeks at his parents' house in his village, and gave us details about himself and his parents that would make our reference to his recommendation credible. We thanked him, thinking that it would never come to that, as we expected the Russians to soon reach Szend; they were only a few scores of kilometers from us. The Russian advance was apparently being hampered by street fighting in Budapest, where five German divisions and several Hungarian ones offered fierce resistance for the six weeks following the capital's encirclement on the eve of Christmas 1944. Nevertheless, by mid-January the Russians had advanced to the Tatabánya-Székesfehérvár line, about sixty kilometers west of Budapest, and in the region where we were staying they had reached the village of Oroszlány, just thirteen kilometers east of Szend. When that happened, we hoped they would be in Szend in a day or two. Instead, German and Hungarian troops reoccupied Oroszlány and the front was stabilized for a while in the hills just east of Oroszlány.

With the onset of February, we had to decide what to do when our certificates expired. We could have gone to Szimö on the invitation of the soldier whose parents lived there, but that was about eighty kilometers to the north, which meant a risky walk of two or three days and would take us further away from the front line. Instead, we filled out our next pair of certificates for the village of Oroszlány, which was just behind the front line. We had no acquaintance there, but we figured we would seek shelter by offering to work in exchange. Thus, on February 4 or 5 we took leave of Feri and his wife and embarked upon the three-hour walk to Oroszlány, a coal-mining village, with some farming.

We walked on a country road with almost no traffic, and reached Oroszlány early in the afternoon. We examined several houses and finally chose one that belonged to an old couple with a daughter-in-law, the son being away in the army. They were poor farmers with very little land; they lived on potatoes and tea and their house consisted of only a kitchen–living room and a bedroom. But they were very friendly and agreed to take us in after we explained our situation. Although they had little or no work for us to do—there was not even firewood to cut, since their stoves ran on coal—they knew that convalescent soldiers like us had the right to food rations, and were hoping that we would get some. After our successful experience with the gendarmes who had examined our identity papers in Szend, we felt encouraged to try to obtain food rations using our certificates. We managed to get some flour, sugar, and a small quantity of bacon, which we contributed to the household, though it was very little. In spite of that, our hosts were very kind to us. Like the rest of the family, we would have tea in the morning, with sugar but no milk, and at noon and in the evening, we had baked potatoes with salt. Most of the time, that was all. We had no separate room, of course, and slept in the kitchen–living room.

While in Oroszlány, we had no access to a radio or any other source of news. It was only later that we learned about the fall of Budapest, which occurred on February 12 after more than six weeks of encirclement and bitter fighting. All we knew was that in our area the front was quiet and the Russians were not advancing. We figured that they might be waiting for spring to start a big offensive. After about a week spent with the poor family, we found out that there was a military unit in the village assigned to work in the local coal mine. The unit consisted of soldiers physically unfit for combat, including some who were convalescing from their wounds. It seemed to us that if we could join them, this would be a good way of legalizing our status and protecting ourselves from the time bomb that threatened us—the expiration of our fake certificates. Also, we could earn some money and thus be able to eat more. So we said goodbye to our friendly hosts and went to try our luck with the military. We presented our papers to the officer in charge of the mine unit; he looked at them rather superficially, obviously uninterested in our background, and said that we could join his unit if we wished, but the pay was very low, just a token. We moved into the barracks housing the unit, where we were given two bunks, and the next morning we went down into the mine.

I had always known that coal mining was hard work, but had never imagined anything close to what we encountered. We went deep under the ground through a shaft, in a shaky elevator that was a platform open on all four sides. Down below, the mine consisted of a network of long corridors and passages. A few of them, the main arteries, were comfortably wide and high, but most of them were just a few feet wide and less than six feet high, dimly illuminated by electric bulbs. The floor of the corridors had rail tracks on which small wagons, some empty and some filled with coal, were pushed by hand. The ceiling of the corridors was intermittently supported by woodwork, mostly vertically placed beams six to ten inches thick.

At the end of each corridor or passage the miners were busy attacking the coal face: some of them bored into the wall with electric-powered drilling machines, others knocked down coal from the wall with large, heavy mattocks, axlike tools for picking. The soldiers worked alongside the professional miners. We, as newcomers, had three tasks: to shovel the coal into the wagons, to push the wagons filled with coal, and to carry on our backs beams to be put in place as the corridors advanced. As far as I was concerned, the easiest task was to push the wagons. It required a strenuous effort when you had to push uphill, as was often the case, but at least you were moving around and could breathe. The shoveling was extremely tiring. Never in my life, either before or since, have I seen a shovel of the shape and size that was used in that mine. The metal scoop, shaped like a huge fig leaf bent up at its edges, was about two feet by one-and-a-half feet in size. When pushed by its long wooden handle into a pile of coal, it would pull out fifteen to thirty pounds, which you then had to lift to the brim of the wagon, about three to four feet high. You could do it for half an hour, but doing this work for many hours in a row was excruciatingly difficult. And you could not loaf: you were constantly supervised, and the number of wagons you filled was counted. The only thing even more unpleasant than coal shoveling was carrying beams. Imagine yourself carrying on your shoulder a beam weighing fifty to sixty pounds, along corridors so low that you had to stay bent over all the time, watching your step along the rails and occasionally maneuvering to avoid the wagons being pushed past you.

When we returned to the barracks in the evening, we fell on our bunks completely exhausted, and mused aloud about what a pleasant convalescence this was for wounded soldiers. The next morning we could barely move. The second day was as tough as the first; the third became more bearable; on the fourth day our bodies and limbs ceased to hurt;

and by the end of the week we felt that we could go on living as coal miners until the Russians came. However, Karcsi and I were disappointed, though not surprised, to learn that neither of us had produced enough to meet the norm, and we did not earn any money beyond the value of our food and shelter.

The following week we were allowed to use the mattocks, a change for the better because it meant more diversity and a little better pay (if we succeeded in meeting the norm). We would have probably gotten used to our new way of life and even earned our living as coal miners but for an unexpected turn of events: at the end of the second week several miners came down with typhoid fever, and we learned that the whole mining complex was going to be quarantined the following Monday to prevent the disease from spreading. Karcsi and I discussed this new situation and quickly reached the conclusion that being under quarantine was not exactly our cup of tea. Among other things, a secluded group would be easier to control in case of an emergency and therefore more likely to be pressed into evacuation. Less than an hour after we heard about the quarantine we said goodbye to the cheerful life of coal mining and were on the road again.

The end of February was now only three days away and our certificates were to expire in the first week of March. I thought we should complete our last pair of certificates for a month to be spent in Szimö, and walk the eighty kilometers with one or two stops for the night. But Karcsi was tired of waiting for the Russians to come and bored with the life we were leading; he suggested that, as close as we were to the front line, now was the time to take a risk and try to cross over to the Russian side. We knew that the front in our area was held by the Hungarian army and there were no German troops in sight. Not knowing enough about front lines to fully assess the actual risk, I did not like the idea; it seemed to me too adventurous and the risk not worth taking. I argued that as long as we still had certificates that could keep us going for another month, it was not worth risking our lives; we should do this only when our last certificates expired, if the Russians had not caught up with us by then. But my arguments had no influence on Karcsi, and he felt a strong compulsion to undertake the contemplated action. Although I felt quite strongly that reason was on my side, I also knew that rational considerations could take into account only a tiny fraction of the events and factors that would ultimately decide our fate. So when I saw that rational arguments were not able to allay Karcsi's itch for "action now," I went along with him rather than break up our team. We spent one more night at the house of the friendly poor family, and early the next morning we headed for the front line.

We had learned from soldiers that the front line ran through the hills about seven to ten kilometers east of Oroszlány. We knew that Várgesztes, the next village southeast of Oroszlány, was still on our side of the front line, so we could use it to explain where we were going in case we encountered patrols on our way ("We must have lost our way trying to reach Várgesztes . . ."). I remember the date that could easily have been our last day on earth: February 26, 1945. We started out on the road, but soon had to leave it. From then on we walked first across empty fields, then started climbing the hill along a trail. We were going east as well as we could. There was plenty of snow on the ground, at least two feet deep, but the weather was mild and the snow was melting, which made walking very slow and cumbersome. It was well into the afternoon when we heard the first shots in the distance. From that time on, our ears became our main guides and we kept walking in the direction of the shots. At one point, as we were climbing a trail and approaching a bend, two Hungarian soldiers suddenly appeared from behind the bend, coming down the trail toward us. They had guns on their shoulders and were carrying the body of a small deer strung out on a wooden pole. As we approached, I addressed them, and, to avoid their questions about where we were going, made a joke about the dinner they were going to have. But the precaution was not necessary: they were not in the least interested in us.

We continued climbing the trail until the sound of gunshots started coming from our left; then we left the trail and walked through the deep snow in the direction of the sounds. Soon we heard the gunshots quite close; the front line seemed to be just a couple of hundred feet away. Stray bullets hit branches of the trees around us. By this time it was dark. We got down on our bellies and started crawling toward the source of the sounds, side by side in the snow. When we had been walking in the snow, our feet would sink in deeply at every step and make a noise; but now that we were crawling on our bellies, our bodies did not sink in and our progress, though slow, was noiseless. We may have crawled for half an hour or an hour—the shooting was now coming from quite close by—when Karcsi stopped and whispered, "Look," pointing forward to the right. I looked; there was a small light, not at ground level but higher. As we kept looking, trying to guess what we saw, the light started moving, now to the left, now to the right. Finally Karcsi whispered, "smoking sentinel." The sentinel was maybe fifty feet ahead of us. He could not see us—we would not have seen him had it not been for the cigarette in his mouth. We had run into a frontline bunker guarded by a sentinel.

We knew that the contemporary technique of improvising a front line was not the classical one of digging a trench; there was usually no time for that under the prevailing mobile warfare techniques. The modern way was to dig and build bunkers for a few soldiers, close enough to each other to form a "line." Our attempt at crossing the front line would be to find an opening between two neighboring bunkers wide enough for us to cross unobserved by the soldiers on each side. After having crossed the line held by the Hungarian army, so our reasoning went, we would then crawl toward the Russian lines and put up a white handkerchief at the opportune moment. Having just approached one of the bunkers of the Hungarian line, we decided to move to the right far enough to leave behind the sentinel with the cigarette. We crawled rightward but before the flickering light of the cigarette had disappeared behind us, we stopped for a new reason: ahead of us we heard the sounds of speech, indicating another bunker, two of whose occupants were talking outside their hiding place. Bad luck, we concluded, let's try the other direction. Slowly, very cautiously, we crawled back to where we had come from. The soldier with the cigarette was still there. We continued to crawl, this time leftward, until we left behind the light of the cigarette. Fortunately, we had become used to crawling and managed to move without making any noise, which was the main thing that saved our lives. Suddenly Karcsi stopped and grabbed my arm. Without a word, he pointed to our right. I did not see anything at first, but after a few seconds I noticed in horror a soldier's silhouette, with his gun at his feet, less than thirty feet from us. We remained glued to the snow for several minutes, hoping the soldier would walk away, but he did not. Finally, very cautiously, we started crawling backward, away from the silhouette; it took us quite some time to gain enough distance to be able to turn around without the risk of being heard, and start crawling faster in the opposite direction. When we got far away enough to be able to talk, Karcsi said: "The network of bunkers is too dense. The front has been in this place for several weeks, and they've obviously had enough time to build out the line.

Let's go back." Needless to say, I did not argue with that conclusion; I felt a thousand-times lucky that we had not been discovered. We crawled for another half hour, then started walking, and got back into the village without further adventures well after midnight. Our hosts were surprised but accepted us; I do not remember the explanation we gave.

■ ■ ■

Having had a close look at the front line, it occurred to us that a safer way to go over to the Russians would be to join one of the units deployed on the front. We knew from conversations with soldiers at the coal mine that one of those units, a Cyclists' Battalion, had its headquarters just outside of Oroszlány. We figured that membership in this unit could not require very special training (we both knew how to ride bicycles), and we decided to ask to join the battalion on the grounds that our convalescence leave was coming to an end and our unit had been destroyed during the battle of Székesfehérvár (we knew the number of such a unit), so we could not possibly rejoin it. I felt a little uncomfortable about the risk of giving myself away through my lack of military training, but I thought I would just watch what the others were doing and do the same. So we left our hosts in Oroszlány and showed up at the headquarters of the Cyclists' Battalion, asking to see the officer on duty. After a long wait, a second lieutenant came to see us, listened carefully to our story, took our certificates, and disappeared behind a door. We waited for more than an hour; then the officer came back in the company of a field-gendarme with a bayonet-armed gun on his shoulder, to whom he handed over our papers with the brief introduction, "These are the two." Field gendarmes belonged to a special branch of the gendarmerie in charge of policing the army and supervising the behavior of its members. Before we could ask or say anything, the officer disappeared behind the door and the gendarme, putting our certificates into his pocket, turned to us with a resolute, "Let's go." I asked where we were going. "You will find out soon," he replied, and motioned us to get in front of him. In the courtyard he untied his horse, got into the saddle, and told us to walk at his side; he had orders to take us to the field gendarmerie's headquarters in Várgesztes. This was the village, about ten or twelve kilometers southeast of Oroszlány, whose name we had planned to invoke during our failed attempt to cross the front line.

The walk to Várgesztes took about three hours. It was a sunny after-noon that we could have enjoyed had it not been for our situation, which was more than precarious. We had naturally been uncertain as to whether our attempt to join the Cyclists' Battalion would succeed, but we had not counted on being arrested. Although we could not discuss our thoughts while walking alongside the gendarme on horseback, we could commu-nicate with each other through signs and gestures. We briefly contem-plated the possibility of attacking the gendarme. After all, the situation seemed desperate, and there were two of us against one of him, with almost no traffic on the country road that we were following. However, the gendarme had more important factors going for him: though he lacked our desperation, he had the advantage of being on horseback, he had a gun with a bayonet, and he was trained for situations like this. So we quickly abandoned this line of thought. After a while we tried to engage the gendarme in conversation. I started by telling him how lucky we were, all three of us, that we had such wonderful weather for our walk. He answered something, from which it became clear that he did not mind talking to us. We then slowly, piecemeal, told him our story about how we had been wounded and hospitalized, trying to make him understand how bad it was to be cut off from home when we most needed it and to have to recover among strangers after the ordeal we had gone through. Finally, we said how ridiculous it was that, having had our own unit destroyed, it should be so complicated to get back into the line of duty.

I don't remember the details of our conversation; but by the time we reached Várgesztes the field gendarme was quite friendly, sympathetic to our ordeal. Since the office was already closed, he said he would hand our papers to his commanding officer, a certain field gendarme lieuten-ant whose name he gave to us, and we should report the next morning to the lieutenant's office. With that he dismissed us.

After a more than tense afternoon, we now felt enormous relief. Our first thought was to fill out our last pair of certificates and head directly for Szimö, rather than report the next morning to the gendarmerie. But a little reflection told us otherwise. If we did not show up, the field gendarmerie would start searching for us. Our physical appearance was unmistakably unique, easy to recognize, and impossible for us to change. Our names would become unusable. If we completed the certificates with different names, we would not have any supporting civilian documents. Besides, if we did not show up, our current certificates would be scrutinized, and the validity of another pair of certificates using the same gimmicks, such as the X-shaped pair of letterhead stamps used in place of the round stamp, would become highly suspect. On the other hand, if we did show up, there was a good chance that, as on previous occasions, our health recovery certificates, coupled with our supporting civilian papers and our rather credibly detailed story, would work. So that is what we decided to do.

We arrived at the office around nine o'clock in the morning. We knocked on the lieutenant's door, he said, "Enter," and we entered the room, where we found the lieutenant in front of the window, using it as a mirror to shave. We told him who we were and he immediately recognized our case. Without putting down the shaving blade, he reached with his left hand for something on his desk, picked up our two certificates, and handed them to us, saying: "You should report in Nagyigmánd." This was the name of a middle-sized town about twenty kilometers southwest of Komárom, apparently an army enlistment and redistribution center where soldiers who had lost their units were supposed to report. We thanked the lieutenant for the information and left. We had survived another brush with death.

There was now nothing left for us but to fill out our last pair of certificates and hope that we would be liberated before the end of another month. We did so, choosing the village of Szimö as our residence for the month of our convalescence. This was the village of the soldier whose acquaintance we had made in Szend. We had his parents' address and his verbal message to them, containing enough details to confirm that we had indeed talked to him.

Szimö (Zemne in Slovakian) was about forty kilometers northeast of Komárom, close to eighty kilometers from where we were; we had two days of walking ahead of us. We started off on a sunny morning in the early days of March 1945, walking due north toward Komárom. At this point we were still using the certificates made out for Oroszlány, which were valid for another couple of days. We had been walking perhaps three to four hours due north on the main road to Komárom when we spotted ahead of us a small military car, a convertible, facing us but at a standstill, with a driver and a high-ranking officer as passenger. By the time we noticed the officer it was too late to get off the road to avoid the encounter, so we continued to walk ahead. As we got closer, Karcsi identified the car by its markings as belonging to the general staff; the officer was a captain, but one from the general staff. As we approached the car, we saluted the captain, who was reading something, and he returned the salute without paying attention. We had passed the car and continued walking with great relief when we heard the officer yell at us to come back. We returned to the car, painfully aware of the strange way we looked in our ridiculously mixed outfits, but putting on the most confident, self-assured expressions we were capable of. Standing at attention, we handed over our health recovery certificates, then our civilian papers, explaining that our convalescence period was about to expire in two days and we were heading to the military enlistment and recruiting center at Nagyigmánd (which was near Komárom), following the instructions of the gendarme lieutenant in Várgesztes, whom we identified by name. The captain examined the papers carefully, looked us over from top to bottom, and shook his head as if saying, "My God, what has become of our army?" Then he handed back our papers and dismissed us. We continued our trip and the next day reached Szimö without further adventures.

In Szimö we found the soldier's family without difficulty. They listened to our story, interested in what we had to say about their son; when we described our situation and asked whether they could take us in for the period of our convalescence—offering, of course, to do whatever work they could find for us—they responded in a friendly manner, saying that they wanted to help us. After some discussion among themselves, they came back with the following proposal: their house was not large enough to take in two persons; therefore they would take in one of us and have one of their neighbors take in the other. We said that would be fine if the neighbor agreed, upon which they conferred with the neighbor in question, who gave his consent. It was decided (I no longer remember on what basis) that I should stay with the family and Karcsi with the neighbor.

My hosts gave me the royal treatment. They had an unused room with a bed, and that is where they installed me. They had me eat with them at their table and were interested in having frequent conversations. Until 1938 this region of Hungary had been part of Czechoslovakia, a democratic republic with much more freedom and somewhat better living standards than Hungary. This was still noticeable after six and a half years; for instance, most families in the village had at least one bicycle, which was not the case in other parts of Hungary. The political atmosphere was also very different: most people in Szimö did not like the Germans and what they represented, and were rooting for an early ending to the war. Also, they did not seem to be very afraid of the Russians.

Karcsi and I met every day and spent much of our time together, either at his place (he was also very well treated) or mine. Occasionally we would do some work for one or the other of the two families, but they did not give us much to do. It had been about two months since the battle lines had frozen, and we expected the start of a Soviet offensive any day. Szimö was not close to the front line and there were no German troops in sight. We started feeling a little relaxed and a little optimistic.

It was in this relatively calm and hopeful atmosphere that I was again struck by a thunderbolt. One morning around six o'clock I woke up to strong and aggressive knocking on the outside door. I heard somebody open the door, and several people yelling commands came into the house. A minute later the door to my room was opened and two armed soldiers with Arrow Cross armbands burst in, shouting, "Here he is, we found him!" upon which two others followed them into the room. They seemed to be members of the much-dreaded Arrow Cross militia, known to shoot on the spot Jews, deserters, and fugitives of any kind. "Out of the bed, bastard, we caught you!" they yelled at me. I was both scared and surprised; I just could not put together the pieces to understand what had happened. I got to my feet, protesting loudly that there must be some mistake, and handed my papers to the nearest militiaman. He stared at the health recovery certificate and I could see that his eyes were glued to my name, disregarding the stamps, signatures, date, and so on. After a couple of minutes another militiaman stepped behind the first one and also started looking at my certificate. "What do you say your name is?" the first one asked with suspicion. "András Hegedüs," I said, "as you can see." There was some hesitation, and finally the first militiaman, who seemed in charge of the group, said to the other: "Fetch the guy who knows him." The man disappeared and returned with a villager who looked at me and shook his head. "It's not him," he said. In a few more minutes they were gone.

What had happened was this: the family's younger son had run away when he had to enlist in the army and had become a wanted person. Needless to say, I would not have chosen to stay with the family of a deserter, had I known this; however, I could not blame the family for not having warned me, as they thought my papers were genuine and I had no reason to fear the Arrow Cross militia. Later we found out that every third or fourth family in the village had a member who had deserted military service and was hiding. Early morning raids by the Arrow Cross militia were not unusual. When they caught a deserter they would often shoot him on the spot.

Toward the end of March, the last of the withdrawing Hungarian troops told us there was nobody between them and the Russians, so with the help of our hosts and some other villagers Karcsi and I got rid of the military parts of our outfits. The day of our liberation was, if I am not mistaken, March 30. Most people preferred to stay inside their houses, but I wanted to witness the coming of the Soviets and went out. For the last few days I had been practicing the few Russian words and sentences I had learned before my arrest; now I was looking forward to meeting our liberators. Toward noon, the first Soviet soldier appeared.

The German soldiers that I had encountered were always well dressed, shaved, well equipped, and motorized. True, I had not seen them at the front, much less in battle. Now I was facing a soldier of the mighty army that had beaten the hell out of the Wehrmacht. What I saw was different from anything I had anticipated, and it stuck in my memory for good. The Soviet soldier approaching me was running in pursuit of the hated enemy. He was barefoot, his boots in his hand, his uniform in tatters, his gun tied to his shoulder with a string; he had no hat. Although he was in a hurry, I made such an enthusiastic gesture when I saw him that he could not ignore it. I also yelled some greeting in Russian. He stopped for a moment, smiled at me, then, as if remembering that he had no time to lose, asked, "Gde Berlin?" ("Which way Berlin?") Silently, I pointed to the west, and he resumed running.

I went into the house trying to digest this encounter. Why was he barefoot? Probably because he was a peasant, for whom boots were always a nuisance. He must have taken advantage of the first warm spring day to loosen up and go barefoot. I remembered that in the village of Somkerék my grandfather's coachman always went barefoot or wore a kind of moccasin made of used tires: you had only to glance at his feet for a second to realize how difficult it must have been to force them into shoes or boots. Why was the soldier in such a hurry? It could not have been because he had lost his unit or been left behind; he was obviously ahead of everybody. So what was driving him? He did not ask for directions to Komárom, or Györ, or Brno, or even Vienna—not to any of the cities on the way to Germany that could be reached in a day or two. No: he asked for directions to Berlin. Obviously, that was on his mind more than anything else, and he probably did not know any of those other cities. I tried to imagine the events that must have transformed this obviously simple-minded peasant into the ferocious fighter that he now was. Had the Germans burned his village, raped his sister or his wife, killed his mother or his child? They must have done something terrible to him, for his rushing ahead in pursuit of the Germans, running barefoot "to Berlin," was fired by a hatred that could only have been caused by personal injury. I was reminded of this scene some fifteen years later, when I read Solzhenitsyn's magnificent poem "Prussian Nights," in which he describes his emotions as he entered German territory as a Red Army captain in pursuit of the German troops. He came driven by that same hatred fueled by personal injury; but, unlike the simple peasant I met, he was a sophisticated intellectual, and his hate for the murderous, criminal enemy mingled in his soul with an unspeakable but irrepressible admiration for those clean, manicured, picturesque German villages that seemed to be from another planet.

During the next couple of days, as the front advanced beyond Szimö, Soviet troops on trucks and troop carriers, as well as on foot, passed the village and sometimes stopped to rest. When they came into the house, I tried to converse with them, but my vocabulary was minimal. Once a group of three or four soldiers sat down at the table to eat something, and one of them opened a copy of *Pravda*. On the front page was a photograph of Stalin surrounded by some members of the politburo. I looked at the paper with undisguised curiosity and the soldier, noticing this, pointed to Stalin's picture and said, "Stalin." Upon which I nodded, pointed to another picture that I knew, and said, "Beria." He almost fell off his chair in amazement, looked at me at some length, and said, "*Budesh bolshoy chelovek*," meaning "You will be a great man."

After a few days, around April 1, we said goodbye to our hosts and started walking toward the next small town to the east. We intended to go to the local Soviet army command, explain our situation—this time under our real identities—and ask for some papers that would help us on our way home. We started out on foot, but soon encountered a Soviet soldier driving a horse-drawn carriage in the direction we were going. I asked whether he would let us ride with him and he readily agreed. On the way he asked us several times—he had to repeat the question, since we did not understand each other very well—if we knew what time it was; and I told him what I thought was the approximate time. When he asked again and wanted to know the *exact* time, I was very impressed with this spirit of punctuality in a simple soldier. A few days or weeks later, when I came to know our liberators a little better, I realized that what the soldier was interested in was not really the exact time, but whether we had watches. The Soviet Union did not manufacture watches for many years after the revolution, so a watch was a great treasure. The soldiers of the victorious Red Army loved to collect wristwatches: some of them wore five or six on each arm. Sometimes they bartered for them with food or whatever they had to offer, but more often they took them away from their owners at gunpoint. Some soldiers did not know that watches needed to be wound up; when their watches stopped, they thought they needed repair.

On our way we met Red Army convoys going westward. Every truck in the convoys had a wide band affixed to the top of the driver's cabin, with the inscription *"Na Berlin"* ("To Berlin.") Once we got into the town, we asked for the Soviet army command post, or commandatura. When we found it, we asked to see the officer on duty; and after we somehow made him understand that we were communists escaped from jail who wanted papers to get home, he said that he would ask a soldier to accompany us to the place where our request could be granted. He gave the soldier the address in writing, and the three of us left together to find the place. When we reached the address, a Soviet army office, the three of us walked in and the Russian soldier gave the name of the person who sent him. The officer who received us seemed to be expecting us. He invited us into an office, wrote down our names, then made a sign to a soldier standing by, who frisked us and took away our belongings, belts, and shoelaces. Despite our energetic protests, Karcsi and I were separated from each other and locked up in different rooms that served as improvised cells, each furnished with straw on the floor to sit on and nothing else. We were prisoners of the dreaded SMERSH, the military branch of the NKVD, the Soviet Secret Police.

After all that we had been through, it should have been utterly disappointing to fall into captivity again. But looking back at my mood at the time, I was not too upset: I viewed it as a minor unpleasantness based on a misunderstanding that would be easy to correct. I was too naïve and inexperienced in matters relating to the Soviet bureaucracy to realize what a dangerous situation we were in. The cell where I sat on the floor held another four or five prisoners. We were supposed to sit quietly without talking, but there was no guard in the room, so we could talk. That was somewhat difficult, though, because most of those in the room did not speak Hungarian. Some of them were Russian soldiers, others were Slovakian. The one thing about my roommates that disturbed me was that all of them had spent at least three months with the SMERSH. We were fed gruel made of barley. I did not dislike it, and we got as much as we needed.

My interrogation started on the day of my arrest. It was businesslike, never rude, conducted by a single uniformed SMERSH officer, a lieutenant I think, in the presence of a translator whose quality I could assess as very poor—I often had to correct him. In the first session I tried to explain who we were and why we had come to the Soviet commandatura. The lieutenant said they had no way of knowing whether our claims were true and therefore had to investigate them. With that, he started taking my life history in thorough detail, from the street address where I was born, through the names of all the schools I ever attended, and so on. I was alternately amused and frustrated by what seemed to me an utterly irrelevant exercise, but I controlled myself and tried to be patient. When it came to my involvement in the communist movement, the interrogation became even more detailed. When I reached the point where the Communist Party of Hungary dissolved itself to be replaced by the Peace Party, the lieutenant shook his head in utter disbelief: there could have been no such event; a Communist Party *never* dissolves itself. Besides, he had met and spoken to people who were currently members of the Hungarian Communist Party. I explained that the party was reconstituted in September 1944, but he did not believe me.

In one respect I could not complain: my case was not being neglected. Every day I spent several hours under interrogation, and the file of my biography was steadily growing. When it came to my arrest and the events at the DEF, the lieutenant wanted all the names of all the agents and prisoners. We then continued with the trial and the jail; with dates, names of cellmates, minute events, who was working where in the prison, who was the cook, and so forth. As the days went by and my dossier kept growing, I consoled myself with the thought that such a mountain of details would eventually show beyond a doubt that Karcsi and I were telling the truth. And this, indeed, is what happened in the end. After about a week, we were found to be telling the truth and were finally freed. When we were at long last told that we were "cleared" and free to go, I said to the officer in charge that, having taken a week of our lives to dispel their doubts about our story, they could now at least satisfy our initial request by giving us a paper that would facilitate our return to Budapest. That, the officer told me, was beyond their jurisdiction: they never issued such papers to anybody.

It was not until much, much later that I realized how lucky we were to have gotten off so easily. Many similar stories that I came across over the years took a very different turn, with the protagonists sent to some camp in Soviet Central Asia to help—just for a few years—rebuild the country destroyed by the war.

Free again, we got back on the road and went to the nearest large town where we were told we could find an office of the Hungarian Communist Party. This was Érsekujvár (Nove Zamky in Slovakian). There, at the party office, we finally managed to establish our identities by having the local secretary call the party headquarters in Budapest. Among the four or five names we gave him as likely to be found there, he managed to locate Hazai, and Hazai confirmed our identities based on our story. Thus, we were issued some temporary personal identification papers in our real names, and we started toward Budapest on the main road, hitchhiking where possible, otherwise walking.

We entered Budapest on foot and went to the party headquarters, where I was directed to temporary living quarters while Karcsi went to his parents' home. I spent a few days in Budapest before going home. I met those of my comrades who had jumped from the train: Hazai, Lichtmann, Hegedüs, and others. I also met Grünwald, who escaped from our convoy the day after we did. I found that all the comrades who had Jewish-sounding names had changed them into Hungarian-sounding ones: thus Sándor Lichtmann became Sándor Szikra, László Grünwald became László Gács, Marcel Schiller became Marcel Horváth, and László Fischer became László Földes. I was given to understand that this was the party line, the reason being that there was considerable anti-semitism among the Hungarian population and therefore a Jewish-sounding name was a handicap in interacting with the "masses." I did not question this reasoning at the time, mainly because it was not something invented by the communists but a decades-old tradition among Hungarian Jews, most of whom were as assimilated as German and Austrian Jews. Indeed, the Grünwalds and Lichtmanns were a minority, most Jews having long before changed their names of German origin into Hungarian ones.

By a decision of the Allies first announced in an interview with Stalin as far back as 1943, Northern Transylvania was to be returned to Romania after the war. In fact, at the time of my liberation Kolozsvár and the rest of Northern Transylvania were already under Romanian administration. Before returning home I spent a few days in Budapest, during which I met János Kádár, who had been one of the wartime leaders of the Hungarian Communist Party and the Peace Party. He knew about our activity in Northern Transylvania and invited me either to remain in Budapest and work in the Hungarian party or go home first to find out about my family and friends, then come back later. I had no clear picture at the time of what the differences between the Hungarian and the Romanian party might be—they were considerable, as I was to discover later—but I somehow felt that my place was back in Transylvania and Kolozsvár. I thanked Kádár for the invitation and told him I would consider it, but my first concern was to get home as soon as possible. The party offered to help me with this, as there was a great deal of traffic between Budapest and Kolozsvár, and I got a seat on a truck that was due to leave for Kolozsvár in a few days. I placed a phone call from Budapest to the party in Kolozsvár and found Sanyi Jakab, my party connection and friend, alive and well. He was happy to learn that I was also alive. He did not know anything about anybody in my family, and was looking forward to seeing me. I knocked on his door one late evening in mid-April 1945.

■ ■ ■

At this point in my story I would like to pause and take stock of what happened to my parents and brother, to my larger family, to some of my comrades and friends. Their fate is part of the tragedy that befell the Jews of Hungary in the summer of 1944.

As I have said in recounting my life in hiding, the Jews of Kolozsvár, including my family, were forcibly moved by the Hungarian gendarmerie into a cramped ghetto at the site of the local brick factory in early May

1944, and were deported from there in sealed cattle cars during the last two weeks of May and the first week of June. The destination of the trains was Auschwitz, the huge nazi extermination camp near Krakow in Poland. Here the majority of the deportees were gassed upon arrival; the rest were subjected to subhuman, hellish treatment that very few managed to survive. The Jews of Kolozsvár shared this fate with those from all the Hungarian provinces. Between its inception in 1942 and its liberation by the Red Army in January 1945—less than three years—the death factory of Auschwitz was used by the Germans to kill one-and-a-quarter million people, among them at least a million Jews. The peak capacity of its gas chambers and crematoria was over ten thousand victims a day. This capacity was almost fully used in the summer of 1944, when in less than two months, between the first week of May and the first week of July, more than 130 trainloads of Jews from the Hungarian provinces, a total of 437,000 people, were received and "processed."*

As to the Jews of Budapest—roughly two hundred thousand—their deportation was prevented by the fact that at the beginning of July, as a result of pressures from several neutral governments, Regent Horthy ordered the deportations stopped. Nevertheless, after October 15, when Horthy's rule was replaced by that of Szálasi and his Arrow Cross Party, thousands of Budapest's Jews were rounded up, led to the Danube, shot dead, and thrown into the river. In the end, roughly two-thirds of the Budapest Jews managed to survive the war.

Of the eighteen thousand people deported from Kolozsvár's brick factory ghetto (this number included Jews from neighboring villages and small towns), only a few hundred survived the war—less than 5 percent. Of those who were not deported because they were in Work Battalions at the time, a considerably larger proportion survived, but this category was small in itself, only a fraction of the younger Jewish male population. Finally, a special group of a few hundred Jews were sent to Switzerland and survived the war. Together, the total number of survivors among the Jews of Kolozsvár added up to less than two thousand.

As to my own family, this is what I was able to find out: My father, who was sixty-one in the summer of 1944, was sent straight to the gas

*For detailed information on the destruction of Hungarian Jewry the reader is referred to the monumental research monograph of Randolph Braham, *The Politics of Genocide: The Holocaust in Hungary*, Vol. I–II, Columbia University Press, 1981.

chambers. My mother, who was forty-seven, survived the first selection. I spoke to a woman who was with her at Auschwitz before being sent to another camp early in the fall of 1944. She said my mother was in relatively good spirits, was lucky enough to have her own boots returned rather than confiscated after the disinfection, and seemed healthy and in fair condition when she last saw her. This led me to hope that maybe, just maybe, my mother would soon return from one of the liberated camps in the western part of Germany. I shared this information with a watchmaker called Borgovan, who knew my mother well and had asked me about her a month earlier, when I had not yet heard anything. To my consternation, when I told Borgovan the latest information, he suddenly remembered that my mother had given him her gold wristwatch for safekeeping. Now that her return seemed possible, he gave the watch back to me. I never spoke to him again.

I nurtured this faint hope of my mother's possible return for more than a month; then a younger woman who had just returned from deportation came to see me. She told me she and my mother had left Auschwitz in the fall of 1944 in a transport to some place further west, where they were separated and my mother was put into a group of women that was sent to Stutthof on the Baltic Sea. She later found out that the entire transport sent to Stutthof had been gunned down and thrown into the sea; there seemed to be hardly any survivors. This was the last I ever heard about my mother.

It is hard to explain, but for many years I did not make any serious effort to investigate what actually happened at Stutthof. I did not even try to find the woman who brought this news and talk to her again. Maybe it was self-defense; I had felt very close to my mother and the story was too awful. But forty-some years later, when Raul Hilberg's three-volume work, *The Destruction of the European Jews,* was published, I found there a description of what had happened at the Stutthof camp. In January 1945, when the Soviet offensive came to a halt near Stutthof, a large group of prisoners, including most of the males, was moved further inland. A group of three thousand women was shot on the shore or thrown from the ice into the water. As to the remaining prisoners, upon resumption of the Soviet offensive in the spring of 1945, they were loaded into three barges at Hela on April 27. One of them, with sick inmates, was directed to Kiel; the other two arrived in the early morning hours of May 3 at Neustadt, twenty miles north of Lübeck. As the victims waded ashore during the day, they were shot at by SS men and naval personnel, while German officers photographed the scene from gardens in their homes. This happened five days before the German capitulation.

During the late summer of 1945 I also heard the story of my brother Bobby's life from his deportation to his death, from a friend who was with him at Auschwitz. This friend, Imre Székely, was between me and my brother in age, and he worked at Dermata until he was deported. He was one of the few survivors among the deportees who remained in Auschwitz until its final evacuation, and he came to see me upon his return. He related that Bobby had survived the first selection at Auschwitz and was soon recruited for the camp orchestra. Yes, there was a prisoner's orchestra at Auschwitz (actually two—a larger men's and a smaller women's orchestra), and my brother became one of its clarinetists. From early morning to late evening, in the open air, in hot and cold weather alike (in my brother's case, from June to January), the orchestra had to play music ordered by the camp commander (in July and August, this was Hoess). Bobby apparently managed to cope with this physically exhausting and psychologically devastating routine until the evacuation of Auschwitz at the end of January 1945. By then, however, he had become very weak; his lungs were dilated and he was suffering from emphysema. At the time of the evacuation, the prisoners were started on a long death march to the west. Bobby marched alongside Imre for quite a while, maybe a couple of weeks. When they arrived at their destination, Bobby was seriously ill and was admitted to the hospital barracks. A few days later, when the Red Army approached their location, the SS ordered a new march to the west. Those in the hospital barracks were ordered to join the march. Imre had a chance to talk to Bobby and told him that anyone who could not get up would be killed. Bobby understood and tried, but he was not able to get up, even with Imre's help. He was killed by a lethal injection along with everyone else who was unable to march.

As to the rest of my family—grandparents, uncles, aunts, and cousins—out of thirty people alive in May 1944, twenty-three were killed and seven survived. Of the survivors, five were in Work Battalions and thus escaped deportation. Of those taken to Auschwitz, only two returned: a cousin on my mother's side and one on my father's side.

Among my friends and comrades whom I recruited for the underground communist movement, three had died: Willy Holländer was killed in an air raid while in jail; Dezsö Nussbächer and Menyhért Schmidt perished in Work Battalions. The others fared better: Ede Lebovits, who acted as a member of the technical group, survived, lived for a short while in Cluj, then went to Budapest to study medicine, and became a physician specializing in lung diseases. He changed his family name to Laczkó. We remained in touch and are good friends to this day. Mayer Hirsch, the Dermata electrician who later became my co-worker at RAVAG, survived the war, returned to Cluj, and lived there under the name of Tibor Hida; in the seventies he emigrated to Israel. György László, the textile worker who loaned us his room for party meetings, survived his service in a Work Battalion and returned to Cluj. After a while he left for Sweden with a fellowship to study engineering; later, he founded a moderately successful small business in Malmö, Sweden. We still communicate occasionally. Of the remaining people who participated in distributing the leaflets of the Peace Party in the summer of 1944, György Havas survived the war and lived in Romania for at least a decade before I lost track of him; Misi Schnittländer survived the war, lived for a while in Cluj under the name of Mihai Sava, and later emigrated to the United States.

CHAPTER 6

■ ■ ■

Postwar Cluj

When I returned to my hometown in April 1945, its official name was once again Cluj. Northern Transylvania, liberated in September–October 1944, had been returned to Romania. During the six months following the August 23 coup by which Romania switched sides in the war, several governments led by generals had succeeded one other. None of them had more than limited authority, as the country was controlled by the Red Army, and the real power lay in the hands of Marshall Malinovsky's troops.

During these months the Romanian Communist Party, which had emerged from the underground with about a thousand members, started organizing itself energetically, enrolling those workers who could be politically activated as well as some intellectuals. In the countryside, the communists were active mostly through a left-wing organization called the Ploughmen's Front, which had been started in the thirties and had numerous "crypto-communists" (a perfectly apt term unknown to me at the time) in its ranks. Some of these were in leading positions, and the organization closely followed the communist line. Together with the Social Democratic Party and the Central Trade Union Council, the Communists organized several mass rallies in February 1945 to demand a new government with popular representation. The Soviets used these demonstrations to pressure King Michael into appointing a government "capable of guaranteeing the stability of the home front," which was needed to pursue the war to its successful conclusion.

On March 6, 1945, as a direct result of Soviet pressures, the king appointed a new government headed by Dr. Petru Groza, president of the

Ploughmen's Front. Groza was publicly known as a lawyer with demo-cratic inclinations who had opposed the nazis and their Romanian aco-lytes. It was his personal tragedy that he ended up as a communist puppet. Three of his ministers, among them Teohari Georgescu (Interior) and Lucrețiu Pătrășcanu (Justice), were Communists. The most impor-tant position was that of minister of the Interior, who was in charge of the police and security apparatus. The Ministry of Foreign Affairs went to Gheorghe Tătărescu, head of a dissident faction of the Liberal Party which was aligned with the Communists. The remaining ministries were headed by Social Democrats and members of Groza's organization. Thus the key centers of power in the Groza government belonged to the Com-munists. Although the Western Allies refused for more than a year and a half to recognize the Groza government, there was little they could do to prevent it from consolidating its power.

At the local level in Cluj, the Communist Party firmly controlled the key positions in the administration and in the city's cultural and political life. The prefect of the county, the mayor of the city, and the chief of police were all Communists, with a Social Democratic deputy here and there. Communists and Social Democrats shared the leadership of the trade unions. The Romanian university, returned from Sibiu and named Babeș after a famous Romanian medical scientist, had as its rector (presi-dent) a well-known archeologist named Daicovici, who aligned himself with the Communist Party. The Hungarian university, named after the famous mathematicion from my hometown, Bólyai, was headed by Rec-tor Csögör, a member of the Communist Party. There were three local newspapers, a Romanian one and a Hungarian one published by the Communists, and a Hungarian one published by the Social Democrats.

The party itself was locally led by a Regional Committee in which my former PC, Sanyi Jakab, played a key role. However, he was not the actual head of the committee. The regional party secretary, or secretary of the Regional Committee, was Vasile Vaida, a Romanian Communist from Transylvania who had been appointed by the Central Committee. In his early forties and a shoemaker by profession, he had spent many years in jail, where he had had a chance to read and acquire a certain degree of education, mostly political. Vaida struck me as a very practical man, level-headed and calm under stress, fair-minded but unyielding when the party's interests were at stake. The most delicate issue he faced was that of the ethnic Hungarians, who were a minority in the country

but a majority in Cluj. There were strong pressures from Romanian nationalistic circles, both locally and in Bucharest, to restrict in various
ways the Hungarian population's right to representation, cultural institutions, use of their own language, and so on. Vaida resisted these pressures as best he could. During the period from 1945 to 1947 that I spent
in Cluj, the Bólyai University functioned unhindered. There was a Hungarian theater in addition to the Romanian one; there were Hungarian
high schools and elementary schools, newspapers and cultural magazines, and free use of the Hungarian language at official places. As a
result of this, real progress was made in the relations between Romanians and Hungarians, both in Cluj and in the surrounding villages. This
changed for the worse—much worse—a few years later, but a good start
was made after the war.

Like all other party members who had been arrested during the war,
upon my return to Cluj I had to undergo a process of clearance by the
party, called verification. The outcome of the process depended on the
behavior of the individual under arrest. Those who had betrayed any of
their connections were excluded from the party. My verification took a
few days and ended with my confirmation as a party member. Several
of those whom I had drawn into the movement and who had participated with me in various actions survived the war without being arrested—Jakab, Hirsch, Havas, Schnittländer, Galambos—and were thus
living testimony to the fact that I had not betrayed them. I was then
asked to work for the party as a member of the County Committee. At
the same time, I was advised to change my name. Though unstated, the
reason was clearly that Blatt sounded Jewish. A party activist, though
not expected to hide his Jewishness, was not supposed to publicly adver-
tise it either. Having seen this happen to my comrades in Budapest, I
was neither surprised nor upset. I chose the name under which I had
played in Ping-Pong tournaments as a teenager: Balázs, a common Hungarian family name sometimes used as a first name.

The County Committee was under the Regional Committee and dealt
with local matters, although all issues of political importance, even local
ones, were handled at the regional level. Our task was to build strong
party organizations at every plant and institution in town, as well as in
the city districts and surrounding villages, and to instruct and educate
the members through meetings, seminars, and the distribution of literature. The meetings were conducted in whichever language was spoken

by the majority of members in the particular organization, so my fluency in both Romanian and Hungarian came in handy. For example, I would conduct meetings at the Dermata organization in Hungarian and meetings at the railway yards organization in Romanian. The purpose of these meetings was to elucidate the party's program and goals so that the members would internalize them and become active in promoting them. We measured the strength of a party organization not so much by the number of its members as by their dedication to the cause and their ability to win acceptance for it in the community to which they belonged.

My private life was almost nonexistent; I poured all my energies into the party. I lived on a modest salary in a one-room studio apartment at the party residence, and used whatever free time I had to study the writings of Marx and Lenin. *State and Revolution,* Lenin's book on the communist theory of the state, was new to me and highly relevant to our situation. Less relevant, but also of interest, were many other books that now became available, and I started to study Marx's *Capital.* My circle of friends consisted primarily of the Jakabs and the Kleins. Sanyi Jakab's marriage was highly controversial in party circles. His wife, an attractive, very bright, highly cultivated, and widely traveled woman around thirty, was none other than Magda Farkas, the oldest daughter of the family that owned Dermata; she was previously married to Endre (Bandi) Klein, a lawyer. In spite of her family background, Magda became a communist during the war and helped the party financially and by hiding Sanyi for a while. She and her first husband, Bandi, who also became a communist during the war, had a seven-year-old daughter, Edi (Edith). In May 1944 when the Jews were ordered into the ghetto, Bandi was with a Work Battalion. His group was released a few days later and, in a more than daring undertaking, he managed to enter the ghetto and smuggle out Magda and Edi. He found them a hiding place in a nearby village, with a Hungarian schoolteacher who had agreed to hide them for a sizable amount of money. Both Magda and Edi survived the war there.

After his divorce from Magda, Bandi Klein married Regina Josepovits, the pediatrician whom I had met in 1944 while both of us were in hiding. Regina herself had an almost fatal episode a few weeks before liberation. She had three sisters, and the four siblings had rather similar facial features. In early September 1944 a man recognized Regina on one of the main streets of Kolozsvár and called a policeman to arrest her. He said Regina was Jewish but mistakenly gave her name as that of a sister who had been deported in May along with the rest of her family. Regina was taken to the police, where she admitted to being Maria Josepovits, that is, her own sister. She wanted to avoid being identified as a communist and handed over to the DEF. But Maria had a child, and Regina was pressed to tell where she was living and hiding the child. This she refused to do, upon which she was beaten for several days without any result. "You can kill me," she insisted, "but I won't betray my child." She was held by the city police, not the DEF, and word went around quickly among the personnel about the stubborn Jewish woman who would rather die than give away the hiding place of her child. The police officer who took her to interrogation and returned her to her cell after every beating would ask on the way back, "Did you tell them?" When she shook her head, he would encourage her, saying, "Don't tell them!" Regina was liberated after about two weeks, when the Soviets entered Kolozsvár. She and her husband became very good friends of mine. Bandi was a wonderful storyteller with a superb sense of humor, always ready to crack a good joke. Regina, called Juci by her friends (a diminutive of Julia, the name under which she had hidden during the war), was an exceptionally decent and generous woman. I developed a strong attachment to her and regarded her as a kind of aunt.

Although my immediate family and my relatives in Northern Transylvania had been killed, I had one relative left in the city of Arad in Southern Transylvania, which had remained part of Romania in 1940. My mother had a cousin of her own age, called Tibor Rényi, who lived in Arad with his family. He was a wonderful man and very close to us. I remember that his occasional visits to our family during my childhood were a constant source of joy. My very first soccer ball was a present from him. Rényi, a successful pharmaceutical entrepreneur, became a communist during the war and organized the sending of food packages and other help to the prisoners of Vapniarca, an infamous detention camp in Transnistria. He survived the war, but lost his wife and son, who were on their way to Palestine on the Turkish ship *Struma* when it was sunk in the Black Sea apparently by a Soviet submarine. He later remarried and had a son and a daughter. I resumed contact with him after my return, met his new family, and we became close friends.

There was one person in my environment who tried to persuade me to take a different course in life. This was Teofil Vescan, the young Romanian mathematician who, back in 1941, had organized an informal calculus course for Jewish students who could not enroll in the university. He was also a communist and a member of the Regional Committee. He spoke to me as a friend, arguing that I had great mathematical talent and, instead of devoting myself to a political career, should enroll full time in the university and study mathematics. I wish now that I had listened to him. I loved mathematics, but at the time I was a true believer in marxism. I saw myself as a soldier in the service of the cause, and the task of building a new society overshadowed everything else.

Immediately upon my return to Cluj, I looked up Ilona Hovány. Although less than two years had passed since our love affair in the summer of 1943, I found her much changed. She looked much older and felt rather miserable. She had lost her—our—eight-month-old son to an unknown disease sometime in January; moreover, she had been excluded from the party for allegedly weak behavior during her arrest. She had a job at Dermata, an educational position, and did not complain about it, but she was very lonely. I offered her my friendship but when she realized that I did not intend to go beyond that, she became even more dejected. I was overcome by a strong feeling of compassion, and when I saw her for the second or third time, I caressed her and finally made love to her, without thinking through the consequences. I saw her a few more times, then stopped seeing her. After two or three months I found out from her sister that she was pregnant. This came as a shock to me; it somehow had never crossed my mind that this could happen. I went to see Ilona and suggested that she have an abortion, as it was very uncommon in those days for a single woman to have a child. Abortion was legal and easily accessible, and of course I was ready to pay the expenses. But Ilona did not want to hear about it; she wanted the child. When I argued that a child should be brought into the world only if both parents were ready for it, she became angry with me and declared that it was none of my business. She said she was going to have the child whether I liked it or not, and it would be *her* child and hers alone. Ilona was a proud and stubborn woman; at the time I did not think of it, but she was thirty-six years old and may have felt that this was her last chance to have a child. Later, after the child (a girl called Anikó) was born, I tried to send her help, but she refused to accept anything from me. I finally found a common acquaintance who from time to time gave Ilona the things I wanted to send her without saying explicitly that they were from me. Three or four years later Ilona married a man with a daughter of his own, and he turned out to be a very good father to Anikó. Although I inquired about Anikó whenever I had the chance and knew that she was doing well in school, I did not get to see her until she was thirty-two, when—divorced, with two children, and living in West Germany—she contacted me and we arranged to meet. That was a big event in my life.

In October 1945 I was sent to Bucharest as one of two dozen delegates from the Cluj region to a major political event, the national conference of the Romanian Communist Party. It was an interesting experience, in some ways an early eye-opener, although one with a delayed effect. At the time I simply registered the stifling atmosphere and other negative phenomena—my marxist convictions were too solid to be affected by them—but later they came back into my consciousness. First of all, for the entire duration of the conference (five or six days) the whole delegation was locked up in a guest house without permission to go out. We were not allowed to do any sightseeing or contact any personal friends we might have in the capital. This was justified by a need for vigilance and self-protection against potential enemies of the party. I found it utterly ridiculous and said so to Vaida, who headed our delegation and was the only one among us to have any contact with the conference organizers. He was visibly uncomfortable and tried to find excuses for the measure, but of course he was not in a position to change anything. Next, the party leaders, most of whom I saw and heard for the first time, made a mixed impression. On paper, the Central Committee was the decision- and policy-making body of the party and its reelection was one of the crowning events of the conference. But it was a fairly large body, with several dozen members, that met only on rare occasions and was in no position to direct the day-to-day activities of the party. The real power belonged to the political bureau (politburo), a committee of fewer than ten members that met frequently and whose decisions were the ones that really mattered. Four members of the politburo were secretaries of the party, and the general secretary was the overall boss.

Gheorghe Gheorghiu-Dej, the general secretary, delivered the main speech at the conference. An electrician from the region of Moldova who had worked for a while at the railway yards of the small Transylvanian town of Dej (its name was attached to his in order to mark this association), he had been one of the organizers of the nationwide railway yards' strike of 1933. He had been jailed from then until August 1944, and became a leader of the party while in prison. A solidly built, good-looking man in his mid-forties who spoke slowly and deliberately, his demeanor was that of a cautious but firm leader of the working class who was aware of the awesome responsibilities that lay on his shoulders. He was not a good orator; in fact, he read most of his speech. The part that stuck in my mind was a brief account of the party's wartime history. He told us that Ştefan Foriş, the party's general secretary during much of the war, had proved to be a traitor and had been kidnapped by a party detachment in early 1944. We were not told what happened to him after his kidnapping. Although at the time I had no reason to doubt the truth of this revelation, I found the secrecy surrounding it rather disturbing. Years later I learned that Foriş was killed after the war by emissaries of the party, allegedly for his treason but without a trial. Decades later he was rehabilitated as having been an innocent victim of unwarranted suspicions. Besides the revelations about the party's history, Gheorghiu-Dej's speech dealt with the current situation and the party's policies. Part of the speech criticized the justice minister, Lucreţiu Pătrăşcanu, for his nationalistic tendencies. Pătrăşcanu had been personally involved in the negotiations with King Michael that prepared the coup of August 23, 1944, and he played a prominent role in its preparation and execution, but this was mentioned only briefly, the emphasis being on his subsequent mistakes.

Ana Pauker, another party secretary and politburo member, was the oldest of the leaders and the only one whose name was internationally known. A good-looking Jewish woman in her early fifties, rather imposing and very bright, she became involved in the movement as a student, and soon rose to a leading role in the party. In the early thirties she was sent to France by the Komintern (Communist International) for a couple of years, then returned to Romania, where she was arrested in 1935 and sent to jail. Her husband, Marcel Pauker, also a party leader known under the code name Luximin, was criticized by the Komintern for engaging in factionalism in the late twenties. He later went to the Soviet Union and was executed there as a traitor in 1938. He and Ana had a son and a daughter. Ana also had a daughter from a love affair with a French communist leader. In the spring of 1941 she was sent to Moscow from her jail cell in Romania as part of a Soviet-Romanian exchange of political prisoners. She spent the war there and returned with the Soviet troops in 1944.

Ana Pauker reported at the conference on the international situation and its impact on the party's daily struggle. She described the difficulties arising from the fact that the Groza government had to maintain the appearance of a coalition government, even though the Western Allies did not recognize it as such, because relations between the Soviet Union and the West did not permit an immediate communist takeover in Romania. She outlined a strategy that, in retrospect, I would call "surreptitious power grabbing": the Communist Party would gradually but unobtrusively take into its hands all the levers of power while outwardly preserving the semblance of a democratic coalition. Interestingly enough, my most vivid memory of Ana Pauker at this conference is her answer to a question (that I no longer remember) to the effect that "we must do many things without calling them by their names."

The third most prominent party leader who spoke at the conference was Vasile Luca, also a secretary and member of the politburo. A man in his late forties, Luca was a charismatic speaker and a born agitator. Of Hungarian extraction, he spoke Romanian with a strong accent; nevertheless, he was thoroughly assimilated and did not consider himself Hungarian. Indeed, he would lean over backward to avoid being accused of Hungarian nationalism. A self-educated worker who had led many strikes, he was jailed in the thirties for his communist activities and freed by the Soviets from a jail in Cernauti in 1940, when they took Bessarabia and Southern Bucovina from Romania. Like Pauker, he had spent the war in the Soviet Union. He was the party leader who dealt with Northern Transylvania, which had special problems as a region just regained from Hungary. He had visited Cluj several times during 1945, and I had met him and talked to him on those occasions. I heard many good things about him from Sanyi, although my personal impressions were much less sanguine: he seemed to me emotional, impulsive, vain, and rather subjective in his judgments.

Another speaker whose presence was memorable in more ways than one was the minister of justice, Lucreţiu Pătrăşcanu, who would be shot as traitor nine years later. Unlike most other members of the party leadership, Pătrăşcanu was an intellectual. He was quick, witty, educated (well known also as a lawyer), and a good speaker. He made a very strong impression at the conference, partly because the delegates were told in advance by their group leaders that he had displayed nationalistic deviations. There was some basis in reality for these accusations, in that

Pătrășcanu had indeed advocated a more nationalistic line toward the Hungarian minority. However, as it turned out, this was used primarily as a pretext by the leading group around Gheorghiu-Dej to isolate him within the party, besmirch him, and ultimately—three years later—arrest him. The root of the conflict seems to have been personal animosity and jealousy on the part of Gheorghiu-Dej, who correctly saw in Pătrășcanu his only viable competitor for the position of party leader. At the conference, where he was attacked by several people besides Gheorghiu-Dej, Pătrășcanu gave an impressive talk, in which he admitted some mistakes in a dignified manner, without the self-flagellation that later became the hallmark of "self-criticism," and pledged to support the agreed-upon party line. At the time, although I was attracted to Pătrășcanu's intelligence, straightforwardness, and dignified manner, I had strong reservations about him as a result of prior information we had all been fed about his deviations and his allegedly anti-party attitudes. He earned my deep respect many years later, when I found out what happened to him after his arrest and how he behaved during the tragedy that befell him.

A much younger intellectual, Miron Constantinescu, in his late twenties, was also active at the conference. A highly articulate, sophisticated, and educated young marxist, he was being promoted to some extent as a counterweight to Pătrășcanu. His character defects were not visible at the conference, and he made an excellent impression on me. On the other hand, I remember well the strongly negative impression I had of Iosif Chișinevschi, the party's propaganda chief. A little gnome-faced man in his forties, Chișinevschi was a Jewish tailor from Bessarabia who had entered the movement as a young man and, like the other leaders, spent years in jail. He spoke with a lisp and a Bessarabian accent. He was narrow minded, was Talmudistic in his argumentation, and had all the traits opposite of those needed by a successful propaganda chief. The reason he got the assignment was probably that the chief of propaganda was also—in fact primarily—the party's ideological watchdog, whose task was to impose the correct line on the party press and all the party's ideological work from journals and seminars to schools for the cadres. In that capacity Chișinevschi managed to eliminate every trace of color and liveliness from the party newspaper, *Scinteia* (*The Spark*), and from the journals he controlled.

Six years later, three of these leaders—Ana Pauker, Vasile Luca, and Teohari Georgescu—were branded right-wing deviationists and destroyed.

But in 1946 they all seemed to be united against Pătrăşcanu; at least none of them voiced dissent during his condemnation at the conference.

Back in Cluj, it took me some time to digest the party conference. After the stifling atmosphere that had dominated it, I felt good about the air of openness and straightforwardness in confronting difficult issues which was the hallmark of my own immediate working environment. I attributed this mainly to Sanyi, who had been primarily responsible for putting together the organization after September 1944 and had carried on the discussions for integrating it into the Romanian party. I admired him for his courageous and skillful leadership of the underground movement in the war years; I respected him even more when I realized what an enormous burden he had taken upon himself by marrying the woman he loved in spite of her family background. For a communist leader to marry the daughter of the biggest capitalist in town was tantamount to sacrilege. No matter that Magda had helped the party in good faith and at great risk to herself; no matter that she had divested herself of her possessions, donating them to the party: In spite of all this, there was an unending torrent of gossip and innuendo against the party boss who had married the daughter of the class enemy. Needless to say, there were people within the party who would use these circumstances against Sanyi at the first opportunity.

Early in the spring of 1946 an incident took place in Cluj that increased my respect for Sanyi still further. One morning, on one of the minor national holidays, a crowd of several thousand demonstrators gathered in the city's main square in front of the local party headquarters, shouting nationalistic slogans and demanding that the Romanian flag be hoisted on the building. The red, yellow, and blue flag of Romania was the nation's official symbol, but in the past it had often been used as a symbol of oppression against minorities, especially the Hungarians, and those memories had not yet faded. The party was therefore waging an educational campaign to convince people that the flag was now the symbol of a democratic Romania, where minorities enjoyed full and equal rights. On the day in question, whoever was in charge of the headquarters had not deemed it necessary to hoist the flag. There were many discussions after the fact, with differing opinions as to whether the flag should have been hoisted in the first place, but everyone agreed that this should not be done in response to a demonstration. I arrived at the party headquarters about the same time as Sanyi, and we both entered the building through a back entrance. Inside there were several members of the Regional and County Committees, other party workers, and a few workers from the party garage. Vaida was out of town, so Sanyi assumed command. Outside the building, the crowd—mostly Romanian nationalist students—was shouting ever more loudly in an increasingly hostile manner and pushing threateningly against the gate of the building. This gate opened into a vaulted entrance space that led to an inner courtyard with side doors leading into the building. Made of solid wood and bolted, the gate seemed to be holding up well, although scores of demonstrators were wildly pushing against it, trying to break into the building. There were no police or military personnel around to protect the building, and we had no weapons other than a few pistols. I personally had no idea of what to do, but Sanyi had a clear battle plan. He gathered everybody in the vault inside the gate, and said, "They want to come in, so we'll open the gate for them." He had some heavy furniture (a desk or two) placed behind the gate so that one side was blocked and could not be opened, while the other could be opened no more than a foot and a half. Then he asked for a few strong comrades to stand at the gate and, when it opened, pull in the nearest two or three people who were pushing against it, while another comrade discharged his pistol above the heads of the demonstrators. The rest of the comrades would then close the gate and bolt it again. He calculated that the shock of seeing the gate open and several people disappear behind it, immediately followed by pistol shots, would scare the crowd and produce a panic. His scenario worked perfectly; there was frightened yelling outside and the crowd quickly dispersed. The demonstration was over. The two men who had been pulled in were roughed up a bit and released with minor bruises an hour later.

The year 1946 brought national elections. The parties of the Groza government formed an electoral bloc called the National Democratic Front. The two main opposition parties were the National Peasant Party and the Liberal Party, the two major bourgeois parties of the interwar period. They campaigned freely, although none of them had means comparable to those of the government parties. The Front did well among the industrial workers, whose political orientation tended to be either communist or Social Democratic; but among the other city dwellers and in the villages, the opposition parties, especially the National Peasant Party, did better; and in 1946 industrial workers formed a relatively small segment of the population, more than two-thirds of which lived in the villages.

The organization of the elections was in the hands of the attorney general, Râpeanu, who scrupulously followed the instructions of the Communist Party in order to avoid being exposed as a former member or supporter of the Iron Guard. Râpeanu set up a system for counting votes which, while theoretically involving all the political parties, in fact made cheating relatively easy. And cheating did occur, mainly but not only at the center. As a result, the front won the elections with a safe majority (something like 80 percent), but everybody knew that this was the result of cheating.

In trying to remember my reaction to what happened, I recall that although I did not like the way the elections were conducted, I was not too upset at the time. Some of the arguments I heard in defense of the fraudulent elections went along these lines: (1) the Romanian peasantry is very backward, having been kept in the dark for centuries, and when it votes for the National Peasant Party, which is the party of the landlords and rich peasants, it is voting against its own interests; (2) elections were always fraudulent under the old bourgeois regime (this was true: Romanian politics had been very corrupt), so the bourgeois parties were merely getting a taste of the same treatment they always gave to the opposition; and (3) according to Leninist theory, electoral votes typically do not reflect the true interests of the voters; rather, they reflect the relative success of the various parties in shaping public opinion. As weird as these arguments may sound to a person free of the marxist warp of mind, I more or less accepted them at the time.

This account of the election would be incomplete without mentioning that a large segment, perhaps the majority, of the peasantry was illiterate in 1946. Because of this, the contending parties had electoral symbols rather than names on the ballots, and each voter had to affix a rubber stamp on the chosen symbol. The front's symbol was the sun; the National Peasant Party's was an eye. On election day, our observers reported seeing peasants, mostly older ones and women, coming out of the voting booths with their eyes blackened by the rubber stamps which they mistakenly thought had to be put on their *own* eyes if they wanted to vote for the National Peasant Party.

In retrospect, I believe it would not have made much difference if the elections of 1946 had not been stolen. The outcome of an electoral victory for the opposition would probably have been the formation of a new coalition government with a more than symbolic participation of the

National Peasant Party; a government without the communists would have been opposed by the Soviets as being unfriendly toward them. Their understanding with the Western Allies gave them the right to have friendly governments in the neighboring countries; and after all, they were solidly in control, with hundreds of thousands of troops still in Romania. Had a coalition government with the National Peasant Party been formed, Romania would still have moved, though somewhat more slowly, along the same path followed by all the Eastern European countries under Soviet control: after one or two years, during which the National Peasant Party would have been largely compromised in the eyes of the peasantry, new elections would have been called or some other way would have been found to throw them out of the government. The decisive factor was the presence of the Soviet troops; everything else was secondary.

In the postwar decades it came to be a widely held view in the free world that the Western leaders had made a fatal mistake at the Yalta Conference by conceding hegemony over Eastern Europe to the Soviets. In my view, this is rubbish: the Western powers did not concede anything beyond what the Soviets had already taken. At the time of the Yalta conference, Romania, Bulgaria, and the greater part of Poland and Hungary had already been conquered by the Red Army. What leverage did the Western powers have in February 1945 to impose conditions on what should happen in these countries? Besides, what happened in Romania was not exactly according to the Yalta script, which had provided for free elections in the liberated countries. So why blame Yalta for it? In fact, the fate of Eastern Europe was not decided at Yalta, but much earlier, when the western powers concluded that they could not invade western Europe while the Soviet troops were still on the Volga, as had been originally planned. The only way to bring about a free postwar Eastern Europe would have been for the Western powers to get there before, or at the same time as, the Soviets. This could have happened if the western European second front, which Churchill and Roosevelt had originally undertaken to open in 1942, had been opened no later than 1943, when the Red Army was still on the River Don. That might have shortened the war considerably, saved millions of lives, and changed many things in postwar Europe for the better. But it would have required risks and sacrifices that the Anglo-American leadership deemed unacceptable.

One of the accomplishments claimed by the Groza government was land reform. The Ploughmen's Front played the leading role in the political campaign for implementing it, but the scenario was written by the communists. Since I was not involved in its execution, I do not remember much about it, but one episode stands out in my mind. It was the party line that, as part of the land reform, the Gypsies should be given land and settled on it. In the county of Cluj, the Gypsy community of several thousand people received land in one of the villages and were told to settle there. We had a communist activist among the Gypsies, an exceptionally bright woman in her late thirties who had considerable influence within the community. I remember how taken aback I was when she complained to me that she was unable to convince her people to abandon their nomadic life-style and settle on the land which they now owned. We created all kinds of incentives for the Gypsies to settle down. From being nomadic semibeggars they had now become landowners, and we told them that if they worked they could become respectable, well-to-do farmers. We set up courses to teach them how to work the land and gave them all kinds of financial advantages. Settling the Gypsies successfully was for us a matter of party prestige, one way of exposing the falsehood of the racial prejudice that held Gypsies to be inherently lazy, inclined to thievery, and disinclined to work. But it was incredibly hard. We did not give up, of course—communists never give up, nor do they admit defeat. But in order to accomplish what the party wanted, the Gypsies had to be literally forced to stay on the land and forbidden to leave the village under threat of arrest. Of course, forced farming cannot be good farming, and the Gypsy village, poor at the start, remained poor.

Some time in 1946 we had a visit from Bucharest by Miron Constantinescu, the young intellectual who had made a good impression on me at the national party conference. He came to Cluj to address a gathering of party activists from all of Northern Transylvania, occasioned by recent acute economic hardships. Since the large majority of the more than two hundred activists who attended the meeting were Hungarian-speaking and understood Romanian poorly or not at all, Vaida suggested to Constantinescu that his speech be translated, so that the delegates could understand its ideas in detail, not just its general outlines. Constantinescu liked the idea but did not want to be interrupted after each sentence by the translator. So it was decided that he should deliver his entire speech in Romanian, after which the translator should deliver it in Hungarian. Vaida proposed that I do the translating, and Constantinescu agreed to this, but added that he had no written text and I would have to take notes. I agreed. All this was decided ten minutes before the meeting. When Constantinescu started talking, I took some notes in longhand and tried to memorize what he was saying. He talked for about an hour, after which I stepped to the microphone and gave an almost verbatim translation of the speech during the next hour. Almost, for I made one change.

Constantinescu spoke about the terrible drought that had stricken Moldova, Romania's northeastern region, leading to a partial famine which the government was trying to alleviate through various emergency measures. But in reality that same drought had no less affected the Székely region (of Hungarian population) in the southeastern tip of Transylvania, and there was considerable famine there, too. To omit mentioning the drought in the Székely region in a speech addressed partly to the activists of that region was a political blunder of major proportions; so wherever Constantinescu had said "Moldova," I substituted "Moldova and the Székely region." Constantinescu, who had some knowledge of Hungarian, followed the translation carefully and was obviously pleased by its accuracy, as I could see from the smile on his face and his occasional whispers into Vaida's ear. But he stopped smiling after I came to the passage about the drought. When the speech was over, he shook my hand, said that I had given an excellent translation, and thanked me for correcting his omission of the Székely region. I said I was sure that when he talked about Moldova he actually meant both regions hit by the drought, and that was why I took the liberty of making the insertion. After the meeting I asked Sanyi what he thought about it. He said, "It's hard to tell what effect it will have on him. He certainly learned that you're a smart and politically astute fellow; but he also learned that you dared to correct him—a sign of independence that he may or may not appreciate."

The Communist Party was reorganized in the spring of 1947. The politburo decided to abolish the Regional Committees, which had a certain degree of autonomy in deciding local policy and appointing local cadres, and to subordinate the County Committees directly to the Central Committee. This was accompanied by a reorganization of the County Committees, carried out in each region by a special commission that spent about a week on the spot and was empowered to decide upon everyone's fate. The commission that came to Cluj was headed by Miron Constantinescu and had two additional members who played insignificant roles. There were several meetings at the regional level at which the work of the Regional Committee was assessed; then the composition of the new, enlarged County Committee was announced, along with the decisions concerning the former members of the Regional Committee. Vaida, the regional secretary, was to be promoted to head of the Central Committee's Agrarian Section. This was a clear recognition of his accomplishments as regional secretary. At the same time Sanyi Jakab, Vaida's closest collaborator and the *éminence grise* behind most of what had happened to and in the party in Cluj since October 1944, was shunted aside and put at the disposal of the Central Committee, where he was left to languish for several weeks without an assignment. He was criticized for having a private life (meaning his marriage) incompatible with that of a communist leader but, as far as I know, no fault was found with his work. In the end Vasile Luca, who had learned to appreciate Sanyi's intelligence, courage, and organizational skills, hired him for his staff, and a few months later, when Luca became minister of finance, he made Sanyi one of his three deputy ministers. As I had been closely associated with Sanyi since the underground years, I expected also to be relieved of my job, but that did not happen: I remained on the new, strengthened County Committee.

The National Assembly that emerged from the 1946 elections had a majority of representatives from the parties of the government coalition, meaning the Communist Party, the Social Democratic Party, the Ploughmen's Front, and the Tătărescu faction of the Liberal Party. This last group was small, intimidated, and unimportant, and it was eliminated in the fall of 1947 by the forced resignation of its leader. The representatives of the Ploughmen's Front were either crypto-communists or followed the party's instructions in a spirit of opportunism; they could be relied upon to dissolve themselves and join the Communist Party whenever the latter so desired, which they eventually did. The only significant group independent of the Communists was the bloc of Social Democratic representatives. The Communist Party's next move was to neutralize the Social Democrats. This was done by starting a campaign around the middle of 1947 for the merger of the two parties. Titel Petrescu, the country's leading Social Democrat, naturally opposed this plan, recognizing it as tantamount to the liquidation of his party. But others led by Lothar Rădăceanu and Ștefan Voitec, the minister of education, who were closer to the Communists, saw it as a way to assure their own political (and perhaps physical) survival, and to exercise some moderating influence on political developments. In the end they prevailed, and the two parties were merged in early 1948 under the name of Romanian Workers' Party. The Social Democratic leaders who favored this merger were co-opted into the leadership, but they were figureheads without the slightest influence.

In the meantime, some changes had occurred in my private life. In late 1945 or early 1946 a law was enacted to rectify the injustice done to people whose education had been interrupted during the war years for political or racial reasons. Voitec's law, as it came to be known, allowed such people to make up at least partly for what they had lost, by following an accelerated curriculum and sometimes taking exams without attending courses. I decided to take advantage of this law and enrolled as a student in the Economics Department of Bólyai University. This did not require me to give up my political work, as it could be done on a part-time basis. Studying economics seemed the right kind of preparation for somebody whose main goal was to build a society with a planned economy. In my judgment at the time, once the communists were in power, the importance of party work, meaning political work, would diminish in favor of building a new, planned economy, for which a whole new science of planning would have to be elaborated. Besides, I was already in the midst of a thorough study of marxist economics, which was the main content of the economics course at the university. All the other subjects—accounting, finance, law, and so on—seemed easy in comparison. So I simply intensified the pace at which I was working my way through the three volumes of Marx's *Capital*. During 1946 and 1947 I took all the first- and second-year exams, so that when I left Cluj in the fall of 1947 I was already a third-year student. I came back to Cluj to take exams in 1948, and finally got my degree, a license in economics, in the spring of 1949.

My study of *Capital* in 1946–47 reminds me of an episode that took place several months later in Bucharest. *Capital* is a very difficult work to read and, as I often found the Romanian translation unsatisfactory and felt the need to check with the original, I decided to buy a German version of *Das Kapital*. So I went to one of the major bookstores in the

Egon in 1946

center of Bucharest and asked a senior salesman whether they had *Capitalul* (the Romanian title of the work) in the original. "Of course," he said, pointing to one of the shelves: "That's where we keep the Russian books." Looking back on it, I realize that the vast majority of people in Bucharest probably would have said that Marx was a Russian; some might have added that he was a Russian Jew.

On an even more personal level, between the fall of 1945 and the fall of 1946 I had several short affairs with women, of which only one was serious and lasted eight or nine months. Then, on a lucky evening in November 1946, I met Edith, my future wife, friend, and lifetime companion. It was a Saturday night and there was a ball of some sort, a place to dance. I went there basically to look around, for I was not a dancer. I had not learned how to dance in high school and looked down on those who did; it was too frivolous a thing to do in times as grave as ours. In the underground movement we had other priorities, and after liberation

Edith in 1946

I had no time for dancing. As I looked around the ballroom, I saw a young girl whose face caught my eye.

"She can't possibly look so pretty close-up as she seems from a distance," I thought, and started walking toward her to convince myself. As I got closer, the impression was even stronger. I was overcome by a strong feeling of "she's the one!" The girl was talking to a fellow whom I knew, Tibor Lusztig, a Jewish youngster who had gone to the same Romanian high school where I had studied in the thirties. He later became a physician and today lives in Israel. We are still friends and see each other whenever I visit Israel. But on that evening, when I joined the two of them by addressing him with some commonplace remark, I waited in vain for him to introduce me to the girl that he had taken to the ball. I stood there for five or ten minutes, talking to Tibor and looking at the angel in his company, yet he would not make the introduction.

Then suddenly the girl turned toward me, held out her hand, and simply said, "I am Edith Lövi." I introduced myself, and from that moment

Tibor was no longer there—he was still standing in the same place as before, but Edith and I became immersed in a conversation that was just between the two of us. She told me that in 1940 and 1941 she had been a fifth grader in the Jewish Lyceum where I had been in the twelfth grade at the time. I remembered having seen her acting in a play staged by the literary circle. She had known my brother, Bobby, well, and so she knew about me, too. She was not yet fifteen at the end of May 1944 when she was deported to Auschwitz, and she was one of the few who returned. In Auschwitz she had accidentally met my brother, who did not recognize her without her hair. She addressed him, "Bobby"; he looked at her blankly, and when she said who she was, his face changed and he exclaimed: "Edith, is that *you?*" That was all, it only lasted a few seconds—they had to go in different directions. I asked Edith to meet me the next day and tell me more. She consented. This is how it all started.

Edith was seventeen at the time, and I was twenty-four. I found her not only physically attractive, but very bright, open, and straightforward. These were my first impressions—later I learned that she was also absolutely honest and dead serious. She was then in her junior year in high school. I talked to her about my life, my beliefs, about marxism and the better society that we were about to build. She listened and absorbed what I said. I gave her books that she read. We fell in love.

For almost a year after we met, we would get together two or three times a week, mostly in the evenings, which was after work for me and after school for her. For Edith was in high-school, in the same Jewish Lyceum that we had both attended under the Hungarian regime, which had reopened some time in the fall of 1946. Most of the teachers had been killed, but a few had survived and there were new ones. Edith loved music, but she decided against resuming her violin lessons. She was an avid reader and many of our discussions were about books. I had access at the time to a motorcycle from the party. We would sometimes take trips to the countryside surrounding Cluj, Edith sitting behind me on the motorbike. The area around Cluj is hilly and parts of it are beautiful, so these excursions—which never lasted more than a few hours—were very pleasant. I came to know Edith's parents and had lunch at their apartment every Sunday. In the summer of 1947 I went with Edith to visit my uncle Tibor Rényi in Arad. We spent a very pleasant vacation there, taking long swims in the River Mureş. We also tried to go canoeing, but on our first attempt the canoe overturned and we had to save ourselves by swimming. In November 1947 I was transferred to a new job in Bucharest, while Edith remained in Cluj to study for her baccalaureate. We remained in touch through frequent correspondence.

■ ■ ■

It was hard for Edith to talk about her deportation: it was too gruesome, too horrible. She would tell me fragments of it now and then, but this was so painful for her that I never pressed her to talk about it. She did not tell the story of her deportation to our own daughters until more than forty years later. Even after she had lived in America for many years, whenever she was forced by circumstances to talk about this subject, she would forget her English, make elementary grammatical errors, and be unable to find the words she needed. It seemed as if the effort of recalling these painful memories took her back to the time when the events actually happened, a time when she did not speak English. Thus, some of what I know about Edith's deportation she told me soon after we met, and some much later; I no longer recall exactly when I received the information. But here is her life story in brief, up to the point where we met.

Edith was born in Cluj on June 20, 1929, the daughter of Sándor (Alexander) Lövi and Klara *nee* Rooz. Her grandparents on both sides were small-town people of modest means. Sándor left home and began earning a living at thirteen. Life was his school and he was a good student. An extremely energetic, capable man, he managed to make himself indispensable in whatever job he held. During the thirties he was a leading salesman in a big textile and garment shop. Klara, whom he married in the mid-twenties, had artistic inclinations, and learned artificial flower making at a three-month course in Budapest in the early thirties. She had a small workshop where she made the most beautiful artificial flowers in the country. The family lived in a small apartment, which also housed Klara's workshop. Edith went to the Neolog (Reform) Jewish elementary school, where her main recollection is of an unfriendly teacher whose threatening attitude made her allergic to mathematics. Edith was eleven years old when Northern Transylvania was transferred to Hungary in September 1940, and from the fall of that year she went to the same Jewish Lyceum in Kolozsvár that I had attended during my last year of high school. Here she fared much better than in elementary school; in fact, she was first in her class. Her parents also had her take private lessons: she played the violin for several years, until her deportation, and studied French. She was finishing the fourth grade of the lyceum—which corresponds to the eighth grade of the American system—in May 1944, when disaster struck: like all the Jews of Kolozsvar, the Lövis were forcibly evicted from their apartment by the Hungarian gendarmerie and moved into the ghetto at the brick factory.

Edith had a schoolteacher, Gizi Deutsch, who in the spring of 1944 informed her and some other students that she had heard on the BBC about the mass extermination of Jews in Poland, and in particular about the use of poison gas. So when the order came to wear the yellow star and a month later to move into the ghetto, Edith and her parents expected the worst. Yet there was no certainty—rumor had it that people were being sent to Kenyérmezö, a (nonexistent) labor camp somewhere in Hungary. In the ghetto, where the Lövi family spent about two weeks, they lived in an improvised tentlike construction together with Klara's sister, Irén. Sándor, like many others, was beaten by the gendarmes to tell where he had hidden jewelry, gold, or other valuables. Toward the end of May, the family, along with many others, was put on one of the trains that came daily into the courtyard of the brick factory to take away Jews. They were loaded into a cattle car that was sealed from the outside. They were allowed to take along some food and water, but little baggage. The car was empty except for a bucket that served as a latrine, and the only light came through a narrow slit under the roof. People stood or sat on their luggage. The journey lasted for three days, and after a while it became clear that the train was not going to Kenyérmezö or to any other place in Hungary, since through the narrow slits one could read the names of Slovakian towns left behind. On the third night, the name of Krakow could be read through the opening, and the passengers realized they were in Poland. Putting that together with what many, if not most, of them had heard about the extermination camps in Poland, they expected the worst.

Soon after that the train reached its destination. Through the narrow opening under the roof Edith and her parents saw an enormous chimney from which a hellish fire rose to the sky, and they figured that they had arrived at the last station of their lives. They cried and said goodbye to each other forever, before the car doors were opened. They were ordered to get off the train, and found themselves on a long platform, facing SS men with monstrous dogs. While the SS men were barking orders, some prisoners performing menial jobs mingled with the newcomers. One of them, a Polish Jew, whispered to Sándor in Yiddish, "How old is the girl?" Edith was to become fifteen in about three weeks. Sándor whispered back, "Fourteen." He probably figured that it was better for Edith to be taken for a child than for an attractive young woman. The man whispered back "sixteen" and moved on. It took several minutes for Sándor to understand the meaning of this exchange, but when he did, he instructed Edith to claim to be sixteen. This saved her life in the first selection, because children under sixteen were sent directly to the gas chambers along with adults over fifty and mothers of small children. Edith was left in the company of her mother and her aunt—who were respectively thirty-six and thirty-two at the time—but they were separated from Sándor, who went with the "young" male prisoners, while they went with the "young" female ones. They did not see him again until after the war.

Taken to a shower and disinfection facility, Edith, Klara, and Irén had their heads shaved and their clothing taken away, to be replaced with some nondescript, ill-fitting dresses without any underwear. They were then beaten with a stick over their freshly shaved heads by an SS woman and taken to Camp (Lager) C, a part of the Auschwitz-Birkenau complex designated for transitional female prisoners. Several hundred of them were herded into Block 20, a barracks with an earthen floor and no bunks or any other furniture. At night they had to lie on the bare, often wet, ground, crammed together like sardines in a can, unable to change position unless those in front of and behind them did the same. So horrible were the sleeping conditions that Edith spent several nights on foot, unable to get used to them. During the day they would spend hours at the Appellplatz, an empty square in front of the barracks. Their food was mainly soup made of grass and some cereal, so bad that in spite of the chronic hunger that they soon experienced, they had to force themselves to eat it. There were frequent selections in which some prisoners were chosen for extermination, and often they had a hard time guessing which column meant life and which meant death.

Soon after Edith's group arrived at Block 20, they were joined by Edith's cousin Eva Wohlberg, a girl of Edith's age, who had been deported from Hajduszoboszló, a small Hungarian town near the old Romanian border. The four women—Edith, her mother Klara, her aunt Irén and her cousin Eva—formed a coherent, tightly knit group with a strong spirit of mutual help and solidarity, a factor that played a crucial role in their survival.

It was in Auschwitz that Edith met Bobby, whom she knew well from school. Although the encounter lasted only a few seconds, it was imprinted forever into Edith's memory. It was also in Auschwitz that Edith witnessed a horrible event—the taking of the entire Gypsy community of the camp to the gas chambers. One evening in early August 1944, Edith was offered a bunk for one night in the neighboring barracks. Soon after going to sleep she was awakened by unusual sounds and shrill voices from the courtyard. Looking out through the window from her upper bunk, she saw thousands of Gypsies being loaded onto a long caravan of trucks: men and women, children and old people, who were crying, screaming, begging, and cursing desperately, their voices partly covered by the wild barking of the hounds and occasional gunshots. It was clear that the Gypsies had somehow found out that they were being taken to the slaughterhouse, and they behaved accordingly. The scene was so shocking that Edith vividly remembered it fifty years later, when she read an article in the *New York Times* on the anniversary of this tragic event.

On August 12 a large group of women prisoners, including Edith and her three companions, were taken out and ordered to undress. They were kept naked in the courtyard for hours. It was not cold, but the situation felt ominous and again they thought that their last hour had come. After a while they were given prison garb with stripes and loaded onto a train that was leaving Auschwitz. Without knowing their destination, the prisoners experienced a wave of relief and happiness—nothing could be as bad as Auschwitz, the lowest of all hells. They were taken to Unterlüss, a small town in northern Germany close to the picturesque city of Celle. The Unterlüss concentration camp was a labor camp, and there were no gas chambers or crematoria. The work of the prisoners was of three kinds: cutting wood in the nearby forest, breaking stones for building a road, and working in a nearby ammunition factory. Edith worked mainly on woodcutting. At first, the food was better than in Auschwitz, but it soon deteriorated to almost the same starvation level. The other major threat to life was cold, against which the prisoners had very poor protection. They had no coats, and nothing to wear under their thin dresses. They took empty paper bags that had held cement and made them into shirts. They were also allowed to make a fire in the forest, around which they could gather and warm themselves for half an hour during the lunch break, in the middle of a workday that lasted from six in the morning till late afternoon. Most important, Edith discovered in herself a rare talent for locating mushrooms in the forest, and while cutting wood she collected enough mushrooms to supplement her and her companions' meal in a meaningful way.

Edith's aunt, Irén, was taken to work at a local ammunition factory. The environment was frighteningly toxic—Irén's face and hair became yellowish-rusty—but she received a glass of milk every day, which under the circumstances was a very significant advantage. The camp had an infirmary barracks with about a dozen bunks, where prisoners who became sick could spend a few days and were sometimes—but only sometimes—treated by a paramedic. Anybody who could not return to work within a week was sent to an unknown destination.

Edith and her group spent eight months in Unterlüss. The prisoners were sometimes taken to work through the center of town, and on such occasions Edith remembers young townswomen instructing their three- and four-year-old children to throw stones at the dirty Jewish women. But she also has some different memories. When several prisoners got scurvy, a paramedic assigned to the concentration camp lined up the prisoners and asked all those who had sores from the disease to step forward. Several dozen prisoners, Edith among them, did and showed him the sores on their skin. He then offered to inject them with vitamin C, but nobody wanted a shot from a German: the practice of administering lethal injections was known to be widespread. The paramedic then took a vial of vitamin C, showed the inscription on it, and injected himself with it. This worked: the prisoners accepted the injections and were cured of their scurvy.

While in Unterlüss, Edith contracted typhoid fever. She had violent nausea and high fever for several days, and was unable to eat either the bread or the soup that the prisoners were given. Then Irén brought her glass of milk from the factory and Edith was able to drink that. Irén continued the practice for a week and Edith recovered. Edith and her companions learned from these tumultuous experiences how capricious human fate can be and how little separates life from death. Irén worked daily at the ammunition factory for more than seven months. One day in early April there was a bombing raid on one of the nearby cities, and it was announced—for reasons that were not clear to the prisoners—that the next day nobody would be taken to work in the ammunition factory. On that very day, the first which Irén spent away from her regular workplace, the factory was obliterated by a daytime American bomb attack.

One morning around mid-April 1945 the prisoners discovered that their German guards had disappeared during the night. The Allied troops were closing in on the Wehrmacht and the German army abandoned Unterlüss. The German cook, a civilian, came in to tell the prisoners, "You are free. The troops are gone." There was great joy which, however, did not last long. After a few hours of "liberty," the good citizens of Unterlüss, with guns on their shoulders, (a "civilian guard"?), surrounded the camp and lined up the prisoners to take them away. Before this could happen, however, the cook distributed among the prisoners the potatoes he had in the cellar. There were about nine hundred prisoners and each received six or seven potatoes. Edith believes that this saved her life over the next ten days, when she had nothing else to eat. The armed civilians then forced the prisoners onto trucks and drove them to the not-too-distant concentration camp of Bergen-Belsen, where they delivered the prisoners to their rightful wardens, the nazi executioners.

Bergen-Belsen had not started out as an extermination camp, but by mid-April 1945 it was probably the most hellish place on earth, Auschwitz having been liberated in January. Infested with typhus and a host of other contagious diseases, the camp was virtually a huge open-air repository of rotting corpses, which were piled up everywhere in large and small mounds. There were no guards inside the camp, as the Germans had pulled out their soldiers earlier, sealed off the camp, and left the prisoners inside to die of hunger, thirst, and disease. To prevent those who could still move from breaking out, a unit of Hungarian soldiers had been given the task of keeping guard until the Germans came back— or, if they did not come back, to blow up the camp (whose premises had been mined) along with the prisoners. Thrown into the moribund camp, Edith and her nine hundred fellow prisoners had the worst week of their lives. The conditions there are impossible to describe. It is enough to say that within a few weeks all but two hundred of the prisoners who were delivered to Bergen-Belsen from Unterlüss died, even though none were shot, gassed, or killed by direct violence. Everybody suffered from typhus; the newly arrived prisoners started getting it in a few days. The typhus victims had high fevers and many were delirious: it was impossible to sleep at night, for the dying, hallucinating prisoners would crawl over the bodies of the healthy ones. There was nothing to eat. Every day Edith and her companions each ate one of the raw potatoes they had brought from Unterlüss. This hell lasted for about a week to ten days, until the British army liberated the camp. The Hungarian army guards decided not to follow the German order to blow it up.

However, the arrival of the British did not stop the wave of dying among the prisoners. The liberators had neither the expertise nor the equipment to deal with the situation. For instance, Edith and many others ate canned beans on the first day after the British arrived. The bodies of the half-starved prisoners reacted violently to the beans. Scores of inmates did not survive this first meal. Edith remembers the terrible nausea and vomiting she went through after her first copious dinner, with beans coming out through her nose. Fortunately, neither she nor her three companions had contracted typhus. Edith had the initiative to take a tent from the warehouse abandoned by the Germans and set it up in the yard of the camp, away from the crawling sick prisoners. Her example was followed by many of the inmates who were still healthy, and a small forest of tents arose in the yard, which can be seen in some photographs of the camp taken soon after its liberation.

A few days later Edith's group and a few others were able to move into the wooden building that had formerly housed the German guards. There were no bunks, and they slept on the wooden floor. It was here that the typhus finally struck them. There was no medical or any other help. To understand this, one must realize that the British army units that liberated Bergen-Belsen were part of a fighting force, moving forward with the front in pursuit of the enemy. Those who came behind them—and they did not arrive immediately—started evacuating the sick prisoners, taking them to a hospital in small Red Cross vans. But there were thousands of sick prisoners, most of whom were dying. The task simply overwhelmed the liberators. Left to themselves, Edith and her companions helped each other. The will to survive and the knowledge that they were liberated helped them defeat the typhus. Edith remembers that their guiding rule was to go—to crawl, since they were unable to walk—to the toilet whenever the urge came upon them, no matter how hard it was to get moving. It was common knowledge that whoever ceased to go to the toilet would soon die. Thus when Irén reached the limits of her strength and refused to go out when she needed to, the others forced her to get up from the floor and crawl out. They had to do this only once or twice; then the crisis passed. In the end, all four women survived the disease.

After her liberation, Edith and her group spent another four months around Bergen-Belsen before being able to return home. When they were liberated, she and her mother each weighed less than sixty pounds. In the next four months they gradually recovered their normal physical appearance, weight, and strength. Edith and Eva went to work for the British army in a laundry. There was no news of Sándor. Finally, in late August, a group of Jewish prisoners from Romania, Hungary, and Czechoslovakia managed to "buy" a locomotive and a few railway cars to take them home. One of them had discovered a case of wristwatches hidden by the Germans, and they used these, along with other goods they had managed to collect after their liberation, to pay for the train. The journey to Cluj lasted three weeks, with a stopover in Budapest, where Klara and Edith found out that Sándor was alive and Eva learned that her parents were dead. Eva stayed behind with an uncle; Klara, Irén, and Edith went on to Cluj and were happily reunited with Sándor, who had been liberated in the concentration camp of Mauthausen in Austria.

Of the several thousand Jewish families that were deported from Kolozsvár in the spring of 1944, the Lövi family of three was the only one to survive the deportation in its entirety.

CHAPTER 7

■ ■ ■

The London Legation

In November 1947 I was transferred to Bucharest, to the Agrarian Section of the party's Central Committee. The Agrarian Section was headed by Vasile Vaida, the former regional secretary in Cluj. The name is misleading, since the section dealt neither exclusively nor primarily with agriculture, but with party policy toward the peasantry, the majority of Romania's population. Land in Romania was still privately owned; the order of the day was to consolidate land reforms enacted by a succession of laws from 1945 to 1947. The collectivization of agriculture was to be put on the agenda at a later time. My transfer to the Agrarian Section was triggered by a request from Vaida, who felt that he could use someone like me, although my qualifications for the job were nil. I had no experience in dealing with peasants; I had grown up in Cluj and had always been a city dweller. In the past, I had dealt successfully with industrial workers and intellectuals, but never with peasants; nor did I have any agricultural expertise. When I voiced these doubts to Vaida, he answered by expressing confidence in my learning ability. Well, I started learning.

Vaida's deputy at the section was a man in his early thirties called Nicolae Ceauşescu. A shoemaker by profession, he entered the movement in the thirties and spent time in jail with Gheorghiu-Dej. This gave him a certain standing in the party, and he was spoken of as Gheorghiu-Dej's apprentice. To stress the importance of the Agrarian Section he had been named Vaida's deputy. Ceauşescu was a little shorter than average and had a slight speech defect; he was more shrewd than smart and was above all very ambitious. I did not have many contacts with him during

186

the four or five weeks that I spent at the section, but the few that I had were not friendly. Although at that time he showed no sign of the megalomania that was to characterize his subsequent career when he became the leader of the country, he was not pleasant company and we did not talk to each other much. There were a couple of other party workers in the section with whom I got along reasonably well. The environment as a whole was unattractive, but the tasks seemed important and challenging.

However, my career in the Agrarian Section did not last for long. At the end of 1947 King Michael was forced to resign and Romania was proclaimed a People's Republic. About this same time, the foreign minister, Gheorghe Tătărescu, was ousted from the government and his party was removed from the governing coalition. The newly appointed minister of foreign affairs was Ana Pauker, one of the foremost leaders of the Communist Party. As soon as she took over, she started cleansing the ministry and the embassies of old school diplomats, considered sympathetic to the bourgeois parties, and replacing them with communists. This process was in full swing in December 1947 and January 1948. As the leaders of the ministry were searching for intellectuals with communist credentials who could fill sensitive diplomatic posts, somebody called their attention to a young economist who spoke English, French, and German but was tucked away in the party's Agrarian Section. Although I had not yet finished my studies, I was considered an economist in party circles on the basis of some lectures I had given on various aspects of marxist political economy. Thus, in January 1948 I moved over to the Ministry of Foreign Affairs, where I was appointed secretary of the Romanian legation in London. The spelling of my name was changed from the Hungarian Balázs to the more Romanian-sounding Balaş.

While preparing for my mission, I met the leaders of the various ministry offices. I saw Ana Pauker herself face to face for just a few minutes. Her deputy, and the person who actually ran the ministry, was Ana Toma, called Anuţa (the diminutive of Ana, pronounced Anutza) to distinguish her from "comrade Ana," as Pauker used to be called. Anuţa was a bright, extremely shrewd, energetic woman, power hungry, whimsical, vindictive—a real bitch, and a powerful one. She surrounded Ana Pauker with a thousand small attentions, and took care of all her personal problems better than any personal secretary could have done. At the same time she ran Ana Pauker's schedule and decided who could or could not see her. She was a master of intrigue and whomever she did not like, Ana Pauker ended up not liking either. She never spoke for herself, but handed down the decisions of comrade Ana. On top of everything else, she was married to General Pintilie (Pantyusha) Bodnarenko, the head of one of the two secret services.

The legation in London that I was to join was Romania's second most important diplomatic outpost in the West (after the one in Washington). When the Romanian minister in London had either defected or been recalled (I no longer remember which), a first counselor called George Macovescu was sent from Bucharest to take over as chargé d'affaires. He was now back in Bucharest to put together the team needed to run the legation. His role as chargé d'affaires was terminated by the appointment of a new minister, Mihail Macavei, an old Romanian gentleman and former landowner who became a communist in the early twenties and divided up his lands among the peasants, like a character in a Tolstoy novel. A generous but somewhat naïve man in his late sixties, he was supposed to serve primarily as a figurehead, the legation being actually run by Macovescu, the first counsellor. Macovescu was a journalist in his mid-thirties, who had sided during the war with the antinazi forces and later married a communist Jewish woman, Teri. He more or less enjoyed the party's confidence but, as I was soon to find out, sometimes more and sometimes less. I was to be the third member of the team, with the diplomatic rank of secretary of legation; and there was also a fourth member, in charge of consular affairs, as well as two secretary-typists.

We went to London by train, since we had several heavy cases to carry. On the way, we stopped for two days in Paris. This was my first encounter with the West, and I liked Paris a lot. I went sight-seeing from morning to evening, mostly with Macovescu and his wife, both of whom I befriended during the first days of our trip. They were knowledgeable about the West, having spent time there before or during the war. In the evening Macovescu—Mac, as his wife and friends called him—took me to theaters and cabarets, where I enjoyed the atmosphere and the music. During the day, the kind of sight-seeing I liked most was just strolling on the large boulevards, observing the people, and admiring the generous, imposing architecture and the many impressive monuments of the city. I remembered much of what I had learned about Paris in high school and thoroughly enjoyed being able to experience it for myself.

Finally, on March 18, 1948, we arrived at Victoria Station in London and were driven to the main building of the legation, the minister's residence at 1 Belgrave Square. The legation's offices were in Cadogan Square, not far from the residence. The residence was large enough for several families. Mr. and Mrs. Macavei lived on the ground floor, Mac and Teri lived on the second floor, and my room was on the third floor. The residence had an Italian cook, and those of us who lived there usually took our meals together. The two diplomats inherited from the former personnel, counsellor Barbu and press attaché Murgu, lived outside the residence; they had been in London for many years and had comfortable homes.

In the first few days after our arrival I spent much of my time getting to know London. I took sight-seeing tours in the red double-decker buses characteristic of London, and traveled for hours trying to absorb what I saw. I was deeply impressed by the scale and efficiency of the subway system, the "tube," as Londoners call it: the density of the network, which offered a station only a few minutes away from almost any place in central London; the speed and frequency of the trains; the cleanliness of the cars; and the civilized manner of the passengers (more so then than now). Above all, I was struck by the image of the huge escalators that took you deep underground, while on the opposite side passengers were being carried up to the surface; this daily kaleidoscope of the mass of people going to or coming from work, reading newspapers and books as they stood on the stairs, with the colorful panoply of equal-sized and yet so varied posters hanging on the walls flanking the escalators—for some reason this image made an indelible impression on my memory. For many days I spent hours walking through the center of London, from Hyde Park Corner, close to our residence, through Piccadilly, along Green Park to Piccadilly Circus, looking at the shop windows on Regent Street, then down Haymarket to Trafalgar Square or through Shaftesbury Avenue to Leicester Square, looking at the movie theaters. I loved strolling in Hyde Park and listening to some eccentric shoot off his mouth at the Speaker's Corner; I wondered how long it would take Romania's communist society to establish itself firmly enough for such freedom to be affordable. Yes, I thought, it was just a matter of time, because freedom was one of our ultimate goals. It was just a matter of priorities: first justice, the elimination of class privileges; then the abundance that would come from the planned economy and the elimination of capitalist waste; and finally, democracy and freedom. For the time being, unfortunately, freedom was a luxury we could not afford.

The English people seemed to me not only better dressed and much better off than those in my country, but also more civilized, more courteous, and better behaved in a way that made social contacts more pleasant. Could it be that the average level of decency was higher than the one I was used to? Certainly, people were also more naïve. I remember going to Austin Reed, a leading manufacturer of underwear, to buy some shirts (as a diplomat, I was supposed to dress well). I bought several shirts, paying for them with a five-pound banknote. As the pound sterling was worth four dollars and the dollar was worth many times today's dollar, five pounds was equivalent to two or three hundred dollars in today's currency. The five-pound banknote was larger than the usual size, completely blank on one side and with the sole inscription of "five pounds" on the other side in cursive letters; but it was made of a special, thick paper with a watermark that could be seen upon holding it up to the light. The young lady behind the cashier's desk handed the note back to me along with a pen, explaining that because of the high value of this type of banknote, it was customary for the person paying with it to write his name and address on the back of the note, so its origin could be traced in case of some problem with it. Would I mind doing so? "Not at all," I said, wrote my name and address on the back of the note, handed it over, and was preparing to show her my passport. To my surprise, the young lady looked at the note, put it in her drawer, thanked me, and gave me the change that was due, without asking to see my passport or any piece of identification. Since I wanted to understand her behavior, I remarked that in the absence of an identity check I could have written *any* name and address on the banknote. She looked at me incredulously, and with genuine consternation said, "But sir, you wouldn't do a thing like *that*, would you?"

I also needed a dark suit for receptions and a lighter one for everyday use in the office, and went to a Savile Row tailor, where diplomats had their suits tailor-made. In Romania we always had our suits tailor-made, mass production having not yet conquered this trade, so I was used to having measurements taken. But in Bucharest or Cluj a tailor would measure one's shoulders, chest, hips, the length of the arms and legs, the thighs, and buttocks—eight or nine measurements altogether. The tailor in Savile Row took forty or fifty measurements. Since this required quite some time, I talked to him during the process. At one point in the middle of the conversation he asked, "On which side do you wear it, sir?" As I did not understand the question, I thought he was referring to something I had said in the conversation. "Pardon me?" I asked, to which he answered, "You see, sir, we need to know how you like to wear it. I mean, do you usually wear it on the right side or on the left side?" When I finally understood what he was getting at, I panicked in my embarrassment: I had never thought of it before, and I discovered that I did not know. It took me quite some time to establish the facts and give him my answer. What a provincial customer I was! As slow and elaborate as the process was, it produced a splendid pair of suits that fit me better than anything I had worn before or would wear after. Actually, I still have one of those suits, the dark one, and when in 1992 I wore it to the president's ball at my university, it was a hit: wide lapels were again in vogue and I was congratulated for my new suit in the latest fashion.

As to the personnel of the legation, the minister was a nice old man, but nothing more. The Legation was run by Mac, who was both knowledgeable and well informed, as well as alert and attuned to the party line. He took his mission very seriously; he seemed to have longed for a role like the one he now had, and being a successful diplomat was his main ambition. For this he was well prepared, and he continued to improve his skills. His English was fluent and correct, though accented, and he had a reasonably full vocabulary. He also spoke good French. He was very quick and had an enormous capacity for absorbing information in a short time. He would read seven or eight newspapers in an hour and a half, and not miss a single interesting news item. We both bemoaned the flatness and emptiness of Scînteia, the Romanian party newspaper that we received daily and, as we were far from home, scrutinized for news. There was none; nothing seemed to be happening at home. Mac complained to me that he could read Scînteia from beginning to end in the car during the five-minute trip to the legation.

As to the two people whom we found there upon our arrival, the press secretary, Murgu, was a lightweight who enjoyed drinking and pursuing women and had no more serious ambitions than those. He stayed on for a couple of months after our arrival, then resigned, guessing correctly that the communist government would not keep him for long and preferring to preempt his dismissal by defecting for political reasons. Zevedei Barbu, the counsellor, was a different story. Unlike Murgu, he was an intellectual with a degree in philosophy and a clean wartime record (for some reason he had spent the war years in England). He was playing with the idea of becoming part of the new Romanian environment and of joining the Communist Party, many of whose goals he shared, although he also had differences here and there with the official line. It was, of course, naïve in the extreme to believe that this was possible: the slightest disagreement with the party line entailed immediate expulsion. That summer, Barbu received a letter from the ministry suggesting that he might want to visit Bucharest in the near future to renew his ties to the homeland. He decided not to take the risk, and resigned. At the time I viewed this as a loss for us; in retrospect, I think Barbu probably saved his life by resigning.

We had a Romanian driver at the legation, inherited from the old personnel. Petre was in his late forties or early fifties and, although he had no schooling, he was useful to us in many ways, primarily through his knowledge of London gained through many years of living there. I remember a funny exchange we had as he was driving me to some place I had to visit. We talked about movies and it turned out that he liked thrillers and Westerns. I said I liked some of them, too, but I was disturbed by the fact that almost everybody got killed. Upon which he turned to me and said, "Why, isn't it the same in Hamlet?"—which struck me as true. To Mac's and my regret, two months later Petre had to be fired on strict orders from Bucharest, and we hired a local driver recommended by our left-wing friends.

My tasks at the legation were of a general political nature. I was to familiarize myself as well as I could with the British political situation, the parties (primarily the governing Labour Party), and the trade union movement by reading the press carefully; by getting acquainted with journalists, writers, politicians, and members of Parliament; and by attending public meetings. I was to report on my experiences, mostly those involving important political events, by describing and interpreting them. First, I set out to make acquaintances. In this I was helped by Mac, who introduced me to all his contacts, and by Murgu, who knew a number of journalists. From time to time the Macovescus would give a party, where

I could meet a couple of members of Parliament, "friends of the people's democracies,"* as well as some trade union leaders and other left-wing politicians. One of the people with whom I became friendly and had long conversations on trade union matters was a member of the Trade Union Council's executive committee. I met Harry Pollitt, the general secretary of the British Communist Party, and was not too impressed with him. In general, I was unpleasantly surprised by the weakness of the Communist Party in Britain: it had no more than a few thousand members; had few articulate, persuasive representatives; and had received a very small number of votes in the last elections. Among the communist intellectuals I met Palme-Dutt, the author of several well-researched, if biased books. I read and respected the marxist economist Maurice Dobbs, another communist intellectual, but never got to meet him. Among the members of Parliament, a couple of noncommunist left-wingers like Solley and Platts-Mills would occasionally show up at our receptions. D. H. Pritt, a well-known author and chairman of the Peace Committee, was a frequent guest at our parties, as was Commander Edgar Young, a retired seafarer who sympathized with the new Eastern European regimes, although he was acquainted primarily with Yugoslavia and knew little about the other countries.

Another source of information was our contacts with the other Eastern European embassies and legations. I soon came to know Pavlov, the first secretary of the Soviet embassy, who had acted as Viacheslav Molotov's interpreter during or immediately after the war. Molotov was Stalin's first deputy and the foreign minister of the Soviet Union. Pavlov was a small, thin, blond man in his thirties, with a narrow face and intelligent blue eyes framed by gold-rimmed glasses. It was interesting to listen to his interpretations of various events. But undoubtedly my most interesting contact in diplomatic circles was the first counselor of the Czechoslovak Embassy, Eduard Goldstücker. He had spent the war years in London and knew the British political scene inside out. Ten years older than me

---

*"People's Democracies" was the euphemistic but official designation of the regimes that came to power in the wake of World War II in the lands occupied by the Soviet Union. The term was meant to describe a broad popular coalition as opposed to a single-party communist system. Thus Romania was called the Romanian People's Republic, Hungary was the Hungarian People's Republic, and so forth. A decade or so later the pretense was dropped and the Romanian People's Republic became the Socialist Republic of Romania.

and much more experienced, he nevertheless seemed to enjoy our discussions, and we spent many evenings together. Sometimes his colleague Kavan, also a counselor at the Czechoslovak embassy, joined us. Goldstücker was a passionate collector of china; I once accompanied him on a shopping trip where he did a lot of looking and little buying. His name became well known worldwide during and after the Prague Spring,* in which he played a leading role on the positive side. Another interesting contact was the first secretary of the Yugoslav embassy, Milyutinovich, whom I greatly admired for his wartime activity as a partisan in Tito's army.

One of my tasks at the legation was handling encoded messages. Every legation had a codebook with numbered pages, an exact copy of which was in the possession of the ministry headquarters in Bucharest. Each page was filled with a random sequence of characters, with many holes (missing characters) randomly distributed on the page. To send a coded message, I would take a page of the codebook, fill in its holes with the message, putting one character in each hole; then transmit the full contents of the page, including the filled-in holes, as a cable. At the ministry in Bucharest, the person receiving my cable would put it in the page format of the codebook, then retrieve from his codebook the exact same page that I had used for sending the message, cover the formatted cable with the page, and read the message through the holes. Coded messages were used only for matters judged to be urgent; otherwise, reports were forwarded by diplomatic pouch, a bag carried by a courier who would arrive at regular intervals once every few weeks.

I read a lot while I was in London. First of all, at the legation it was my duty to read or browse through all the major newspapers, and Mac and I would discuss the news daily or every other day. Next, I tried to understand the economic news, stock market reports, company statements, and so on. I was eager to learn about the British and world economies. Occasionally I also read American newspapers and magazines. I read or looked over many books on economic subjects, but at this point I was interested not in Western economic theory but in practical, mana-

---

*Prague Spring is the popular term for the period of political thaw in Czechoslovakia that preceded the Soviet invasion of 1968. Under the leadership of Alexander Dubcek, the Czechoslovak Communist Party tried to reform the communist system and bring about a transition to a more tolerant and flexible version of it, sometimes called "socialism with a human face."

gerial economics, whose lessons could be easily applied to a socialist economy. Besides, I was preparing for my exams in various economic subjects at the university back home. I enjoyed visiting the large book-stores around Charing Cross Road, where I would sometimes spend hours browsing. I soon became conversant with the economic problems of the day. At the same time, I learned to describe the situation in Roma-nia and the problems facing the government there in terms suitable for a Western audience, stressing the social and economic injustices of the past and the efforts being made to correct them: the redistribution of the land, the granting of equal rights to national minorities, free education and health care for everybody, and the beginnings of the drive toward industrialization. I had a couple of invitations to lecture, one from the University of Leeds. I went there by train and gave a talk attended by about twenty students. Afterwards they asked a lot of questions, most of them naïve but none of them hostile.

George Enescu, the famous Romanian composer who was living in Paris, visited London some time during the spring or summer, and Minister Macavei, who knew him personally, invited him to dine at the legation. The Macovescus and I were also invited. Although I liked those pieces of Enescu's music that I was familiar with—the *Romanian Rhap-sody* and a few others permeated by Romanian folklore—my musical culture was rather limited, and I was a little worried about whether I would be able to keep up my end of the conversation. It turned out, though, that with the exception of Teri, the others knew even less about music than I did, and the conversation quickly shifted to other subjects. The minister, seconded by Mac, attempted to persuade Enescu to return to Romania, painting a rosy picture of the enthusiasm that would greet his return and the warm welcome he would receive from the authorities. Fortunately, Enescu was not impressed by this, and stated frankly that, judging from what he had seen in Romanian newspapers, he did not think he would like the atmosphere there. Mac, wisely, did not insist or try to defend the atmosphere; instead, he pointed out that the country was experiencing a difficult transition and that maybe, after things had settled and conditions improved, the maestro might change his mind about returning. And that's where they left it. Enescu, of course, never returned and eventually died abroad.

In early June I returned to Romania to take my exams at Bólyai Uni-versity. As this had been prearranged, I did not need approval from

Bucharest to return; I just bought the ticket and left for two weeks, this time by air via Prague. Back in Bucharest, I reported to the ministry, had interviews with Anuţa Toma and some others about how things were going at the legation, and left for Cluj to take my exams and spend a few days with Edith. It was a great joy to be with her again. She was busy studying for her baccalaureate, the toughest exam of all, which was due in a couple of weeks. I took my own exams successfully, though not without a hitch. One of the exams was in international law and the professor, Buza, was known to be strict and unyielding. He had a very personal way of examining: he would hold in his hand a narrow sheet of paper containing a list of seventy to eighty short, concrete, factual questions that he would fire at you in a forty-five-minute face-to-face session. He would countenance no deviation from the subject: you either knew the answer to a question or you did not, and there was no room for displaying your general familiarity with the subject or your ability to judge the merits and demerits of a point of view. Many of the questions dealt with specific paragraphs of the United Nations charter, which I did not know by number or in great detail. Since I was duty-bound as a diplomat to know these things, I felt awkward. To this day I remember it as the most unpleasant exam I ever took. I passed, but it was a low pass, and I felt ashamed. On the other hand, my economics exam with Professor Kelemen was quite pleasant. I was obviously more familiar with marxist economics than Kelemen himself; so at the end of the exam, after giving me the maximum grade and congratulating me, he asked whether I could explain a marxist concept he had never really under-stood, namely the fetishism of capital. I did, to his satisfaction. The other exams went uneventfully. I had basically completed my degree, although I received my diploma only in the following spring.

Either before my trip to Cluj or just after, Commander Young, the British seaman who was a friend and occasional visitor to our legation, came to Bucharest with his wife for a few days' visit. I had instructions from Macovescu to take care of him while he was in Bucharest. In order to make his visit interesting, I invited him to dinner at the Jakabs.' Natu-rally, this had to be approved by the Foreign Ministry, and it was. As protection against any kind of suspicion, I also invited Louisa ("Lulu") Năvodaru, who at that time was working for one of the secret services. We had a reasonably pleasant and uneventful evening. Later, I had ample reason to regret that event, but at the time it gave me the feeling of having done my duty more than adequately, and I was grateful to Sanyi and Magda for giving the dinner, which they had enjoyed as well.

During my stay at the Jakabs,' Magda asked me to meet her sister Edith, who was married to a Frenchman and was living in Paris, on my return trip to London when I was supposed to stop in the French capital, and give to her Magda's love and a small present, a gold cigarette-case. I knew Magda's sister from Cluj, which she had visited in 1945 or 1946. During my stopover in Paris, on my way back to London I called her, met her, and gave her the cigarette case. I had no inkling at the time that this seemingly innocuous episode would later become the source of a major headache.

A couple of days before returning to London, I was summoned unexpectedly to the party's Central Committee. There I was given a new task, to be kept absolutely secret. It had to do with the Cominform, the Communist Information Bureau set up in September 1947 by those European Communist parties that were either in power or had large followings, with the task of organizing a regular exchange of information. The member parties were those of the Soviet Union, Poland, Czechoslovakia, Hungary, Romania, Bulgaria, Yugoslavia, France, and Italy. The headquarters of the organization had been in Belgrade until the spring of 1948, when the dispute between the Soviet and Yugoslav parties erupted and as a result, it was moved to Bucharest. I already knew about this dispute from the party press, where it was portrayed as a struggle of all earnest communists against the treacherous actions of the Yugoslav deviationists. The Cominform had a monthly publication dealing with problems of marxist theory and communist policy, whose articles were written by leading ideologues from the various member parties, and occasionally from nonmember Communist parties. The Cominform journal needed organized contacts with the leadership of various Communist parties, and it would be my task to handle the contact with the British party, that is, with Harry Pollitt, its secretary general. I was to get in touch with Pollitt upon my return and hand over to him a letter, given to me in an unsealed envelope, informing him of the Cominform journal's agenda and asking him to contribute an article on a subject of his choice within the next six months. I was then supposed to transmit Pollitt's article to Bucharest. All this cloak-and-dagger business was obviously unnecessary. The Communist Party of Great Britain was perfectly legal, and what it was suffering from was not official persecution, but a lack of followers. The whole exchange could have safely taken place through the regular mail, but I agreed to do what I was asked to do. The most unpleasant part of my interview at the Central Committee was a question concerning my colleague Macovescu: Had I noticed anything suspect in his behavior? The questioner's intonation made it clear that he thought he had good reason to be suspicious. When I protested that I had never noticed anything suspect and that I considered Macovescu a person eminently qualified for and fully dedicated to his job, who made every effort to closely follow the party line, the response was a skeptical "we'll see" and an admonition to observe him carefully.

Back in London, I contacted Pollitt and told him that I had a message to deliver. I let him choose our meeting place and, to my surprise, he suggested that I visit him at home one evening. He lived in one of the working-class suburbs of western London, and I went to his place by subway and bus. He read the letter, then asked several questions about the Cominform, which I answered to the best of my knowledge. He then said he would write the article and would let me know when it was finished.

Several times during my stay in London I attended sessions of Parliament. The House of Commons was the more interesting chamber, where the real debates took place. I was fascinated not only by the substance of those debates, but also by the language, the oratory, and the manners. The famous British attachment to everything traditional culminates in the opening ceremony of the Commons at the beginning of every parliamentary session. A man comes into the House of Commons, introduces himself as the king's messenger, and attempts to hand a written message to the Speaker of the House. The Speaker refuses to accept it, reprimands the messenger for entering without knocking on the door (a custom even the king's messenger must follow), and sends him back to do it all over again according to the rules. The messenger then goes out, knocks loudly on the door, and is told to "Enter!" whereupon he comes into the house again and repeats his introduction. I found this ceremony highly amusing. Speaking of the English love of tradition, a more common expression of it is to be found in the shape of the London taxicabs. In 1948 the cabs looked very much like the ones seen in films made in the twenties and thirties, and forty-some years later they still look much the same.

At some time during the summer of 1948 I had my most interesting political assignment while in England: I attended the national conference of the Labour Party in Scarborough, which was open to the public. This was a unique experience for me. I spent a whole week witnessing the struggle between various groups and orientations within the Labour Party, and listening to scores of speeches, some stupid, some clever, and many demagogic. I spent time talking to delegates, left-wing and otherwise; I observed the voting process and tried to guess the outcomes. To put it briefly, it was the most thorough schooling that I could have imagined in British politics. I no longer remember the many platforms that were debated and voted on, but after attending this convention I was in a position to discuss competently most of the issues in British politics at the time. I also made some new personal contacts.

■ ■ ■

Soon after the conference, two new diplomats arrived from Bucharest to serve as a commercial mission: Jacques Berman, commercial counselor, and Ion Măgură, commercial third secretary. They both reported to the Department of Foreign Trade in the Ministry of Commerce, Berman being Măgură's boss, but they were under the control of the legation. I was put in charge of supervising the work of the commercial mission on behalf of the legation, probably because I was considered an economist—something I was trying to become but, in my own estimation, still fell somewhat short of being. My regular weekly meetings with Berman, at which he reported to me about what he was doing, enhanced my economic expertise. The commercial mission's task was to expand the rather meager trade between Romania and the United Kingdom; it was supposed to find export outlets for Romanian products and arrange for the purchase of certain British products. Jacques Berman, an architect in his late forties or early fifties, had some wartime communist connections and some experience with foreign trade. He spoke fluent but heavily accented English.

My most interesting experience with Berman was a visit to the Ford automobile plant in Dagenham. Berman had been invited to visit the plant through his business contacts, and he asked whether I would be interested in joining him. I was definitely interested; the Dagenham plant was a relatively new facility, incorporating the latest technology in automotive manufacturing. I found the visit exhilarating, as I was generally an admirer of advanced technology and had never before seen such a large, modern factory. Parts of it were fully automated. "This is the kind of thing we need in Romania," I thought. I envisaged the building of socialism as the construction of scores of factories like this one. Since communism had come to power in industrially underdeveloped countries, historically its most urgent task was to industrialize; thus, the tasks of industrialization and social transformation merged in my mind.

About this time I was promoted to the rank of first secretary. This was an important recognition and also meant a substantial increase in salary. As I had to spend a lot of money on dressing like a diplomat, and there was no special allowance for such "setup costs," the raise came in handy. It also made it easier for me to get married on my next trip to Bucharest and bring Edith back with me to London. With my earlier salary we would have had to live on a very tight budget. As far as my actual job was concerned, it was hardly affected by my promotion. The only change was that, in addition to what I was doing before—including the supervision of the commercial mission—Mac put me in charge of protocol. This meant learning the language of diplomatic correspondence (in which, for instance, a "verbal note"—*note verbale* in French—*always* means a written memo). I also learned to write invitations to receptions and verify guest lists to avoid diplomatic blunders, write letters accepting or declining invitations, make seating arrangements at receptions, teach the personnel how to pour wine at the table (always from the right) and how to serve food (always from the left), and many other details of this sort. This task was hard for me to learn, not because it was inherently difficult but because I found it utterly boring and contemptible.

A central issue on the Eastern European political scene was the growing rift between the Yugoslav Communist Party and all the others, who were grouped around the Soviet party. There were detailed accounts in the party press about the Yugoslav "deviationists," mild at first and only ideological, then sharper and spilling over into the political realm, where they bordered on "treason to the international communist movement." The Yugoslav press in turn refuted all the allegations and claimed that the Yugoslav party was the victim of a campaign to discredit and besmirch it. I had good relations with the first secretary of the Yugoslav embassy, Milyutinovich. I now contacted him and proposed that we get together to discuss the situation. Mac had warned me against having any contacts with the Yugoslavs, but I told him there could be no harm in attempting to steer one of their diplomats in the right direction. In our long discussion I told Milyutinovich how disturbed I felt about the split in the ranks of the Communist parties and how worried I was about where this might lead. I asked him whether in his partisan days, when he was fighting the nazis and dreaming about being liberated by the Red Army, he could have imagined a situation in which he or his party would oppose the Soviet Communist Party on any grounds whatsoever. My question stirred him up quite a bit; he said no, he could not have imagined such a situation. He told me that he was as disturbed as I was, even more so, as he was more directly involved. He claimed that the Yugoslav party was doing everything in its power to avoid a rupture. He had detailed stories about what had occurred behind the scenes for many months. But a situation had been reached in which the Yugoslav communists could avoid the split in only one way: by refuting their own leaders and throwing them out. This they were not willing to do, because they were convinced that their leaders were right and were actually protecting vital Yugoslav interests. We finished our conversation by agreeing to disagree and wished each other personal good luck.

Some time during the summer of 1948 the Soviets closed all land access routes to Berlin. Berlin, situated deep within the Russian-occupied zone of Germany, about two hundred kilometers behind the east-west demarcation line, was at the time divided into four sectors: Russian, American, British, and French. According to the Potsdam agreement among the four powers, the Western Allies had free access to their own sectors through several highways and a rail connection designated for this purpose. This was why West Berlin had remained free of Soviet control despite its location. The Soviet action came in response to the fact that the Western sectors of Berlin had adopted a new currency created in the three Western occupation zones of Germany. By closing the access routes, thereby threatening to strangle the completely isolated city (its supplies of almost everything came through these routes), the Soviets meant to force the Allies to abandon West Berlin. The Soviet action created an acute crisis in East-West relations, but also a moment of high tension for the Western leaders: how should they respond to the Soviets? The press was full of alarming news reports; the world seemed on the brink of a new war. The Western response was to stay put and to organize what became known as the Berlin airlift, which every month for fifteen months carried more than 150,000 tons of goods into West Berlin, thus assuring its survival as a free city. In the end the Soviets backed down, but at the beginning it was far from clear what would happen. For instance, the Soviets might have tried to interdict the flights over their occupation zone. If the Western powers had refused to comply, this might have led to the shooting down of Western airplanes, with far-reaching and unpredictable consequences. In reporting on the situation from my vantage point in London, I tried to convey as accurately as I could the prevailing mood in the press and the country, which favored continuing the airlift.

An important event in my diplomatic career occurred some time in the fall of 1948. Our friend on the Executive Committee of the British Trade Union Council contacted me one day, saying he needed to see me immediately. When I met him, he told me in great secrecy that the Executive Committee had just decided that the TUC would pull out of the World Federation of Trade Unions, where the communist-led French and Italian unions, along with the Soviet and Eastern European ones, had acquired a majority position. This decision was to be implemented at the organization's next meeting, scheduled within a couple of weeks. The American unions—the AFL and the CIO—were at the time no longer members of this organization, and the hope was that the pullout of the TUC would prompt the other labor federations not dominated by communists to do the same. Our friend said the decision was confidential, only a few people knew about it, and he asked me to inform the Soviet embassy, so that he could avoid contacting them directly. I promised to do so. I then contacted Mac and told him about what had happened. Here we ran into our only serious disagreement during my tenure at the legation. Mac wanted me to hold off telling the Soviets for a few days, so that Ana Pauker could get the news first from our coded message and have time to tell the Soviets herself, before they found out from their embassy in London. I could see the logic in Mac's thinking—he wanted to earn some brownie points by giving Ana Pauker a head start in conveying what seemed to be an important piece of information to Molotov, the Soviet foreign minister—but I disagreed. The issue seemed not only important but urgent: If the Soviets could do something to prevent or counter the move, time was obviously of the essence; if not, time was still important for organizing a response. Besides, I had promised our informant to alert the Soviets, and his request implied the urgency of the message. For all these reasons, I did not want to delay informing the Soviets, and told Mac that we ought to do both things simultaneously:

send the coded message to Bucharest and let the Soviets know about the TUC's plan. He disagreed and tried to "order me" as my superior at the legation to proceed according to his plan, but I refused to obey and immediately contacted Pavlov. It was now around 10 o'clock in the evening and Pavlov wanted to meet two days later. I told him I had to see him right away, upon which he invited me over. At the Soviet embassy I gave him our friend's message, which he said he would forward to Moscow within the next half hour. My relations with Mac soured momentarily, but they bounced back to normal in a couple of days.

At the beginning of 1948 the United States had launched the Marshall Plan to assist Western Europe. Originally, all the European countries ravaged by the war were invited to participate, but the Soviets declined and the other Eastern European countries, including Romania, followed their lead. The British press was full of news about the plan, and I set out to study all available materials, as this seemed an important event in the economic, and by implication, political, history of Western Europe. I was fascinated by the boldness, the imaginativeness, and the scale of the plan, but perhaps more than anything, by what I somewhat unconsciously—I could not admit it to myself at the time—perceived as the plan's *generosity*. This was something that did not fit into my world picture of capitalism in its imperialist stage. The more I read, the more perplexed I became. I knew from the communist press that the Marshall Plan was viewed by my comrades as an American tool for subjugating Western Europe and tying it politically and economically to the United States, so I carefully scrutinized the published documents for onerous clauses hidden in the fine print. But I could find none. There were practically no conditions attached to the huge grants provided by the plan. I concluded that if this was indeed a plan of conquest, then it was a very confident and far-sighted one which had no need to impose any explicit obligation on its recipients. It might indeed lead to a certain loss of independence on their part and to the establishment of U.S. hegemony over Western Europe, but if so, then this would be an indirect consequence of the plan, not something provided for in its clauses.

At the beginning of December I was again given an opportunity to visit Bucharest for a couple of weeks. I flew there again via Prague, but this time I had to interrupt my trip in the Czechoslovak capital, because either there or in Bucharest the airport was fogged in and the flights between the two cities were suspended. This gave me an opportunity to visit this magnificent Central European capital and do some sight-seeing in the medieval sections of the city. I was very impressed, and when I saw the old Jewish cemetery I was struck by its intricate little tomb-stones. Since the airline could not guarantee a departure date, I decided to continue my trip by train, a journey a little longer than a day and a night. I sent a cable to Bucharest and took the train. There I ran into Grigore Preoteasa, the de facto head of our legation in Washington, who had just completed his assignment there and was on his way home. I had met Preoteasa earlier but had never had a conversation with him. I knew him as an able Romanian communist intellectual in his mid- or late thir-ties. We now had a long talk in which we discussed the situation both in the United States and in England. He expressed his appreciation for how well informed I seemed to be about conditions in England. I drew him into a discussion of the Marshall Plan, since I assumed that, having been stationed in Washington, he knew more about it than I did. This turned out not to be the case, and as he listened to my explanations and interpretations he agreed without questioning anything that I was saying or adding anything to it.

Upon my arrival at the Gara de Nord, the main railway station of Bucharest, Edith, who had come from Cluj to meet me, was just coming up the stairs at the front entrance, accompanied by our friend Bandi Klein. I was surprised by how thin and pale Edith looked; she explained that she had just recovered from a bad flu with high fever. By now she was a freshman at Bólyai University, in the Department of Philosophy. We were invited to stay with Sanyi and Magda Jakab, who were living in an elegant house in the most beautiful suburb of Bucharest, near a large park named after Stalin. Sanyi was now one of the three deputy finance ministers and was known as the right hand of Vasile Luca, the party secretary who was minister of finance. Edith and I stayed there the first week after my return. During the day I was tied up full time with official matters, but in the evening, when we were sitting around the dinner table, I would try to describe my life and adventures in London. It felt very good to be with Edith, and I felt that our relationship had been tested and was strong enough to warrant the seal of marriage. I asked Edith to marry me. She agreed, and during the next few days we worked out the details.

Right after my arrival in Bucharest, I requested and obtained an ap-pointment with Gheorghiu-Dej, the general secretary of the party and supreme boss of the country. Here is what led to this audience. At some time in 1946 or 1947, King Michael had sent to London two hunting guns of British manufacture that needed repair. The legation took them to a repair shop specializing in that particular brand of guns. With the king's abdication at the end of 1947, everybody had forgotten about them, but when the belongings he had left behind were inventoried, somebody found correspondence relating to the guns and communicated his findings to the party. Gheorghiu-Dej liked hunting, so it was decided to try to recover the guns. In November, the legation received the request, and Macovescu dropped the matter into my lap. The head of the repair shop said that the repairs had long been finished, but that he was not sure whether he should return the guns to the king, whose personal property they were, or to the legation that had sent them to the shop. I gave him the legal argument on the basis of which the legation was laying claim to the guns, suggested that he consult a lawyer, and asked for a definitive answer within two weeks; otherwise, we would sue him. I also mentioned that while the former king may have been a good client, he was now just a *former* king, whereas Romania was a country with many hunters who might bring him business in the future. Ten days later he called and asked me to pick up the guns, which I did. This was a week or two before my departure for Bucharest, at which time the legation was in the process of arranging for the transportation of the guns. Because of the personal nature of the matter, Mac wanted to avoid the official channel of correspondence through the Ministry of Foreign Affairs and suggested that upon my return I ask for an audience with Gheorghiu-Dej, who was eager to get hold of the guns, and tell him what the legation had arranged.

So now I was sitting in a chair facing the most powerful man in Romania. I was meeting him for the first time, although I had seen him before at the party's 1945 national conference. He was obviously pleased by what I had to tell him, and asked me to convey his thanks to whoever was involved in recovering the guns. Then he reclined in his chair and, with the intonation of a person who is the perfect master of his time, said: "Tell me about England: what kind of a place is it?" I did not quite know what to say. The man and his level of understanding were unknown to me. Also, I had no idea whether I had five minutes at my disposal, or twenty-five. After almost fifty years, I do not remember what I said. But I do remember that I decided instantly: describe, don't analyze.

Give facts; not statistical facts, but direct observations; the raw material, not its interpretation. Be frank, be blunt, but stick to the facts. And so I started describing England as I experienced it. Gheorghiu's face showed keen interest as I described London's working-class suburbs, how the workers lived, how their houses looked, what they were able to buy for their salaries. He enjoyed my description of the subway system and the double-decker buses. I related several episodes of the Labour Party conference at Scarborough, and told him about the health care plan that was being introduced. He asked about the British Communist Party and I gave him, without comment, the number of members and the number of votes they got in the last elections. The picture that I was painting must have surprised him, since it was utterly different from what he was reading about England in the party press. He winked at me a couple of times, as if to encourage me to say things that are usually not said. He listened to me for a little less than an hour, then said that he had learned a lot from what he heard and wished me good luck. I had the impression that he meant what he said.

■ ■ ■

Two days later I had to give a report on the situation in England at the Ministry of Foreign Affairs. The forum was a gathering of all the heads of political directorates, chaired by Anuța Toma, Ana Pauker's deputy, with the additional participation of a few Romanian diplomats who happened to be in Bucharest, among them Grigore Preoteasa of the legation in Washington with whom I had traveled from Prague. Again, after almost fifty years I don't remember in detail what I said in my report, but I know that I drew a picture of the economic and political conditions in England, starting with and emphasizing throughout the facts I had personally experienced, and continuing with some statistical data. My report consisted of about 80 percent facts, but I also included some interpretation, the gist of which was that the British working class was currently not a revolutionary force, that conditions in Britain were more or less stable, that Britain had survived the dissolution of its empire surprisingly well, and that our party's policy, if it was to be successful, must be based on these realities. I also described the basic facts of the Marshall Plan. My report, which lasted about an hour, was followed by an uninterrupted sequence of attacks. I don't remember who was the first to give the signal, but speaker after speaker criticized my report as embellishing the situation in England, misjudging the temper of the working class, being taken in by bourgeois propaganda, not wanting to see the cracks under the surface, and so on and so on. My "mistakes" were diagnosed as manifestations of bourgeois objectivism. What upset me most was that Preoteasa, our envoy to Washington with whom I had spoken for several hours on the train about much the same subject and who had then agreed with almost everything I said, never contradicting or correcting me, was now one of the most vociferous critics of my report.

Contrary to party etiquette, in my answer to the critics I refused to recant and exercise self-criticism. Instead, after refuting with facts some of the concrete criticisms, of which there were few, I replied to the general criticism by pointing out that two days earlier I had had the privilege of a lengthy audience with comrade Gheorghiu-Dej, to whom I related basically the same things that were described in my report. The fact that I had not encountered any disapproval on his part led me to believe that he could not possibly have found my views so wrong. "But be that as it may," I said, "since this forum finds that I see things the wrong way, it does not make sense for the ministry to send me back to my post. Instead, I should be replaced with somebody who sees things correctly." At that point Anuţa Toma angrily suspended the meeting, saying that it had dragged on too long anyway, and that perhaps she should talk to me before we resumed our debate. She then took me to her office where she dressed me down for the way I reacted to the criticism—the help that the comrades were offering me. "Everybody who makes a report is criticized," she said, and told me I must learn to listen to the criticism even when it is only partly justified, and learn from it. As to my suggestion about not being sent back to my post, she would discuss it with comrade Ana, but she personally disagreed with me. She thought I should be sent back.

The next day Anuţa told me she had talked the matter over with comrade Ana, and they both thought that I was doing a good job at the legation and should be sent back. As to my report, we were not going to resume the meeting. I should talk individually to those of the participants with whom I felt I had something to clarify, and heed the general advice about being more careful in interpreting the facts. In the future, I should not restrict myself to observing surface phenomena, but should try to see the deeper underlying connections and trends. I did not follow up on the suggestion of trying to clarify things through individual discussions; I thought it would not make sense. From what had happened, I concluded that the leadership's real objection was not to my way of seeing things but to my way of talking about them, of presenting them. If they had meant what they said, if they had really thought that my report did not describe the situation accurately and that I did not see things as they were, it would have made no sense for them to send me back to my post. "Obviously," I thought, "you are allowed, even required, to assess reality accurately and use your assessment as a guide to action. But you are not allowed to voice your assessment, even in a high-level meeting. It's all right to speak openly with the party's general secretary in private; it is not all right to speak openly in a conference, even one of high officials and policy makers."

Before returning to my post, there was an important personal problem to be solved: Edith and I wanted to get married. Since I had only a few days to spend in the country, we decided to get married quickly and simply before a civilian forum in Bucharest, then to visit Edith's parents in Cluj for a couple of days and pick up the things she wanted to take to London. When I announced at the ministry that I intended to marry Edith, I was told to inform the secretary of the ministry's party organization, Lenuţa Păsculescu (who was also the director of the cabinet), and talk over the matter with her. She asked me a few questions about Edith and was relieved to hear that she was a party member. She wanted to meet Edith, which she did next day, after which she gave us her enthusiastic blessing, congratulating me on what a sweet comrade I had found. Our brief marriage ceremony took place on December 21, which happened to be the birthday of both Edith's mother, Klara, and Stalin. We needed two witnesses; one was Juci (Regina) Klein, my old pediatrician friend from the underground; the other was the driver who took us to City Hall. As soon as the ceremony was finished, we left for Cluj in a car belonging to the Ministry of Finance that Sanyi lent us. In Cluj there was great joy in the Lövis' household. Although Klara and Sándor would have liked a fancy wedding, they accepted the way it happened as being in tune with the new times. They were happy for Edith and gave us their blessing. Their love and care accompanied us throughout our adventurous next eighteen years in Romania.

Back in Bucharest, I cabled the legation to announce that I was returning with Edith. I introduced her to a few colleagues at the ministry, and we picked up her passport. At the end of December we took the train to London, with a stopover in Paris. It was one of the most pleasant train rides I ever had. The train stopped in Vienna for an hour and a half, and we went for an evening walk in the quarter surrounding the railway station. In Switzerland, at the border station of Buchs, Edith was ecstatic about the mountains of high-quality chocolate, which was unavailable in Romania. We stayed at the Paris legation for several days, which we spent sight-seeing and shopping. Once I took Edith to a very elegant restaurant, where we started our meal with oysters—Edith was having them for the first time—and used the wrong forks for eating them. When the waiter removed our plates, he also took the forks we should have used—that's how we learned the rule. I also remember Edith's consternation when she saw the bill, which was considerably higher than what we had paid two hours earlier for a pair of Bally shoes. In Romania at the time the price of a pair of shoes was several times that of a meal for a couple. We also bought Edith a black dress that she could wear for diplomatic occasions. It looked wonderful on her, and I got my first taste of that basic difference between men and women that I was to experience all my life: Edith was genuinely happy about owning that dress; she radiated when she put it on.

We went to the Moulin Rouge and to some other places, and, of course, we took the elevator to the top of the Eiffel Tower. There a photographer offered his services and naturally, as we were on our honeymoon, we accepted. He took us around the balcony on top of the tower to decide which of the four sides we wanted as background. After due deliberation we chose the one that seemed most memorable, upon which he invited us inside the building. There his camera was set up in front of a series of panels. He chose one bearing a picture of the background we had selected, put it on top, ordered us to stand in front of it, and took the picture. We still have it; it looks like one of those pictures that maids in our hometown used to bring home from an outing at the fair.

We arrived in London in the first days of January, and Edith was an instant success: everybody liked her and Teri Macovescu in particular congratulated me warmly on my "choice." Our living quarters were to be on the third floor of the residence at Belgrave Square, the same place where I had lived before, except that now we had an apartment instead of a single room. Edith spoke only a little English, so she started taking English lessons at the Berlitz School on Oxford Street. The two of us went

Together in England, early 1949

on several sight-seeing tours. Among other things, we visited the National Gallery, where, to my great surprise, Edith recognized many of the
paintings by Gainsborough and others from photographs she had seen.
We went to Sadler's Wells where we saw *Swan Lake* in a very good
performance. We went to movies. On weekends we would drive out,
usually with Mac and Teri, to Windsor, Brighton, or elsewhere. The

English countryside was always very beautiful, and in the winter of 1948–1949 the traffic was still quite moderate, so driving through the countryside was a genuine pleasure. By this time the personnel of the legation had increased by the addition of a new press attaché and his wife, but we did not spend much time with them.

An interesting cultural experience was a concert given by Paul Robeson at the Royal Albert Hall. It was a magnificent performance by this uniquely great American singer. A giant of a black man, he had a voice that made you fear that the roof would fall in. He sang a wide range of songs in ten or more languages, from English and French to Russian, Italian, Spanish, German, and Yiddish, among others. He had an inexhaustible repertoire of pieces, each more beautiful than the next. We heard many of the songs for the first, and some for the last time, and were completely overcome by their charm. Before the concert, there was a reception in Robeson's honor at the Soviet embassy, where a new film was shown, a Soviet wartime story dealing with the emotionally charged events of that period. Edith, who sat near Robeson in the audience, saw him cry during the film.

I think it was at this reception (but it may have been on some earlier occasion during the winter of 1948–49) that Pavlov, the first counselor of the Soviet embassy, approached me saying he had some information meant not just for me, but for the entire Romanian legation. He understood that Commander Edgar Young, who passed as a friend of the people's democracies, was a frequent guest at our legation. I confirmed this. He also used to be invited to the Soviet embassy, Pavlov said, because they also considered him a friend; but unfortunately he had recently sided with the Yugoslavs in their dispute with the Soviet Union and the rest of the people's democracies, and had gone so far as to become a mouthpiece for the Titoist propaganda machine. The Soviet Foreign Ministry now considered him an enemy agent and the embassy had stopped all contact with him. The next day I informed Macovescu, Macavei, and the rest of our diplomatic staff, and Young disappeared from the legation's guest list.

Barely five weeks after Edith and I arrived in London, Minister Macavei was summoned to the British Foreign Office. I accompanied him to translate. The official at the Foreign Office protested the expulsion from Romania of two British diplomats, who were implicated in what he claimed was a show trial and accused of spying. The official asserted categorically that the two diplomats were innocent and that the charges were trumped up. Macavei replied that he had no personal knowledge of the details of the trial, but he did not believe that his government would accuse the two British diplomats without a reason; after all, what purpose could that serve? All he could say, added Macavei, was that his task in London was to try to improve the relations between his country and Great Britain, and he was doing his best toward that goal. He asked whether there was anything that he had not done and could do in order to improve those relations. The British official answered that Minister Macavei should not deceive himself about the relations between our two countries: they were *bad,* he said, very bad. The minister should let Bucharest know that His Majesty's government was not disposed to tolerate such treatment and would retaliate in kind in the very near future.

Less than a week after this audience, the legation got an official letter from the Foreign Office to the effect that First Secretary E. Balaş and Commercial Third Secretary I. Măgură of the Romanian legation in London were declared persona non grata by His Majesty's government and were expected to leave the country within six weeks. On the day when the legation was notified of this decision, a press release by the Foreign Office informed the public about the step taken, describing it as retaliation for the Romanian government's expulsion of the two British diplomats. It was specifically stated that the measure was not directed personally against the two Romanian diplomats, but that their ranks corresponded to those of the two British diplomats expelled from Bucharest.

Although I would have preferred having a few more weeks to show Edith around, I did not at all mind returning home; in fact, I had felt a little sidetracked in London and was eager to get back and participate in shaping the new society. Specifically, I wanted to work at the State Planning Commission, where it seemed to me that the country's immediate future was being worked out and decided upon. The State Planning Commission was in charge of elaborating the country's economic plans, which affected everything else: education, science, urban development, social spending, and so on. But this was not in the cards, for reasons that will become clear later.

So Edith and I set out to make the best use of the six weeks at our disposal. Professionally, my main concern was to finish a study of the

Marshall Plan, for which I would have no sources at home. Edith generously offered to type what I was writing, although she modestly said that she was not a good typist. On this occasion I discovered what a master of understatement she was. Fortunately, it did not matter much, because what was urgent was to extract all the information I needed from the available sources. The typing itself could be finished at home. On a personal level, we took a train trip to Scotland for our own pleasure, visiting Glasgow and, very briefly, Edinburgh.

Our expulsion from Britain aroused some public interest in our personalities. As we were under orders not to give any interviews, the reporters who were hanging around the residence tried to find out what they could about our daily lives. One morning an article appeared in the *Daily Mirror* under the title "Black-Haired Edith Balaş Takes Her Last English Lesson." It described the event in the title and a little more, all based on guesswork of about the same accuracy as the description of Edith's hair color, which was light brown then as it is now. Obviously the reporter assumed that a Romanian woman *must* be black-haired. We did some shopping before we left. Among other things, we bought two Atkinson blankets that we did not stop using until eighteen years later when we left Romania for good. When the day of departure finally came, we said goodbye to our friends and to England, and took the train home.

CHAPTER 8

From Top to Bottom

Upon my return from London at the end of March 1949, I was appointed head of the Directorate of Economic Affairs in the Foreign Ministry. This office had been newly created to take charge of all foreign economic relations except for trade, which was the domain of the Department of Foreign Trade in the Ministry of Commerce. For a first secretary of a legation to be appointed a director in the Ministry of Foreign Affairs was a promotion, and I was somewhat surprised after what had happened three months earlier when I was accused of "bourgeois objectivism." But it turned out that whatever suspicions existed concerning my possible contamination with bourgeois ideas were dispelled by my expulsion by the British Foreign Office. My bosses assumed that when the Foreign Office chose me from among the Romanian diplomats for expulsion from the United Kingdom, they must have meant to deprive the legation of its most useful member. So my expulsion from Britain was held in my favor in Bucharest, and in fact triggered my promotion. Fortunately, by the time I returned from London I already had my degree as an economist, so I had at least that much qualification for the job. I also had the experience gained from supervising the activities of the commercial mission in London.

I had to organize the directorate from scratch. I brought in two bright young men from Cluj, Iván Köves, an economist, and Iuliu Bojan, a journalist; and a young economist from Timisoara, Tibor Schattelesz, who had considerable knowledge about economic facts and some knowledge of economic theory. I was also given the option of recruiting from among the personnel of the ministry, and I managed to attract two members of the Directorate of Consular Affairs, both of them well qualified and serious. In addition to these five, I was "given" a female party member who had good intentions but little training, and later another young woman recruited for the ministry from among fresh university graduates. With this team, plus two typist-secretaries, I divided the tasks of the directorate between three or four sections. The one whose work interested me most was devoted to economic studies of various international issues and events, and it published periodic economic bulletins for the information of the other directorates of the ministry. These bulletins, which we introduced at our own initiative, soon filled a gap, and came to be in high demand. The studies were uneven, but some of them stirred interest. Within three or four months of its inception, the new directorate was making a difference in the ministry's internal life, and we came to be viewed as a group competent in its own field, an exception to the amateurism that pervaded the rest of the ministry. When Ana Pauker took over the Foreign Ministry in November 1947, she fired all the old "bourgeois" experts and replaced them with party people, in whose selection the main criterion was political devotion. Thus, professional expertise was a rare thing in those days, and this explains how somebody with so little experience and such relatively poor training as myself could in a few months achieve the status of the ministry's top economic expert and become a man whose professional competence—unlike his devotion to the party line—nobody ever dared to question.

In addition to my job at the Ministry of Foreign Affairs, I was appointed a lecturer at the Institute of Economic Studies and Planning, a college-level institution whose Romanian acronym was ISEP. The course I taught at ISEP, World Economics, required the students to work hard and familiarize themselves with institutions and concepts they had known next to nothing about; nevertheless, it was quite popular, mainly because it gave the students more information about the outside world than all their other courses combined. In a country where foreign news was only available through the lens of the party newspaper, and facts about foreign countries were reduced to caricatures of reality, it is not surprising that a course that conveyed information about the world economy was popular with students. I enjoyed teaching it, and because this was a senior-level course, two of my graduating students were hired by the institute a year after I started, and one of them became my assistant.

The president, or rector, of ISEP appreciated the fact that my course, although demanding, was popular with the students, and we got along well. I cannot say the same for the provost (prorector), who was a party hack called Manea Mănescu. He had a degree in statistics or commerce, and during the war he had had some involvement with the communists, though it must have been perfunctory; he never showed the courage of his opinions. Mănescu always strictly toed the party line in its latest and most extreme version, and would ferociously attack anybody whom he perceived as deviating from it. While ferocious toward those below him or outside party circles, he was the most subservient flatterer of his superiors and party leaders in general that I ever came to know. One episode that I remember from my early teaching career was a conflict with this provost. To put it in context, I must briefly digress to describe the political atmosphere at the time.

In early 1949 the Communist Party launched the first campaign, intensified in 1950, for collectivizing the agriculture. It was accompanied by a rather brutal persecution of the kulaks or rich peasants (defined as anybody who had over twenty acres of land or used hired labor), not to mention the landlords, who were arch-enemies. All this was part of the "sharpening of the class struggle." Following the Soviet example, the Romanian Party leaders decided to start some public works in which the "class enemy" could be employed in forced labor, so they began building a canal between the city of Cernavoda on the Danube and the Black Sea, which came to be known as the Danube–Black Sea Canal. A glance at the map will convince anybody that the Canal did not make much economic sense. Its main declared purpose was to shorten the navigational distance to the sea for ships coming from the upper course of the Danube; in this respect it saved about 150 miles, not a big deal. Its secondary purpose was to provide water for irrigation in an arid area of Dobrogea, the region along the seacoast, but this could have been achieved with a fraction of the effort required to build a waterway for seafaring ships. In fact, the principal motivation for the canal was to create a place where "enemies of the people" could be sent to expiate their crimes by working for the republic. Such a concept is harsh and repulsive enough in itself; but the real tragedy was that the "enemies of the people" were not individuals who had acted against the people or the regime purporting to represent them—police control was so tight that no organized resistance was possible on anything but a negligible scale—but individuals whom the regime had singled out as its enemies on the basis of their social backgrounds. Adding to the senseless cruelty of forced labor on a useless project was the fact that a person could be sent to the Canal without a regular trial: a so-called administrative sentence, which required no legal justification, was sufficient.

It was in this atmosphere that, at the end of a semester, the best student in my class and the only one to receive a grade of 10 (corresponding to an A+) turned out to be the son of a landlord, or former landlord. His name was Răducan or something similar. I was not aware of his background, as I was interested in the students' talents and seriousness, not in their parents' social status or politics. The provost, Manea Mănescu, asked to see me; I went to his office and found him very upset: he could not understand how a person with my standing in the party and with my past in the underground movement could so completely abandon the principles of class struggle as to give the maximum grade to a class enemy, the son of the well-known landlord Răducan. "This is absurd," he said. "This son of a bitch has no place in our institute; you must change his grade to a failing one."

I answered that, first, I was not in charge of admissions; he, the provost, supervised the admissions office; and if it had admitted a class enemy who should have been rejected, that was his responsibility, not mine. Second, in my class Răducan had never expressed views hostile to the regime or to the party, so I could not support the contention that he was a class enemy. His father may have been a landlord, but he had to be judged primarily on the basis of his own behavior. If Mănescu had evidence that Răducan was indeed a hostile element, he should expel him from the institute on that basis. He could do so openly by proving his accusations, and did not need to resort to the subterfuge of a failing grade in my course. Third, to use the grading system to get rid of elements whom the Provost wanted to get rid of without specifying the true reason would compromise the grading system in the eyes of the students. Why should they work hard and learn what was required of them when they saw that grading was not based on their performance but on other criteria? I refused to do this, I told him, and would not change Răducan's grade; I regarded such a procedure as contrary to the interests of the educational system and ultimately harmful to the party. If the provost disagreed with this point of view, I was willing to go before a party forum and discuss the issue.

Mănescu could have eaten me alive; but he did not know what to say or do and left the issue—and me—alone, at least for the time being. He found no reason to expel Răducan, who got his degree at the end of the year. But of course, Mănescu never forgave me, and gave vent to his hostility later when he grew more powerful and had the opportunity. Fortunately for me, I had already left Romania when Mănescu reached the peak of his power as prime minister under Ceauşescu in the eighties.

Besides my job at the ministry and my teaching position at the ISEP, I joined the editorial board of the monthly economic journal *Probleme Economice*. The editor-in-chief, Mircea Oprişan, a Jewish journalist and economist who was above all an astute political manipulator, later made a career as minister of domestic trade in the mid-to-late fifties. At the time, he courted me assiduously because of my "strategic position" at the Ministry of Foreign Affairs. The adjective "strategic" refers to the fact that I was working in the entourage of Ana Pauker, who was viewed as one of the leaders of the party and the country, second in importance only—if at all—to Gheorghiu-Dej. So Oprişan gave me the royal treatment, asked for my opinion on many matters, and covered himself with carefully thought-out excuses whenever he did not want to follow my advice. He would say, for instance, that unfortunately the Propaganda Section of the Central Committee had advised against my recommendation, which of course closed the issue.

When we returned from London at the end of March 1949, Edith and I spent a couple of weeks at Sanyi's and Magda's house. Soon after that Edith went to Cluj to take her first-year exams at Bólyai University, upon the completion of which she transferred to the University of Bucharest (called C. I. Parhon after a famous Romanian medical scientist). During the spring we were allocated a two-bedroom apartment in a small family house at number 12 Strada Tokyo, in a quiet, pleasant quarter not far from the ministry. Our apartment had a living room, dining room, and kitchen on the first floor, and two rooms on the second floor, one of which we used as a bedroom, the other as a study. We put into the house some nice furniture that we received as a wedding present from Edith's parents. I also had at my disposal a chauffeured car from the ministry. Although I would have much preferred to have the car without the chauffeur so that I could drive it myself, this was not permissible. I could drive the car occasionally, but the driver assigned by the ministry was responsible for keeping it in good condition at all times. Cars—an imported item—were so expensive, and drivers—local labor—were so cheap, that the luxury I was enjoying was in fact the car, not the driver.

In September 1949 something strange happened in Budapest that shook up the entire communist world. László Rajk—one of the few homegrown leaders of the Hungarian Communist Party, a former underground fighter and participant in the Spanish civil war, minister of the Interior for a while after 1946 and foreign minister thereafter—was publicly tried and confessed to being a Trotskyite, a Titoist, and for many years an agent of the Western espionage services. He was in the dock with several other people who all pleaded guilty. The trial lasted for several days, during which the depositions and testimonials gave a detailed, perfectly consonant picture of a complex and dangerous conspiracy. Rajk and two other participants were sentenced to death and executed; the others got life or heavy prison sentences. It was, of course, a show trial, but at the time neither I nor any of my friends in Bucharest or in Budapest knew that.

To understand how I and others like myself, including many experienced people who were anything but gullible, could believe such a thing, one has to bear in mind the following circumstances. For one thing, this was the first trial after World War II in which a communist leader was accused of treason. Although those who had lived through the show trials of the late thirties in the Soviet Union might have taken a more skeptical view, I and most of my comrades had not. My experience with this kind of thing was nil. Second, the trial was superbly staged by its diabolical organizers. The depositions sounded utterly credible: all of the detailed accounts told essentially the same story in different words, sometimes with minor contradictions which were then straightened out in a seemingly impeccable fashion. In those depositions, fiction mingled with facts. Many of the most fantastic allegations were true, although they did not, of course, prove the guilt of the accused. For instance, during the civil war in Spain, Rajk was relieved of his position as party secretary of his military unit for expressing Trotskyite views and, though not excluded from the party, he was sent to the front line. Also, after returning to Hungary, where he became one of the leading members of the underground party, he was arrested and tried by a military tribunal in November 1944. In that same trial, the leader of the Small Landholders' Party, Bajcsi-Zsilinszki, a militant, outspoken, noncommunist antinazi, was sentenced to death and executed; but Rajk was spared the death sentence as a result of the energetic intervention of his brother, a fascist and secretary of state in the Arrow Cross government of Szálasi. Both of these facts were true, verifiable, and somewhat strange. Although they proved nothing, they made other strange admissions by Rajk more credible. Finally, I along with many others reasoned along the following lines: if Rajk's confession at the trial was not true, then he must have been totally, utterly broken by his interrogators between May 1949, when he was arrested, and September of the same year, when he came to trial. But, though I had not known Rajk personally, I knew that he was a tough underground fighter during the war, one who had been arrested by the DEF in 1944 and had not given anyone away (if he had, he would have been excluded from the party after the war). If the DEF, whose terribly efficient methods I knew all too well, had been unable to break this proud communist even to the extent of divulging a single name, how on earth could anyone have forced him to accuse himself in a calm, deliberate voice of precisely those crimes that he must have considered the most despicable on earth? I could not conceive of such a possibility; therefore, as naïve as this may sound, I believed Rajk's testimony.

A few weeks after Rajk's trial, in October 1949, I was sent to Budapest for a few days as a member of a Romanian team to negotiate an agreement with the Hungarians on railway transportation. It was a routine affair with no political implications and no serious economic ramifications, handled mainly by the railway experts who were part of the delegation, so I had time to look up some of my wartime comrades. Naturally, I discussed the Rajk affair with them. They were all shocked by it, but none of them expressed any doubt as to the truth of the matter.

While I was in the Hungarian capital, I had some important news from Edith. Before leaving for Budapest, I had asked her what she wanted me to bring her. Material for a dressing gown, she said, and she added that she needed three meters. When I called her from Budapest, she told me she had something important to say. "What is it?" I inquired. It concerned the material for the dressing gown, she said: it had better be four meters, not three. I guessed what this meant—that she was pregnant—though I was not quite sure. She confirmed it upon my return.

From 1949 to 1951, busy though I was with my work, Edith and I made sure not to miss important cultural events. We were occasional operagoers; the Bucharest Opera was quite good, and it sometimes had world-class guest singers. The symphony orchestra was also good, and occasionally there was a famous visiting violinist or pianist. Romanian theater was of high quality; one of the stage managers of those years, Liviu Ciulei, later made it to the West and worked for a while in the United States. Contemporary plays were pretty bad because of political control, but we saw many classical plays superbly staged. Among the highlights of our cultural experiences I remember several visits by the Bolshoi Theater and the Kirov Ballet, as well as the unsurpassed folk dancing troupe of Moiseev.

On several occasions I was asked to lecture on economic matters at the party school. My lectures usually went well, and I had the reputation of a good speaker. However, my greatest success, in terms of its repercussions, was a lecture I improvised the night before I gave it, on somebody else's behalf. That somebody was Alexandru Bârlădeanu, a leading member of the government. He was minister of commerce in charge of both foreign and domestic trade, and was also in charge of coordinating several other economic ministries. He was a Romanian communist intellectual in his early forties, of Bessarabian origin, fluent in Russian, very bright and widely read, with the reputation of being the country's most knowledgeable practical economist. He was a friend of Sanyi's, and one evening complained to him that he had just been scheduled for an audience with Gheorghiu-Dej for the next morning, when he was supposed to deliver a lecture at the party school. Sanyi suggested that he ask me to lecture in his place, and guaranteed that the audience would be satisfied. When Bârlădeanu, whom I had not met before, called me with the request, warning me that I had only that night to prepare, he was disarmingly flattering, saying that he was burning with curiosity to meet the rare person who could make a skeptic like Sanyi sound enthusiastic. Needless to say, I did not turn him down, and I gave a lecture which, according to Bârlădeanu, was very well received. He told me I had saved him from a very unpleasant situation. As I said before, this turned out to be my most important lecture in terms of its repercussions: sixteen years later, when I was fighting the final battle of my five-and-a-half-year war to be allowed to emigrate, Bârlădeanu was one of the two or three persons most likely to have been instrumental in my getting the emigration permit.

In late 1949 or early 1950 I was assigned to participate, as the representative of the Foreign Ministry, in negotiations conducted by a Romanian team with a delegation of the Swiss government for the purpose of settling Swiss claims on behalf of former owners of Romanian nationalized

Sanyi Jakab around 1949

enterprises. A number of Swiss bank accounts had been frozen because of these claims, so settling them was important to Romania. The Romanian delegation was headed by Gogu Rădulescu, deputy minister in the Ministry of Commerce, in charge of the Department of Foreign Trade. Besides Rădulescu and myself, the delegation had representatives from the Ministry of Finance, the State Bank, and the Department of Foreign Trade.

Gogu Rădulescu was a friend of Sanyi and I had had some earlier contacts with him. When I returned from London, I had called Rădulescu and told him about some pending issues concerning the activity of the commercial mission in London. He asked me to come over to his ministry, where I had a friendly conversation with this strange, bitingly ironic man whose tongue everyone feared. He was physically strange; he looked like a Mongol warlord, the way I imagined Genghis Khan had looked. Moreover, his favorite mode of conversation was to ask seemingly naïve questions, then to deride his interlocutor if he missed the answers. He could not stand hypocrites and flatterers, and anybody who tried party sloganeering with him was interrupted and sometimes thrown out of his office. For a while he could afford to be provocative and disdainful of party demagogues because of his background; everybody knew that he had spent the war in the Soviet Union and was seemingly on good terms with some Russians who were in Bucharest at the time. This was enough to shield him against attacks. But his situation eventually changed, and the enemies he made in the late forties took their revenge on him in the fifties.

Though my contacts with Rădulescu started on a good footing, my mission on the negotiating team was nevertheless an unpleasant one. Romania's main economic relations with the outside world were of two kinds: joint enterprises with the Soviet Union and foreign trade. The first was under the control of the Ministry of Finance, and the Foreign Ministry did not feel any urge to stick its nose into what was happening there. The second was being carried out by the Department of Foreign Trade, but Ana Pauker's Foreign Ministry was arrogating the right of political control over it. Naturally, Rădulescu, as head of the Department of Foreign Trade, resented these attempts and resisted them fiercely. After all, he was a party member and expected to be trusted. This led to an ongoing conflict between the two ministries, now more latent, now more open. Of course, the conflict was never with Ana Pauker herself— that would have been unthinkable in view of the great difference between her party status and Rădulescu's—but with Anuța Toma, the main deputy foreign minister and *totum factum* of the ministry. Rădulescu did not hide his contempt for Anuța Toma, to whom he would often refer sarcastically in conversation with others. My own opinion was that the Department of Foreign Trade should be allowed to conduct its business according to commercial criteria and that politicizing its activity could only be detrimental to the development of Romania's trade relations. In being appointed the representative of my ministry in the negotiations with the Swiss delegation, I was now thrown against my will into the middle of this conflict. I spoke to Rădulescu openly about my discomfort with the situation, and assured him that I would play as constructive a role in the negotiations as I could and that he need not worry about my reporting anything behind his back to the party, my ministry, or anyone else. If I had any objections, I would tell him before anybody else. He appreciated my straightforwardness and we got along very well.

The negotiations were difficult. The Swiss delegation was led by an experienced Foreign Ministry official called Troendle. The Swiss came with a list of claimed properties, evaluated at what our side considered exaggerated prices. They were well prepared, knew what they wanted, and had supporting documents for every claim they made. On our side, Rădulescu had no time to prepare for the negotiations in advance, and was following a strategy of "playing it by the ear," something he was pretty good at. The other members of our delegation were knowledgeable about the issues affecting their specialties, but knew nothing about the rest; nobody seemed to have a good grasp of where we stood, what was to be done, which of the claims could be contested, and how. I was completely ignorant during the first few days. Not only did I have less than a week's warning, but the actual claims were unknown to anyone before the arrival of the Swiss delegation. It did not occur to anybody on the Romanian side to ask the Swiss to present their claims in writing a month before the start of the negotiations, so that we could study them. I took the materials with me after the meetings and spent several nights familiarizing myself with them, and after a few days I was able to dispute certain claims and argue about interpretations. The representative of our Finance Ministry was able to dig up evidence of tax evasion on the part of the former owners, as well as outright cheating and bribery used to avoid tax payments. When these taxes owed by the former owners to the Romanian state were calculated, along with the associated interest and penalties, it turned out in many cases that their value exceeded the owners' claims. At first, the Swiss delegation questioned the legitimacy of the Romanian claims, but after a while it adopted a new strategy, abandoning those cases where the indebtedness of the companies exceeded the owners' claims, and asking instead for full compensation in the other cases. Here I argued that we were not dealing with the individual owners, who indeed had no responsibility for each other's debts, but with the Swiss government as representative of the whole group; and if the Swiss government wanted to settle the outstanding issues between the two countries, it could not claim to represent only those who had a favorable balance of claims against the Romanian government—it must also be accountable for those who had an unfavorable balance. Rădulescu liked my argument and embraced it, since the total indebtedness canceled out a large part of the claims. I no longer remember the details of the settlement, but the Romanian side ended up recognizing only a fraction of the claims.

The negotiations lasted about three weeks. Once a week I was supposed to report to Anuṭa Toma about what was happening. Every time we spoke she would try to get me to say something negative about Rădulescu's conduct of the negotiations, but I ignored her enticements and reported that, as far as I could see, things were headed in the right direction. When the negotiations ended without my reporting any deviation or misbehavior on the part of the Department of Foreign Trade, I expected Anuṭa to dress me down on one pretext or another. To my surprise, she instead greeted me with a broad, friendly smile and gave all kinds of signs of her appreciation. I was puzzled; I suspected a trap. But soon I had the explanation from Anuṭa herself. Apparently the Secret Service was in complete control of the Swiss embassy's communications with Berne. The embassy was thoroughly bugged and any letter dictated to a typist became available even before it was sent: Possibly some other channels of communication were also controlled by the Secret Service. Suffice it to say that Anuṭa read to me with great satisfaction the report that Troendle sent home after two weeks of negotiation. It said that the leader of the Romanian delegation had a good sense of humor but absolutely no knowledge of the subject at hand, causing everything to go very slowly; that the experts were obtuse, each one so enclosed in his own field that one could not get an idea across to them; and that the only capable negotiating partner was the representative of the Foreign Ministry. Anuṭa's satisfaction came not so much from the praise that I—and through me her ministry—received, as from the derogatory remark about Gogu Rădulescu.

In the spring of 1950 I was sent for a month to Orşova on the Danube, to do some troubleshooting as acting director of the administration of the Iron Gates, the straits through which the River Danube crosses the Carpathian Mountain chain. For about 150 kilometers, from Baziaş, due south of Timisoara, to Gârla Mare, due south of Turnu Severin, the Danube forms the border between Romania and Yugoslavia. A little less than halfway between Baziaş and Gârla Mare, the Danube crosses the Carpathians through the straits called the Iron Gates. Before the straits, the Danube is almost a kilometer wide; in the straits, it narrows to 150 meters. Naturally, the passage of the water becomes swift, the river bottom

Egon and Edith in 1950

is rocky, and ships need to be guided through the straits by professional
pilots trained on location for this purpose. This pilot service and other
navigational services were provided by a joint Romanian-Yugoslav administration, whose functioning was threatened by the political conflict
between the two countries. My task was to find a modus vivendi that
would safeguard vital Romanian interests. I acquitted myself of the task
to the ministry's satisfaction.

Edith joined me in Orşova in late April. She was in her eighth month
of pregnancy and I was eager to make her life as comfortable as possible.
We enjoyed the wild, stark beauty of the area. We took a couple of trips
on the Danube by motor boat, up the entrance to the straits, then down
to the exit, then back to Orşova in the middle. The mountains facing the
river are several hundred feet high and the straits look as if the gods had
literally cut a passage in the mountain chain. There are still traces of the
Romans who ruled this area for 170 years back in the second and third
centuries. Near Turnu Severin one can see the remains of a bridge across
the Danube built by the famous Roman architect Apollodorus of Dam-

ascus. What is even more interesting, on the southern, Yugoslav bank of the river, the Romans had built a suspended road, or carriageway, scores of kilometers long. The road no longer exists, but all along the southern bank there are deep holes in the rock, about a foot in diameter, spaced at regular intervals of six to ten feet, at a level of twenty to thirty feet above the water. These holes held the beams that carried the road—a stunningly impressive feat of engineering. The stark beauty of the area makes it one of the most remarkable sights in the world. I remembered the novel *The Golden Man* by Jókai, a famous nineteenth-century Hungarian writer, that I had read as a teenager and whose action takes place at the Iron Gates, and I relived some of its story. Edith also remembers the weeks spent there as a magnificent experience, and her memories are, of course, colored by her advanced pregnancy. Because of her condition, she tended to be hungry much of the time, so she recalls that we could not cook where we lived, and that we ate in a small restaurant in the village, where the food was spartan, being little more than bread and omelets. She also remembers our watching the Greek Orthodox Easter procession, in which I recognized several party members. Edith claims to remember that I was unusually nice to her because of her pregnancy— a great compliment on her part, because in general I was not very good at being nice.

We returned to Bucharest in the second half of May 1950. I resumed my work at the ministry and Edith went to her parents in Cluj to give birth. Anna, our first daughter, came as a present to me on June 7, my own twenty-eighth birthday. She was born at home with a complication: she had swallowed some liquid in the womb, part of which went into her lungs, and when she saw the light of day she could not breathe at first. Edith had been anesthetized and when she opened her eyes, she saw the doctor holding a blue, motionless baby by its feet and shaking it, the baby's head hanging down and giving out a rattling sound. She thought the child was dead or dying. She lost consciousness again, and when she opened her eyes a second time she found a beautiful baby at her side. Fortunately, Anna and Edith were in the hands of an excellent gynecologist, Dr. Büchler, and everything turned out well. (A few years later Büchler, harrassed by party hacks, committed suicide.) Anna was a big baby who needed a great deal of milk, and Edith had plenty. They returned to Bucharest and, after a while, when the summer heat set in, Edith left with Anna for Predeal in the mountains.

Edith and I had a common friend in Cluj, Elza Katz. In the late forties she had married Vasile Vaida, the former regional party secretary of Cluj who had earlier divorced his first wife. They lived in Bucharest. In the summer of 1950 she and Vaida had a daughter, Veronica. It happened that Elza did not have enough milk, and Edith had more than enough, so for a while Edith breast-fed Veronica Vaida. Two decades later the same Veronica Vaida had a brilliant student career in America, where she got a Ph.D. in chemistry and an assistant professorship at Harvard. She was being courted by a young American colleague who wanted to marry her. As her parents were away in Romania and she felt the need to involve somebody she trusted in her decision, she called Edith and asked that she accompany her on a first visit to her colleague's parents in Ohio, not far from Pittsburgh where we were living. Edith agreed; and when they entered the house of the young man's parents, the first thing Edith saw on the wall was a decoration that the father had received for having participated during World War II in the bombing of the Ploesti oilfields and refineries in Romania. Such is life's irony.

Anna developed in a very short time into a well-built, rosy-cheeked, friendly child, a constant source of joy. The mountain air of Predeal proved very good for her. She had large, expressive eyes, which I thought came from Edith; nicely shaped red lips, a copy of my brother Bobby's lips; and a smiling, round face with two prominent dimples. She started talking early, and her first words expressed a down-to-earth, no-nonsense realism: when I took her into my arms upon coming home from work and, instead of inquiring whether she was hungry or needed anything, I stupidly asked, "Do you love Daddy?," she blurted out, "Love meaty!"— and, of course, she got meat. She also loved chocolate and, yes, occasionally she gave convincing evidence that she loved Mommy and Daddy.

Unfortunately, Mommy got sick. Back in June Edith could not take her exams because of the childbirth. We knew in advance that this would happen, so she made arrangements to take all her exams in September. This, followed by the 1950 fall semester work as a junior-year student, required a strenuous effort which, coming shortly after the childbirth and breast-feeding, led to a serious case of hyperthyroidism, which was diagnosed some time in the spring of 1951. Medication and complete rest were required for two or three months. Edith again went to Predeal and returned only in the late fall, almost completely cured. She then resumed her student activities as a senior.

While I was in London, my friends from Cluj, Bandi and Juci Klein, had moved to Bucharest, where Bandi became deputy director at one of the state companies of foreign trade, while Juci went to work as a pediatrician. Also, some time in late 1949 or early 1950, my uncle from Arad, Tibor Rényi, came to Bucharest with his family to work for some economic agency reporting to the Finance Ministry. Edith and I maintained close contact with both families, who were—besides Sanyi and Magda Jakab—our best friends.

In 1949, soon after my return from London, I started studying Russian. An elderly Russian lady called Natalya Konstantinovna (first name and patronymic—she never used her last name) gave lessons to several directors and deputy ministers at my workplace, so I decided to try her. She turned out to be not only an excellent teacher, but in many ways a remarkable person and I continued taking Russian lessons from her until 1952. By 1951 I could read not only the newspaper *Pravda* and *Izvestiya*, which did not require a particularly rich vocabulary, but also economic journals and Chekhov's stories. I could carry on a conversation with the Soviet professor of political economy at the ISEP, as well as write letters. Natalya Konstantinovna (she always had to be addressed by both names, as Russian—not Soviet—etiquette demanded) was in her late seventies. She was either widowed or divorced; it was hard to know because she never revealed any personal information, and knew a hundred times more about the personal lives of her students than any of them knew about hers. I called her a lady, not a woman, and a lady she was: in style, dress, attitude, demeanor. She was always well dressed, with her blond hair elaborately styled, polite but proud, always erect, brave, healthy-looking. One winter day she blurted out inadvertently during our lesson that sometime before noon she had slipped in the street, fallen, and broken her rib. To my question as to why she was not in a hospital, she laughed and said that a broken rib was no big deal; it just needed a bandage around the chest, which she had put on herself. She was rather strict about homework assignments, and got me into considerable trouble with Anuța and several other colleagues by berating them as lazy and holding me up as an example of the progress she expected a student to make. When I discovered the source of the trouble I asked her to stop, but it was already too late. Natalya Konstantinovna had fled Russia during or after the revolution and made no attempt to appear favorable to the Soviet Union; she simply avoided any political discussion. It was a miracle that she was not thrown out of the ministry, something which I assume she expected would happen sooner or later. But I admired her dignity and courage. She did not hide her contempt for certain linguistic innovations the Russian Communists had introduced. Whenever I would use one of the forms or expressions that I had picked up from the Soviet press, she would correct me; and when I would point out the source, she would say, "Never mind; that is not correct Russian." Edith also took lessons from Natalya Konstantinovna, and they liked each other very much.

Late in the spring of 1950 I decided to attempt to get transferred to the State Planning Commission, since it was my main ambition to get involved in what I felt were the real problems of building socialism in Romania. I talked about this to Sanyi, who advised me against it because the State Planning Commission was headed by Miron Constantinescu, of whose character (though not intellect) he had a low opinion. But I was undeterred by this, since my interest was not in making it to the top at the commission, but in participating in the process of economic planning on a grand scale, of learning the skill "on the job."

I decided to take up the issue with my top boss herself, and asked for an audience with Ana Pauker. She received me after a few days and was very friendly at the beginning of our conversation. I thanked her for her confidence and for appointing me to such a responsible position in her ministry. Then I went on to explain that I had chosen to become an economist because, ever since the liberation of our country and the party's coming to power, my dream had been to participate in the construction of the planned economy, in the elaboration of the economic plans underlying our development. I respectfully asked that she allow me to pursue my dream and work in my chosen area at the State Planning Commission. She listened thoughtfully, then said, "Well, maybe we should talk to comrade Constantinescu."

I took this to be a positive answer and said, "I would indeed be very grateful."

But then Ana Pauker started talking about something else. She said that she had some plans for developing the Directorate of Economic Affairs and that as the head of the directorate I would of course, be part of these plans. I said that the important foreign economic issues were handled either by the Department of Foreign Trade—insofar as commerce was concerned—or by the Ministry of Finance—insofar as the

Soviet-Romanian enterprises were concerned—and that beyond these two areas there was not, and could not be, any important foreign economic activity. She said that I was wrong about this, that the recently formed Comecon (Council of Mutual Economic Assistance) implied economic cooperation between the participating countries beyond foreign trade, that the Foreign Ministry would probably get involved in this, and that this involvement might open up for me entirely new perspectives and possibilities, such as entering into working relationships with such persons as comrade Molotov in the Soviet Union. She probably intended the dropping of Molotov's name to be a bombshell that would provoke an ecstatic reaction on my part. Instead, I had a rather low-key reaction. I thanked her again for her confidence and assured her that, whatever was decided, I would do my best; nevertheless, I still preferred to work on economic planning. She ended the conversation with "We'll see," and nothing came of my request. Nor did the work with Comecon come into the Foreign Ministry's sphere, as she had apparently hoped.

About a week after this conversation Sanyi told me that, without asking me, he had suggested to Luca that he ask for my transfer to his ministry, where I could get involved in some really important domestic economic issues. Luca cautiously sounded out Pauker about me before asking for anything and got a rather negative reaction: He is a capable fellow, she said of me, but rather phlegmatic. This was a very unfavorable characterization at a time when enthusiasm and party devotion, the opposites of phlegmatism, were the qualities most sought after. Obviously, my phlegmatism consisted of being unimpressed by the possibility of working with such important personalities as comrade Molotov and the Grand Lady herself. Luca did not pursue the matter further.

• • •

In the fall of 1951 Edith and I, together with Gogu and Dorina Rădulescu, took a three- to four-day trip by car to visit the famous painted Moldavian monasteries. There are several of them in the northeastern tip of the country; their exteriors were painted in lively, time-resistant colors in the fourteenth or fifteenth century, at least one of them by Greek monks from Mount Athos. They are a unique phenomenon. The trip itself, through the mountains of southern Bucovina which we were seeing for the first time, was very beautiful; and the monasteries were a real treat.

On this occasion I found out a few bits and pieces about the lives of Gogu and Dorina. The rest of their story I learned a few years later, when we grew closer to each other and the political atmosphere became a little more relaxed.

Gogu Rădulescu was the leader of the communist students in Bucharest in the late thirties. Himself a Gentile, he had a Jewish communist fiancee called Dorina. When Romania ceded Bessarabia and Northern Bucovina to the Soviet Union in the summer of 1940, Dorina, who was close to being arrested, went over to the Soviet Union, following a plan she and Gogu had concocted that was supposed to bring them together again soon. (It took five years, but in the end they were reunited and got married.) In the spring of 1941 Gogu was called up by the army, and in June he was sent to the Soviet border as an army lieutenant.

Late on the evening of June 21—the night of the German attack on the Soviet Union—he and the other Romanian officers on the Soviet border received their orders: "Get your troops ready; we are attacking at three in the morning." Being a Communist and a wholehearted supporter of the Soviet Union, Gogu decided to go over to the Soviets to warn them, hoping they could use the few hours at their disposal so as to not be completely unprepared. He left his unit with the intention of crossing the border, at the risk of being shot either by his own or the Soviet border guards. He managed to avoid the border guards, and just before midnight reached Soviet territory, where he gave himself up as a Romanian deserter with a message. Since he was an officer, he got an immediate audience and gave the Soviet officer the information he had about the impending attack. He was not believed. He was called a provocateur, a spy sent by the Romanians on some obscure mission, and was arrested. He protested and kept repeating, "You will see very soon," but to no avail. At three in the morning the Romanian attack started, in close coordination with the German troops. Instead of being freed, Gogu was sent behind the front as a valuable prisoner, a spy. It did not matter that he had been proved right; nobody had time to examine the details of his arrest. All they knew about him was that he had arrived under suspicious circumstances and therefore was likely to be a spy. Not *certainly* a spy, but could one take such risks in time of war?

Gogu spent most of the war, more than three years, in various prisoner camps and stations of the Gulag, the Soviet network of detention centers. He came to know several of them quite well. At the beginning, he found it hard to believe what had happened to him. It was obviously a misunderstanding, and he expected every day to be released. Gradually he learned about other "misunderstandings" and came to view his own fate more skeptically. Although he did not lose faith in marxism or in communism as a better future for mankind, he became more than a bit skeptical about the merits of Russian communism. During his more than three years of wandering between prisoner camps, amidst hunger, disease, cold, and hopeless despair, he learned Russian. He also learned the taste of the Gulag and developed some instincts for avoiding it. When in 1944 he was approached by the organizers of the Tudor Vladimirescu Division, a Romanian Army unit set up to fight against the Germans alongside the Soviets, he signed up and thus managed to return to his country alongside the liberating Soviet army. Later he managed to find his fiancée, whose wartime story was no less fantastic than his, and married her.

Gogu's story stuck in my mind, but that of Dorina, his finacée, I have mostly forgotten. Dorina went over to the Soviet Union in the spring of 1940. During the ten days between the Soviet ultimatum and the actual entry of Soviet troops into Bessarabia it was possible to move over by simply traveling to any place in the region and being there when the Soviets came. She first settled in Chişinău (Kishinyev in Russian), the capital of the region. When the German attack started in June 1941, she fled along with those lucky civilians who managed to muster enough courage to leave everything behind and go East by whatever means—by train when possible, by horse carriage, by foot—and thus survived; as opposed to those who got trapped by this or that difficulty and fell under German occupation, to be killed. Dorina had wonderful stories about her wanderings from Chişinău in Bessarabia to Alma Ata in Central Asia, of which I remember only one recurring scene. Every new place where they arrived required registration. There was always a long line in front of a desk where a colorless bureaucrat sat, asking an interminable sequence of questions in a monotone voice and writing down the answers. He would ask Dorina her name, when and where she was born, her parents' names and occupations, where she went to school, and so on and so on, never looking up from his papers—until he got to the question: "And where have you spent time in jail?" To which Dorina would say, "I have never been in jail." At that point the bureaucrat would put down his pen and look up in bewilderment at this unheard-of phenomenon: a human being, past twenty, who had never been in jail!

•   •   •

More than a year before our trip to the monasteries, a world political event of tremendous importance took place: on June 25, 1950, North Korea launched a full-scale invasion of South Korea across the demilitarized zone. The North Korean leaders were good students of history: like the nazi attack on the Soviet Union nine years earlier, their onslaught was launched shortly after midnight on Saturday. They had the advantage of complete surprise and the superior strength of a well-trained, communist-controlled army of a society on a full wartime footing in peacetime. They immediately conquered Seoul, the South Korean capital, and within a few weeks managed to occupy a large part of the country. The invasion was perversely described by the North Koreans and the Soviet press as a riposte to a South Korean attack. Nobody in my circles believed this, and it was viewed as a diplomatic lie demanded by the circumstances. It was also clear that the North Korean attack could not have taken place without Stalin's approval.

At the time this happened, party cadres in Romania were expecting something else. The Romanian region adjacent to Yugoslavia, the Banat, was filled with more Soviet troops than ever before. The press campaign against Tito, that arch-traitor of the world proletariat and inveterate lackey of the imperialists, was becoming more and more violent. Yugoslavia was excluded from the Cominform; the various people's democracies friendship treaties with Yugoslavia were denounced one after the other; and the need for brotherly help to the peoples of Yugoslavia in the form of armed intervention by the Soviet Union and its allies was being more or less openly discussed in party circles. When war broke out on the opposite side of the globe, our interpretation was that, because of Korea's peripheral location, whatever the Western powers' response might be, the Russians must have considered this adventure less likely to provoke a world conflagration than a move on Yugoslavia. I remember Sanyi calling the North Korean invasion "Stalin's trial balloon," meaning that if the reaction of the Western Allies was limited to fulmination, protests, and condemnation, then the stage would be set for "liberating" Yugoslavia. As it happened, the United States managed to get the United Nations involved on the side of South Korea, and General MacArthur's troops soon pushed back the North Korean attackers well beyond their starting point. So "Stalin's trial balloon," if indeed that is what it was, failed. It is quite possible—we will probably never know for sure—that the American action in Korea saved Yugoslavia from an attack from its neighbors, led by their Big Brother.

After the Chinese intervened, the Korean War dragged on for quite a while. Romania, like the other European people's democracies, did not interfere militarily, but sent North Korea nonmilitary aid, including doctors and medicine. Among the doctors who spent several months in North Korea was a friend of mine by the name of Avram (Abraham) Farchi. When he returned from Korea in early 1952, he was a little reluctant to talk about his experience, as he was under strict orders to keep everything secret, but I was curious to know the truth about Korea. I said that if he knew any real military secrets he should certainly not tell me about those, but there could be no harm in his telling me, a director in the Foreign Ministry and a wartime party member, about some facts of life in Korea. So he came to my office and we had a long conversation, in which I asked him questions about everything: the quality of life in the country of Kim Il Sung, the quality of the Soviet armament of the Korean military, the performance of the MIG airplanes the Koreans were using compared to that of the American fighter planes, the morale of the North Korean army and population, and so forth. At the time I did not know that my office was bugged and that every question I asked Dr. Farchi and every answer he gave me were reported to the Secret Service. Actually this event triggered my discovery of that fact, since Farchi was soon taken to task and dressed down for having disclosed state secrets to me, and he had the courage to tell me about this. When I asked him who else knew about our conversation and he said nobody, I was finally able to draw my conclusions.

There were other occurrences that could be interpreted in hindsight as indicating a lack of confidence in me, or preparations for my replacement. Some time in 1951 I was given a deputy: Bazil Şerban, who had fought in Spain in the ranks of the international brigade and later in the French resistance, and who from 1948 to 1950 had had some assignment as a diplomat, was now appointed deputy director of economic affairs. True, before this happened Anuţa Toma called me in and explained that they had no immediate task for Şerban abroad and simply wanted to keep him at home for a while. As this job was nearest to his qualifications, would I mind introducing him to the tasks of the directorate and helping him to make himself useful as my assistant. Of course, I did not mind, and Şerban and I actually worked together smoothly and without conflict: We discussed and agreed upon all the problems that the directorate had to decide or solve. Even if Şerban's appointment had been intended from the beginning as a step toward my replacement, I would have seen nothing wrong with that: after all, I had asked Ana Pauker to let me move to the State Planning Committee.

A few weeks after my conversation with Farchi, Anuţa Toma questioned me about it in an icy, hostile atmosphere. I tried to explain to her that as a communist and as someone who closely followed the international scene, I was deeply interested in the unfolding of the most important political-military event of our time and was not ashamed for wanting to know as much as possible about it. But ominously, the point of Anuţa's questioning was not to dress me down for having enticed Farchi to talk to me about Korea when I knew he was under orders to be silent. No, the point was quite different: she wanted to know who gave me the task of finding out Korean military secrets, to whom I was supposed to relay the information and by what means, and so on. Of course, I indignantly rejected her insinuations, but that did not get me out of trouble. For by the time this happened, around February 1952, I was indeed in trouble, and not because of Farchi. The problem was my friendship with Sanyi Jakab.

Sanyi was my closest friend and I spent time with him at least once or twice a week. We both liked walking and felt the need to stretch our legs after sitting at our desks all day, so we took long walks, usually in the evening. Sanyi was considered to be the right hand of Vasile Luca, the party secretary and finance minister. Although there were three deputy ministers of finance, it was Sanyi whose opinions Luca relied upon most. The Ministry of Finance had come to play a very important role in the Romanian economy. Immediately after the war, the Soviet and Romanian governments had formed a number of joint companies (Sovroms as they were called, for Soviet-Romanian) as part of Romania's reparation for its participation in the nazi-led invasion of the Soviet Union. These companies, taken together, embraced at least half of Romania's entire mining and industrial production capacity, and they were controlled on the Romanian side by the Ministry of Finance. Sanyi was involved, at least for some time, in supervising the directorate of the ministry that dealt with these companies. There was a Soviet counselor to the Ministry of Finance, one Dobrohotov, whom Sanyi had to deal with. I met Dobrohotov in Sanyi's office and was struck by the friendly, informal, and relaxed atmosphere that seemed to characterize their relations. Sanyi had started taking Russian lessons in 1948 and, although he was not very good at learning languages in general, his sustained effort enabled him to conduct a rudimentary conversation with Dobrohotov in Russian, the only language the latter spoke. This gave Sanyi some advantage over his two colleagues and many others who had dealings with the Russians, since none of them knew the language and all had to rely on translators. Although at that time, in 1949–50, Sanyi had quite good relations with Dobrohotov and, through him, with the Russians, that situation changed in 1951, when Dobrohotov was recalled and replaced.

Sanyi's reputation in his own ministry was that of a tough, demanding, and knowledgeable boss who could not easily be misled. He was known to judge matters on their merits, unaffected by the political weight of the persons who expressed a different opinion. In an atmosphere of general sycophancy, where at meetings everybody watched the boss's and other important people's facial expressions to get their cue as to how to react to what was being said, his demeanor struck a discordant note. As far as I know, he had no important conflicts within his ministry: few people dared to take issue with him, since he was usually well informed, and besides, he was known to have the ear of Luca. On the other hand, conflicts tended to develop with other ministries that were violating budgetary constraints, and mainly with the State Planning Commission, whose plans were often unrealistic and tended to follow the wishes and dreams of the party leaders, even when those were economically unsound. Nobody, including Sanyi, could of course question the wisdom of clearly stated party directives; but he would come to these meetings well armed with facts and data, would point out contradictions in the proposed plans, and would ask unpleasant questions about them which showed that the emperor had no clothes. In 1949–1950 these conflicts were still incipient, but during 1950 and 1951, they developed into skirmishes that gradually grew into a major confrontation.

The skirmishes came to be viewed as differences of opinion and approach between the people around Luca (primarily Sanyi) and the people around Gheorghiu-Dej, since the head of the State Planning Commission, Miron Constantinescu, would never have dared to take issue with Luca on anything without the direct support of Gheorghiu-Dej. In this gradually evolving but still latent conflict between Gheorghiu-Dej and Luca, the third leader, Ana Pauker, who to a large degree held the balance between them, tended to side with Luca, and the fourth leader, Teohari Georgescu, usually supported Pauker. Although Pauker was more or less maintaining the balance between Gheorghiu-Dej and Luca, this balance was slowly but surely shifting in favor of Gheorghiu-Dej. The reason for this had more to do with human factors than with the substance of the issues. On the issues, Luca was almost always right: he had a better grasp of the economy, a better feel for the economic process than Gheorghiu-Dej, and probably had better advisers. But Luca was an impulsive, emotional person, prone to occasional fits of rage and not at all given to political intrigues and strategic games; whereas Gheorghiu-Dej, though less astute in economic matters, was cool, calculating, and knew perfectly well how to play political chess. Whereas Luca did not suffer fools gladly, Gheorghiu-Dej worked to attract anybody whom Luca had alienated. He assiduously courted important members of the Central Committee to draw them to his side, and rewarded them for any support given to him or to his people in meetings. In other words, he was systematically building a personal constituency within the party. To appreciate his success in this undertaking, one must bear in mind that Gheorghiu-Dej had spent the war in a Romanian jail, whereas Pauker and Luca had spent it in Moscow. So at the beginning Pauker and Luca were Moscow's emissaries, while Gheorghiu-Dej was an unknown quantity to Stalin. Moreover, it was well known to the upper echelons of the party that nobody could gain control of the Romanian party without at least the approval, if not the active support, of Moscow. Thus, on the face of it, Gheorghiu-Dej's chances of getting the upper hand over Pauker and Luca must have appeared slim to the people around them. Yet, between 1949 and the end of 1951 Gheorghiu-Dej managed to do just that.

How did he do it? First, he patiently and painstakingly built up support among the party cadres. Next, he set out to win over the Soviets. This was not easy, but two circumstances helped. First, Iosif Chişinevschi, the watchdog of ideological orthodoxy, was also a Moscovite, and after a while became the Soviet party's main informer in Romania. Whereas Luca treated Chișinevschi as a despicable worm, Gheorghiu-Dej was generous in expressing his appreciation for Chișinevschi's important services to the party. As a result, the Soviets started getting less favorable information about Luca than about Gheorghiu-Dej. Second, the fact that Luca was responsible for the Sovroms, the joint Soviet-Romanian enterprises, helped Gheorghiu-Dej. Anybody who has ever run a joint enterprise knows that there are always differences of opinion among the partners. Any differences that arose in connection with the running of the Sovroms became disputes between Luca and the Soviet representatives. None of these disputes ever got out of hand, since nothing was further from Luca's intentions than to confront the Soviets or do anything that might have been perceived as harmful to them; nevertheless, disputes were unavoidable. Cumulatively, with the help of Chișinevschi's subtle and not-so-subtle interpretations, the Soviets came to see Luca as a comrade who sometimes put the narrow interests of his party or country ahead of those of the world proletariat and its representative, the Soviet Union.

If this growing conflict had been simply a contest between Gheorghiu-Dej and Luca, the former would have won hands down and much earlier than he actually did. But it was not that simple. The main complicating factor was that Ana Pauker, a Moscovite like Luca himself and internationally the best known leader of the party, would more often than not side with Luca. Worse for Gheorghiu-Dej, early on Pauker had Chișinevschi hanging to her coattails: nobody sang her hosannas more ardently than comrade Ioshka, as Chișinevschi was known in party circles. A further complication came from the fact that Georgescu, the fourth party secretary and minister of the interior, who also controlled one of the two secret services, usually sided with Pauker and therefore, by extension, with Luca. Thus Gheorghiu-Dej's first real coup occurred when he managed to drive a wedge between Pauker and Chișinevschi and to draw the latter into his camp. Soon after that, Gheorghiu-Dej managed to take control of the other secret service, circumventing Georgescu. By 1951, Chișinevski had managed to feed the Russians enough negative information on Luca to make him suspect in their eyes. From then on it was just a matter of patiently preparing the ground and working out the details of the "right-wing deviation" that Luca was to be accused of in the spring of 1952, and in which Pauker and Georgescu were also to be implicated. By that time the Soviets were not only alienated from Luca but also ready to accept, based on the convincing if circumstantial evidence furnished by comrade Ioshka, the regrettable complicity of Pauker and Georgescu: a real *tour de force* for the odd couple, Gheorghe Gheorghiu-Dej and Ioshka Chişinevschi. All of this has to be placed in the context of the general atmosphere of suspicion, bordering on paranoia, that Stalin and his agents were fomenting in all the satellite countries after the break with Yugoslavia and the Rajk trial in Hungary. In fact, the pressure to find deviationists and enemies of the party came to a large extent from the Soviets; the function of the local leadership was mainly to fill in the roles and identify the culprits.

Around mid-1950 the two Romanian secret services were merged into one, the Securitate, and placed under the control of the Ministry of the Interior. This seemed to be a setback for Gheorghiu-Dej, since it put security matters squarely in the hands of Georgescu. There is no evidence, however, that it was meant as a move against him. It was probably demanded by the Soviets, to make the Romanian organizational structure more closely resemble the Soviet one. Anyway, Gheorghiu-Dej countered by taking direct responsibility, as secretary general of the party, for all political trials, and having the head of Securitate, General Pintilie (Pantyusha) Bodnarenko, report to him directly on all important matters. As a result, although Georgescu was Bodnarenko's administrative boss, his party boss was Gheorghiu-Dej.

In January 1952 the party and the Council of Ministers ordered a drastic monetary reform in order to stabilize the Romanian currency. It restricted everybody to exchanging only small sums of money, and all cash savings and bank deposits were practically confiscated. While the measure was a heavy blow for anyone who had savings, it did stabilize prices and, of course, helped to balance the budget. Although the underlying principles and general thrust of the currency reform were decided by the party and the government, the Ministry of Finance was in charge of implementing it, and later certain details of the execution were presented as attempts to help the kulaks and were held against Luca and his deputies, among them Sanyi.

Sanyi was not a talkative man and he had lived for many years in an atmosphere of secrecy, where nobody was supposed to know more than he needed to function effectively. For this reason, he generally refrained from discussing his work with me. Yet he occasionally described certain episodes, mainly after mid-1951. At the time neither he nor I could see the issues and the forces at work as clearly as they now appear in hindsight; even so, as the storm was gathering toward the end of 1951, Sanyi once told me that he could have saved his skin by accepting an indirect overture from Gheorghiu-Dej—he had only to agree to turn against Luca, but he was unwilling to do this. In this he was, of course, an exception. Most of the people in the entourage of Luca and Pauker became turncoats. The most spectacular turnaround was the stab in the back that Anuţa Toma gave to Ana Pauker by joining Chişinevschi in early 1952 and attacking "from within the ranks" the Grand Old Lady she had until then worshiped like a deity.

Before the campaign against the "right-wing deviation" was started, neither Sanyi nor I expected to be arrested. Nevertheless, we discussed what happened when somebody was suspected of wrongdoing and arrested for investigation. We believed that, although false accusations and erroneous arrests might occur, in the end the truth would always come out. We knew that it could take a long time for that to happen: There was the case of Mihai Levente, a member of the communist underground during the war and a state secretary at one of the ministries in the postwar years, who was arrested in 1949 under suspicion of being an enemy agent. He was found innocent and was freed after two years. Sanyi also told me that, for communists mistakenly arrested, the period of investigation was usually on the order of two years. But could an innocent person be convicted? We both felt that the Rajk trial was genuine, but in 1950 or 1951, there was the case of Traicho Kostov, the general secretary of the Bulgarian Communist Party, tried in Sofia for Trotskyism, Titoism, and collaboration with the Western espionage services. Kostov, according to the act of indictment, had confessed to all these crimes and given detailed accounts of how he carried them out. Numerous witnesses were brought forward who supported the accusations in minute detail. But at the peak of the trial, when Kostov himself was questioned, he retracted his earlier depositions and denied everything. The communist press did not tell the truth about what transpired at the trial, and the live radio transmission of the trial was immediately interrupted when Kostov began his denials; nevertheless, the two or three minutes that one could hear were enough to convey the gist of what had happened. Based on this, we both concluded that Kostov was probably being tried on trumped-up charges.

There was also the case of Pătrăşcanu, the Romanian party leader arrested in 1948. There had been no trial yet, but in November 1949 Gheorghiu-Dej had denounced him at a Cominform meeting as an imperialist agent. Everybody was awaiting the consequences in the form of a public trial, but no such thing had yet taken place. In the spring of 1951 Emil Calmanovici, a prominent Jewish civil engineer who had worked during the war with the underground Communist Party and had donated all of his assets to the party, was arrested. His brother-in-law, Mirel Costea, a well-known member of the Personnel (Cadres) Section of the party's Central Committee, shot himself a week or two later. These were alarming events, but since the Pătrăşcanu affair was still under investigation, we could not draw any firm conclusions.

I heard from Sanyi that one of the most effective methods for interrogating communists was to appeal to their Party loyalty, to their communist conscience, and to ask them to examine their acts self-critically. We agreed that such an appeal was completely misplaced, and that once a communist found himself under arrest and investigation by the Securitate, he had every right to defend himself. The place for self-criticism was the party meeting, not the prison cell or torture chamber.

My description of these events and circumstances raises a basic question: In view of the abuses of power that were taking place, of the infighting in the party and the government, and the general lack of principles in the party leadership, how could Sanyi and I still keep our "faith," our communist conviction? For the fact is that we both did at the time. This is not easy to explain, yet it is a rather widespread phenomenon. A genuine, deep ideological conviction is not easily overturned by facts of life that seem to contradict it. This is doubly true of a conviction or worldview that one has absorbed as a young man and for which one has sacrificed his freedom and risked his life. Besides, Marxism as a general philosophy and worldview is one thing; attempts at its practical implementation are another. Communism as the future of mankind is not necessarily the same as its primitive implementation in a backward society with an underdeveloped industry and working class. Also, as a practical matter, I was to a large extent shielded from the truth concerning the Soviet Union, about which I entertained many illusions based mainly on the extraordinary performance of the Red Army and the Soviet people during World War II. I attributed most of the anomalies around me to weaknesses in the Romanian party. After all, Romania had not had a revolution and its Communist Party had very weak traditions. Romanian communism was essentially an imported commodity. It took a long time before I was able to see beyond these mental subterfuges and rethink the very basic issues of marxism, communism, and social justice versus freedom and democracy. I was not yet ripe for such a basic re-evaluation of what was the main axis of my spiritual life at the time of these events.

At the beginning of March 1952 Vasile Luca was accused of a right-wing deviation, excluded from the politburo and the Central Committee of the party, and relieved of his position as finance minister. Shortly after that, Teohari Georgescu and Ana Pauker were expelled from the polit-buro and relieved of their government positions. The three of them—Luca, Georgescu, and Pauker—were branded as the right-wing deviationist group within the party. A new minister of the interior was appointed in the person of Alexandru Drăghici. The alleged right-wing deviation con-sisted of favoring the class enemy and trying to slow down the party's drive to transform Romanian society and lead it toward socialism. The main charges were directed at Luca, who allegedly had favored the well-to-do strata of the peasantry by keeping their taxes low; had attempted to slow down the collectivization of agriculture; had been opposed to the currency reform; and in its execution had again favored the well-to-do strata of the population. These accusations were based on distortions of facts, slanted interpretations, and sometimes the exaggeration of genuine mistakes. The truth is that, while there had been many disagreements between the leaders about specific measures and tactical moves, these were not of the "left or right" type and were not about principles. In fact, Luca had no specific policy of his own in opposition to that of the party. Georgescu and Pauker were accused of having supported Luca's right-wing policies. The truth in this allegation was limited to the fact that the two disagreed with the finding of a deviation and were opposed to the isolation and condemnation of Luca.

Simultaneously with Luca's expulsion, Sanyi became the object of a party investigation. We continued to meet almost daily. I had been Sanyi's friend for a decade, having worked under his direction in the wartime underground. It was well known that we were close, and we saw no reason to try to hide this fact. Nor did I feel any inclination to distance myself outwardly from Sanyi, as was the general habit in party circles. As soon as the first communiqué about Luca appeared in the press, Sanyi became a pariah: nobody except me (and of course, his wife) would talk to him. At our meetings, Sanyi complained that the "party investigation" that he was undergoing was absolutely hostile, and lacked any objectivity. The atmosphere was such that he expected to be arrested. At the end of March, during a dinner at our house, Sanyi was urgently summoned by telephone to the party Central Committee. That is where he was arrested, as I found out the next day from Magda, who told me that Sanyi had not returned home. Three months later Magda was also arrested. In August Luca was arrested.

I spent the spring in an increasingly hostile atmosphere at the Ministry of Foreign Affairs. In June I was dismissed from my job amidst accusations that I was a hostile element who had infiltrated the Communist Party and had managed to camouflage himself as an allegedly useful technical expert. At a party meeting held at the ministry in mid-June to discuss the right-wing deviation, I was attacked as one of its local incarnations. This was a ritual like the *auto-da-fé* from the days of the Inquisition. It was a public political execution. Everybody was supposed to "criticize" (that is, viciously attack) the target of the meeting, and whoever refused to play by the rules had to suffer the consequences. I had but one day to warn a couple of my friends not to foolishly try to defend me, since at that stage it would have been useless to me and very dangerous for them. I explicitly remember having talked to my directorate colleague Bojan in this sense. Subsequently, I judged the speeches at the meeting as follows: whoever regurgitated the official accusations without changing the wording, was OK, but I considered hostile those who tried to be original and concocted accusations of their own, based either on facts taken out of context and distorted, or on outright lies. And there were plenty of speeches of this latter type. One of them was that of Bazil Şerban, my deputy. He had performed some deeds of courage in his life—fighting in the Spanish civil war, joining the French resistance—and he still carried some bullets in his body when I met him. But at that meeting his courage completely evaporated, seemingly squeezed out by his preoccupation with making sure that he would be the one to replace me as I was obviously being kicked out. He suddenly discovered the class enemy in me, and did his best to corroborate his discovery with alleged or distorted facts. I felt contempt and pity for his complete loss of dignity.

After being fired from my job, I was told that I would also have to move out of the house where I was living. We were shown a couple of alternative, much smaller apartments, and we were fortunate enough to find one that was not only acceptable but definitely pleasant. True, it was very small: a living room, a bedroom, a kitchen, and a bathroom. But it was a penthouse, on the top (fifth) floor of a very nice apartment building near Stalin Square, at Bulevardul Stalin number 72, overlooking the Stalin Park, and it had two large balconies. Edith took Anna to Cluj and left her with Klara and Alexander for the summer; then she returned to Bucharest and we moved into the new apartment. After a few weeks without a job, I was given some routine work at a company, where I started on August 1. Edith and I discussed the possibility that I might be arrested, since I was close to Sanyi, and his wife had also been arrested. I wanted Edith to be prepared for a long wait, so I mentioned the case of Levente as an example of a comrade arrested, held for two years, then found innocent, and released. At that time I still had a pistol which I had acquired while in Cluj and brought with me when I moved to Bucharest. I had not applied for a permit and I thought it prudent to dispose of it. I asked Edith to take it in her purse and drop it into the nearby lake when there was nobody around, which she did.

On the night of August 12–13, around two o'clock, our doorbell rang persistently. I got up, and heard knocking on the door: "Open, it is the militia!" The militia was the name of the police, but this was not the police. Three plainclothes Securitate men were waiting outside and they had a search warrant. I let them in, upon which they asked me to open the back door, where there was a fourth Securitate man. They made a long, meticulous search and took everything written and every photograph in the house. They were not rude. On the table in the living room there was a picture of Anna, taken a couple of months earlier around her second birthday, in which she looked particularly charming. The head of the Securitate detail, a young man with a moustache, looked at the picture, asked where the child was, and upon my answer that she was with her grandparents, said to me, "How can you live without her? If I had such a child, I could not be without her for a day." I came to remember that remark a few times over the next couple of years. After about two hours, with the search completed, they showed me what they were going to take away and had me sign the list of items, saying, "We are done."

After I signed, the leader of the group turned to me and said, as if it were an afterthought, "Would you please put on your clothes? You are going to come with us for a little while." In English the sentence sounds awkward; in Romanian it is *Veniți puțin cu noi*, equivalent to the French *Vous venez un peu avec nous*. It was a hot August night, but I put on my warmest suit, a brown one made from English wool. The man advised me to also take along a sweater. "What about pajamas?" said Edith. "He won't need those," the man replied, upon which I saw Edith's face turn even darker than it had been. She was close to crying, and I would have liked to lift her spirits. I soon had the opportunity: before taking me away, the leader of the group suggested that if I wanted to eat something before leaving I could do so. Upon which I turned to Edith and asked for the chocolate torte she had made a few days earlier. She brought it from the refrigerator and I ate two big slices, ostentatiously showing how much I enjoyed them. I saw her face visibly light up. I kissed her and said something to the effect "Don't worry. I will be back." Then we left.

It must have been around four or four-thirty in the morning. We took the elevator down. I was put into the back seat of a car between two of the men who arrested me, and one of them covered my eyes with what I will call for lack of a better term a metal blindfold, a pair of eyeglasses with tin in place of the glass and tin on both sides, so that I could not see where I was being taken. We drove for a while, and I had the impression that the car was going in circles. Then we stopped. I was taken out of the car and into the basement of a house; the blindfold was taken off and I was told to sit down on the floor of the dark corridor where I found myself. I spent the rest of the night there. In the morning I was again blindfolded and led to a car. This time I was driven for perhaps forty minutes, and because of the blindfold, again had no inkling of where I was being taken. Finally we arrived at the place where I was going to spend quite some time. The car stopped; I could hear a heavy gate opening, then closing behind us. As I was to learn later—much later—I had arrived at the infamous interrogation center called Malmezon. The name was derived from Malmaison, the private mansion of Napoleon Bonaparte and Josephine de Beauharnais near Paris.

From the top echelons of the society in which I had been living, at the age of thirty I now fell to the darkest bottom of the sea of life.

CHAPTER 9

. . .

The Malmezon I

When I was taken out of the car on the morning of August 13, 1952, still blindfolded, I was in the prison courtyard. Neither then, nor later during my long stay at the Malmezon, did I ever actually see the courtyard. I was led into a building and my blindfold was taken off. I was standing in a registration office, where my name was entered into a book. My wristwatch, wallet, pen, telephone book, belt, and shoelaces were taken away, as were the contents of each of my pockets except for a handkerchief. I was blindfolded again, then led through a long corridor into a cell, where the blindfold was removed and I was left by myself.

The cell was about eight by fourteen feet, with a bunk, a small table (about two by two-and-a-half feet), and a chair, all wooden. There was a straw mattress on the bunk and a tin drinking cup on the table. The door, made of heavy wood reinforced with steel, was built into one of the shorter walls. It had a window of metal blinds, about four inches by twelve inches in size, that could be opened only from the outside and was used for handing in food or other small objects without opening the door. There was a peephole above the metal window, about one-half an inch in diameter, covered on the outside with a metal lid. High above the door was a narrow glass window; this too could be opened only from the outside. As the window faced the corridor, which in turn had windows to the outside, it let through some daylight on bright days, although neither the source of light nor any part of the sky itself could be seen from the cell. The floor of the cell was made of some stony material; the walls were of brick. In the ceiling there was an electric light that was permanently on, day and night.

The prison rules were as follows. You were allowed to lie on the bunk or sleep between ten o'clock at night and five o'clock in the morning. The beginning and ending of bedtime were signaled by loud knocks on the door from a guard who went from cell to cell. Two or three minutes after the wake-up knock the guard would check through the peepholes to see if everybody had gotten up, and for those who had not there was trouble of various sorts. During waking hours it was strictly forbidden to lie down. Food was served three times a day through the window with metal blinds. Breakfast was a black liquid that looked like but did not taste like coffee (probably chicory) and a piece of bread (about half a pound) which was to last for the whole day. At noon there was a barley or gruel soup with some vegetables in it and, once or twice a week, some traces of meat. In the evening, there was soup again. The meals were served in tin containers; the coffee was poured into each prisoner's tin cup. The soup came with a metal spoon, which was taken back along with the tin dish after each meal. This was the food regime when I arrived in August 1952, but in 1953 it became worse: the noon meal was eliminated and the evening meal was served earlier. This twice-a-day food regime was in force for about a year, after which the earlier three-times-a-day regime was reinstated.

Three times a day, in the morning, after lunch, and after dinner, you were blindfolded and taken to the toilet, a hole in the concrete floor that was flushed with water. There you had to do your business with the door open, under the watchful eye of the guard, in at most three minutes. One day, I first stood over the hole and urinated, then discovered that I also needed to defecate. When I turned around, let down my pants, and squatted over the hole, the guard raised hell: "Those two things are to be done together!" You were given one sheet of toilet paper a day. Once a week you were taken to a shower.

There were no reading materials, and no paper and pencil except when an interrogator explicitly ordered them for writing an autobiographical supplement. In such cases the sheets were numbered and you had to return them all, whether used or not. It was strictly forbidden to speak aloud, to sing and play games, to knock on the wall, or to attempt in any other way to communicate with another cell, not to mention the outside world. You were being continuously being watched, day and night. The long corridor in front of the row of cells was covered with a running carpet, and the guard on duty wore slippers so that he could not be heard when he approached the cell to look through the peephole. The frequency with which the guards looked into your cell varied from once every two minutes to once every seven or eight minutes. If you were caught with your eyes closed, even though you were sitting, not lying down, the guard would bang on the door to wake you up. If this happened repeatedly, you would be punished by having to stand for an hour or by being beaten. At night, the lights would stay on, and you were not allowed to cover your eyes, nor to put your hands under the blanket. The guard had to be able to see your eyes and hands through the peephole throughout the night. These were precautions against suicide attempts, mainly through cutting your veins—although, of course, you had nothing to cut them with. The guards were not permitted to conduct any conversation with you; furthermore, no guard was allowed to open the door of a cell by himself: if the need arose, he had to call for a second guard to be present when the door was opened. All this made it impossible to gain influence over a guard in order to use him to establish contact with the outside world or with other prisoners. The isolation of the prisoner was complete.

These conditions were pretty harsh, but they were nothing when compared to the nightmare of the interrogations that went on for weeks at a time. Every evening before bedtime, for almost four weeks after my arrest, I was taken to interrogation and not returned to my cell until an hour before wake-up time. After half an hour or, at best, an hour of sleep, I was forced to get up and walk or sit. Whenever my eyes closed, the banging on the door would wake me up, hour after hour, day after day. During the first two or three days I was given paper and pencil to write my autobiography in as much detail as I could remember. When I finished, the pencil and every sheet of paper were taken away, and I just had to stay awake.

The first interrogation started on the day after my arrest. The door of my cell was opened, and a guard stepped in and told me to get up. Then he put the blindfold over my eyes and took me to an office in another part of the building. Being led blindfolded to the interrogation room and from there back to my cell was a nightmarish experience in itself, one that I was to go through hundreds of times. The guard, firmly gripping my arm, would push me forward at a considerable speed. When we came to some stairs, there would be a brief warning ("up" or "down") and the grip would become a little firmer. Nevertheless, I would stumble from time to time, sometimes falling down. I would then be lifted with my blindfold still on, and the march would continue. When the guard reached the intersection of two corridors, he would stop and give a warning signal to the guard on duty in the other corridor, to inform him that he was approaching and that no one else should enter the corridor from the other end or open a door until he and his prisoner had passed. The warning signal was a snap of the thumb with the middle finger. I heard this sound so many times and got so used to it that fifteen years later, when I saw the film *Doctor Zhivago* and heard Evgraf, Zhivago's commissar brother, snap his fingers, the sound sent a chill down my spine. This confirmed what I had learned before, namely that the Securitate's prisons were copied exactly from the Lubyanka and other NKVD prisons, as was the rest of the system, including the methods of interrogation. The snap of the fingers as a means of communication was a Soviet invention.

In the interrogation room my blindfold was taken off, the guard left, and I found myself facing a uniformed Securitate lieutenant. He was young, tall, and hostile. He did not give his name, neither then nor later. His first question was why was I here. When I said that I had no idea and was hoping to learn the answer from him, he became angry, as though I had said something insolent. He informed me that I was where I was in order to answer questions, not to ask them. "I ask the questions and you answer them, not the other way around!" he shouted, then asked again: "What do you think? Why were you arrested?" Upon my repeated assertion that I did not know, he kept insisting that even if I did not know for sure, I must have *some* idea, I must have assumed *something*— so what was it? I said that my arrest was obviously a mistake; I assumed that I was suspected of something, but had no idea of what. "The party does not make mistakes," he said, "and your arrest has been ordered by the party."

The interrogator lectured me about the basic choice that I was facing, which he put roughly in these terms: After long concealment on my part, the party had finally come across detailed information about my hostile and dangerous activities; this was the circumstance which led to my arrest. My choice lay between adopting an attitude hostile to the party and to the Securitate, which was in charge of executing its policies, as I seemed inclined to do; or coming forward with a sincere confession and trying to help the party clean up the mess that my accomplices and I had created. The first road led to perdition—the party knew how to deal with its enemies: it destroyed them. The second road held the promise of lenient treatment and possible ultimate rehabilitation. He told me that after being led back to my cell I would receive paper and pencil, which I should use to write an exhaustive autobiography, describing in full detail all my activities and not leaving out anything important. This autobiography would be a major test of my sincerity.

Back in my cell, I was given a pencil and a stack of paper whose sheets were numbered, and I started writing. I described in detail how I got into the movement, with whom I had worked, my activities during the war, my time in hiding, my arrest in August 1944 and my treatment and behavior at the DEF, my fourteen-year sentence, my time spent in prison, my escape and liberation. I then described my activities in Cluj after the war, my mission to London, my expulsion and return to Bucharest, and my work in the Foreign Ministry.

It was only after this that my true interrogation started. Everything that I wrote was questioned, subjected to disbelief. I was punished for my alleged lack of sincerity with continuous nighttime interrogations, without being allowed to sleep during the day. In the interrogation room I was kept standing, with my arms raised in a vertical position, until I collapsed. Whenever I lowered my arms, I would be hit or kicked. Once, when I was standing with my arms raised, the interrogator looked at a report which he said contained the truth about my activities, not the fairy tales that I was trying to sell him. Then he put it down and left the room. When that happened, I lowered my arms and stepped toward the desk in an attempt to see what was in the "report." But the thing turned out to be a trap, for as soon as I moved toward the desk, the interrogator re-entered the room, barked at me wildly, and hit the back of my neck with a karate chop that almost made me pass out. While still in pain, I realized what the trap meant. He needed an excuse for beating me and apparently was not supposed to do it as a routine matter, at least not at that stage. However, he was allowed to keep me under constant nightly interrogation, leaving me less than an hour for sleep, for a period of several weeks. I suffered more from this than from the pain caused by the occasional beatings. Of course, systematic beatings of the kind I had been administered at the DEF would have been another matter.

The form of interrogation practiced at the Securitate was for the interrogator to write down in his own handwriting his questions and the prisoner's answers, and at the end of the day (or rather the night) to have the prisoner sign every sheet. At the beginning, my interrogator tried to transcribe my answers rather liberally, making them more to his taste than to mine, but after I had several times refused to sign the sheets he wrote, forcing him to rewrite them, he understood that I would not sign anything that differed from what I had said, no matter how tired or sleepy I was.

Everything that had happened in my life was questioned. My underground activity, for example, was a fairy tale I had invented to create credentials for myself in the party. I pointed to people who could confirm every single act that I had described. Then, asked the officer, how did I explain that, when every active communist in Cluj was arrested in the fall of 1943, I was not? I explained that I had gone into hiding on October 1, 1943, because at that time I had reached the age for military service and had to show up at an enrollment center, and that none of those arrested knew my hiding place. I went into hiding "just in time," the interrogator said. A month later, he said, I lost contact with my party connection (Sanyi Jakab), but according to my story, after a few weeks I managed to reestablish the contact by accidentally meeting him one evening on the street. This was at a time when both of us were in hiding and went out only when we needed to, in a town of more than one hundred thousand people. What did I take the interrogator for, in assuming he would believe such an absurdity? Wasn't that ridiculous? Since it had indeed been a most improbable event, there was little I could say in defense of my story besides the fact that it was true. My hope, though, was that when they interrogated Sanyi about this episode, he would say the same thing, which would be at least a confirmation of sorts.

Further, the interrogator questioned my behavior at the DEF. My claim of not having betrayed anybody under the wild beatings that broke so many others was not credible. "You are not such a tough guy," he said. "We know that working-class people who grow up in hardship and are used to suffering from childhood do indeed sometimes manage to behave like heroes. But *you*, with your middle-class background?" All I could say was that most of the people who worked with me and whom the DEF was trying to find through me survived the war and could be interrogated: Mayer Hirsch (who after the war had changed his name to

Tibor Hida), György Havas, Misi Schnittländer (who later became Sava), Galambos. None of them was arrested, nor was anybody else through me. As this issue came up many times and I was sleepless and irritated, on one occasion I finally said, "Try me if you don't believe me."

"Do you mean you want us to beat you like the DEF did?"

"Yes," I said, "if that's what you need to believe me." They did not do that—they used different methods, at least in my case.

The next item in my life's story that aroused incredulity was my escape from the transport evacuating the Komárom prison. "Thousands of people were shot throughout the German-occupied territories for trying to escape from similar marches, but you claim to have been an exception. They just forgot to shoot you—right?" All I could say was that I was not alone, that my comrade Fekete who escaped with me was alive and well in Budapest, and the story could be checked with him for all its details. Remarks like this would always send the interrogator into new outbursts of rage. Who was I to teach them what to check and whom to ask? If it were up to me, they would have to stop the investigation and start running after alleged witnesses to check all the fairy tales that I was inventing—an army of investigators would not be enough for that. They knew better what to do. They would find out the truth from *me*, even if they had to make sure that my life became hell before I gave them what they needed. "The time will come when you will sign anything we put in front of you without even reading it," my interrogator assured me.

Soon the interrogation turned to Sanyi Jakab. My close connection with him, especially during the wartime period for which the Securitate lacked witnesses, must have been the main reason for my arrest. "Tell us everything about your relations with this enemy of the people" I said that Sanyi was my best friend, that he was my party connection during the 1942–44 period, and that we remained friends after the war. What did we discuss? Many things; current events, things that happened in our lives. Did I realize in what company I was placing myself when I spoke of Jakab as my friend? Hadn't I read the party materials according to which he was an enemy of the people? Did I dare question the wisdom of the party, the judgment of our experienced leaders? I said I wasn't questioning anybody's judgment; all I could say was that in my presence Jakab had always behaved like a good revolutionary, and if he had indeed been an enemy and a traitor, he had managed to hide his true face masterfully, because I never observed any behavior like that.

This again sent my interrogator into a rage. How did I explain the fact that in 1941, when all the party leaders were arrested, Jakab, who was one of them, escaped? I knew a little bit about this, and I could explain it. The party leaders were warned that arrests had started, and Jakab went into hiding the minute he learned the news. Others, like Hillel Kohn, decided to go into hiding but first went home to say goodbye to their families, upon which they were of course arrested. Besides, Jakab was not the only one to escape arrest, others included Béla Józsa and Ilona Hovány. How did I explain the fact that in 1943 he again escaped arrest? Well, none of those arrested knew where he was hiding, and he did not go to any appointments after the arrests started. Finally, how did I explain the fact that of all the leading party activists in Northern Transylvania, Jakab was the only one who managed to avoid being arrested till the very end? Beyond the explanations I had given for 1941 and 1943, I said, he could have been arrested in the wake of my arrest in 1944, had I given away our meeting place and time, but I had not, and nobody else who was in contact with him at the time was under arrest. What did I know about Jakab's sabotage at the Ministry of Finance? I knew nothing about that; we did not usually discuss his work.

Changing his tone, the interrogator then adopted a different attitude. Didn't I realize what a dangerous game I was getting into? There was incontrovertible evidence that Jakab worked for the Gestapo during the war. Maybe I did not know it at the time, but now that this fact had been revealed to me, rather than trying to whitewash him, I should make a serious effort to recall elements of his behavior or episodes in our work that would corroborate the facts known to the party. If I were to help the party in this fashion, that would certainly influence my own situation. He did not want an immediate answer, but told me to think it over. I answered that there was nothing for me to think over, that I never saw any sign of Jakab being anything but a revolutionary. If the Securitate had evidence to the contrary, that was fine; but I saw no way in which I could support that evidence. The interrogator launched again into one of his long diatribes of assorted threats, and assured me that they would make me pay the price of my stubbornness.

At some point I was also questioned about my conversation with Dr. Farchi after he returned from North Korea. Who gave me the task of interrogating Farchi, I was asked, and to whom did I report our conversation? I explained that I had the conversation with Dr. Farchi on my

own initiative, and did not report on it to anyone. Why was I interested
in North Korea? Because it was the most burning issue of the period
from 1950 to 1952, I answered. But, said the interrogator, the precise
questions I had asked Farchi came directly from an espionage repertoire.
I did not know about that. So why, he asked, was I taking him for a fool?
Didn't I realize that I was caught red-handed? What sense did it make
to keep denying the obvious once I had been caught? And so on, and so
on. Did I tell my wife what Farchi said about North Korea? No, I did not.
Did I tell any friends, in particular Sanyi Jakab? No, I did not (in fact I
may have told him about the more interesting parts of Farchi's story, but
I thought my poor friend had enough trouble without this).

My interrogation was conducted every night by the same young,
ambitious, hostile investigator. But several times during the sessions a
senior Securitate officer, a major or colonel in his late forties or early
fifties, came into the room and stayed for a couple of hours, though
never for a whole session. He rarely spoke, and when he did, it was to
advise me in a fatherly tone to stop my ill-considered, hostile behavior
and start cooperating with the investigation in my own best interests, as
that was the only attitude that offered me the hope of some way out of
my desperate situation. Every time I heard this argument either from
him, or from others before and after him I said essentially the same thing
in different forms: that I was willing to fully cooperate in establishing the
truth, and for that purpose I was giving the most detailed information I
could, which unfortunately was not being followed up. I kept naming
witnesses, I said, who could testify to what I was saying, but my interrogator, instead of questioning the witnesses and checking on the facts
that I was stating, kept calling me a liar and pressing me to make false
declarations. This I refused to do. I do not remember all the threats that
were thrown at me and the exact circumstances under which they were
made. But it was repeatedly explained to me that the place where I found
myself had only two exits: one to the firing squad and from there to a
mass grave in the cemetery, the other to the courthouse for a trial followed by a jail sentence whose length, and the kind of prison where it
was to be served, depended entirely on my attitude.

After twenty-five to twenty-seven days with almost no sleep at night,
I was in pretty bad shape: I was shaking most of the time and felt cold
in spite of the heat outside. When it came to eating I felt like vomiting,
but I still forced myself to swallow the food and managed to keep it

down. I remembered that on the second day after my arrest, when I was taken to the toilet, we were stopped at the end of the corridor to let another guard pass with his prisoner. The blindfold on my eyes was not very tight and through the lower left corner I could see the carpet on which we were standing. As the other guard and his prisoner passed, I raised my head as much as I could without being observed. I could, of course, not see the prisoner's face, but I could see the lower end of a jacket he was wearing. I shuddered: the temperature was in the upper nineties, I had nothing over my shirt and still felt hot as hell, yet this prisoner felt cold enough to put on his jacket. I knew from my experience at the DEF and in prison that prolonged torture, coupled with poor food and poor sleep, makes you prone to feel cold. Still, I could not have imagined that within less than a month I would find myself in the same state.

At that point my interrogation suddenly stopped. Bedtime found me in my cell for the first time in almost a month, and boy, did I ever sleep until five o'clock in the morning! The next day passed uneventfully, although I was almost as sleepy during the day as before; the evening passed without my being taken to interrogation, and I had a second night of perfect sleep. By the third day I felt a lot better, and on the morning of the fourth or fifth day, when things seemed almost normal, I started doing my usual morning exercises. Although there was no rule forbidding this, I somehow tried to avoid being seen by the guard. In a few days it turned out my instinct was sound: apparently the guard saw me exercising once and reported the fact, as he was supposed to report everything he noticed about every prisoner.

So I was taken again to the interrogation room, where I faced the same officer who had completed my interrogation a week or ten days earlier. He addressed me with irony in his voice: "I hear you are exercising. Trying to keep your morale high? Well, listen: I finished your interrogation because we have concluded that you are not yet ripe to be questioned. We have room here to keep you, and time to wait for as long as it takes to make you change your mind. In the meantime your wife, who was informed about the true face of the monster she had married, has started divorce proceedings which the court will grant automatically. Your child will be raised with the help of the state in the right spirit, and will reject her traitor father as soon as she's old enough to understand the situation. As for you, you may rot here to the end of your days if you so choose. We have no time to waste on you; we have more urgent things to do. If you ever change your mind, just tell the guard, and then, if we have time, we will talk to you." With that he called the guard and sent me back to my cell.

The things my interrogator said sounded terrible, but by that time I had developed a healthy reflex of automatically rejecting everything the interrogator said as false and meant to mislead me. So I did not believe a word of what he said about Edith. That Edith should divorce me now, when I was in trouble, was inconceivable to me. That was not like her. Perhaps five years from now, if she realized that I was hopelessly doomed, she would ultimately decide to start a new life for herself and our child. But certainly not now, not today or tomorrow. As to the rest of the sermon, about the Securitate having time to wait for me to change my mind, I knew that to be true to a large extent; but there was nothing I could do about it. So I just tried to put myself in the state of mind of having to endure for a very long time, probably years. But I somehow had the firm conviction that if I did not give in and did not provide them with ammunition by admitting or inventing things I had not done—in other words, if I resisted the pressure and stuck to the truth—then sooner or later (probably later rather than sooner) they would simply have to let me go. I was thirty years old when this calamity fell upon me. I felt young and strong; my conscience was clear and my morale was high. The main thing, I kept telling myself, was not to let them crush my spirit. And I had hopes for the long run, because I believed that if they did not break me, there was nothing they could do to me. In light of what I subsequently learned, this belief was naive. Things could easily have taken another turn, and I could have been dragged off to trial, sentenced on the basis of other people's depositions, and shot. Or I could simply have been killed without a trial, as happened to others. Moreover, this is what most likely would have happened had it not been for the death of the Father of All Peoples in 1953. But my naïve belief certainly helped me to keep my morale, and in that sense it may have saved my life.

During the weeks that followed I tried to find ways to cope with solitary confinement. I decided that I needed to put my body and brain to work. For my body, I did physical exercise in the morning for about fifteen minutes, and took long walks in my short cell every few hours. These walks became feasible only when I realized that by choosing the right length of step, so that I took an odd number of steps between the two ends of the cell, I could alternate between right turns and left turns.

Prior to that, when I was taking four steps in one direction, turning, taking four steps in the other direction, turning again, and so on, I would get dizzy after a few minutes, because I was always turning in the same direction. The only way to turn in alternating directions was to make the walk between the walls either three or five steps long. I did both; that is, I took three-step walks with bigger steps and five-step walks with smaller steps, but avoided the four-step walks completely.

As to my brain, I tried to devise various mental exercises. Every morning I went through a number of sessions in which I tried to remember everything that I had ever learned. I soon discovered that if I systematically concentrated upon a subject for a while, many things that I did not remember at first would come back upon a second, third, or eleventh try. I would hold a session on physics, for example, which was rather poor at first, with huge gaps. As I tried to fill in the gaps, things would gradually fall into place and after a while my physics session became much richer. I held mathematics sessions in which I tried to reproduce techniques I had learned and to formulate and solve problems—all this took place in my head, of course, since there was nothing to write with or to write on. I developed a feel for time—the only "clock" available was the rattle of dishes that marked the approach of the midday and evening meals, although my stomach soon became an equally reliable clock—and I divided the time between meals into three or four sessions on different subjects. A variety of subjects was necessary to avoid becoming very tired. I held literature sessions, in which I mentally recounted novels in as much detail as I was able to remember. I tried to remember—not with much success—poems that I had once liked. I had language sessions, in which I would conduct conversations in English, Russian, French, or German. Many words that I could not remember at first came to me upon repeated trials.

Two or three times a week I "went to the opera" or to a concert. Going to the opera meant concentrating first on the overture, then trying to reconstruct act 1, act 2, and so on. This musical part of my program was not meant just as an exercise of memory, but also as a kind of entertainment. Upon trying to recreate Beethoven's Ninth Symphony, for instance, I relived the concert where I had first heard it (from a record player) and got quite a pleasant evening out of it. I was able to reproduce several operas and symphonies to a substantial degree, although never, of course, completely; from others I managed to reconstruct only small fragments.

I discovered that if I "went to" Gounod's *Faust* (my favorite opera) on Monday, and it was "on" again the following week, the second "show" was often more complete than the first. Naturally, this effect of increased accuracy ceased after two or three repetitions.

I decided to try to play chess. Playing any kind of game was strictly forbidden, so I had to do it unobserved. I saved a piece of toilet paper, pulled a straw from my mattress, dipped it in the morning coffee, and drew a rather pale chessboard, two inches by two, on the toilet paper. I sat in my chair facing the door with the peephole, placed the small table in front of me, and put my tin cup on the table. The chessboard went right in front of the cup, facing me. When the guard flipped the cover of the peephole and looked in, all he could see was me sitting peacefully at the table, plunged into my thoughts; his view of the chessboard was entirely blocked by the cup. This is why the chessboard had to be so small. I made tiny chessmen out of bread stolen from my precious daily portion; the black ones were bread mixed with coffee. A pawn was about a tenth of an inch (two or two and a half millimeters) in both height and diameter; the other pieces had the same diameter but were about one and one-half times as tall as the pawns. Chess is a game that requires two players, but one can play it against himself. After I started playing chess, I got so enthralled by the game that I had to make an effort to stop doing it all day long and get back to "work," doing my brain exercises.

It is hard to describe how tiny my chess set was. The guards conducted frequent, unexpected searches of the cells. These searches were extremely thorough. I underwent five searches while at the Malmezon, and not once was my chess set discovered. The chessboard I simply kept in my pocket as the toilet paper of which it was made; the lines I drew on it were pale enough to be missed unless somebody was looking carefully for precisely that kind of thing. The chessmen I kept in a handkerchief that was folded in the usual way. Once an inspecting officer picked up the handkerchief, held it by one of its corners, and shook it open to make sure there was nothing hidden inside. The pawns and pieces were so tiny that they were simply taken for crumbs. They fell to the ground, where some of them were inadvertently crushed under the boots of the inspecting officer. After the search was over, I remade the few pieces that had been destroyed and everything was "back to normal."

My cell was in a building that could not have been very far from some street or boulevard, I concluded after a while. In the early fall, when schools began everywhere, I occasionally heard the distant, barely discernible ring of a bell, followed by the sound of a group of children rushing into the schoolyard and starting their games. Everything was very distant and muffled, and I could not discern at once what I was hearing. Actually, the first time I managed to give it the right interpretation was when I realized that the noise was repeated after about an hour, meaning that a class was over and the next break period had begun. The acoustics varied from day to day, and the sounds disappeared later in the fall when the windows of the corridor were shut, except for short periods when they were opened for ventilation. Other signs of outside life that occasionally penetrated my solitude and stirred my emotions were screeches that could have come from a street car at a great distance, and a couple of times the song of marching soldiers, again from a great distance. The soldiers were singing a tune that was new to me and that seemed extraordinarily melodious. It gave me such intense pleasure—I could not make out the words, of course—that, although I heard it only for a few weeks in the fall of 1952, it became imprinted in my memory forever. Years later, when I sang the tune to Edith, she said she had heard the song and that part of its words read, "When Lenin is watching us from the heavens," which gave us a good laugh.

Some time in the late fall of 1952 I developed a urinary problem: I had to pass urine more often than the three daily rounds to the toilet. The way to address the guard about anything was to wait until he approached the cell and then knock on the door. The guard would then open the metal window of the door and ask what the prisoner wanted. To my first such request, the guard agreed, and after keeping me waiting for about ten minutes, blindfolded me and took me to the toilet. But when I kept asking for the same thing more often, the guards would sometimes go along and sometimes refuse. The refusals led to very painful situations; after a while I started banging on the door, upon which I was reprimanded and threatened with beating. Since I was unable to cope with the situation, I asked for a doctor and told the guard that from that moment, whenever he refused to take me to the toilet, I would urinate into a corner of the cell. The situation did not change, however, until I started actually doing this. At that point—after I was duly harangued for my filthiness and the mess I had made of my cell—a doctor finally arrived and examined me. He did not say anything but obviously I had a urinary tract infection, and he gave me some medication which cured it. I was given tools to clean my cell, and life returned to "normal."

Between my first interrogation, which ended with the first week of September, and the next one, which started in December or January, I spent about four months without talking to anybody except during the incident with the doctor and on two occasions when I was taken to an interrogation room. On the first occasion, in late September or early October, I found myself facing a new interrogator, another young uniformed officer, taller than the first one. He was much more polite than my first interrogator and, after asking a few introductory questions about my relations with Sanyi Jakab, he focused on my visit to Bucharest in June 1948, when I returned from London for two weeks, part of which I spent with the Jakabs. He wanted to know whether Jakab or his wife had asked me to take anything to the West when I returned to London. I said no, and he suggested that maybe I had forgotten because it was a small thing. Nevertheless, it was important for me to remember so that the facts could be clarified. I thought further, but could not remember anything. He then asked whether I knew that Magda had a sister in Paris, and I said of course I knew. Had Magda asked me to take something to her sister, a small present, a cigarette case? I then remembered that she had. Was it a gold cigarette case? Yes, it was. And what happened then? he asked. I gave the case to Magda's sister in Paris, I said, along with Magda's greetings and good wishes.

Officially it was illegal to take or send precious metals out of the country, and the gold cigarette case was made of a precious metal. But this was obviously a trivial violation of the law, one that every diplomat and every traveler was likely to commit, and I did not hold it in the least against Magda that she had not tried to hide it: after all, more was at stake here, and she probably wanted to prove her sincerity so she would be believed in more important matters than this. Nor did I have the slightest hesitation in admitting that I had taken the cigarette case to Magda's sister: I knew that this was not the kind of thing the Securitate wanted to indict me for. Next, the interrogator asked who else was present when Magda gave me the cigarette case to take to her sister. Nobody, as far as I could remember, I said. But the interrogator persisted: "Try to remember who else was present; it is important." I tried to remember whether Sanyi was present. I did not think so; according to my recollection my conversation with Magda had taken place during the day, when

Sanyi must have been at work. Next the interrogator asked, as if wanting to help me remember, whether the Jakabs had a maid. Yes, I said, they had a maid called Ági. Was Ági present when Magda gave me the cigarette case? Quite possibly, I said, since she came and went through the house while I was talking with Magda, and the doors were open. The interrogator tried to pin me down to a flat statement that Ági was present, but I genuinely did not remember and was unwilling to budge from that position. He was dissatisfied with this, but finally gave me the interrogation record to sign. It reproduced my statements more or less accurately, and I signed it. That was the end of the session and I was sent back to my cell.

Two or three days after this I was again taken to the same interrogator, who, to my surprise, confronted me with Magda Jakab. We were both asked who the other was, and we stated each other's names. Magda's face was very drawn, and I imagine mine looked pretty bad, too. She smiled at me with an expression that said, "Look what it has come to." The interrogator asked me to repeat what I had told him about the cigarette case. I repeated the statement that I had given him. He then asked Magda whether she now remembered it. I immediately understood from this why the interrogator had insisted that Ági was present in the room when Magda gave me the case: it was Ági, not Magda, from whom the Securitate had learned about it, and my confirmation of Ági's presence was necessary to make my statement concur with hers. I felt awful about having to assert something that Magda was obviously denying for one reason or another, quite possibly to protect me from the consequences of having broken the law by taking her present to her sister. And indeed, when she was asked for her reaction to my statement, Magda, obviously not wanting to lose her credibility by reversing herself, said she could not remember having given me a cigarette case for her sister. Upon which the interrogator addressed her rudely, yelling at her, "What kind of behavior is this? Aren't you ashamed of yourself? Your husband's best friend tells you that you asked him to take a small present to your sister, and you are shamelessly denying it! How do you expect us to believe you in more important matters, when you lie even about such a trivial thing?" Now I understood the purpose of the whole exercise: it was to humiliate Magda, to enmesh her into a contradiction with a friend, to make her feel both guilty and ashamed for having lied. I felt terrible for being drawn into this situation. I was feverishly trying to think of what

I could say to alleviate Magda's situation. Having admitted that I delivered the cigarette case, I could not credibly retract that admission. Such an attempt would have served no purpose.

Next, the interrogator turned toward me and asked emphatically, "Well, Mr. Balaş, what do you think about the behavior of your friend Magda?" The fact that he called me Mr. Balaş instead of "you rotten traitor" or some similar epithet made me feel doubly guilty for having allowed the Securitate to use me in this fashion. So in answer to his question I said the exact opposite of what he wanted me to say. It was quite possible, I argued, that Magda should have forgotten this episode. It happened four and a half years ago and had no significance. A cigarette case was a standard object for a small present. There was nothing special about it to remember; it did not even have a name inscribed on it, nor was I aware of any memorable aspect of our discussion. So, I said, I don't see the significance of her remembering or not remembering this episode. As I was talking, the interrogator's face turned red. I turned halfway toward Magda, in an attempt to convey to her the feeling that we were on the same side, that despite the confrontation and our differing memories of this trivial event, I was not in league with her torturers. The interrogator tried to interrupt me several times and finally yelled at me (which I liked a lot better than the "Mr. Balaş"). He got up from his chair, gave me the record of the confrontation to sign, and got rid of me as quickly as he could, calling the guard to take me back to my cell. There is one thing I should add to the account of this episode: Ági, the Jakabs' maid who, for whatever reason, told the Securitate about the cigarette case, later revealed a very decent attitude toward her former employers: she took in the Jakabs' five-year-old son and sheltered him for many months.

After these two sessions, I never saw the investigator who conducted them. He was apparently not assigned to my case and was only interested in organizing the confrontation with Magda in order to affect her behavior. Nor did I ever again see my first interrogator, who must have concluded my case inconclusively, without any "positive" findings, and therefore been removed from it. It was not until three or four months later, during the winter, that I was again taken to an interrogation room, this time to face a new interrogator. Unlike the other two, this man was not young: he must have been in his late forties. Also, from his demeanor and way of speaking, I judged that he must have been a former worker recruited from the factory floor to help the party enforce the dictatorship of the proletariat by strengthening the Securitate. He started by inquiring about my health, and asking how I felt after five months in jail. I told him that a few weeks earlier I had had a urinary infection that had been taken care of, and other than that, I was OK. Did I have any complaint? Only one, I said, namely, that I was kept in jail without any reason, that my case was not being investigated, that my depositions were not being checked out, and the persons who could confirm what I was saying were not being questioned. As a result, I was still languishing in my cell. He seemed taken aback by what I said. Why, he asked, did I think that my statements were not being checked out? Who told me that? I did not need to be told, I said. The fact is that if the Securitate had questioned the people whom I named, they would know by now that I was telling the truth and would have sent me home.

He then told me that he was my new interrogator; he had just been put in charge of my case and had studied my voluminous folder. He would do a full investigation from the beginning, he said, starting from scratch, and he advised me to cooperate. He assured me that the Securitate had more information on me than I could ever suspect, that they had questioned people named by me and others not named by me, and that they knew all about me. Their method, however, was not to tell me what they knew, but to let me tell them first; this way they would know whether I was sincere. As long as there was a single fact that they knew and that I was not telling, they had evidence that I had not yet made up my mind to come forward with the whole truth. In this contest between us, he said, time was on their side, because they were in no hurry, and could wait as long as it took for me to make up my mind.

He then asked me again how I felt and if I had any complaint about my conditions, about the food, the air, the cell, the sleeping hours. All these conditions could be changed if I wanted it: I could have a daily glass of milk; I could have a daily half-hour walk in the prison courtyard; I could have an hour of rest or sleep every day after lunch; finally, I could have books to read. It all depended on me. Why didn't I think it over and start to cooperate with the investigation? I thanked him for his good intentions, and explained that I had every reason to cooperate in establishing the truth about my activities, since I had nothing to hide and the sooner the truth was established, the earlier I would be released. But when I was asked to admit things I had not done, I obviously could not go along. My interrogator then countered that I had too simplistic a view of the truth. There was no such thing as a *unique* truth; there were *many* truths. Whose truth did I mean to support? That of the party or that of its enemies? I said I was sorry, but I remained a prisoner of my simplistic view of the truth: I knew of only one.

We then started going through my life in even more detail than in the first investigation. There was no hurry; there was much less yelling than in the previous interrogation; and I did not have to stand up for hours with arms raised. There were long sleepless nights, but usually I had three to four hours left for sleep, unlike the first time around. I was again asked the same questions I had answered in my first interrogation, but whenever I attempted to start my answer with "As I said when I was asked about this the first time," the officer became irritated and interrupted me with "I am not interested what you were asked before and what you answered. This is a new investigation and we are starting from scratch." In his irritation I detected apprehension about the fact that I remembered what I had said before. You apparently were not supposed to do that; you were supposed to be sufficiently confused by the continuous nightly interrogations and the lack of sleep to forget what you had or had not said. I quickly learned this rule of the game and stopped displaying any recollection of what I had said before, giving the same old answers as brand new ones.

None of the interrogations yielded any new results. The interrogator felt that he was left empty-handed after every session, and he did not hide his frustration at this. "You are making no effort to help our investigation," he said. "All you do is try to convince me, to convince us, of your way of looking at things. This will not get you anywhere." A number of times he tried to undermine my basic position. "You claim to be a communist," he said, "but how could you ever have been a communist? You just joined the party for some other reason. The Communist Party is the party of the working class. What do you have in common with the working class? How can you claim to be a communist when your father at one time was a banker, then a merchant, and your grandfather was a landlord?" I reminded him that Marx himself was not exactly a son of the working class, and that his friend Engels owned a sizable factory where he employed several hundred workers.

"Let's be serious," he said. "Don't give me stories like that: those were certainly great men, but they were scientists, philosophers, men of ideas. If they had foreseen that as a result of their ideas they would lose their factories, be assured they would have changed their minds." Since my interrogator did not commit his ideas on this matter to the interrogation record, I am afraid I was the sole (captive) audience of these deep philosophical revelations. I must admit that I did not dispute him on these issues. However, in his complaint about my trying to convert him to my point of view, I seemed to recognize the echo of criticism he may have received for succumbing at times to my seductive arguments. In the meantime, since our long sessions kept producing no tangible results—many sheets were signed, but not a single "useful" one—my interrogator could not, or would not, grant any of those privileges that he had described to me in such minute detail.

Toward the end of this investigator's "tenure," around mid-March, he started pressing me for the names of all the people whom I had met while in England. I gave him as many names as I could remember—and there were quite a few—with descriptions of the occasions when I met them and sketches of what we talked about. If I did not remember what we talked about, he would come back again and again to the name in question until finally I would get fed up and say that we talked about the health of his wife, the weather, and—this always had to be an integral part of the list of topics—nothing else. "Are you sure you discussed nothing else?"

"Yes, I am quite sure." The alternative that was more to my taste—"We may have discussed some other things too, but they must have been insignificant since I don't remember them"—never worked; so after a while I gave up and adopted the simple, plain, categorical style they preferred, except, of course, when some real issue was at stake.

Such an issue soon came up, following the question, "Did you meet a certain Mr. Thompson?"

To this I answered, "Not that I recollect."

"Think about it and answer the question: Did you, or did you not, meet Mr. Thompson?"

"I don't remember having met anybody by that name," I said, "but you must realize that as a diplomat I met hundreds of people, and the name Thompson is as common in England as Ionescu is in Romania, so it is quite possible that a Mr. Thompson was among the guests at some reception that I attended and that I met him without remembering it."

Not only was the interrogator completely dissatisfied with my answer, but he saw in it a "diplomatic" attempt at avoiding a clear answer to his question. He became angry. "You must answer yes or no. If you don't remember, think until you remember. But you must tell us where and when you met this Mr. Thompson and what you discussed with him."

We finally settled on an answer that went roughly like this: "Throughout my stay in England, I never met and had discussions with any person by the name of Thompson, except possibly as part of a large crowd at some reception that I attended and that was also attended by many people whose names I don't remember." He did not like it, but I would not budge—and that is where we left it.

Then he asked: "You say you have not met Mr. Thompson. What was the name of your espionage contact in England?" I said as plainly and simply as I could that I had no espionage contact in England or anywhere else. Then came the next question: "Have you ever been on a street called Park Laahne?" He was giving the Romanian pronunciation of Park Lane, the elegant boulevard along Hyde Park in central London. "Yes," I said. His face lit up and he leaned back in his chair. "So, finally, you have made up your mind to talk. Wonderful—it is never too late. So tell me, what happened at that meeting on Park Lane, who exactly was present, and can you remember the number of the house, or give a description of it, and the date of the meeting?"

This time my task was easy—I could give a very clear, simple, categorical answer, though not the one my interrogator wanted to hear. "I never attended any meeting on Park Lane and I have never visited anybody on that street."

My interrogator came back to this subject several times in various forms. He had me describe occasions when I walked through Park Lane, as if my saying that I crossed it on my way to a movie or some event in Hyde Park could be construed as a partial admission. I had not yet come to the point of admitting my espionage meetings on Park Lane, but I was already forced to admit that I was a not-infrequent visitor to that nest of crime. Mr. Thompson's name was also brought up on every occasion: How did he look, even if I did not quite remember my conversation with him? What was his general appearance, and most of all, what kind of tasks did he assign me? I was assured that in time, if I thought hard enough, I would remember all these things and many others which I would have to tell without being specifically asked about them, if I intended to prove my sincerity.

But before the issue of my alleged espionage in England was ever broached, during the first week of March 1953, more precisely on March 5, something unusual happened as I was walking up and down in my cell. By the way, from the beginning I had made a conscious effort to keep track of the date. Because of the many sleepless nights, I realized the danger of losing track. So I made it a habit to "move the calendar ahead" by one day in my head every morning as I woke up. In addition, as a safety device, I also scratched tiny little lines onto the wall in an unobtrusive place with my spoon during lunchtime. So I did not lose track of the date.

On March 5, 1953, around eight or nine in the morning, in the quiet of my cell, I heard something that sounded like a sequence of artillery shots at a great distance. The distance may have been an illusion due to the fact that my cell was separated from the outside world by several layers of walls and windows, and as the beginning of March was still winter, the windows to the outside were closed. When I heard the first shot, I was not sure—it was rather muted, and if there had been any other noise at all I would not have noticed it—but I started listening intensely. There was a second shot, then a third and a fourth, all at regular intervals. I started counting the shots and when the sequence stopped at twenty-one I had no doubt about what I had heard: a twenty-one-gun salute. I instantly remembered two things: a Soviet film about the war, in which the German capitulation was celebrated with a twenty-one-gun salute on Victory Day; and the description of Lenin's death in the party bible, *The History of the Communist party of the USSR*; the entire nation mourned, and the tragic event was marked by a twenty-one-gun salute. So that was it: either Stalin or Gheorghiu-Dej must have died. With the precedent set in the party bible, they would not dare to fire a twenty-one-gun salute for anything or anybody but the supreme leader, either of the Soviet party or of the Romanian party. I instinctively felt that what had happened was an important event, although I must admit that I did not realize what enormous significance Stalin's death held for the fate of so many people, myself included. I knew that Stalin's leadership bore the stamp of his personality, but I still viewed him as the supreme commander of a solidly constructed, well-oiled machine—the party apparatus—whose functioning was governed by firm and well-thought-out rules, and which would not be affected in any major way by the passing of the command to a new person. I was, of course, dead wrong about this. Anyway, I kept watching for any sign from which I could deduce which of the two alternative events had happened, but in vain: Nothing had changed in my daily routine. I was not to find out for more than a year and a half.

■ ■ ■

My interrogations had now become more sporadic; my interrogator seemed to have lost all hope of achieving anything. On one occasion I was taken to an officer who seemed to be senior in rank to my interrogator, probably as a way of checking on what the latter was reporting about my allegedly intransigent behavior and of feeling me out in an attempt to find my weak spots. This officer spoke with a Hungarian accent and his face had Jewish traits. His first question was: When would I finally come to my senses and stop the charade I was indulging myself in? To which I answered that I did not understand what he was talking about. He started swearing at me with the worst kinds of four-letter expletives, mentioning various sexual organs, my mother, my relatives in the animal kingdom, and so on. At first I felt my blood rush to my head in outrage, then I forced myself to stay calm: I decided that if I was going to be beaten badly, it would have to be for an issue of substance, not for protesting the interrogator's style. So I simply shut my mouth and did not answer him. When he started shouting and swearing again, I simply looked away, contemplating the wall. Then an amazing thing happened. Without any transition, he asked a perfectly sensible question in a perfectly normal voice. I could not believe my eyes and ears. A second earlier he had seemed uncontrollably enraged, and now he had suddenly become—how shall I put it?—mildly bored. I answered his perfectly sensible question in a perfectly sensible way, to which he re-acted with another wild outburst of rage, with even more colorful pro-fanity, this time bringing in my grandmother and expanding on the animal domain. However, as my initial shock had now passed, I watched him carefully and noticed that his rage was entirely artificial: inside, he was as calm as on a sunny afternoon in a city park. The rage was obviously theater, and it occurred to me that perhaps the theater was not meant just for me. I had a strange feeling that the room was bugged, the session was being taped, and the man, a Hungarian Jew like myself, wanted to make it absolutely clear that he was as hostile to me as any interrogator with a healthy orientation ought to be. I never found out the truth about this, but it was my impression at the time. Normal questions followed by normal answers on my part again led to feigned angry outbursts on his part, although his repertory of curses only seemed rich and colorful during the first fifteen minutes; after that, he kept repeating himself. We went through all the major questions broached by the previous interrogators, which I answered in exactly the same manner as before, and the session ended with the officer's vivid description of the scene in the not-too-distant future when I would crawl on my belly, pleading for mercy and ready to sign the interrogation sheets without reading them. On that note we parted company and I was sent back to my cell.

The days passed uneventfully until one night in the second half of March I was told to collect my things in order to leave my cell. It happened in the middle of the night, without any premonition, like most of the significant events in the accursed place that had become my residence. I was awakened by the noise of my door being opened. A guard stepped into my cell. I opened my eyes and sat up. "Get up," he said, "and take all your things." I was wearing my underwear in bed. Now I put on my pants, jacket, and shoes; grabbed my things—two shirts, two handkerchiefs (one of them containing my chessmen among its folds), a pair of socks, and a sweater—let myself be blindfolded by the guard and be led out of the cell. I had no idea where I was being taken: to the courthouse for a trial, to another prison in Bucharest or elsewhere, or merely to another cell in the same damned prison. We traversed the long corridor, then went out into the courtyard. Although blindfolded, I could sense the outdoors from the quality of the air I was inhaling. It was a pleasure to smell fresh air for the first time after seven months, even though it lasted only a couple of minutes. Then we entered another building, descended some stairs, traversed another long corridor, and stopped. A cell door was opened; it sounded even heavier and more metallic than my previous door. I was pushed in, and my blindfold was taken off.

I was in an underground square-shaped cell whose sides were about eleven or twelve feet long. There were two concrete bunks built into two adjacent walls facing the door. The two bunks met at their heads, where they also served as seats for at a "table," a concrete slab of about two-and-a-half-by-two-and-a-half feet and about five inches thick, built into the wall. In the corner opposite the one that held the table, there was a

Turkish toilet, that is, a hole in the concrete floor and a handle for flushing it with water. Above the Turkish toilet, a shower was affixed to the ceiling. This was a better-equipped cell than the one I had left, in the sense that it had a toilet and running water. It was also a more "modern" cell in that it had nothing movable, the two bunks and the table were solidly built into the walls, and there was no chair. What disturbed me, though, was the fact that there was no window at all, only some venti-lation onto the corridor in front of the cell, so that even the little daylight that could occasionally be seen in my previous cell had disappeared. In a way, this underground cell was even more isolated from the outside world than my previous lodging. The door had the same structure as the one of my earlier cell—metal blinds and a peephole—but it was heavier and more metallic, so at night when doors were opened and shut, they made a deafening bang.

When I was brought into the cell in the middle of the night, one of the bunks was occupied by somebody who was asleep, facing the wall, and he did not turn around to see why his door had been opened. The guard who took me to the cell motioned me to lie down on the free bunk, which I did after putting my things in a bundle on the floor under the table. In spite of being emotionally upset by the change, which at that point I perceived on the whole as positive, because of the toilet facility and the (as yet unknown) company, I fell asleep after a few minutes and woke up only when the guard knocked on the door in the morning. My companion was a man in his mid-thirties, tall, well built, and seemingly in excellent physical condition, which made him suspect in my eyes from the moment I met him. We introduced ourselves, but I cannot remember his name. My first assumption—that he was an informer for the interro-gators—was based not only on how healthy he looked (fat would be an exaggeration, but he was anything but thin) but also on the fact that I could see no other reason why my interrogators should have suspended the most potent psychological pressure they could exert on me, namely solitary confinement. If I had any doubts about my assumption, they quickly disappeared at breakfast time: I got my coffee, and my cell mate got his, plus a glass of milk. He was a little embarrassed and said that he had the milk as a result of a medical prescription and therefore needed to drink it, but he did not mind if I wanted to taste it occasionally. I thanked him and said that, since I did not have a medical prescription, I probably did not need it. In the middle of the morning the guard came to take my roommate into the courtyard for a walk. I asked him afterwards how the courtyard looked, but he said that the area where he was taken to walk was a square-shaped place, specially created for the purpose, about twenty to twenty-five feet in each direction and surrounded by four walls. Apart from the walls, the only thing he could see was the sky and, of course he could smell the fresh air. In this respect he was probably telling the truth—it is hard to imagine that somebody would invent a thing like that—but I never found out, since throughout my long stay at the Malmezon I was never taken out for a walk. I never got to "belong to the club." After lunch, my cell mate explained that, as part of the same medical prescription, he had the right to sleep for an hour. I did not mind, and I used the time while the cell was free to do my daily long walk. Exactly one hour after he went to sleep, the guard knocked on the door to wake him up.

Despite my antipathy toward the role my cell mate was playing, I decided to try to make the best of the situation and enjoy whatever conversation I could have with him. I tried to make him talk to me about his life, his work before he was arrested, and so forth, but he either had very little to say or was afraid of saying the wrong things. When I asked why he had been arrested, he told me that he had been involved with a pro-Tito group. It did not seem very convincing. More likely, I assumed, he had been involved with the Iron Guard, was now being blackmailed into playing this role, and had been instructed to tell me he was a Titoist in order to make me more sympathetic toward him. When he in turn inquired about my reason for being arrested, I told him that it was a mistake, that in fact there was no reason for me to be where I was. But still, he said, what was I being accused of? I told him that I was a friend of Jakab, who had been arrested as part of the right-wing deviation of Luca and others. I also said that I had a history of underground activity during the war, various aspects of which were now being investigated— or rather should be investigated, because unfortunately the interrogators didn't seem to have questioned the people who knew about my activity; otherwise they would have found out long ago that I was innocent and would have sent me home. He shook his head in commiseration and asked how long I thought I could resist in this situation. This sounded like the kind of thing he was supposed to find out from me; I said that unfortunately I had no choice, that it was not a question of my resisting, but of how long it took the investigation to establish the truth, a thing over which I had no control. Judging by the slow pace at which things seemed to be moving, it might take the Securitate five to six years to reach a conclusion. Did I think, he asked, that I could survive that long under my current regime? I shrugged and repeated that I had no choice but to wait patiently until the truth was established, even if it took a decade. He shook his head again, and then we changed the subject. I was hoping he would report exactly what I had said to him, which he probably did. Our cohabitation lasted less than a month. That time was probably sufficient for the investigators to find out that switching me from the single to the shared cell had been a fruitless exercise, and consequently to decide to put back on me the psychological screws of solitary confinement.

. . .

Before that happened, however, my second interrogator concluded my case as fruitlessly as had his predecessor. In our last session he told me with reproach in his voice that he had done everything humanly possible for me. He had offered me all available options, that is, either confessing to any of the assorted crimes that were laid out to me, or at least declaring honestly that Sándor Jakab had been a nazi agent and giving the party all the information I had on this. Had I agreed to go along with either of these options, or had I shown any interest in helping the party in some other way, I certainly would have been punished, but I would have been treated leniently and given a chance, after some time, to return to a normal life. But in my blind obstinacy, I had rejected his helping hand.

"I don't really understand you," he said. "Where do you think you find yourself? You are acting as if you wanted to get out of here with an untarnished record, with your head held high. But there is no such thing, young fellow. You did not appreciate my efforts to help you. Well, you will then have to answer to others. I am finished with you." With that he dismissed me, and I was left alone for about a week or ten days, until a new investigation started, with a new man—for the third time, from scratch.

CHAPTER 10

■ ■ ■

The Malmezon II

The third investigation of my case started around mid-April 1953. My new interrogator was again a young, uniformed lieutenant, more intelligent and open-minded than the last interrogator. On our first encounter he said something to the effect that he had heard bad things about me, that I had caused his colleagues a lot of trouble, that I had developed quite a reputation for refusing to cooperate with the investigation. "It seems that you have adapted yourself to the environment here and have settled in for the long haul," he said. Instead of summoning the courage to tell the truth and abandon my attitude of futile denial, he said, I was trying to convince my interrogators of my own point of view, to sort of win them over. It would make no sense for me to try this with him, he said. Any such attempt on my part would be doomed to failure. On the other hand, if I stood by what I had said—namely, that I was willing to cooperate in establishing the truth—then there was a common ground on which we could understand each other. So we would start from the beginning, review all my activities, and bring out the truth, not as I wanted it to look, but as it was in reality.

And start we did. I was taken to interrogation sometimes every night of the week, so that I got hardly any sleep; sometimes only every other night; sometimes, for a change, in the daytime; and sometimes not at all for several days. My cell mate was taken out of the cell after we had been together for less than a month, so when I was not being interrogated I was again by myself. The food had become more meager, and not just for me; this was a change in the Malmezon's food regime. There were now only two meals a day, and the half-pound of bread was replaced with half a pound of cornmeal, cooked and allowed to cool and solidify. Although the quantity of cereal was the same, cornmeal contains fewer nutrients than bread. My new cell had an advantage over the old one in that I did not have to wait to be taken to the toilet and could relieve myself whenever I liked. You have to be a prisoner, it seems, to discover some of the basic pleasures of life. Normally the water tap in the cell— the shower—provided only cold water, but once a week there was hot water for a couple of hours, during which I could take a hot shower and also wash a shirt, a handkerchief, or a pair of socks (I had a change of each of these). I had now spent about nine months at the Malmezon, and my socks and my sweater had developed holes. I set out to mend them, using a straw from the mattress as needle, and a thread that I pulled from the bedsheet. The straw needle did not have a hole, but I made a crack in it that held the thread quite well. I sewed very clumsily at first, but developed some dexterity, so that after a while my sweater and socks looked as though they had been darned by an expert seamstress.

One day something strange happened. In the morning I usually ate a thin slice of the cornmeal mush with coffee and left the bulk to be eaten later during the day. I used a thread pulled from the bedsheet to slice the cold mush, so I could bite from it without making crumbs. On the day in question I had eaten my morning slice and left the remaining piece of mush on the table when I was taken to interrogation. I was returned to my cell three or four hours later, before the afternoon meal was served. To my consternation I found the piece of mush in the exact place where I had put it, but with a big bite missing. I was flabbergasted: why would the guard want a bite of my mush? He could not possibly be hungry, and besides . . . it just made no sense. Did he want to mock me? Was this a plot to make me feel that I was losing my senses? Or was I indeed hallucinating? Maybe I *did* take a bite before being taken out of the cell. The trouble was that I knew my own bite, and this bite was definitely not mine. For a fraction of a second it crossed my mind to knock on the door and complain, but I immediately realized how ridiculous my complaint would have sounded, so I gave up the idea.

Nevertheless, the thing kept intriguing me and at night I did not sleep well. The next morning after breakfast, as I was sitting quietly, deeply submerged in my thoughts, I heard a tiny noise from the toilet, as when a small object falls into the water. I did not pay attention at first, but when I heard it a second time, I suddenly realized that I had heard it before. I cautiously approached the toilet, but before I could see the hole I heard the noise again, this time quite distinctly; and when I looked at the hole, there was nothing to be seen in it but water. I chose a position on the other bunk from which I could clearly see the hole and sat motionless for about half an hour, intent on identifying the event that had caused the noise. But the noise did not recur. Finally, after a while, a grayish rat stuck his head, then his body, out of the hole. It was more than half a foot long without its tail. I did not budge, and the rat made a few steps in my direction. Then I made an involuntary move—I may have shuddered—and the rat noticed me, turned around, and disappeared with a jump under the water in the hole, making the very noise whose origin I wanted to establish. So now I understood: it was His Excellency the Rat who had tasted my mush the day before!

My first reaction was to alert the guard: he would probably put some pesticide into the hole that would kill the rat or chase it away. Then I changed my mind. In my free life I did not like pets. I could get along with dogs and could even like certain individual specimens, but I hated cats. This reaction may have developed during my childhood, when I raised pigeons and the neighbor's cat would kill them whenever it managed to catch them. However, with my life so boring as it was now, any prospect of entertainment, even from a rat, had its lure. I remembered my teenage readings about taming animals and Jack London's novels about dogs, and I decided to try to tame the rat. Everything has a price, and in spite of the constant hunger I was suffering by now, next morning I sacrificed a small piece of mush and placed it on the floor between myself and the hole. By the way, the water in the hole was as clean as in any toilet after the water had been flushed, and although the rat was more likely than not coming from a sewer, by the time he reached my toilet he was washed clean—or so it seemed. He took quite some time to show up, but toward the end of the morning he finally arrived. He immediately noticed the piece of mush, but he was also aware of my presence. For a while he sat in the hole with only his head out, looking first at me, then at the mush, again at me, then again at the mush. I patiently waited until hesitantly, slowly, he started to approach the piece of food. Then, with a quick forward-and-backward movement, he grabbed it in an instant and disappeared with it under the water in the hole. I took another tiny piece of mush, this time holding it in my hand, and waited until the rat returned, which, as I expected, happened very soon. When he stuck out his head, looking at me and at the empty floor, I slowly moved my hand, holding the food between my thumb and forefinger, until I made sure he saw it. Then, ever so slowly, I leaned forward and put the piece of mush on the concrete floor halfway between the rat and myself, and ever so slowly, avoiding any sudden movement, withdrew my hand. The rat stayed where he was, waited for a while, then came out of the hole, a little less hesitantly than before, and grabbed the food.

I repeated this procedure for several days and the rat soon came and went in a more or less relaxed fashion. He would even spend a few minutes in the cell, sitting and walking around, and for a while I had fun watching him. But as soon as I tried to approach him he would run away, . . . and he was a lot quicker than I was. The fun did not last very long, however; after a few days I got bored, and when next I was taken to interrogation, I realized that there was no safe place in the cell where I could leave my unconsumed piece of mush. I took a bite and slid the rest in my pocket, but this was not something I wanted to do on a regular basis. So, as I was being taken out of the cell, I told the guard on duty that there was a rat visiting it regularly through the toilet. He said they would take care of it, and they must have done so, because the rat disappeared.

At some time during the spring of 1953 the monotony of my daily existence was interrupted by a rather somber episode that sent chills down my spine whenever I thought of it for months afterward. Early one afternoon I heard noises coming down the corridor from some other cell. Apparently a prisoner was banging his cell door, and the guard was berating him in a muffled voice: "Keep quiet, shut up, . . ." and I could not make out what else. Then from the cell came a loud, clearly audible, articulate roar: "Seven years! I have been here for seven years! Do you hear me? Seven years, seven years!" He kept shouting this message until, his cell door having been opened, something like a blanket must have been thrown over his head and in a few seconds he was subdued. Perfect silence followed. That evening, as sleepy as I was, I was unable to fall asleep. The man's loud, clear voice, with the two carefully selected words repeated over and over—"seven years, seven years"—reverberated incessantly in my ears. We were now in May 1953; he had been arrested in 1946. Why was he being kept here for so long? After all, this was not a place where people served prison sentences, but a place of interrogation. Could somebody be investigated for *seven years*? It sounded insane and horrible, and it shook my morale.

My new interrogator went through the same motions as the previous two had done. This time, when asked questions that I had answered more than once in the past, I carefully avoided saying, "As I said earlier, . . ." and acted as if I were answering the question for the first time. Everything went according to the old script: we covered my underground activities in detail; I repeated the names of people who could testify to most of the essential things that I was saying; we went through my arrest by the DEF and my interrogation there. Again, I had to endure the incredulity of the investigator, to which I said—this time no longer as an outburst of rage, but quite calmly—"If you don't believe me, test me." Like the earlier investigator, the man was taken aback: "You don't mean to say you want me to beat you on the soles as they did at the DEF? Damn it, if that's what it takes to make you talk, I'll do it right away." He opened the drawer of his desk and pulled out a sizable rubber truncheon, the sight of which was very familiar to me, although I had not seen one since 1944. He grabbed it and started hitting the desk with it, as if to demonstrate how heavy it was.

I said something like, "It is a terrible experience to be beaten with a truncheon like that, on the soles or elsewhere; an experience that I know very well. But if that is what it takes for you to believe me, go ahead and do it. I am willing to sign this statement so you can cover yourself."

He was visibly upset. He put down the truncheon and ordered me, "Stand up!" I did. "Get out!" I turned around and started toward the door. As I was putting my hand on the doorknob, he yelled at me, "Stop!" I stopped and turned toward him. "You are completely crazy," he said. "Aren't you afraid of anything? Don't you realize that the minute you step through that door the guard will shoot you? He will assume you have killed me or knocked me down. Nobody without a uniform walks through this door unattended!" In fact, it had not occurred to me that I was engaging in such a dangerous adventure in following his orders, but I did not mind if he wished to interpret my action as a sign of fearlessness (which it was not, as I was far from fearless). As to my repeated statements that I did not mind being beaten if that was what it took for my interrogators to believe me, I had said it at first out of frustration and desperation; but when I repeated it, that was partly out of calculation, since I quickly learned the supreme rule that you do to the prisoner what he fears most and finds least palatable. So I believed that my statements along those lines did not increase, but perhaps actually decreased the chances of my being beaten.

One day the investigator made me resume my story from the date of my arrival in England. I had to list the names of all the people I had met in England, and there were plenty of them. I did it from scratch, never mentioning my earlier interrogations on the subject. When he asked me whether I had met Mr. Thompson, I gave him the same detailed answer I gave the first time, but he seemed more understanding of my argument that the name Thompson was too common for me to flatly deny ever having met a person by that name. He did not insist on learning whether I had ever been on a street called Park Lane, but asked instead whether I had ever participated in a meeting or office visit on Park Lane, to which I flatly said no.

And then he threw the bombshell. He looked at me gravely and wrote down, then read out aloud for me, the following question: "Jacques Berman, your colleague at the Romanian legation in London, has declared that he and you worked together as spies for the British Intelligence Service. Do you admit this?"

The question, as awesome as it was, seemed to me so ridiculous that I literally laughed it off. My answer was, "No, I do not admit this, nor do I believe that Jacques Berman has ever said anything like it."

He refused to write down my answer and got angry: "I am not asking you what you believe; I am asking—and answer my question squarely— whether you do or do not acknowledge that you spied with Jacques Berman for the Intelligence Service."

"No," I said, "I never spied for the Intelligence Service, with or without Jacques Berman."

He then wrote down and read out the next question: "Does Jacques Berman hold any grudge against you? Does he have any reason to harm you?"

"No," I said. "I have no basis for believing that Jacques Berman holds a grudge against me, nor do I see any reason why he should want to harm me."

The interrogator cautioned me: "Think before you give your answer. On the one hand, you claim that what Berman says is not true. On the other hand, you say he has no reason to harm you. Think again. Maybe he does. Otherwise, why would he say what he says if it is not true?"

"I don't believe for a minute that Berman said what you claim he did."

"Why?"

"Because he is a decent, level-headed man, and he could have no interest in inventing such a horrendous lie."

"So then who invented it? Do you dare to say that we, the Securitate, are inventing things?"

"I don't know. I can only say that I am convinced Berman never said those things."

"Well, I will bring him here and he will repeat them to your face. What then?"

"That will never happen," I said.

"Why?"

"Because Berman will not do it."

"How the hell can you be so sure of yourself, and not only of yourself? Let's suppose for a moment that I bring Berman here and he tells you to your face that you spied jointly for the Intelligence Service. Will you then admit that you did it?"

"If that happens," I said, "then I will ask Berman for details: What did our alleged espionage consist of? What kind of secrets did we sell the British? How did we come across those secrets? Espionage is a very concrete business; he would have to provide facts, and he cannot have facts, because they don't exist. So he will be caught from the beginning in the most elementary contradictions and he will have to retract his allegations, which I repeat, I do not believe to be his."

My interrogator was quiet; he looked at me at some length, studying my face. Then in a soft, changed voice he said slowly, "You trust people too much."

I could not help but feel that his last statement was sincere, that it was not part of the continuous bluffing that I was being subjected to. It was not until many years later, in the early sixties, that I found out that this was indeed the case. At that time, Jacques Berman, who had been arrested in the fall of 1952 as an accomplice of Pătrășcanu, and sentenced to ten years imprisonment in April 1954 in the latter's trial, was freed before completing his sentence. He called me and asked whether I was willing to meet him, to which I said yes. He then visited me and apologized for having declared during his arrest, under physical and psychological torture that he could not bear, that he and I had spied for the

British Intelligence Service. Later, however, when given an opportunity, he retracted his deposition on this matter.

■ ■ ■

The "tenure" of my third investigator lasted for about six months, until October 1953. During those six months his attitude toward me fluctuated a great deal. At rare moments I felt that he respected and in some ways even admired me, and that he wanted to help me establish the truth. Most of the time, though, I perceived him as a faceless representative of that murderous machine that was trying to crush me. I think some of these fluctuations reflected the struggle in his mind between what he was hearing from me and what he was being told by his superiors. The reproach I kept hearing for trying to "convince" my interrogators instead of helping the investigation was not for nothing: I did my best to make my case for the truth as persuasively and with as much objective evidence as possible. When I rejected an accusation I did not limit myself to saying it was false: I argued as effectively as I could that the accusation was absurd, that it could not be true, because if it had been true, it would have implied facts that could easily be checked and shown false. I always described in detail circumstances that contradicted the accusation, and gave names of people who could be questioned to confirm those details. Since my interrogator was fairly intelligent and did not seem a blind fanatic, he could not possibly remain impervious to my reasoning.

On the other hand, his superiors were evidently telling him that everything in my past was suspect, that I was admittedly a close friend of the public enemy Sándor Jakab, that my whole behavior proved that I completely lacked the party spirit, and that he should guard against my attempts to enmesh him in my net of false arguments, as had happened to his predecessors. Every time he started a new round of questioning on a new topic, he was glacial and hostile at the beginning, as if putting a wall between me and himself; he acted as if he had thought through and rehearsed his line of questioning, which was supposed to lead me to some admission of guilt. As the questions and answers unfolded—some of them were never consigned to paper; they remained suspended in the air, but they had their impact on his thinking—his demeanor would gradually change, as if he had at least partly accepted my argument.

When we started out the next time, I usually noticed a relapse; obviously he had talked to his superiors, who had dismissed my point of view, perhaps even without considering it seriously. While this was rather frustrating and often seemed hopeless, I felt nevertheless that I had to fight with all my powers of persuasion for the "soul" of my interrogator—realizing, of course, how unequal this struggle was.

Once, during the late spring or summer of 1953, I was taken to an interrogation by two new officers. They were seated at the same desk and one of them did not open his mouth during the whole session, his role being either that of learning or of witnessing, without active participation. The other, who led the conversation, was a tall, thin man in his mid- or late thirties—an intellectual, sophisticated and knowledgeable. He was hiding his rank, but was probably a captain or major. He seemed to me Jewish. He spoke softly and did not yell at me, but was full of an irony meant to be biting. "I am reading your depositions. They are fairy tales. All of them. You describe yourself as a hero, as immaculate as the Virgin Mary in the New Testament. You claim to be absolutely clean. You don't seem to realize that you are throwing away your life. I am here to explain to you that it is high time for you to make up your mind. This is your last chance. We have been very patient with you, but enough is enough. Unless you make up your mind to come forward and talk, you will be crushed irrevocably. You will then regret what you have done, but it will be too late. Listen to me, I want to tell you about a case that you could learn from. Have you ever heard of Radek?"

"Yes, I have."

"Well, Radek was involved in the trial of the Bucharinist-Zinovievist Center, whose members were all executed by firing squad, as traitors deserve to be. But Radek, because he chose to help the party and confessed his own crimes as well as those of the others, was spared and received a sentence of ten years. Let me tell you his story."

At this point I got so irritated by the parallel he drew, which I felt was completely out of place, that I interrupted the officer and said angrily: "Don't tell me Radek's story. I know it and it has absolutely no relevance to my case." For the first time since I had been arrested, I felt that I was losing my calm. The officer seemed to be taken aback by my reaction and, judging from his facial expression, wanted to raise his voice to put me in my place. But he swallowed his intended rebuff, kept calm, and said, "Listen, I am here to help you." But this was too much for me; I lost control. Unintentionally, I raised my voice and yelled at the officer, "I don't need your help! I need you to do your duty and establish the truth. Don't help me!"

Bewildered, he rose from his chair and slowly approached me. I was ready for a slap, a kick, or a more thorough beating. Instead he came closer and closer, looking at me as you might look at some curious insect, and mumbled between his teeth, "Oh yes, sweetie, you have no idea how much you need it. You have no idea." He stopped with his face five inches from mine, piercing me with his eyes, and repeated "You have no idea how much you need our help." Then he stepped back, called the guard, and sent me back to my cell. I never saw him again.

From the summer of 1953 on, my interrogations became very sporadic. I spent long days, sometimes weeks, without seeing my interrogator. Although my morale was holding up pretty well, physically I felt much weakened. The food, which for months now had consisted of only two meals a day, was grossly insufficient and I was permanently hungry. Once, when I found my interrogator in one of his better moods and he inquired about my health, I told him that I was not yet sick but that the food I was getting was a starvation diet. He told me that he would like to help, but he was bound by the rules and could improve my situation—in terms of food, sleeping time, walks in the courtyard, and so forth—only if I changed my attitude. The food that I was getting was the standard portion at the time; everything above that had to be earned. This was the rule and he could not change it. I continued to follow my program of physical and mental activities, although my walks became shorter, as I was getting tired earlier.

I sometimes had dreams at night, some bad, some good. I do not recall any dreams about Edith or Anna, maybe because I often daydreamed about them. Most of my dreams I forgot soon after I had them, but a couple stuck in my mind forever. In a nightmare that was as disturbing as it was clear, I saw Sanyi Jakab's dead body laid out on a high catafalque. It was a very powerful image, which I still remember. It was visually so sharp that I could not help feeling that something must have happened to Sanyi on that night. I even tried to remember the date, so that if I ever had a chance to talk to him again, I could ask what had happened to him on that night.

Another time I dreamed about the future as I apparently had subconsciously imagined it. I was visiting a factory, something like a steel mill or a metalworking plant of the next century. I was being led through a huge workshop hundreds of yards long and wide, bustling with activity performed with fantastic, otherworldly equipment. Huge machines reaching to the sky, each manned by a single person, clean and smart-looking, were molding hot metal into all kinds of objects, which were then stored in neat piles a few yards away. Everything was on a gigantic scale; everything was clean, fast-moving, neat, and automated. The hot metal was red; the cold steel was for some reason shiny. Everything on the shop floor was continuously moving; enormous cranes and forklifts, operated by just a few people, were rearranging everything. Further ahead of us, a waterway loomed up, with an enormous bridge that had one of its ends pivoted and lifted to the sky. I occasionally asked questions that were answered politely. It was not clear what my connection to the whole thing was, but I experienced a warm feeling of pride and pleasure at the sight of this futuristic industrial landscape that "we" had finally managed to bring about: I was witnessing the bright future of mankind as I had imagined it in my communist dreams. A rather strange dream to have in my situation—I tried to understand why I had it, but in vain.

Some time during the fall of 1953 I had my last session with my third interrogator. I did not know, of course, that it was to be the last. He said something to the effect that he had done his best to clarify the many unsolved problems that surrounded my case, but that I had not helped him and so he had not accomplished much. He intimated that if I had shown some flexibility and acceded at least to some of the minor charges, then perhaps the other ones could have been fended off; but with my attitude of blank denial of everything there was nothing he could do.

I sank back into the solitude of my cell. Weeks, perhaps months, went by without anything happening. Some time during the winter (I don't remember even the approximate date) the prison's food regime reverted to the three-meals-a-day model; it was a most welcome change. The extra daily ration of soup and the reintroduction of bread instead of corn meal made a palpable improvement in my—and everybody's—diet. In the meantime my digestive tract had developed an acute sensitivity to any kind of irritant. The single most rewarding meal, usually served only once a week, was a rich, thick split pea soup. I loved it, and felt that it gave me more nutrition than three or four of the usual thin soups I was getting on most days of the week. After a while, however, I developed a nasty reaction to the split pea soup, several times experiencing bouts of diarrhea with cramps within a few hours after consuming it. The diarrhea was so severe that it left me feeling as weak as if I had been literally emptied of all my juices. As this happened every time I had the pea soup, I tried various strategies to avoid it. Once things got so bad that I refrained from eating half the soup and sent it back, despite my strong desire to eat the rest, in the hope that a smaller quantity would not provoke the same violent reaction. In the end I adopted the following procedure: I would restrict my breakfast to coffee only and save my entire portion of bread for the midday meal. Then if that meal was pea soup, I would mix the soup with bread. This way, the diarrhea was much attenuated and became bearable.

At some point during the winter of 1953–54 I was again taken to an interrogation room. Again I faced a new interrogator, the fourth one. He was a short, stocky officer—lieutenant, first lieutenant, or maybe even captain—in his late thirties or early forties. Like the others before him, he informed me that he was assigned to my case and that he planned to review with me everything I had done from the earliest days of my political activities to the day of my arrest. I felt frustrated at the thought that all my efforts to clarify the suspicions against me had been in vain, and that after a year and a half in jail, under terrible conditions, I was back to square one, starting again from scratch. This fresh effort by a new investigator was the fourth in a line of failed attempts to establish not the truth, but my guilt. I tried to console myself with the thought that it was still better to be investigated than to be completely forgotten and left to rot in my cell for months without ever talking to another human being.

This time the investigation seemed to follow two distinct trends. On the one hand, I was periodically submitted to the same sermons as before about the futility of my stubborn denials and the shortsighted stupidity of my attempts to delay the day of judgment, which was bound to come anyway: wouldn't it be nicer to swallow the bitter pill and get it over with once and for all? The by-now ritualistic phrase, "Well, have you finally made up your mind?" was repeated every time I was taken to interrogation after a break longer than a few days. On the other hand, the specific questions I was asked and the interrogation records put on paper were aimed at settling any discrepancies, however slight, between differing versions of the same event that the Securitate either had heard from me or somebody else, or had simply come up with as its own hypothesis.

Thus, from the period of my underground activity, I again had to describe in detail the partial strike (refusal to work overtime at RAVAG in 1942) and the accompanying police interrogation. Why had I not been detained? I explained the handwriting test, which was unable to establish anything, and I pointed out that others had also been interrogated by the police on that occasion and nobody was detained. Then we went through the details of my recruiting activities for the party and the actions we organized. Asked for my view of what led to the arrests by the DEF in the fall of 1943, I said that those events had been analyzed at the time by the persons under arrest, who were in the best position to determine what had happened. A pretty clear picture had been established by consensus, and this had been reconfirmed after the liberation of Cluj during the party's investigation into the behavior of those arrested. According to this consensus, the chain of arrests started with the apprehension of a man in the technical group, who then was cruelly beaten and gave away Ilona Grünfeld. In turn Grünfeld, who was also cruelly beaten, gave away everyone she knew, either by name or by recognizing them in pictures shown to her. Less well understood were the circumstances leading to the first arrest. One hypothesis was that the arrested man had been in contact with an old-time ex-communist who had become a DEF informer after the Vienna Diktat, and had somehow aroused the suspicion of this informer. All this had been established by others; I was not involved in these investigations, I said, so I could not vouch for their accuracy, but if the Securitate was truly interested in finding out the detailed story behind the 1943 arrests, the witnesses were alive and could be questioned.

My investigator retorted that Ilona Grünfeld had told a very different story of the 1943 arrests from the one I was giving, and that she placed the blame for her arrest squarely on me. I found this strange but not unbelievable, since I knew Grünfeld to be a rather weak woman who in 1943 had betrayed to the DEF everything she knew, going as far as to point out faces she recognized, of people whose names she did not know, on a high school graduation photo. I also imagined that she could not harbor very warm feelings toward me, since I did not have much respect or liking for her and had never talked to her after the war. Finally, I could even imagine that upon hearing about my arrest as a suspected enemy of the people, she might have reexamined our 1942–1943 contacts in the light of this "discovery" and talked herself into believing that I had

somehow caused her arrest. So I did not react to my interrogator's assertion with the same dismissive attitude as in the case of Jacques Berman's
espionage story, but asked instead how I could have betrayed her when
I was not in contact with her at the time, did not know her by name, had
no idea where she lived, and simply had no way of putting the DEF onto
her trail even if I had wanted to. My investigator then said that, according to Grünfeld, I had sent her a typewriter which ultimately led to her
arrest, because she had used it to type party materials and its font had
been tracked down by the DEF. To the best of my recollection, my answer centered around the following points:

First, I never sent a typewriter to Grünfeld. I myself never had one,
did not know how to type, and had no business getting involved in the
procurement of typewriters. Grünfeld should be asked who actually
brought her the typewriter in question, and why she thought it came
from me. Second, I explained that in the underground Communist party—
both in Romania and in Hungary—political work (which meant work
with people, trade unions, other mass organizations, recruitment of new
followers, educational activities, and so forth) and technical work (which
meant work with duplicating or printing machines, production and
duplication of party materials, and the like) were kept separate for conspiratorial reasons. This was a basic organizational principle of party
work, of which Grünfeld, veteran party worker that she was, must have
been aware. How could she then tolerate such a crass infringement of
this basic rule as my sending her a typewriter? To whom did she mention this aberration at the time? Hadn't she complained? Why not? Third,
there had been a detailed party investigation of the 1943 arrests in early
1945. I asked my investigator to obtain the records of that party investigation, if he did not yet have them. I was not involved in that investigation in any way; I was not even back in Cluj at the time when it took
place. Why had Grünfeld given a different version at the time? Why did
she not raise then the issue of the typewriter allegedly sent to her by me,
at least as a possibility in explaining her arrest? Fourth, if I had set a trap
for Grünfeld which led to her arrest by the DEF—which seemed to be
what her version of events implied—how did this jibe with the fact that
none of the people whom I had recruited for distributing the Peace party
manifesto were arrested?

Unlike on previous occasions, I was under the impression that my
interrogator was not simply dismissing my explanations; in fact, he was

taking them down in writing in minute detail, including my proposed questions to Grünfeld. Actually, he wrote more than one interrogation report on this issue, because three days after concluding the session he reopened the question of the typewriter and, to my delight, came back with a series of supplementary questions. This showed that he and his bosses were now finally paying attention to what I was saying. Naturally, I welcomed any question, no matter how hostile in tone, that opened up an opportunity to give additional details about our activity in 1943. I had nothing to hide, and the more details were consigned to paper, the harder it would be for anybody to ignore or distort the record. So we wrote record after record with extra details, all duly signed by me after I made sure that nothing was changed in my deposition. And this time no attempts were made to change my statements either in substance or in tone by writing them differently from the spoken version.

When it came to my arrest by the DEF in August 1944, the interrogator pressed me to explain how my hiding place had been discovered. I repeated for the umpteenth time that I did not know, and laid out the various possibilities that I thought were plausible. He retorted that the most likely person to have informed the DEF was Sándor Jakab, since he knew my hiding place. I refused to accept this hypothesis, arguing that the single most important piece of information the DEF wanted to find out from me after my arrest was the time and place of my next appointment with Jakab. Then we went again through the story of my interrogation by the DEF, with all the details. This time I managed to get the officer to write down the names of all the persons whom the DEF had tried to identify, find, and arrest through me, but who had not been arrested, had survived the war, and could be questioned. When it came to my escape, I repeated the story in all its details and gave again the name of Károly Fekete, my comrade and companion in the escape, who was living in Budapest and could be questioned.

Finally, we came to the postwar period and my mission to London. Once again we went through the motions of the espionage accusation based on Jacques Berman's alleged testimony. I flatly repeated that I did not believe that such testimony existed. The interrogator did not want to commit this to paper; but he argued without rancor that it would not help my case to show contempt for the Securitate by asserting that I believed it capable of inventing false accusations. I realized that he had a point and dropped the objectionable part of my answer, restricting myself to denying categorically having ever spied for the British Intelligence Service with or without Jacques Berman.

When we came to the end of my story, the officer suddenly relapsed into the role of chief inquisitor. He said he had committed all my statements to paper as I intended them to be committed, but that these were useless, since they simply showed that I had still not made up my mind to come forward with the truth. On some minor issues of detail I might have spoken the truth, but on the whole my testimony was still a cover-up. He would now send me back to my cell where I would have plenty of time to think; but it should be clear to me that as long as there was a single item they knew about and that I was trying to hide—and there were plenty of questions they had deliberately avoided asking me—they would continue to know that I had not yet made up my mind to tell the truth. With this he remanded me to my cell, and I did not see him again for several months.

While I was still being interrogated, at the end of February 1954, I suddenly faced a difficulty in deciding the date: was it the first of March, or the twenty-ninth of February? I had forgotten the exact rule for identifying leap years, and was not sure whether 1954 was one or not. I decided to ask the guard, but I knew that he was not likely to answer my question unless it somehow caught him by surprise. So I knocked on my door to signal that I had something to ask, and he opened the metal blind to see what I wanted. I then said that I wanted to wash my shirt, and was wondering when there would be hot water. He said, "You have to do that on Saturday when you have your shower," which of course I knew. I then said, "Thank you. I will do it on Saturday. By the way, is the first of March today or tomorrow?" His face changed as he said, "I don't know," and closed the metal window.

My attempt at clarification having failed, I set out to find the answer on a different basis. I knew for a fact that every fourth year is a leap year, but I did not know where to start the counting. The information that eluded me was that you simply count year 1 as the first one; that is, to find out the answer for any given year of the calendar, you simply determine whether the year is divisible by four. Since 1954 is not divisible by four, it was not a leap year. Although I did not know this rule, I did know some other facts. Fact 1: On June 22, 1941, the Germans invaded the Soviet Union, and to make the invasion as big a surprise as possible, they timed it for three o'clock on a Sunday morning. Fact 2: On June 25,

1950, the North Koreans invaded South Korea, and to make the invasion as big a surprise as possible—"learning from historical experience" as the communists liked to say—they timed it for shortly after midnight on a Sunday morning. These two facts I knew; and they meant that both June 22, 1941, and June 25, 1950, were Sundays. From this it was just a matter of counting the weeks between the two dates in order to establish that there were two leap years between those events, rather than three. But if 1954 was a leap year, then so was 1950, 1946, and 1942, which gives *three* leap years between the two dates instead of two. From this I concluded that 1954 was not a leap year and that the date was March 1, not February 29.

I had barely finished my calculations when the guard opened my cell and took me to the interrogator, who was visibly upset. "You asked the guard whether March 1 was today or tomorrow. What made you believe that it was today or tomorrow? Who told you so?"

"Nobody," I said, "but I knew the date when I was arrested and kept counting the days."

He did not want to believe me. "Since when have you been trying to have conversations with the guards? Which other guards did you talk to? Don't you know the rules, don't you know that you are not allowed to talk to the guards unless asked?"

I told him that I regretted having asked the guard, that it was all the fault of my laziness, since I could have found out for myself without asking, as I actually did after the guard refused to tell me the date. "What did you find out?" he asked.

"The answer to my question," I said.

"What answer?"

"Well, the fact that today is March 1, 1954."

"And what difference does it make to you whether that is true or not?"

Not much, I had to admit: "In either case I am on my 546th day under arrest."

He had no comment on that and sent me back to my cell after thoroughly admonishing me to respect the rules and never again attempt to conduct conversations with the guards, or else I would be seriously punished.

Some time during the summer of 1954, after about three months of complete solitude without any interrogation, I underwent a sort of psychological crisis. It occurred to me that during my four investigations, each one of which went through the episode of June 1948 when, during my brief stay in Bucharest I had invited Commander Young to dinner at the Jakabs, I had never mentioned the fact that during the following winter the Soviets warned us that Young had sided with the Yugoslavs and therefore was to be treated as an enemy agent. There was no reason to hide this fact, since we fully complied with the Soviet directive, except that mentioning it would have made my earlier invitation of Young to dinner seem more suspect. It now occurred to me that if there was any truth to what my current interrogator and his predecessors had said—to the effect that as long as there was anything that they knew about and that I was not telling them, that was a sign that I had still not decided to tell the truth—if there was anything to this, then, well, here was something they might hold against me. Despite repeated questioning about Commander Young, I had never mentioned the crucial fact that in the winter of 1948–1949 the Soviets warned us that he was an enemy agent. The more I thought about this, the more stupid it seemed to me that I had not mentioned this fact as unpleasant as it was in terms of appearances. When one is alone for months and his fantasy runs wild, things get distorted, blown out of their normal proportions. After three or four days I could not think of anything else: my daily schedule got screwed up; I was unable to concentrate on my chess game; the idea became an obsession. I was unable to take my mind off the subject.

I finally decided to correct my omission and asked the guard to take me to the interrogator. He said he would tell the interrogator, but nothing happened. The next day I told the guard again, and again nothing happened. The third time I insisted that I had something urgent to tell the interrogator, that it was not a complaint but it had to do with the investigation. All this was to no avail. The guard answered my insistence by saying that my interrogator had been informed of my request but was busy with other cases. I finally realized that I had fallen into something that was obviously a regular pattern with prisoners in solitary confinement: after a while they break down psychologically and feel the need to talk to their interrogators. Not responding to them, keeping them waiting for weeks, was part of the psychological torture, part of the process of "mollifying" the prisoner. As soon as I realized this, I started feeling better: No, I said to myself, you won't get at me this way. Don't want to talk? Fine, I can wait. I no longer asked the guard anything; I slowly resumed my daily program and managed also to play chess. The crisis passed. After more than two weeks the interrogator finally had me taken to his room. I told him I had something to declare that I had not declared before, and told him about the Soviet warning. He took down my deposition and asked a couple of questions that I answered: Had I met Young after the Soviet warning? No. Had anyone else in the legation met Young after that warning? Not to my knowledge. Then he asked why had I not declared this when I was first questioned about Young. Obviously, I could not claim that I forgot to mention it; so I stated frankly that I was afraid that mentioning the Soviet warning would make my invitation of Young to dinner during his visit to Bucharest the previous summer look suspect.

The officer concluded the record, had me sign it, then said, "Is this all? We knew this all along. When you said you had something to say to me, I thought you had finally made up your mind. But I see now that I was mistaken. Have a good time in your cell; maybe you need another few years to make up your mind." With that he promptly sent me back to my cell. In spite of this sinister dismissal, I felt relieved. On the one hand, the interrogator's reaction showed that I had been naïve to fear that they would hold against me the fact of not having talked about this before. His saying "we knew this all along" made it clear to me that they had *not* known it: misleading the prisoner was a very elementary rule of interrogation that I had learned at the beginning. But it also made it clear that the information had no significance, because they were basically not interested in the truth, but in breaking the prisoner so he could be made to sign the statements the Securitate wanted. As to the final sermon, that no longer affected me—I had gotten used to it and did not take it seriously.

Months went by, and toward the end of the summer of 1954 I developed a problem that prevented me from walking for any extended period of time: my left foot started hurting whenever I stepped down on it. At first I tried to ignore the pain and continued walking. But it became gradually worse, so I had to stop my walking exercise and replace it with other exercises, such as lying on my back on the floor and bicycling. I now started doing this several times a day in place of walking. In my free life I had sometimes needed to wear arch supports in my shoes. When I was arrested I had not been wearing supports for a long time, so I did not bring them along when I was taken from home. I now figured that, as a result of the poor food, the many sleepless nights, and the lack of air and sunshine, my body had considerably weakened and so I probably needed the supports again. Ignoring this need and trying to walk in spite of the pain must have exacerbated the problem. I tried to manufacture something equivalent to a support by molding the inner soles of my shoes with bread in the shape of a support, then letting the bread dry and harden. This failed to accomplish anything: The bump that I shaped into my inner sole would not stay in place and quickly broke. Willy-nilly, I asked to see the interrogator, specifying clearly that I had a health problem, lest he be led to believe that I had decided to confess my crimes. I was taken out fairly promptly, after just a few days, and I told him what my problem was. I also gave him my interpretation of it, and said that I had the right kind of supports at home; the only thing that was needed was to ask my wife to send them.

I did not really expect any positive outcome from this audience with my interrogator; I was just trying my luck. But to my pleasant surprise, he did not say what I expected: namely, that I first had to decide to tell the truth. Instead, he asked me whether I had any other health problems: Was I able to sleep at night? Did I feel any other pain besides the one in my foot? Was my digestion normal? Did I cough? I said that at the moment I had no other health complaint. I added that, although a foot is just a foot and one does not die because one's left foot hurts, nevertheless this was a serious problem for me because I was unable to walk, and not being able to walk was a very grave condition. I then repeated my request. Again to my pleasant surprise, he did not reject it outright. What I was asking for was difficult to do, he said, because prisoners under investigation were usually not allowed any contact with the outside world, and asking for something to be sent in was a form of contact with the outside world. So it was difficult, but not impossible. He proposed— proposed!—that I wait for a few weeks and see how my problem evolved; maybe it would heal or go away by itself. If it did not, I should then ask to see him again and he would try to do what I wanted. This was a change of tone that I certainly appreciated, and I agreed without hesitation to wait and try to let my foot heal by itself.

One morning in the first half of September, a guard opened my door, entered the cell, and ordered me to collect all my things. I was blindfolded as usual, then taken out of the cell, led through the long corridor into the prison courtyard—I could smell the fresh air—then into another building, through another corridor, and finally into another cell where my blindfold was taken off. I found myself in a cell of the kind I had been in for the first seven months after my arrest, with no toilet, a wooden table and chair, and some daylight coming in from the corridor through the glass window high above the door. The only difference from that earlier cell was that this one had two wooden bunks, one on top of the other, with the lower bunk occupied by somebody. I was told to take the upper bunk, and the door of the cell was slammed shut.

My new cell mate was a rather strange fellow. At first I thought that this was a new trap, with a new informer who was supposed to find out from me what I was unwilling to tell the investigators. But I soon abandoned this hypothesis. First of all, I was not currently under investigation. My fourth investigation had been concluded months before. And there were other reasons, related to the personality of my cell mate. Teodor Bucur—this was his name—was thirty-six years old, of medium height, very thin, mostly bald, with a high forehead and a narrow face. As soon as I was introduced into his cell, he asked me how long I had been arrested and what was the latest news I had heard from the outside world. I told him the news from the summer of 1952. He had been under arrest for five years when we met, but he said he had more recent news because he had had several cellmates. He told me that Stalin had died in March 1953 and that Beria had subsequently been executed, but he did not know who the current leader of the Soviet Union was. The news about Stalin's death seemed credible in light of the twenty-one-gun salute I had heard on March 5, 1953; but the news about Beria having been executed seemed weird and I took it with a grain of salt (although, of course, it turned out to be true).

About himself, Bucur told me that he had spent the war as a student in Berlin; he went there not out of sympathy for the nazis, he said, but because he obtained a fellowship and this gave him the opportunity to avoid being drafted into the Romanian army. He studied history there and became a historian. He did not like sports and did not play games, but he liked reading. His main hobby, as well as his chosen profession, was history. He also liked to read novels, see plays, and travel. He had traveled extensively in Germany and the surrounding countries in the aftermath of the war and was able to give wonderful descriptions of beautiful places and monuments. Listening to his travelogues was an unmitigated joy for me, intensified, of course, by my hunger for this type of conversation after two long years of deprivation. I remembered for many years Bucur's painstakingly detailed description of Stephansdom, Vienna's magnificent cathedral, and was reminded of it again when, after many more years, I finally saw it. Bucur had found a job as a historian at some research institute in West Berlin. He had fallen in love with and married a German girl, and had settled permanently in West Berlin. Nevertheless, he wanted to keep some cultural ties to his native land, so from time to time he would go over to East Berlin to visit the Romanian diplomatic compound where there was a cultural center. There he would read or borrow from the center's library books about Romanian history, literature, geography, and folklore.

Some time in 1949, during one of his visits to the Romanian diplomatic compound in East Berlin, Bucur "forgot to go home": he was arrested by agents of the Securitate, drugged, put on a flight of TAROM (the Romanian airline) from East Berlin to Bucharest, and woke up in a cell at the Malmezon. He was then questioned for many months about his connections to Romanian emigrant circles in Berlin, which he said were nil or at best perfunctory. He told the Securitate everything he knew again and again, but the interrogators were never satisfied, the bastards—here he interrupted his narrative to let out a long, colorful stream of swear words—kept pressing him for things he did not know and could not say anything about.

At certain points in his story he would unexpectedly stop, say, "Excuse me for a moment," walk up and down as if immersed in some inner conversation with himself, then after a while come back and resume his story as if nothing had happened. On one such occasion he said, "They wanted something; I *had* to answer them." I did not understand why he *had* to answer them and asked for an explanation, upon which he said, "Oh, you don't know about it? They are not doing it to you?"

Doing *what* to me, I asked.

"Well, the electromagnetic connection." I did not understand. Then he explained that at some point during his long interrogation the Securitate— here again there was a break for a long curse—had put him to sleep and implanted an electromagnetic device into his brain. By means of this device, he explained, they could call him up at any time to ask him questions and he had to answer them—not necessarily aloud, because the most hateful aspect of the device was that it also read his thoughts. But he had to answer in his thoughts, or else they would submit him to various kinds of mental torture. So he had developed a habit of never refusing to answer or trying to hide anything. "It doesn't make sense, you see, when they read your thoughts anyway."

I told Bucur that I was not aware of anybody having implanted a device into my brain, and that I did not think a device of the kind he was describing existed. I did not see the scientific principle by which it could function, I said. Besides, this would be such an important discovery, with such a huge effect on everybody's daily life beyond its uses by the Securitate, that if such an invention existed or was even close to being feasible, we would have certainly heard about it.

"Your reasoning is absolutely impeccable," he answered. "My first reactions were along the same lines; I just didn't want to believe it. But then circumstances opened my eyes and revealed to me what was happening."

"What circumstances?" I asked. Then he told me the following story.

After a while the Securitate—pause, a long curse—tried to treat him differently, giving him reading materials. But what he received was all shit—"Forgive me for the expression," he said—brochures of the Communist party—and now came a stream of oaths three times as long as the one for the Securitate. Not having anything else to do, he said, he set out willy-nilly to read one of the brochures. It so happened—and he assured me that this was absolutely spontaneous and unintentional—that when he first came across the name of Gheorghe Gheorghiu-Dej, he was overcome by a need to fart, which he could not resist. Soon after that he was taken to interrogation, and what he had feared turned out to be true: the interrogator knew that he had farted when he read the name of Gheorghiu-Dej. He was berated and lectured at length for his lack of respect and his contempt for the party leaders, and he got nowhere when he tried to explain that the episode was involuntary.

At that point in Bucur's story I gave up trying to talk him out of his belief in the electromagnetic device. I understood that his belief was not based on logic and would not be shaken by rational arguments. I also noticed that my attempt to question the veracity of what he was saying irritated him, and from then on I tried to avoid contradicting him crassly or otherwise annoying him. One of the things in which I did contradict him, and was actually able to help him, was his firm conviction that the cells of the Malmezon were deliberately proportioned in such a way that the prisoner could not walk in them for more than three or four minutes without becoming dizzy. I explained that the dizziness came from the fact that he was always turning in the same direction, always right or always left, and that he had to alternate the direction of his turns. Yes, precisely, he said, but that was impossible to do because of the dimensions of the cell. But when I pointed out to him that the direction of the turn could be alternated by making an odd, rather than an even, number of steps in each direction, he tried it and finally convinced himself. From then on he started taking walks in our cell and professed eternal gratitude for my showing him how to do it.

Bucur was also interested in my background and did not want to believe me when I told him I was a communist. "No, that's not possible," he said. "Maybe it's not possible," I said, "but it is true," to which he retorted, "But you are not like them!" I tried to explain that obviously not all communists were alike, but did not get very far.

At one point Bucur told me a hair-raising story. A long time, maybe a year, after he was arrested, he said, the Securitate arrested his wife, who was living in West Berlin, and brought her to the Malmezon.

"How did you find out?" I asked. "Did they confront you with her?"

No, he said, it was much worse than that. They put his wife in a cell adjacent to his, so he could hear what was going on there, and one night eleven Securitate officers raped her one after the other, laughing and making fun of her, while she desperately cried for help and continually called her husband by name. When he started telling me the story I was inclined to believe it, for, after all, I knew there had been kidnappings from the West by Soviet or Eastern European agents. But by the time he finished, I concluded that the story was unlikely to be true.

First of all, the Securitate people were a nasty bunch but strongly disciplined: whatever they did was strictly calculated, not spontaneous. What purpose would it have served to gang-rape the young German wife of a Romanian emigrant? To break him? But he did not see the rape; he was not even told about it; and he did not have any evidence of it beyond what he thought he had overheard. It sounded more like a hallucination than anything else. Besides, in kidnapping Bucur from East Berlin the Securitate had already committed an act that might have led to bad publicity in the West. After his disappearance from East Berlin, his wife surely would not have gone there, and kidnapping her from West Berlin was the kind of complicated, risky operation that the Securitate would not lightly undertake without a serious reason. It would have carried the risk of a headline—"German wife of kidnapped historian also kidnapped from West Berlin by Romanian secret police"—which was not exactly the image the Securitate was after. Further, if they had kidnapped Bucur's wife, the Securitate would certainly have questioned her, tried to get her to contradict her husband in one respect or another, and confronted him with her. Otherwise the kidnapping would have served no useful purpose. But when I asked Bucur if his wife had been interrogated or if he had been confronted with her, his answer was negative. Finally, Bucur did not really need to be broken. He was perfectly innocent and willing to tell the Securitate whatever he knew, which, of course, was almost nothing. For all these reasons the story seemed unlikely.

Cohabitation with Bucur had its positive and its negative sides. On the positive side were all the exciting stories of his life. But beyond these, there was another matter of major importance: Bucur not only had the right to read but he actually had books. He was probably given this privilege when the Securitate discovered his schizophrenia, or whatever the name of the mental illness was to which he was driven by his torturers. When I was put into his cell, he had a classic of Russian literature, Goncharov's *Oblomov*, from the prison library. I had heard a lot about this novel's masterful portrayal of the "Russian character," but had not read it. Now the opportunity was there: although I was not allowed to read Bucur's book (or any book), still, if Bucur wanted to be my accomplice, I could read it, since only part of the upper bunk could be seen from the peephole in the cell door. And Bucur was more than willing. So, soon after I moved into the cell, I spent the only five or six days at the Malmezon that I could qualify as pleasant, even exciting, as I surreptitiously but avidly read Goncharov for much of the day and forgot everything else, even the food. It was a superb pleasure, akin to the one experienced when drinking the first glass of water after having been deprived of it for days.

On the other hand, my nights became a lot more agitated than before. Bucur would not comply with the rule against covering one's eyes during the night. He claimed he could not sleep with the light bulb shining into his eyes, and he covered them with a black handkerchief. Some of the guards went along with this, making an exception for a prisoner whom they perceived as slightly deranged, but other guards would not tolerate it. They would first bang on the door, which Bucur typically ignored, but which naturally woke me up. Next they would open the door and berate Bucur, upon which he would explain that he simply could not sleep otherwise. This was often followed by instant punishment, such as making him stand for half the night and so on. I tried to sleep through the commotion whenever I could, but often it was impossible.

Some time in early October, Bucur and I were jointly moved into a cell in the other building, which I had inhabited for more than a year before being moved into Bucur's cell. The new cell had the advantage of being equipped with a toilet hole and shower; otherwise our life did not change. There was a little more room for walking in the new cell, but I could not take advantage of it, since my left foot continued to hurt badly as soon as I stepped on it. In fact, before the change of cells the three daily trips to the toilet had become a nuisance, since walking hurt me so badly that I could only limp. Around the middle of October I asked again to see the interrogator for health reasons. He had me brought to his office a couple of days after I asked. I told him that I had waited for several weeks as he had asked me to do, but my foot was not getting better; on the contrary, it had grown worse, and when I tried to walk on it there was swelling as well as pain. He listened, then asked again whether I had any other health problem, to which I said no. Then he asked, "Can you wait for another month, just a month?" I said that my foot hurt badly, but yes, if there was no other way, I would wait for another month. His demeanor and his attitude gave me hope. I could not help feeling that something seemed to have changed, that this was no longer the same murderously hostile attitude that I had been exposed to during the last two years and two months.

As I later found out, my foot pain was not caused by lack of supports; I had a much more serious problem. Two years of meager food, no milk or butter, lack of sunshine or even daylight meant, among other things, complete deprivation of Vitamin D. This had led to massive osteoporosis (decalcification of the bone) in my left foot and to a lesser extent in my right foot. Fortunately, at the time I was not aware of this, and so the pain in my foot did not affect my morale too much.

On the morning of November 12, 1954, as I was squatting at the toilet, the door opened. The guard came in and motioned me to get up to be taken to the interrogation room. He was in a hurry, as always, and could barely wait for me to pull up my pants. I remembered that it had been about about a month since I had been told to wait for another month. In the interrogation room I faced the same officer, my fourth interrogator, sitting behind his desk. From his severe, penetrating gaze and the stern expression on his face I realized that he was again in the role of the grand inquisitor and I did not expect to hear anything good. I thought he was going to let me know that my request for the supports had been rejected because I would not cooperate with the investigation. Instead, what I heard was worse.

"I am asking you for the last time," he said, "to make up your mind and come forward with the truth. Today you have a last chance to do this. If you don't take this chance, tomorrow it will be too late. Today is an important day for you." I sat quietly without saying a word. "Well," he said after a while, "will you or will you not come forward and talk?"

I was rather put off by this development, but said to myself, "What did you expect? You let yourself be deceived by the interrogator's seeming kindness for a fleeting moment and allowed yourself the luxury of a hopeful outlook. Now you must pay the price of your foolishness." To the interrogator I said, "Everything there was to be said I said a long time ago. I have nothing else to declare."

"Well," he replied, "if that is your wish, then so be it. You will now leave this place and go elsewhere. Are you psychologically prepared to move to another place, perhaps worse than this, perhaps better in some respects? Are you prepared to start a new life there?"

I did not quite know how to take this new threat. I assumed that there were other places of investigation besides the one where I was being kept, but moving me to another such place did not seem to make sense. I also knew that there were places like the Canal, where "enemies of the people" were sent, usually without a judicial sentence, on the basis of some administrative ruling; and this now seemed a possible interpretation of what the interrogator was talking about. My uncertainty was reflected in my answer to his question: "I don't know whether I am ready; it depends on the place."

He then said, "Well, what about home for a place?"

"Pardon me?" I said.

Suddenly, his whole face became a big smile: "You are going home."

I did not believe him. I held back the joyous reaction that was building up inside me. "Don't be a fool," I said to myself. "Don't let them fool you again; waking up from the dream will be painful."

"When?" I said aloud, "When do you plan to send me home?"

"In about an hour," he said, "as soon as the car is available." I still did not believe him. What if they put me in a car blindfolded, telling me I was going home, and then the car stops, they nudge me out, the blindfold is taken off—and I am in a new prison? What a psychological coup that would be for them! They might figure that would break me. How could I test him?

"Right now I am in a cell with another inmate," I said. "I have another shirt besides the one I am wearing. It is my only change, but if I am going home, I will not need it. May I leave it with my cell mate, who has been under arrest longer than me and has no change?" I figured that if they were sending me to another jail, they would want me to keep my second shirt, since I would need it there.

The officer's face suddenly darkened. "Who is your cell-mate?"

"Teodor Bucur."

"What do you have in common with him? Why do you care about him?" he asked.

"We spent two months in the same cell, ate the same food, shared the same toilet, and told each other stories," I said.

"What messages did he ask you to take out in case you were freed before him, and to whom are you supposed to take those messages?" the officer asked.

"We did not discuss such a contingency," I said, "and he did not ask me to take any messages to anyone."

"I warn you," the interrogator said, "that if you *do* take a message out of here, you will find yourself back here in no time."

I liked this a lot: it seemed that they were really going to let me out. "OK," I said, "I understand, and I do not intend to take a message to anybody. So may I leave my shirt with Teodor Bucur?"

"Certainly not," he said, "and you are not going to return to your cell either."

"I have some things there, though," I said. I was thinking mainly of my folded handkerchief with the miniature chessmen that I would have liked to keep as a souvenir in case I was indeed being freed, or as a useful toy otherwise. I was also thinking that if their freeing me was only a bluff, I would need my sweater.

"We will get those for you," he said. He called the guard and told him to go to my cell and get all my things. I imagined Bucur's face at the news that he was losing his cell mate: he would have no means of knowing whether I was being freed, sent to another jail, or just put in a different cell.

The guard soon returned with my things. The interrogator then said, "Well, you will now be freed. We hope that the time you spent here was not entirely lost for you. You must have learned a few things, and we hope that in the future you will be more careful about what you say and how you speak. Anyway, I wish you good luck. Where do you want the car to take you?"

"Home," I said and gave the address: "Bulevardul Stalin, number 72."

"Your family no longer lives there. Your wife has moved to her parents in Cluj," he said. "Do you have some friend in Bucharest?"

"It's none of your business who my friends are, you bastards," I thought, but instead I said, "I want to join my wife and daughter. If they are in Cluj, take me or send me there, please."

"I cannot send you to Cluj by car," the officer said, "but I can provide you with a train ticket. There is a train that leaves Bucharest in the evening and gets there in the morning. Is it OK if I get you a ticket for tonight?"

"Perfectly OK," I said.

"And where do you want to spend the day here in Bucharest?" he asked. "To what address do you want us to take you? You will need somebody to spend the day with, to eat with. You don't have a lot of pocket money."

"Don't you worry about that," I said, "just leave me in the street, anywhere around the place where your people picked me up. I will find my way from there."

"You seem to have difficulty walking," he said.

"Yes, quite a bit. I could use a walking stick, if you have a spare one." He told a guard to go find some sort of stick; then, after being blindfolded, I was led to another room to wait for the car to become available. When that happened, I was again blindfolded and taken to the registration room where my things had been deposited when I arrived. I was given back my belt, shoelaces, wristwatch, wallet, and bag. I was also given a walking stick and a train ticket to Cluj for the same evening. Then I was blindfolded and led to the car. We drove for thirty-five or forty minutes before the car stopped and the person accompanying me took off my blindfolds.

"Here you go," he said, "have a good day." I got out of the car and found myself in my old neighborhood where I had lived before my arrest.

It was two years and three months to the day since that fateful night when I had been arrested and my long, long nightmare had started. For exactly two years and three months I had not seen the sky. On this November morning, the sky looked bluer than ever before. The sun was shining and everything looked unnaturally bright: the trees lining the street, the houses, the fences. There were no people in the street. The car waited for a few seconds, as if to see what I was going to do, but I decided not to do anything until it left. So I just stood there, leaning lightly on my stick, and watched the driver until he pressed the gas pedal and drove off. Then I finally felt free.

CHAPTER 11

■ ■ ■

The Aftermath

From the spot where I was dropped by the Securitate car, it took me about ten minutes, limping slowly, to reach the home of my friends Bandi and Juci Klein. They were both at work—it was between ten and eleven in the morning—and the children were at school; but the maid, who was at home, knew me and let me in. I asked her whether she remembered Edith and knew anything about her. She said, of course, and she knew that Edith and the children were living in Cluj. "What children?" I said. "You must mean my daughter Anna." She was embarrassed: "Sorry, I got confused and thought that you had two children. Your wife and daughter are in Cluj and are well. I saw your wife earlier this year when she visited here." We called Juci and Bandi at their workplaces and they both said they would come home immediately. While waiting for them, I had a chance to look into a mirror and what I saw was a pale, greenish, barely recognizable variant of my earlier face.

Juci arrived first; a little later Bandi appeared. There was great joy, of a quality that only those who have been in similar situations understand. Naturally, my first question was about Edith and Anna, and Juci said, "Edith and the children are in Cluj with Edith's parents, and they are healthy and OK." Like the maid, she spoke of "children."

"What children?" I asked.

"You don't know? They didn't tell you?" wondered Juci.

"Tell me what?"

"That you have a second daughter." This came as a shock. I could not say anything; I just stared at Juci.

"Her name is Vera," she said, and hastened to add, "Her face is very much like yours."

"When?" I asked haltingly. "When did this happen?"

"She was born some time in the spring of 1953," Juci said, "a little less than nine months after you were taken away." I felt a mixture of confusion, relief, and a sort of pride.

Juci immediately started to explain how Edith had discovered her pregnancy ten days or two weeks after my arrest, and how everybody—including Juci herself and Klara, Edith's mother—advised her to have an abortion. They argued that keeping the child in Edith's dangerous situation—after all, she could have been arrested herself—was too risky and would complicate her life enormously. But Edith was adamant about wanting the child. Then they told her, "We hope this will not be the case, but being realistic, you may never see Egon again." "That's why I want at least his child," was Edith's reply.

We tried to call Edith on the phone. She was at work and so was everybody else; nobody was at home at Edith's parents' house. Finally Juci managed to reach a neighbor of the Lövis. After a while her message reached Edith and she called back. The only thing I remember about that conversation was an overwhelming feeling of joy. I gave her the arrival time of my train the next morning.

Juci and Bandi told me that four weeks before my release, in the middle of October, there had been a trial of Vasile Luca and his "accomplices," including Sanyi Jakab. Luca confessed at the trial to have been an informer for the prewar Romanian Siguranța (the political police) from the early thirties on, and to have done everything he could to undermine the party after it came to power. He was sentenced to life imprisonment. Sanyi was indicted for having sabotaged the economy. He tried to defend himself at the trial, admitting to have committed errors but rejecting the accusation of deliberate wrongdoing. He was sentenced to twenty years in jail. The others got lighter sentences; some were acquitted. I found this news shocking. Amidst the horror of the news about Sanyi's sentencing I was nevertheless relieved to hear that he was alive and that the accusation of his having been a nazi agent had been dropped. I was also told about Beria's execution after Stalin's death, and Malenkov's ascent to power.*

I took the overnight train to Cluj and in the morning, as the train pulled into the station, I was standing on the stairs of the railway car when I saw Edith running toward me. We embraced at length. Tears poured down her face. She was as pretty and shapely as ever, but there was a change in her face: between her eyebrows, on her forehead right above her nose, there was a new line that gave her an expression of maturity unknown to me. She asked why I was limping; I could not hide it beyond the first few minutes. I said it was nothing; it would go away shortly. We went home.

It was around eight o'clock, and as we entered the Lövis' apartment I saw a child's bed and in it a little girl asleep. I was overtaken by a warm feeling as I seemed to recognize Anna, hardly changed since I had last seen her. She was about the same age and the same size, or so it seemed to me. As I looked at her, trying to make out her features without waking her up, the door from the other room suddenly opened and a tall, lanky girl, about five years old, with a pretty, smiling face, entered the room and approached me with almost dancing steps, like a ballerina. I suddenly realized that this big, unfamiliar-looking girl, must be Anna, and that the other one was my new daughter. Anna hugged and kissed me with an air of familiarity that contrasted sharply with my own feeling of meeting a new, unknown person. This whole episode lasted only a few minutes; but like all first impressions, it was sharply etched into my memory. I was soon to find out from Edith how much Anna had missed me. She could not be told, of course, where I really was; instead, she was told that I was at work in some other town. She would repeatedly and insistently inquire about why I did not come home, at least for a visit. "Doesn't Daddy love us?" she would ask. She refused to accept the explanations offered. She had an uncle, the husband of Edith's Aunt Irén, who was very kind to her and to whom she felt close. One day she asked him, "Uncle Károly, would you want to be my father?"

*Lavrenty Beria, Minister of the Interior in control of the Secret Police and all branches of the enormous Soviet repression apparatus, was second in power only to Stalin until the latter's death in March 1953. That event was followed by a brief but sharp power struggle between Georgy Malenkov and Nikita Khrushchev on the one hand, and Beria on the other. Beria lost, and in June 1953 he was executed as an imperialist agent who had infiltrated the Communist Party in order to undermine it.

Anna and Vera before Egon's release, in 1954

When I rejoined my family, Anna was four and a half. She talked easily and intelligently, and had many questions. She knew many songs, both children's songs and others. Vera was one and a half, a well-developed, sweet, healthy girl, who sang along with her sister. When taken out for a walk, the two of them were show stoppers. For a while I bathed in the happiness of being their father.

When Edith and I had a chance to talk, I told her what I had been through and she described her life in my absence. In addition to the new feature I had detected in Edith's face, which gave it a more mature look, there was also a considerable change in her personality. The two years and three months that I spent under such horrible conditions were very hard on her, too. She had to face some basic decisions in her life, and confronting them had not only made her mature, but had strengthened her character and given her a new independence of judgment. A week before my arrest, Edith had been assigned a job at the Scientific Publishing House in Bucharest. After my arrest, she went to see the director, told him that I had been arrested, and asked whether she could still take the job. Fortunately the director, a certain Comrade Deutsch, said, "The party knows what it's doing. If you have been assigned to this job, it means you can take it." She started working. Soon she discovered that she was pregnant. In spite of everybody's advice, she stubbornly decided to keep the child. Then she decided to move to Cluj, where she could stay with her parents, who could help her with the pregnancy and the new child. Sándor and Klara were happy to receive her and Anna. But a job had to be found. Luckily, the Scientific Publishing House had its Hungarian-language branch office in Cluj, so she asked to be transferred there, explaining her reasons. The same Director Deutsch who had agreed to hire her in spite of my situation, now agreed to transfer her to the Cluj office. I should mention that the type of decent behavior displayed by Director Deutsch was rather uncommon.

Since Edith did not want to abandon our Bucharest apartment—obtaining another one later would have been an almost impossible task—she decided to cede it temporarily to somebody, on the understanding that the person would return it as soon as I came home. In Cluj, Edith and Anna were surrounded with the love and care of Sándor and Klara. The Lövis had an income well above the average, as Klara made wonderful artificial flowers and Sándor was extremely good at marketing them in his free time. He held a job as the buyer for a state company. In the centrally planned economies of Eastern Europe, with their constant excess of demand over supply, the job of the buyer was a crucial one for each company, so Sándor's work was highly appreciated by his employers. That in itself would not have produced a high income; all salaries were low, though some were lower than others. The main source of the couple's income was private economic activity, namely Klara's artificial flower workshop. Sándor's job required him to personally receive every delivery, whenever it arrived, so people would frequently come to fetch him in the middle of the night. The trouble with this was that whenever the bell rang in the middle of the night, Edith never knew whether the visitor was somebody from Sándor's company, looking for him to receive a delivery, or from the Securitate, coming to arrest her.

On May 8, 1953, Vera arrived. She was born with her umbilical cord around her neck, a complication that was luckily resolved without great difficulty. She was a healthy child from the beginning and showed no trace of the anguish that her mother had lived through many times during her pregnancy. After Vera's birth, conditions in the Lövis' apartment became a bit crammed, and Edith decided to move out with the two girls into a garden at the top of Majális utca, the nice street where I had lived in hiding between October 1943 and May 1944. The garden had a cabin where Edith and the girls slept; a maid would come in the morning and bring food cooked at the Lövis' apartment. They all loved the garden, so the following year Sándor bought a similar garden on the same street, and had a wooden cottage built there with two rooms and bath. Thus, from the end of May to mid-October Edith and the girls lived in the garden on top of the hill. It was a lovely place, and the girls still remember it with delight; they continued spending much of their summertime there, with their grandparents, for several years after my return. While living in the summer house, Edith rode a bike twice daily to her workplace downtown. She would return home at noon to feed Vera, then go back to her job.

At her workplace, Edith edited and supervised the Hungarian translations of scientific books in areas other than the natural sciences, mainly works of classical philosophy. She befriended two of her colleagues and got along with the others and with her boss. However, to our earlier acquaintances, those with party connections, she became a pariah. Some would turn away their heads when meeting her in the street; others would cross the street to avoid her. Such behavior was common; it was a precaution that most party members felt expedient to exercise as a measure of self-protection. During the first few months after my arrest, Edith was expecting the worst. She had no news about me either then or later, could not write or send me anything, and did not even know whether I was still alive. Just as I had been kept in the dark about my family, Edith was given no news about me.

The atmosphere was terrible, and frightening things were happening in some of the neighboring countries. In November 1952, in Prague, there was a trial of the "zionist-imperialist-Titoist center" headed by none other than Rudolf Slansky, the general secretary of the Communist Party, a Jew. He confessed to all the crimes he was accused of and was executed. In the wake of the trial, an anti-Semitic wind started blowing throughout the socialist camp in all of Eastern Europe. Things got even worse in January 1953, when a communique from the Soviet news agency TASS revealed that in Moscow a plot by Jewish doctors to poison some of the party leaders had been foiled at the last moment. Edith expected every day a headline about my indictment or execution as a traitor. At some time during the late fall of 1952, she was called to the Securitate from her office and questioned for two or three hours about my activities. She related what she knew, but the Securitate was not satisfied and wanted more. In particular, they were interested in what she knew about Commander Young, but Edith did not know him or did not remember him at all (she may not have actually met him). When they finally let her go they said that she might be called in again, but this did not happen.

During the winter of 1953–1954, Magda Jakab was released by the Securitate after a year and a half of detention. Magda had gone insane while at the Securitate: she could not recognize anybody, would refuse to eat periodically on the grounds that "they" were trying to poison her, and so on. She needed treatment and internment in a mental asylum. At the mental hospital in Cluj a neurologist who knew Magda admitted her and undertook to treat her. But Magda needed an official guardian and there was nobody to take on that role. Sanyi Jakab had two brothers in Cluj, but apparently they felt so threatened by their association with their brother, the "enemy of the people," that neither of them thought he could assume this additional burden. Edith found out about this and offered to become Magda's guardian. That meant weekly visits to the mental hospital, which Edith found hard to bear. Magda would not recognize her or talk to her, and Edith was never sure whether the things she brought for Magda, mostly food and some delicacies, actually remained in Magda's possession or were simply taken away after Edith left. The sight of the other insane patients also had a very depressing effect on Edith. Nevertheless, she kept up the visits. When I returned to Cluj, almost a year after Magda's release from the Securitate, her situation as a mental patient was unchanged. She never recovered.

One or two days after my arrival in Cluj the best orthopedist in town examined me and, after taking X-rays, found that I was suffering from massive osteoporosis in both my feet, especially the left foot, caused by the vitamin D deficiency. The pain in this foot was from the inflammation caused by my attempts to walk. The doctor ordered complete rest for the foot and put it in a cast for three weeks to ease the inflammation. He thought that rest, good food, vitamins, fresh air, and sunshine would cure my osteoporosis in a couple of months.

While I was confined to bed for more than two weeks, I started receiving visitors and had long conversations with some of my friends. I learned that after Stalin's death there were some changes in the Soviet Union, but the nature of those changes was unclear. One of the mysteries was the strange arrest and execution of Beria in the summer of 1953. For one thing, Beria had been the head of the Soviet Interior Ministry and the security apparatus, and in that capacity he had been involved more than any other Soviet leader in the staging of the trials of Rajk, Kostov, Slansky, and others. I certainly did not mourn his departure. Yet there was no admission on the part of the new Soviet leaders that those trials had been wrong. Quite the contrary: the way Beria was liquidated was as weird as any of the previous sudden downfalls from the heights of power in the Soviet-dominated empire. He was not apprehended for arresting innocent people or for organizing fake trials; no, he was arrested as an "imperialist agent," instantly found guilty, and executed under murky circumstances whose details were unavailable. Was there any reason to assume that with the death of Stalin and the elimination of Beria the nature of the show trials would be reconsidered? One of my friends was of the opinion that they would all turn out to have been erroneous, based on false accusations. I wished this would turn out to be true, but at that point I did not know.

Some of my friends read the Hungarian press and listened to the Hungarian radio, and in Hungary some strange things were happening. As early as the winter of 1952–1953, the head of the Hungarian secret police, Gábor Péter, had been arrested. He had been the chief architect of the Rajk trial, under the guidance of Mátyás Rákosi, the party leader. Furthermore, in June 1953, following a visit to Moscow by the entire Hungarian leadership, the politburo of the Hungarian Party had been reshuffled: Rákosi gave up the prime ministership while remaining general secretary of the party, and a new person, also a former Moscovite, Imre Nagy, became prime minister. Nagy advocated giving priority in the party's economic policy to the development of agriculture and light industry—in other words, to the production of food and consumer goods as opposed to heavy industry. He also encouraged "more openness and straight talk" in the country's political life. Some of these priorities echoed those of Malenkov, the Soviet prime minister. Yet there seemed to be no consensus on these issues; Rákosi, appeared to go along with the new line only reluctantly, and kept warning of the dangers represented by the "class enemy." In the midst of considerable uncertainty about where the ship of world communism was heading, one remarkable fact was certain: after Stalin's death and Beria's elimination, there were no political trials of party leaders either in the Soviet Union or in any of the other communist countries, except Romania.

In reading the brief press reports on the trials of Luca and Pătrăşcanu I tried to put together the missing pieces of the puzzles they represented. Luca's trial was semipublic, meaning that officially it was a public trial, but in reality attendance was only by invitation; the audience consisted mainly of Securitate agents and a few reliable party hacks. Even so, I was able to find out that at the trial Luca had miserably besmirched himself by confessing not only that he had been an agent of the bourgeois Romanian Siguranţa in the thirties, but that during a prewar workers' strike he had actually signaled to the forces of order when and where to shoot into the demonstrating crowd. He also willingly admitted to all kinds of wrongdoing in his capacity as finance minister, committed with the simple and straightforward motivation of harming the party's cause. Several high officials of the Finance Ministry testified against him, either as co-defendants who then were acquitted, or as witnesses. On the contrary, Sanyi Jakab, accused of various acts of sabotage as deputy finance minister, defended himself at the trial by describing some of his actions as economically justified and others as taken in good faith, even if in hindsight they might appear to have been misguided. He provoked the wrath of the party by asking the prosecution witnesses unpleasant questions. Two other high officials who had worked under Luca, though not in the ministry itself, were sentenced in the same trial. I was to find out much later, when Sanyi was freed as part of a general amnesty in 1964, that because of his "uncooperative" behavior during the investigation and the trial, he was kept in solitary confinement after his sentencing under basically the same regime as before, until almost the time of his release— for a total of eleven and a half years.

As to the Pătrăşcanu trial, in the fall of 1954 I could find out only that it had taken place in April of that year, that it was not even semipublic, and that Lucretiu Pătrăşcanu himself, along with Remus Koffler, a leading member of the party during the war, had been sentenced to death as enemy agents in the service of the Anglo-American espionage organizations. Belu Zilber, a well-known economist and statistician; Emil Calmanovici, a civil engineer; and Alexandru Ştefănescu, an industrialist, all of whom had been active in the anti-nazi underground during the war, were sentenced to life in prison as accomplices of Pătrăşcanu and Koffler. The architect Jacques Berman, my former colleague at the Romanian legation in London, was sentenced to ten years imprisonment, also as an accomplice of Pătrăşcanu and the other members of the "espionage ring." Several other people were sentenced to terms of between eight and fifteen years. In the fall of 1954 I was not able to find out anything about the behavior of the accused at the trial, except for the fact that Pătrăşcanu refused to admit anything, which was why the trial could not be public. The press falsely reported that all of those accused in the trial had admitted their guilt.

Many years later I learned that Pătrăşcanu, who denied all the accusations throughout the six years of his detention, appeared at his trial with one foot amputated and rejected the whole indictment as a farce. His last words to the judges were: "Murderers, history will put you in this box where I now stand." He was shot the day after the death sentence was passed, allegedly in his cell, from behind.

Koffler denied all the charges during his interrogation until, gravely ill, he was taken to a hospital where he was visited by a member of the Central Committee. Nobody knows what he was told, but after that conversation he agreed to confess to the most monstrous accusations of treason and espionage, inculpating himself and Pătrăşcanu alike. At the trial, however, he retracted his confession and said that it had been extracted from him under the false pretense that it would serve the interests of the party.

Belu Zilber was broken a few months after his arrest in the late forties, and invented many of the false stories that formed the basis of the indictment against the group. When freed in 1964 under a general amnesty, he asked to be rehabilitated. But the people at the party cynically showed him his confessions and said, "You have repeatedly stated that you committed these things, so what do you want now?" He recounts these and other adventures in a memoir written in the seventies and published in the nineties. Emil Calmanovici rejected the accusations as false, at the trial as well as during his interrogation. After his sentencing, he went on a hunger strike while in prison and was killed by his jailers in a failed attempt to force-feed him.

Finally, Jacques Berman, arrested in late 1952, was soon broken and agreed to the espionage charges brought against him, inculpating Pătrăşcanu and some others. In the fall of 1954 I had no way of knowing whether he had actually made the statements about spying for the British with me that I had been told about by the Securitate. But, as I've already mentioned, in the early sixties, when he was freed before completing his sentence, he came to see me and apologized for having given in to pressure under torture and having implicated me in an espionage story that he later retracted.

Over forty years later, a collection of the main documents of the Pătrăşcanu trial was published in Bucharest (*Principiul bumerangului: documente ale procesului Pătrăşcanu*. Editura Vremea, Bucuresti, 1996). In this volume, I found a long statement made by Jacques Berman while he was under arrest in January 1953. The statement deals with Berman's alleged postwar espionage activities. In it, Berman claims that soon after his arrival in London in 1948 he was recruited by the British Intelligence Service to work for them, and soon after that he in turn recruited me. The two of us allegedly had several meetings with a certain Mr. Thompson of the Intelligence Service in the latter's office on Wigmore Street. In order to enable the two of us to spy more fruitfully, the Intelligence Service allegedly arranged for me to be expelled from Britain in early 1949. According to Berman's story, after my return to Bucharest I worked directly with the Intelligence Service without his assistance, but when he also returned a few months later, he was instructed to sabotage the country's economy and to spy, conveying the information that he was able to gather to the Intelligence Service through me.

In 1997, when the archives of the former Securitate were partly opened to researchers, a young American historian specializing in Eastern Europe, Robert Levy, was kind enough to give me two other statements of Berman's referring to alleged espionage activities performed jointly with me. In these statements, made in March 1953, Berman was asked to elaborate on his earlier statements concerning his joint espionage activities with Balaş. He repeated the same story, but this time placed the meeting with Thompson in the latter's office on Park Lane, not Wigmore Street. He went on to elaborate on the subject of his espionage activities after his return to Bucharest, all of which he claimed to have performed under my direction, handing over to me the results of his efforts to be forwarded to the British Intelligence Service. He had a long list of documents from the Ministry of Construction that he allegedly had given me between November 1949 and June 1952 to be handed over to British intelligence: the chapters of the 1950 and 1951 state plans dealing with the construction industry, quarterly reports on construction plans and their execution, the organizational blueprint of the Research Institute for

Construction, and many others, all described in ' concrete detail. Ominously, his statement goes on to say that he had obtained all these materials from Emil Calmanovici and that they were written in Calmanovici's
own handwriting. He also claimed to have given me materials about
Romania's electrification plan, information about some engineering problems that arose in the construction of the Danube-Black Sea Canal, the
names and functions of the Soviet counselors at the Canal Works, plans
for the capacity expansion of the Hunedoara Steel Works, and many
other items, obtained from two other individuals mentioned by name.
Berman's statements include a detailed account of when and where he
handed over these materials to me: mostly at my home in Strada Tokyo—which in the January statement he mistakenly calls Strada Haga—
but a couple of times at my office in the Ministry of Foreign Affairs.

I will probably never find out why the charge against me of spying for
the British Intelligence Service with Berman and his allegedly numerous
accomplices was dropped: certainly, it was not just because I adamantly
denied it. One plausible explanation, put forward by Robert Levy, is this:
it is well known that, from 1949 to 1952 the NKVD, the Soviet counterespionage service, was actively pushing the people's democracies to organize political show trials. Of all the Eastern European satellites, Romania
was the only one that did not have a trial of leading communists during
this period. For sure, two such trials were in preparation, one against
Pătrăşcanu and the other against Luca, but they were delayed until after
1952 for reasons of their own: Pătrăşcanu's, because in spite of all its
efforts, the Securitate proved incapable of obtaining a confession from
the main culprit; Luca's, because the group supposed to make up the
trial was arrested only in 1952, and by the end of that year, in spite of
Luca's having been broken as early as September, the trial was not ready
to go. Thus, during the winter of 1952–1953, so Levy's reasoning goes,
there was an attempt, initiated by the Soviets, to link the two cases into
a single monster show trial like Rajk's and Slansky's, involving, besides
Pătrăşcanu and Luca, also Pauker, Georgescu, and perhaps others, with
zionist connections figuring prominently among the accusations. The link
between the two groups would have been the alleged espionage activity
for the British Intelligence Service by Berman and Calmanovici from the
Pătrăşcanu group, carried out jointly with, and partly under the direction of, Egon Balaş from the Luca group. Certainly, the pressures exerted
by the Securitate on Berman during the winter of 1952–1953 to come up

with his espionage story and implicate me along with Calmanovici and others support this hypothesis.

As the machinery of the Securitate was methodically and laboriously grinding out this conspiracy, Stalin suddenly died in March 1953. It was about the same time that I was being pressed to admit to having visited that ominous place in London called Park Lane and to having met there a certain Thompson. A couple of months later, in May 1953, I was being pressed to admit to have spied with Berman for British Intelligence. However, in the face of my categorical denial, the Securitate gave up without going to the extremes they were capable of when they were really determined to get something: no attempt was made to savagely beat me, as Jakab, Zilber, and Calmanovici were beaten, in a more decisive attempt to break me. Why? The most plausible explanation is that with the death of Stalin, the Soviet pressure for show trials had stopped. From then on, the Romanian Securitate conducted the preparation of the two trials on its own, without any particular Soviet pressure. This is at least partly corroborated by the fact that in early 1954, when Miron Constantinescu was sent to Moscow by Gheorghiu-Dej to present a summary of the case against Pătrăşcanu to Malenkov, the Soviet premier, and to obtain his approval for the trial, he was told by the latter repeatedly: *"Eto vashe delo"* (This is your business.) Thus, the fact that I survived my ordeal, instead of becoming the crucial link between the Pătrăşcanu and Luca trials, was sheer luck on one plane, historical accident on another.

By the way, I have independent confirmation of the fact that Berman later retracted his depositions implicating me. Robert Levy also managed to retrieve from the archives of the former Securitate the internal memorandum dated October 20, 1954, on the basis of which I was released. This document states that Egon Balaş had been arrested for the following reasons: in the fall of 1943 he had managed to avoid being arrested in a way that indicated possible connections to the Hungarian counterespionage (DEF); after his arrest in 1944, he had managed to escape from a transport to Germany under circumstances that aroused suspicion; finally, during the war he had worked in the underground communist movement with the detainee Sándor Jakab. "For these reasons, and in order to clarify the entire activity deployed by both Balaş and Jakab during the underground period and after August 23, 1944, as well as in order to clarify the nature of their connections with the British Commander Young, Egon Balaş was arrested on August 12, 1952."

After relating how I got involved in the communist movement and how I became a party member, according to my own statements, the document says, "These facts are confirmed by Sándor Jakab." It further states:

> Balaş claims to have organized a strike, to have organized distributions of leaflets, etc. In connection with this, the witness Ilona Grünfeld states that Balaş organized the distribution of leaflets in a way that could provoke the arrest of the comrades (see p. 366). Balaş, on the other hand, states that he took all the necessary precautions in organizing these activities (see pp. 43, 44, 47, 48, 49). The depositions taken from the witnesses Mihail Sava, Gheorghe Havas, and Tiberiu Hida, who had participated in the distribution of the leaflets, confirm Balaş's statements and show that they were not arrested for their underground activities. (see pp. 345, 346, 348 and 393)

About the circumstances of my not having been arrested in 1943, the memorandum reproduces my explanations for going into hiding exactly at the time I did, and of the way I suspended my contacts when the arrests started, and states that these facts are confirmed by Sándor Jakab. It then summarizes the story of my arrest in 1944 by the DEF, my interrogation in Budapest, my sentencing to a fourteen-year prison term, and my escape from the transport to Germany upon the evacuation of the Komárom Star Fortress. It adds:

> Since the persons who know about these facts live in the People's Republic of Hungary, on March 9, 1954, we approached the competent authorities of the P. R. of Hungary with the request that they question certain persons named by us on these matters. On May 18 and July 9, 1954, we repeated this request. Nevertheless, to this date we have no answer. On the other hand, it should be mentioned that in the party file of Egon Balaş there exists a statement by Károly Fekete (who is living in the P. R. of Hungary) confirming Balaş's statements concerning his escape, thus clarifying this problem.

Notice that although I had been arrested on August 12, 1952, and although the question of my interrogation by the DEF and my subsequent escape had been central to my case and figured prominently among the reasons given for my arrest in this same document, it was not until March 9, 1954, a full year and a half later, that the authorities of the "fraternal republic" were approached. This confirms my contention that the purpose of the investigations—mine as well as others'—was not to establish the truth but to coerce confessions, whether true or false. In March 1954, when the first request was made, I was undergoing my *fourth* full-length investigation. Apparently the three earlier ones were simply concluded with the negative result that I refused to cooperate and so nothing could be established: No attempt was ever made to check the information I gave by questioning the witnesses I named.

Finally, with respect to Berman's espionage story, the memorandum says the following:

In the process of investigating Jacques Berman, former economic counselor at the Romanian legation in London (1948–1949) (sentenced in the Pătrășcanu trial), the latter stated that he had established espionage relations with Egon Balaş and had connected Balaş to the British Intelligence Service (see pp. 313, 315, 316, 317, 318). Egon Balaş refused to admit that he had espionage relations with Jacques Berman or with any other person. Subsequently Jacques Berman retracted his statements concerning Egon Balaş, maintaining that he had no espionage relations with Egon Balaş. (see p. 337)

The memo concludes with the admission that "no penal facts" could be established against the detainee Egon Balaş, and therefore recommends that he be set free. There is no explanation given for Berman's change of mind, nor is there any discussion of the circumstances under which Berman's original, absurd espionage story was spawned. Who inspired it and for what purpose? What led the story's inventors to change their minds? We may never be able to find out, but Levy's hypothesis is at least plausible.

Be that as it may, in those days of late 1954 I was not aware of the mortal danger in which I had been. I basically saw in my release a confirmation of the naïve belief I had entertained throughout the long years of my arrest: that if I stuck to the truth and did not give in to pressure, sooner or later the Securitate would have no choice but to let me go.

Three weeks after my arrival in Cluj, the cast was removed from my left foot and I tried walking on it. I could not; it still hurt badly at every step. The doctor wanted me to stay in bed for another few weeks, but I had no patience. During the time that I was immobilized, I had been thinking about what kind of work I wanted to do. I decided to say goodbye to politics. I was still committed to building a better society and I still considered myself a communist, but I was bitterly disappointed with the politics of the Romanian Communist Party and decided that I would not accept any party or government job, even in the unlikely event that one would be offered to me. I wanted a research and teaching job, with plenty of time to learn. When I was in the Foreign Ministry I used to be considered its best economic expert, but I did not feel that I knew enough about economics and was eager to learn, to become a true expert. So I was impatient to start my new life. Also, I had to take the steps necessary to reclaim our apartment. Thus, though still walking with a stick, I decided to go to Bucharest and try to obtain the kind of job that I wanted and get shelter. I also wanted to get a second opinion about my foot.

The orthopedist in Bucharest confirmed the diagnosis of massive osteoporosis. I also underwent a thorough general medical examination, during which I was hospitalized for several days. Everything else was found to be in order, and the prescription for the osteoporosis was as much rest for the foot as possible, and patience (of which I was rather short). So for a few more weeks I walked with a stick and then the pain gradually disappeared. As for work, I was reinstated in my teaching position at the Institute of Economic Science and Planning. Also, after a few weeks, though not without a struggle, I managed to get back our former apartment, the little penthouse on the fifth floor of Bulevardul Stalin number 72. At that point Edith came to Bucharest, followed soon by the two girls and a maid. Edith got a position as assistant professor at the Department of Philosophy at the university. This is how our new life started after my return from the Malmezon.

There are three episodes or features of my subsequent life that I would like to discuss here, since they relate to my life under arrest. About a year after my release, on a street in Bucharest I ran unexpectedly into Teodor Bucur, my former cell mate at the Malmezon. I was greatly pleased to see him free and we then made an appointment to talk. He had undergone a significant change since we had shared the same cell. Gone were the days when he could not pronounce the words *communist* or *Securitate* without cursing. He was now very tame and had nothing bad to say about anybody or any institution. He had been freed a few months after me and given a clerk's job at some state company. What about teaching history, his profession and his hobby? No, that was not in the cards—understandably so, he would say, given his own "history." But he had no complaints about that; people had been good to him by letting him go free and helping him find a job.

How about his former wife and love, the German woman whom he had married? Well, it was one of the conditions of his release that he would forget about her and not try to contact her in any way. Nor was he to contact anybody else in the West. Maybe it was cruel on my part, but I could not refrain from saying, "But for God's sake, she is your wife! How long do you intend to keep your promise?" He sadly shook his head: "Don't remind me of her; I am doing my best to forget her. It was so long ago. She could not possibly have waited for me for more than five years after I had disappeared without a trace. She must have thought either that I was dead or that I had simply left her. What happened to me does not happen in her world, and she could not possibly have imagined what it was. By now she must have a new life. Why should I upset it? Besides, I don't want to return to the place where you and I met. So I started looking for another girl, and I actually found someone, a colleague at the office, whom I will soon marry."

"Do you love her?" I asked, again perhaps cruelly. "Do you love her like you did the other one?"

Again, he sadly shook his head. "Well, this is an entirely different story. But we are getting along well," he said. "Besides, she has a good social origin, which I certainly need to compensate for my own political short-comings." I felt terrible pity, of a kind that I had rarely felt in all my life. More than a decade later, when I first managed to lay my hands on George Orwell's *1984*, I remembered Bucur when I read about Winston Smith after his release from the torture chambers of the Ministry of Love: something had irreversibly changed in Winston, in his innermost being. On that afternoon in 1955, I had felt the same thing had happened to Bucur.

The second episode relates to my party situation. When I was released, my party membership card was not returned to me. I was in no hurry to rejoin a party organization; but sooner or later my status had to be clarified, because everything in our society depended on one's party status: what kind of a job you were allowed to take, what kind of activities you were allowed to engage in, etc. Since I still considered myself a communist at the time and was actively interested in influencing the way things were developing and trying to change them for the better, I decided after a while to ask for a clarification of my party situation. So I turned to the party organization at my workplace and was directed to the party Control Commission, which was in charge of investigating disciplinary matters that exceeded the authority of any particular party organization. It took several months for the Control Commission to take up my case. In the meantime, though I did not belong to any party organization and could not pay my membership dues, I was not formally excluded from the party. I was one of those whose case was "under investigation."

When I was finally called before the Control Commission, a body of ten or eleven members, instead of an apology for having kept me under arrest for two years and three months under the harshest conditions without any valid reason, I got a rude dressing down for not having helped the party unmask the right-wing deviationists, in particular Jakab. I answered that, whatever my shortcomings were as a party member, having passed through the purgatory that I had been put through, I hoped that at least my underground activity would be recognized for what it was worth and that my honesty and devotion to the communist cause would not be questioned. In other words, I expected the suspicions concerning my past activities, to have been once and for all settled, and put to rest as a result of the thorough investigation that I had undergone. Well, this hope of mine was crudely rebuked. In particular, one especially nasty member of the commission, Ion Vinţe, said that I should be under no illusion that I had been proved innocent: what happened was simply that the comrades at the Securitate were not able to prove anything against me—which by no means implied that I was innocent. I would have to prove to the party through my future work whether I deserved to be a party member. For the time being this did not seem to be warranted, and the commission would have to wait and see. And so my situation continued to be in limbo; I was a non-excluded party member who nevertheless belonged to no party organization and paid no dues. In other words my membership status was still under investigation. This status continued until 1959, when my new activities provided a basis for a decision: my expulsion.

The third aspect of my life that I want to briefly discuss is the dreams, or rather nightmares, that haunted me occasionally—though infrequently—during the years following my detention. For eight years after my release, on every night of August 12–13 I would dream that I was about to be arrested, in the process of being arrested, or had just been arrested. On the first two occasions, my memories were still fresh enough to remind me during the day of August 12 that this was the anniversary of the beginning of my ordeal. But after two or three years I no longer noticed the date, and went to bed in the evening unaware of its special significance. Still, I would have the dream. There were two remarkable things about these dreams. First, my body seemed to have some sort of inner clock that told it the date without my being aware of it. I often had this discussion with Edith on the morning of August 13: "Did you realize yesterday that it was August 12?" (there was never a need to explain what that meant). "No." "Neither did I, but nevertheless I had my usual nightmare. Can you remember, did we talk yesterday about anything that relates to that date, and that could have triggered the dream?" "No, I can't think of anything." And so it went, year after year, for eight years. The second interesting feature about these dreams is that, although they were never exactly the same—the chain of events, the persons present, their looks, the surroundings, were different every time—yet, the dreams were all essentially the same, as if parts of a serialized novel. What was the thread binding together the installments of this novel? Not the act of arrest itself, which was physically unfocused and hard to pinpoint. It was the atmosphere, the underlying state of my mind: The arrest was in my consciousness. In fact, I was dreaming that I was aware of being arrested, of being torn from my family for a long, long time, and I was living through the nightmare again and again.

I occasionally had other dreams, some of them also nightmarish, although I would not like to give the impression that this sort of thing in any way dominated my life. I was a psychologically well-balanced, usually calm individual; these dreams were only occasional reminders of that twenty-seven–month period I spent in a different world. By far the most striking and remarkable of these occasional nightmares was along these lines: I dreamed that I was living in a kind of penal colony, in a city inhabited only by politically suspect people like myself. We were all free to move around as we wanted, but could not leave the city. The main theme of the dream was again the atmosphere, the taste of things: Outwardly I was free to do whatever I wanted to, yet I was a prisoner and so were all the others. By the way, there were only men in the colony. My dream had no sexual dimension; women and thoughts about women were completely absent. I would meet my fellow citizens in the street and we would talk to each other cautiously, so as to avoid saying anything politically objectionable. Some of the men had big bellies. We all knew they were "pregnant," but we acted as if we did not notice the obvious fact. The reason for our behavior was that we also knew what pregnancy meant: The so-called pregnant men had informers planted into their bellies. Thus, it was best not to notice the pregnancy and to act as if it did not exist.

The dream had many other ramifications; it was a very long one and when I woke up after it, I vividly remembered all the details. Time has, of course, washed them away, but the image of the pregnant men stuck forever. The penal colony, by the way, was for a while a recurrent theme of my dreams. I say "penal colony," but that is not how it figured in my dreams. The closest description of the place in my dreams would be the admittedly vague phrase "that other world." Years later, when I came across Solzhenitsyn's concept of the Gulag Archipelago, I had this immediate reaction: This is that "other world" of my nightmares.

CHAPTER 12

■ ■ ■

Reform Communist

Although at the Institute of Economic Science and Planning (ISEP) I taught about the world economy, meaning the capitalist economies of the Western democracies, my main interest was in the economics of socialism. I wished to participate in the scientific analysis of the economic processes unfolding under socialism and in the development of a science of economic planning. But alas, everything I read on the subject was pure party propaganda without any analytical content. There was an official Soviet textbook, translated from the Russian, called *The Political Economy of Socialism*. But what it said about the socialist economy had little resemblance to the economy we were living in; it was mostly a description of what *should* be, not of what was; and it was dogmatic rather than analytical, proclaiming such "economic laws" as the continuous improvement of living standards and the balanced development of the different branches of the economy. There were some Soviet textbooks on economic planning, but they were little more than collections of procedural rules, containing no analytical tools capable of providing answers to the questions facing an economic planner. An objective, scientific analysis of how a socialist economy functions simply did not exist. Furthermore, the reasons for its absence were pretty clear: everything pertaining to the economics of socialism was considered ideological and as a result was treated with the same rigidity as the tenets of a religion. Raising questions was simply not tolerated. Had I lived in Hungary or Poland, where the death of Stalin marked the beginning of at least some questioning and some tolerance for it, I would probably have thrown myself passionately into investigating how a socialist economy actually functions. But in Romania this was utterly hopeless. Not only did a thoroughly dogmatic attitude prevail in terms of what one could say, or write, or question, but in addition everything related to planning was top secret. Without facts and data, there could be no analysis, but anyone outside the top leadership who attempted to obtain such data was treated as a spy. "Who put you up to it?" was the invariable question. One of the leaders of the Central Directorate of Statistics, Retegan, spent five years in jail as a spy because he answered a United Nations request for demographic data and sent the UN material that had apparently not been cleared with the appropriate party forum.

In this atmosphere, which made it impossible to study the actual functioning of the economy, I turned to making a normative study of some basic proportionalities that had to prevail in any closed economy, whether socialist or capitalist. The relationship between the two "sectors" of the economy, as they were called, the one that produces production goods (machinery and industrial raw materials) and the one that produces consumer goods, was analyzed by Marx in his schemata of simple and expanded reproduction. Although his analysis focuses on a closed capitalist economy, it is one of the few parts of his work that are also relevant to a socialist economy. I had always been attracted to this early growth model of Marx's, which he put in the form of a system of equations called tableaux. These tableaux struck in me a chord that was planted early on, when, as a high school student, I had been asked by Albert Molnár, the Soviet escapee living in my hometown, to help him work out the solution to the system of linear equations connecting the output of and input into various branches of a miniature economy. This is closely related to Leontieff's input-output model, whose basic idea—as Paul Samuelson notes in his well-known textbook *Economics*—had been anticipated by Marx. I thus set out to see what one could say about Marx's schemata for expanded reproduction from the point of view of economic planning.

In a sequence of three closely related studies, published between December 1955 and March 1957 in *Probleme Economice*, the Romanian economic journal, I attempted an analysis of some basic proportionalities between the production in the two sectors and of the way these proportionalities were affected by technological progress, the productivity of labor, and some other factors. The analysis used an amplified version of Marx's schemata for expanded reproduction and, although I care-fully avoided making ideologically loaded statements and used strictly technical terminology, the fact that I dared to "mess around" with Marx's sacrosanct schemata—in the sense of changing them, mainly by amplification—raised some eyebrows. On the other hand, the technical language of the papers and the inability of the party hacks to follow mathematical reasoning or notation sheltered me from an open attack. In the end, the articles were dismissed in party circles as being "pure mathematics" (an expression of disdain) and I was classified as a "mathematician." Somebody dug out from my past the little-known fact that before getting involved in the communist movement I had been passionate about mathematics. So, whereas in an earlier period of my life, as a diplomat and Foreign Ministry director, I was put in my place as "an economist," meaning a technician who should be given no political weight, now I was being dismissed as "a mathematician," whose papers were of no substantive politico-economic interest. I did not mind this at all.

In fact, the articles and the gossip surrounding them earned me quite a bit of respect in the eyes of academic and nonacademic economists and other intellectuals. I became aware of this when the vice president of the Academy for the Social Sciences, Vasile Malinschi (whom I had known in the 1949–1952 period but whom I had not met after my release) called to congratulate me on the first article, saying that he had spent the week-end reading it and had quite enjoyed it. However, he warned me to be careful: "None of our economists would ever dare to change a comma in Marx, and you feel free to interpret and modify his schemata of ex-panded reproduction? You should buy an insurance policy against her-esy before you do something like this." The second of the three articles was also published in the French journal *Études Économiques*, and the third was also published in Russian in *Revue des Sciences Sociales*, a monthly journal of the Romanian academy. Soon after Malinschi's call I was in-vited by Vladimir Trebici, an official at the Central Directorate of Statis-tics, to become an outside consultant of the directorate. Being on this list of consultants turned out to be very useful to me three or four years later when I lost my research and academic jobs. I was also invited by an official of the chamber of commerce to consult with its study group and was offered access to its reasonably well-endowed collection of foreign publications, which was closed to the public. This was a valuable re-source under the prevailing circumstances.

Another door that opened as a result of my articles was that of *Contemporanul,* the leading cultural weekly in Romania. I was included in a select group of artists, writers, philosophers, and other intellectuals who were invited to attend the regular weekly "tea parties" given by Gheorghe Ivaşcu, the editor-in-chief. Ivaşcu, in addition to responding to the splash made by my articles, may also have felt some sympathy toward me as an ex-inmate, since he had spent close to five years in jail as an alleged "class enemy." His parties were a good place to meet interesting people. There was, of course, no truly free discussion, but sometimes one could at least have a conversation in metaphors. Finally, the main benefit that I drew from my articles was that in the spring of 1956 I was able to join the Institute of Economic Research of the Academy, a major development in my professional life. Here is a sketch of the events that led up to it.

In February 1955 Malenkov was replaced by Nikolay Bulganin as head of the Soviet government, which made the first secretary of the Communist party, Nikita Khrushchev, the de facto ruler of the Soviet Union. The year between the event and February 1956, when the twentieth congress of the Soviet Communist party took place in Moscow, was rich in political developments that shook the world I lived in. These developments, alongside my bitter personal experience, eventually led to a drastic change in my political outlook. Thus, for a period of about four years starting with the spring of 1955 my state of mind was that of a "reform communist."—someone who, having become aware of the anomalies of the communist system as it existed before the death of Stalin, believed nevertheless that the system could be reformed, that its defects could be eliminated, and that a better society could be built, more just and more humane than the capitalist one. In Romania, few of those who thought along these lines were in positions of power or influence; but in the Hungary of Imre Nagy, the Poland of Wladyslaw Gomulka, and the Czechoslovakia of Alexander Dubcek, there were quite a few reform communists who for a while were either in power or had a share in it.

In referring to the anomalies of the system, I have in mind both political and economic aberrations. In the political sphere, there was a complete suppression of freedom and a reign of terror that went far beyond what might have been justified by the need to consolidate the new regime and avoid a counterrevolution. It was not just the classes of the former landowners and bourgeoisie that were oppressed, as the marxist theory of the dictatorship of the proletariat had envisaged; everybody's freedom was suppressed and hundreds of thousands of people were made to suffer various forms of deprivation. And the oppressor was not "the proletariat," but the party and the state apparatus under its control. In the economic sphere, the centrally planned command economy, while making some strides in the direction of forced industrialization, was functioning irrationally and achieving the production targets of the plan at the cost of enormous, unjustified sacrifices. Instead of growing along with the volume of output, living standards seemed to be deteriorating along with the apparent increase in output; this anomaly came to be described as "production for the sake of production."

The political winds that were blowing from the Soviet Union seemed to carry the seeds of change. In early 1955, Khrushchev launched a campaign against the "cult of personality," described as the root cause of all the evil things that had happened under Stalin. However, although the cult had been focused on Stalin's personality, the culprit for the abuses that had taken place was made out to be Beria, the former minister of the interior, who allegedly had misled the great man. Thus, the freshly executed Beria took the brunt of the often bitter criticism of past abuses. Nevertheless, the need for changing the practices that had led to those abuses was generally acknowledged, and all the "fraternal" parties began to search their souls to make sure they had not been affected by the cult of personality. Odes of joy appeared in the Romanian party press celebrating the wisdom of our leaders, who had spared us the mistakes of a personality cult. At the same time, while avoiding the deifying style in which our press had formerly referred to the "Father of All Peoples," more and more articles flattering the new Soviet leader, Nikita Khrushchev, appeared.

In the spring or early summer of 1955, Khrushchev decided it was time to go to Canossa to repair the division between the Soviet Union and Yugoslavia, and he embarked upon a visit to Belgrade in the company of Prime Minister Bulganin and other members of the Soviet top brass. In his speech in Belgrade, Khrushchev took responsibility in the name of the Soviet leadership for the deterioration of relations between the two Communist parties, in particular for having accused the Yugoslav leadership of treason and subservience to the Western imperialists. These accusations had been false, Khrushchev now publicly acknowledged, and in the name of the Soviet leadership he apologized for them. As it turned out, a *public* apology had been one of the Yugoslav conditions for mending relations. However, while apologizing, the Soviet leaders put the blame squarely on Beria, the alleged imperialist agent who had infiltrated the party leadership. The Yugoslavs received these explanations with scornful smiles and sarcastic, hard hitting remarks about the way the pure soul and naïve mind of comrade Stalin had been deceived by the devil Beria without anybody noticing. In the end, although relations between the two countries were mended, they remained cool, far from the hopes of the Soviet leaders who would have liked to simply return Yugoslavia to the fold, meaning the community of "fraternal" Communist parties. Of that project, nothing came.

But the Soviet leaders' apology to Tito had far-reaching implications for the Eastern European Communist parties. If Tito was not and had never been an imperialist agent, then Rajk, Slansky, and the others who had allegedly conspired with him to better serve the CIA or British Intelligence Service, could not have been imperialist agents either. For if everything related to Tito was removed from their trials, what was left was a mess full of inexplicable holes. Although little was publicly said about this matter at the time, this was on the mind of every party activist who read the communiqué on the Soviet-Yugoslav meeting. The Yugoslavs had good reason to insist on a public apology: They understood the political consequences of what was happening. For the party faithful there was an unpleasant uncertainty in the air and worry about the future. For the likes of myself, however, there was a pleasant uncertainty in the air and hope for the future. You could see this on people's faces. I would meet a well-known party stalwart and, without saying a word, point to the communiqué in the newspaper and give him an ironic look. To my amusement, he would turn his head away in bitter disgust.

In fact, soon after the Soviet leaders' trip to Yugoslavia, a partial rehabilitation of Rajk took place quietly in Budapest. A communiqué of the Central Committee asserted that the most serious accusations against Rajk had been unfounded, and it blamed the frame-up on Gábor Péter, the former head of the Secret Service who had been arrested a few months earlier. But this partial rehabilitation did not wash: there was an uproar, and the authority of the party sank to a hitherto unknown low. By that time Imre Nagy, who had been made prime minister of Hungary in the summer of 1953, had been removed from any position of power. Rákosi again reigned supreme as first secretary of the party, and the country had a new prime minister in the person of András Hegedüs—the same Hegedüs whose identification papers I had used after my escape during the war. Hegedüs had been appointed prime minister in April 1955, and in June he and Rákosi came to Bucharest for a three-day official visit. I read about the visit in the newspapers and decided to try to meet him. I called the Hungarian embassy, described my relationship to Hegedüs, and left a message for him with my telephone number, in case he reciprocated my wish to see him. He did not return my call, and when I called the embassy on the last day of his visit I was told that he had not had a single free minute. Years later, on a visit to Budapest, I was told by a common acquaintance that Hegedüs had received my message and would have liked to meet me, but that he had to be at Rákosi's disposal all the time and their schedule was very crowded.

A few months after these events, Khrushchev dropped his bomb. In February 1956 the twentieth congress of the Communist party of the Soviet Union started its deliberations in Moscow. It looked like it would be another typical party congress: the leading personality would make a long report that would be unanimously approved, then there would be a so-called discussion—a sequence of speeches completely devoid of content—and finally a list of the new Central Committee would be submitted to the approval of the participants, who—surprise!—would approve it without change. And so it was—until the last day.

Then the participants were summoned to a "closed" meeting, where Khrushchev made a four-hour secret report. As we learn from his memoirs, the secret report was a surprise not only for the delegates, but also for the members of the politburo. There had been no prior decision to present such a report at the congress. A committee had been set up months in advance under the leadership of a certain Pospelov, an apparatchik at the Central Committee. It was given broad powers to collect all the available facts on the terror that had reigned under Stalin, strictly for the confidential and internal use of the politburo. Pospelov collected thousands of pages of material, which he summarized in a sixty- or seventy-page report describing the arrests, sentencings, and executions of no fewer (according to Khrushchev's memoirs) than hundreds of thousands of innocent people, among them two-thirds of the several hundred Central Committee members "elected" at the seventeenth party congress in 1934. This report had been circulated among the members of the politburo (by that time renamed the Presidium) just before the party congress, but that august body did not have the slightest intention of making it public, an act that most of its members would have considered political suicide. Then on the last day of the congress, during a break, with only the members of the Presidium attending, Khrushchev raised the issue that "it would not be fair" to the participants of the congress to keep them in the dark about what the Presidium had discovered concerning Stalin's crimes (here, for the first time, the "mistakes" became crimes). He proposed that somebody read the report in a secret, closed session. A vehement dispute ensued, in which, according to Khrushchev, most members of the Presidium were initially opposed to the idea. They went along only when it became clear to them that one way or another, Khrushchev was going to make the report public despite their misgivings. Then the closed session was convened and Khrushchev read the report. It was labeled secret and was not published, but it was sent to the leaders of all the important Communist parties in the world, and leaked to the Western press.

I think I read the report in the *New York Times*, to which I had access, with considerable delay, through a couple of libraries. It was an extraordinary document by virtue of the sheer mass of crimes and abuses that it revealed, and by its uncompromising condemnation of Stalin's practices as *criminal*—not as "mistakes," not as "deviations from the party line," but as outright criminal acts. This document was not published in the Romanian press, nor were the Romanian party leaders happy with it. The report described the personality cult around Stalin and pointed to it as the source of all the abuses committed in the name of the party. Gheorghiu-Dej's personality cult never took such extreme forms as Stalin's, but it was of the same type: Anybody who dared cross the boss or displease him in even a minor way could count on retribution. True, Gheorghiu-Dej's retribution was usually much milder than Stalin's, but the principle was the same: the authority of the boss was meant to be absolute, unchallenged by anybody. And when the opponent, doubter, or questioner was serious enough to pose a threat, as in the cases of Foriş, Pătrăşcanu, and Koffler, his retribution was death. Officially, the Romanian party leadership treated the report as an internal matter of the Soviet party, where some regrettable abuses had apparently been committed in Stalin's name. It was good, according to the official line, that the victims of these abuses had been identified and posthumously rehabilitated, but fortunately this was not a problem for the Romanian party:

In Romania, nobody had been sentenced without being guilty, and there was nobody to rehabilitate. Yet the twentieth congress of the Soviet party had an enormous impact everywhere, including Romania. The impact was mostly on people's minds. From that point on, everybody knew that sooner or later abuses would be discovered and that terror could not reign indefinitely with impunity. This knowledge put some fear into the authorities and gave some hope to people looking for a change.

Encouraged by these events and desirous of getting into a research-oriented environment, at the end of February, about a year after my return to Bucharest, I asked to be permitted to work at the Institute of Economic Research of the Academy. This was the youngest of the academy's institutes, having been founded some time in late 1953. Its recently appointed director was Gogu Rădulescu, an old friend of Sanyi's and mine. Gogu had lost his ministerial position in late 1952 and had lingered on in some insignificant job, but he had not been arrested. Three years later he was made director of the Institute of Economic Research as a first step toward rehabilitation. He received me warmly and reacted favorably—meaning without fear—to my stated intention of asking to be allowed to work in his institute. My request was approved, and I was allowed to keep my teaching position at the Institute of Economic Studies (ISE, formerly ISEP) on a part-time basis.

I started working at the Institute of Economic Research in March 1956. Gogu asked me to set up a section on the economies of capitalist countries. He also let me know that for the unfilled position of deputy director of the Institute that he had two candidates in mind: myself and Costin Murgescu, the head of the Section of the History of the National Economy (meaning the Romanian economy). I suggested that he propose Murgescu for the position of deputy director, as I preferred research to administration. My position in this matter had two sides. On the one hand, I felt a huge thirst for learning and therefore wanted a full-time research job that offered the greatest opportunity for this. On the other, after my years spent in jail, for some reason or other, the usual factors that attract people to jobs of administrative responsibility—social prestige, the power to influence things, better pay—had ceased to attract me.

Thus Murgescu became deputy director of the institute and I set out to organize my section. I was given two researchers, both in their forties, knowledgeable about economics in general and the capitalist economies in particular. Besides these two, I received a slot to hire a third one. I managed to attract Tibor Schattelesz, the talented young economist whom I had hired in 1949 for the economic directorate of the Foreign Ministry. In 1952, at the time of my public "execution," he had behaved decently— I don't remember what he said, but he was certainly not among my active critics. Besides, I had great respect for his bookishness, wide culture, and knowledge of economics. Thus, we started with a group of four. A few months later I was given two more slots and I hired two young graduates of the ISEP. The six of us had our desks in one big but friendly office; however, except by special arrangement, we were almost never all present at the same time, as most of our research needed to be done in various libraries. Our research was organized around subjects chosen freely by each individual, the main limitation on this freedom being the need to show that the subject was researchable. Each of us would periodically submit his or her findings to a discussion by the whole group.

■ ■ ■

One of the two young newcomers was the wife of a friend, Miklós Dános, a journalist at the Hungarian-language daily newspaper *Magyar Szó*, published in Bucharest. Unlike his wife, Ninel, who was a very capable but not particularly cheerful woman, Miklós was a born charmer and had an excellent sense of humor. One evening Edith and I were at the young couple's home with two or three other friends of theirs, when Miklós arrived and said, "You will not believe what happened to me earlier today. For the last two weeks I've had a nagging pain in my back, so I went to see a doctor. He took an X-ray and showed it to me—lo and behold, he claimed that I have a spine! Me, Miklós Dános, a *spine*? I assured him that must be a mistake, since I was a journalist and couldn't possibly have such a thing. Even if I had one at one time, I was long ago cured of it."

The newly appointed deputy director at the institute, Costin Murgescu, was a very capable economist in his mid-thirties. His father, a former high-ranking army officer with strongly pro-nazi sympathies, had committed atrocities during the war and received a long sentence as a war criminal. Costin, however, had come into contact with anti-nazi circles in 1943, and had openly turned against his father. Because I did not know all the details, I had some reservations toward Costin; but I basically felt that, if he had indeed done this, he had done all that a decent person could do. Our relations throughout my tenure at the institute were those of mutual respect—less than friendship, but more than I can claim for my relations with many other colleagues. Murgescu's wife, Ecaterina Oproiu, was the best-known film critic in Bucharest, and we usually read her column.

As to my personal life, in the period from 1955 to 1957 Edith worked as an assistant professor in the faculty of philosophy of the University of Bucharest. Our closest friends during this period were the Kleins. Bandi continued to work for an import-export company; Juci continued as a pediatrician. Other friends of ours included my uncle Rényi with his family; Tibor Schattelesz, my colleague from the institute; and Ivan Köves, an old friend from Cluj and colleague at the ISE. Magda Stroe, one of Edith's colleagues at the university and a woman of remarkable character, became a good friend of ours. A few years older than Edith, she was Romanian on her father's side and Hungarian on her mother's side. Under the prewar Romanian regime she was discriminated against as a Hungarian; under the wartime Hungarian regime she suffered persecution as a Romanian. Moreover, she happened to have a big nose and was therefore often mistaken for a Jew. She had several Jewish friends, and when the Jews of Northern Transylvania were being deported in 1944, she gave her birth certificate to one of them, Hanna Hamburg, to enable her to hide. Hanna Hamburg survived the war thanks to Magda Stroe, and lived in Paris afterwards. Had Hanna been apprehended, the certificate would have been found and Magda might have paid for her compassion with her life. Because of this, both Edith and I always felt very close to her.

Another friend of ours was Imre Tóth, a professor at the university who taught the history and philosophy of mathematics. A year older than me, Imre was a Hungarian Jew like myself, born in Northern Transylvania. He became involved in the communist movement a little before I did, and was arrested and sentenced to a jail term in 1941. He was very bright and widely read, with a strong theoretical bent, and rather impractical. He studied mathematics but did not like problem solving; instead, he was interested in the history of mathematical ideas and the philosophical aspects of mathematics, a field in which he came to excel and in which he wrote several interesting and highly original books that were also published in the West. His name became well known in the sixties, partly through his books and articles and partly through a lecture series he gave on Romanian television. When he emigrated to the West around 1969 or 1970, he was appointed professor of philosophy at the University of Regensburg, where he taught until his retirement in the late eighties. He now lives in Paris.

Imre was a great storyteller and had a wonderful sense of humor. About Magda Stroe, our common friend whom we both liked but knew to be extremely naive, he would say: "You know, Magda has lately become very cautious. When she has visitors at her home and wants to have a discussion, she carefully places a pillow over her telephone in case it's bugged. The trouble is that the guy who then sits on the pillow is an informer."

The butt of one of Imre's jokes was Georgi Dimitrov, the former Bulgarian leader. Dimitrov had been secretary general of the Bulgarian Communist party and a leader of the Komintern in the thirties. He had enormous prestige because in 1933 the nazis had dragged him to the trial of the alleged Reichstag arsonists. After having set the Reichstag (the German parliament) on fire, the nazis attempted to blame the communists. A trial was staged, in which Dimitrov appeared as one of those accused of organizing the arson. He defended himself so effectively that his presence at the trial brought shame on the nazi regime. Around 1951 or 1952, when some of the communist leaders in the satellite countries were being executed as traitors, Dimitrov fell ill and went for treatment to Moscow, where he died at a hospital under rather obscure circumstances. There were many rumors about his death, based partly on the assumption that Stalin was jealous of Dimitrov's prestige and popularity. Some time in 1955 or 1956, when the Soviet press started revealing various abuses of power under Stalin, Imre burst into our apartment with the following announcement: "Have you heard the news? They have found out how Dimitrov died." "No, we haven't heard it. So how did he die?" "Of natural causes—pneumonia." "How come?" "The knife was too cold."

In June 1956 Edith and I made a visit to the Soviet Union. It was an eye opener, because we still had some illusions at that time. We went as tourists, by train, with a heterogeneous group of about twenty people, for a two-week tour of Kiev, Moscow, and Leningrad.

For me, the most interesting episode of the trip occurred in Moscow, on our visit to the ZIL automobile factory. This event not only confirmed, but exceeded, my worst suspicions about the credibility of claims concerning Soviet accomplishments. The plant itself left nothing to be desired to the eye of a nonspecialist like myself. The technological process was very similar to what I remembered from my visit to the Ford factory in Dagenham, England. However, at the start of the tour we were addressed by an engineer who had been assigned to us as a guide and obviously specialized in this kind of assignment. He spoke to us for about twenty minutes, reeling off a series of statistics that listed the plant's accomplishments. There were many things that sounded false to my by-then suspicious ears. One that I remember distinctly was the statement that the personnel of the foundry and the forge worked a six-hour day, as such work, like mining, was recognized to be unusually taxing. Perhaps I would not have paid much attention had I not been a foundry worker myself, as well as, briefly, a coal miner. When we reached the foundry, I stepped aside from the group and engaged one of the workers in conversation. I asked him in Russian when they started and finished work, and it became clear that they had an eight-hour workday.

"Do you always work eight hours?" I asked.

He hesitated. "No, not always," he finally said.

"When do you not work eight hours?"

"Well," he said, "when there is some urgent work to do, and we are asked, it is not convenient to refuse working overtime."

"Does that happen often?" I asked.

He was obviously starting to feel uncomfortable, and frequently looked around to see whether anybody was listening. "Well, it happens; there is nothing you can do about it."

"Do you ever work less than eight hours a day?"

He looked at me in surprise. "Less than eight? No, never."

The group had advanced in the meantime to the other end of the foundry. I joined them and asked the guide, "Is this the only foundry in this factory?"

"It is the only one," he said.

"Is this the place where you said the workday is six hours?"

"Yes," he said, "this and the forge. The reason is that the type of work done here and in the forge is physically more demanding than that in the rest of the plant."

I could not, of course, confront him with the testimony of the worker I had talked to without provoking a scandal and, worse, getting the worker into serious trouble, as he was probably not supposed to talk to foreigners. Instead, I decided to check further and make sure I was not missing something. I noticed that in spite of what the engineer had said about the physically demanding nature of foundry work, which I knew from my own experience to be true, there were quite a number of women working there, possibly a third of the employees. Perhaps the women were the clue to the situation; perhaps *they* worked shorter hours. So I struck up a conversation with one of the women.

She told me, without any room for doubt, that the women had an eight-hour workday, the same as the men. When I asked, "Always?" she reacted just as her male colleague had earlier: "No, not always. There is often more work to do than we can finish in eight hours, and then we do overtime." She added, as if to defend the system of overtime, "But when we do extra work we get extra pay."

I went on to ask whether she or her colleagues ever worked less than eight hours per day. "Yes," she said, "if any of us gets pregnant, for the last three (or two? I don't remember exactly) months of pregnancy we work only half a day."

I was shocked by the crass way in which the tour guide had lied. "If this is how they lie about something that is right under your nose and that you can easily find out," I thought, "what about more distant, less easy-to-check matters?"

While in the Soviet Union, Edith and I tried to get as much accurate information as we could on living standards. In Kiev people seemed better fed than in Moscow, and in Moscow much better fed than in Leningrad. Overall, we found the food situation considerably worse than in Romania in terms of the availability of fruits and vegetables, dairy products, and to some extent, meat. Clothing, especially shoes, was way below the Romanian standards; in fact, shoes and apparel imported from Romania were luxury items. In Leningrad, where people dressed excep-tionally badly, we saw men and women wearing clothes from the twen-ties and thirties. Not just old-fashioned, but old: suits which showed the wear and tear of at least twenty years; hats the shape of which was known to us only from silent movies.

But the sharpest distinction between conditions in Romania and in the Soviet Union was to be drawn in the realm of living quarters. There was simply no comparison between the way people were housed in Bucharest, and the way they seemed to live in Moscow, not to mention Leningrad, which had suffered particularly badly during the war. Apartments were extremely crowded, with families living on top of each other with no privacy at all. On one occasion, when we were on a sight-seeing tour near the Kremlin in the very heart of Moscow, Edith needed a toilet. There was no public one in sight. There was also no restaurant, bar, or similar facility that might have had a toilet. After a long and frustrating sequence of failed attempts to get some help or direction in this regard, I literally forced the tour guide to enter the apartment house in front of which we happened to be standing, and ask the tenants' permission for a tourist to use their toilet. When he complied, Edith entered one of the apartments. She traversed a long corridor, from which other doors opened into one- or two-room apartments, each inhabited by a different person or family. At the end of the corridor was the toilet, common for all the apartments. The "room" housing the toilet had a wall on only one of its four sides; each of the other three sides was separated by a curtain from the room or kitchen behind it. We learned that this situation was rather typical.

The paradox in all this was that the Soviet Union had Europe's largest steel and heavy machine industry; its army was among the best equipped in the world; and within a year it would launch the Sputnik, the first spaceship in the history of mankind. It also had plenty of hydrogen bombs and the missiles to deliver them.

On the last day before our departure I had a chance to talk to a representative of Intourist, the agency in charge of our program, who came to see us off. He asked me to convey to him my group's impressions of our visit, how we were treated, and whether we enjoyed what we saw. "We want to learn from the group's experience, so we would like you to tell us not only good things, not only what you liked, but also what you did not like." "OK, if that's what you want, you'll get it," I said to myself. I started out by praising the many wonderful things that we had seen, and describing how impressed we were with the accomplishments of the Soviet Union in rebuilding the country in such a short time after such a terrible war. Then I thanked Intourist for allowing us to visit the ZIL automobile plant. We enjoyed that visit very much, I said, and were very impressed with the factory. And here I added, "Because you want me also to tell you the things I did not like, here is one small item in that category," and I went on to relate the episode about the working hours in the foundry in the same detail as I have described it above. At the end, I said, "The plant is a perfectly equipped, flawlessly functioning marvel of twentieth-century technology; it is most impressive as it is. Why make false claims for it? That does not help the cause; it hurts it. The same engineer who made the false statement about this also claimed many other accomplishments concerning the workers' lives. If he lied about one thing, why should I believe him about the others? I don't think the interests of the party are well served through such practices."

The man from Intourist thought for a moment, looked at me, then stared off into the distance and said, "Frankly, I don't know why those workers tried to deceive you, why they lied to you. But the fact is that what the engineer-guide said is true: workers in our foundries and forges work only six hours a day, since theirs is a very difficult, demanding type of work. And that is true not only at the ZIL factory, but in every factory throughout the Soviet Union, and it is a well-known fact here."

■ ■ ■

Back in Bucharest, there was interesting news waiting for me. It came from Hungary. Ever since the "partial rehabilitation" of Rajk during the previous summer, something ominous had been simmering just beneath the surface of Hungarian social life. You could see it and taste it in the ever more numerous, ever more daring, often devastatingly critical articles that were appearing in Hungarian daily and weekly cultural publications. It had all started back in the fall of 1954, three months after the Hungarian politburo had been summoned to Moscow. Rákosi had been demoted as prime minister and Nagy named in his place, while Rákosi kept the party leadership. In October of that year, the journalists working for the party daily held a meeting in which they blamed themselves for going along for so many years with the orders to write biased and outright false reports. They solemnly pledged never again to publish lies. They could not keep this naïve pledge, of course, yet an account of their meeting—which was not publicly announced either before or after—made the rounds through the grapevine and started the ball rolling. When, in the summer of 1955, the party leaders were forced by the Soviet-Yugoslav reconciliation to admit that Rajk's trial had been rigged and that he was "essentially" innocent, these early stirrings turned into rage. For a while, with Nagy ousted after Malenkov's fall and Rákosi back in the saddle, the control of the party could be sufficiently tightened to avoid an explosion. In the summer of 1956, under pressure from Tito, the Soviets finally forced Rákosi to resign; however, they replaced him with Gerö, who was too closely associated with Rákosi to be considered a change. Thus, throughout the summer of 1956, emboldened by Khrushchev's "secret" revelations at the twentieth party congress, communist and noncommunist intellectuals alike were essentially asking: Where do our leaders stand in this respect? When are they going to reveal their own crimes? Who will answer for the life of Rajk and so many others? None of this, of course, was ever openly said or written; but it was there nevertheless, to be read between the lines, and the leaders were unable to stop it. A quiet revolt of party and nonparty intellectuals was going on; every week new names would join the ranks of the critics.

I remember a typical article by Tibor Tardos in a literary weekly, titled "Seawater Is Salty." It described a beautiful beach at a marvelous seaside resort, on a bright sunny day when the glittering blue waters of the sea tempted people to launch themselves into the waves for a cool, refreshing swim (Hungary had had no access to the sea since the end of World War I). All over the place, loudspeakers mounted on high pillars were singing the praises of the resort: "Citizens, brothers! Get ready for the great joy! You are about to taste the seawater, the sweetest, tastiest, most refreshing drink in the world. Prepare yourselves for the pleasure and the enjoyment. Drink plenty and enjoy yourselves." People rushed into the sea and started drinking the water. A terrible disappointment followed: they discovered that seawater is salty and undrinkable. The celebration turned into an outburst of rage; the marvelous resort turned into a place of bitter disenchantment. The message: Socialism, whatever its merits, had been turned into a bitter hell by false claims on its behalf and the lies surrounding it. Not accidentally, the revolt of the intellectuals was not aimed primarily at the low living standards, the broken promises of a better life for the working people, or other social issues. Instead, it focused on what was perceived as the rule of the Big Lie. "Enough of that," they were saying. "Let's finally speak the truth."

It was in this atmosphere that, in the late summer of 1956, I wrote to Karcsi Fekete, my companion in the 1944 escape, letting him know that Edith and I intended to visit Budapest. Karcsi, who at the time was a minister in the government of Hegedüs, invited us to stay with him and his wife (another Edith). We scheduled the visit for the two weeks starting on October 24. On the evening of October 23, 1956, Edith, the two girls, and I took the train to Budapest. There was a stop in Cluj early in the morning, and we had planned to leave Anna and Vera with Edith's parents for the duration of our stay in Budapest. When the train pulled into the station at Cluj, Edith's parents were waiting for us. I handed to Sándor Anna's and Vera's luggage and we were kissing the girls goodbye when Sándor said, "What are you doing? Haven't you heard the news? You must get off here; it makes no sense to go to Budapest now." We had not heard anything, having left home before the evening news. "There is revolution in Budapest. They are shooting in the streets. You must get off the train," Sándor said quickly. I was exhilarated.

"That's wonderful," I said. "I am not sure what's the right thing for Edith to do, but as far as I am concerned, I want to be there, I want to be part of it."

My father-in-law was nervously trying to talk me out of what my instincts were dictating. "It doesn't make sense; you would be endangering yourself for nothing. You can follow the events from here; we've had our radio constantly tuned to Budapest since last night." But I was bent on going; I felt as though I had started growing wings.

Then my father-in-law overheard somebody say that the radio had just announced the closing of the border with Hungary. I did not want to believe him; I thought he was inventing this to get me off the train. So I went to find the railway official in charge of the train and told him I had important business in Budapest and had to get there. Was it true that the border had been closed, and if so, would the train still continue its trip to Budapest? He answered without hesitation that he had just received instructions to stop the train at the border. "We are not going to Budapest," he said. For a few minutes I continued to inquire about alternative ways of getting to Budapest, but soon discovered there were none. And that is how our well-prepared and much-anticipated visit to Budapest ended in Cluj. We spent our two-week vacation there instead of in Budapest. Much of the time I was glued to the radio, trying to absorb and decipher the news coming from Hungary.

Besides Edith's parents, we had a circle of friends in Cluj. They included the literary critic László Földes and his wife, the writer Marica Földes, both extremely colorful, lively, interesting people; and Ernö Gáll, a marxist philosopher and editor-in-chief of the journal *Korunk*, who nine months later published an article of mine for which he was taken to task in Bucharest. We all followed closely the events taking place in Budapest, and were deeply shocked when after twelve days, on November 4, Soviet tanks crushed the uprising, killing many people. The repression that

followed during the next couple of years included the executions of Imre
Nagy, the communist leader who had sided with the rebels, denounced
the Warsaw pact, and asked for the withdrawal of Soviet troops; of Pál
Maléter, the military leader of the uprising; and of other leaders. In the
wake of the Soviet action more than one hundred thousand people fled
to the West across the Austrian border.

The new Hungarian party leader, János Kádár, was at first hated by
everybody; he had been installed by the Russians and had gone along
with the execution of his former comrades. In the years following these
events, however, he earned a considerably better reputation, as he gradually instituted a regime more tolerant and less harsh than in any of the
other socialist countries. The Soviets allowed him to do it, because they
had learned in 1956 that it was better not to mess with the Hungarians;
there was always the danger of an explosion. Thus, a tacit deal gradually
evolved under which the Hungarian party unconditionally supported
every Soviet foreign policy initiative, but was given a more or less free
hand in running the internal affairs of its own country. Kádár's political
motto became "Those who are not against us are with us," and the resulting social-economic conditions came to be described in the West in
the sixties and seventies as "goulash communism." In Eastern Europe,
Hungary came to be considered—not without a little sarcasm—"the
merriest baracks of the socialist camp." The Western term was intended
to describe the new emphasis on consumer goods and, more generally,
on improving living standards. But an even more important feature of
Kádár's regime was the increased freedom of debate that intellectuals
came to enjoy, which was at the root of the Eastern European characterization. I still recall my amazement when in 1957, only a few months
after the suppressed revolution, the Publishing House for Economic Science in Budapest published a book by János Kornai, *The Overcentralization
of Economic Leadership* (I am using here a literal translation of the original
Hungarian title), the first critical in-depth analysis of the command
economy and its planning methods, which hit its target with devastating
accuracy. In a way, the sacrifice and suffering of the Hungarian revolutionaries of 1956 was not in vain.

In other socialist countries, however, and certainly in Romania, the
consequences of the Hungarian revolution and its defeat were on the
whole negative. The barely discernible ideological thaw that had started
after Stalin's death and Beria's execution, and had been considerably

enhanced by Khrushchev's revelations at the twentieth congress of the Soviet party, fizzled out, and by 1957 the political gears had been put in reverse. The party line hardened, and a period of more repressive policies followed for two or three years.

Mine was one of many fates affected by this backtracking. The trouble I ran into had to do partly with an article I published in 1957, but mainly with my book published in 1958. But my "suffering" at this stage was minor in comparison with that of many others whose lives and careers were effectively thwarted. Just one example: Constantin Noica, one of the best-known Romanian nonmarxist philosophers, had dinner with a group of friends at an outdoor restaurant in September or October 1958. There was music, they drank wine, and since the restaurant was outdoors, they felt at ease and talked freely, making "reactionary" jokes and sarcastic slurs about the puppets of the "ideological front." The men were with their wives, and at one point a Gypsy woman approached the table to sell flowers and asked permission to leave her pot full of flowers under the table. In December of that year, Noica and some of his friends were arrested. The Securitate broke several members of the group by reproducing verbatim their conversation at the restaurant: The flower pot that the Gypsy woman left under their table was bugged. Noica was sentenced to twenty-five years in jail. He was freed under a general amnesty about six years later.

My 1957 article was written under the influence of the economic debates going on in Hungary, to which I had access through some publications. For a year preceding the October 1956 revolution, the Petöfi circle in Budapest had been organizing exciting literary debates, which went well beyond the realm of literature and soon became overarching intellectual debates about every aspect of Hungarian society and contemporary Hungarian life. The economists had their own debates, reflected in the pages of their journal and the press. It was through these indirect channels that I learned about market socialism, an idea launched in the mid-thirties by Oskar Lange and more recently embraced by the Yugoslav economists, whose heresies from orthodox doctrine were tolerated by Tito in the hope that they would come up with a model of communism different from that of the hated Soviet Union. Market socialism is a generic term for a system in which the economic units, while collectively owned in some form, are autonomous agents that pursue their own objectives—for instance, profit—and bring their goods to the market. The planning authority then sets the prices so as to bring demand and supply into equilibrium at the desired level. This would replace the direct planning mechanism of the command economy, in which every firm is given quantitative tasks for the execution of which it is held responsible, with a more flexible mechanism of price incentives, in which firms are induced to produce what the planners want by the setting of appropriate prices. The advantage of this system over the command economy would be greater overall efficiency: whereas in the command economy the arbitrary nature of prices invalidates any comparison of alternative ways of producing the same thing, under market socialism the equilibrium prices would provide an adequate basis for such comparisons and thereby promote efficiency.

Thus, in early 1957 I wrote an article for the magazine *Korunk* about some current issues in economic research, in which I tried to explain the importance of having prices that reflect the relative efforts spent on producing various things. I argued that just because markets and prices play a central role in the functioning of a capitalist economy, there was no reason why they could not serve as useful tools in running a socialist economy as well, once the planning authority understood their functioning and mastered the art of using them. On the contrary, by making the economy more efficient, they could contribute to the strengthening of socialism. Unlike my earlier three studies, which were technical and inaccessible to the party hacks, this one was written in nontechnical language and had the goal of political persuasion. It got me into trouble, along with the editor-in-chief of the magazine, Ernö Gáll, who was summoned to Bucharest for a dressing down some time in 1958. The editorial board had to apologize publicly for its ideological blindness in having accepted such a revisionist piece of writing. My own troubles started about the same time, and not just because of this article.

CHAPTER 13

• • •

Heresy and Expulsion

As one of my activities at the Institute of Economic Research, in early 1956 I started working on a book on Keynesianism, the economic doctrine of John Maynard Keynes. Keynes's general theory of employment, conceived during the Great Depression of the 1930s, was meant to explain those long years of massive unemployment and underutilization of productive capacities. Furthermore, it took the point of view that similar depressions could be avoided by appropriate government policies. In the postwar decade, Keynesianism was the dominant trend in Western economic thinking, and many of Keynes's policy recommendations were being tested in practice. Later these recommendations and some of their theoretical underpinnings became increasingly controversial, but the Keynesian analysis of income-level determination as the equilibrium point between projected investments and scheduled savings entered the mainstream of Western economics and became a basic component of modern macroeconomic analysis. When I undertook my project, Keynes seemed to be the most relevant modern economic theorist to somebody who wanted to break out of the isolation imposed on marxist economists—prisoners of a theory that had been frozen for three generations—and explore some new ideas.

In marxist economic literature, Western nonmarxist economists were described uniformly as ideological lackeys of capitalism, whose theories served the sole purpose of justifying capitalist exploitation, making it acceptable to the working class by depicting it as a system whose functioning was governed by spontaneous processes expressing rational principles of efficiency. Marginal analysis of any kind was anathema, as it did not conform to the labor theory of value. Equilibrium analysis and the use of mathematical techniques was disparaged as a sophisticated way of obfuscating the simple facts of exploitation. In making a departure from this general paradigm, I wrote a book that, while treating Keynes from a marxist, hence critical vantage point, nevertheless analyzed his theories with a view to deriving from them generally valid results that would be useful to marxist economists. The title of the book was *Contributions to a Marxist Critique of Keynesianism.* I took as my starting point the fact that Keynes, unlike the bourgeois economists of earlier times, no longer confined himself to explaining the capitalist economy (in the marxist interpretation, to acting as an apologist for it) but pinpointed and diagnosed its major contemporary weakness: the possibility, and under certain circumstances even likelihood, of underemployment equilibrium, that is, economic equilibrium at a level of underutilization of production capacities, meaning protracted mass unemployment. Furthermore, having diagnosed the disease and its alleged causes, Keynes also offered remedies in the form of fiscal and monetary policies that he believed the government should use to prevent or eliminate this undesirable phenomenon. While an apologist of capitalism had no need to be objective, let alone scientific, I argued, somebody who was aiming at curing a basic disease of capitalism must have tried to use scientific tools; otherwise his attempt at curing the disease would have had to fail, and he could be of no use to the bourgeois system he was trying to help. Hence, the need to look at his work with fresh eyes and a perspective different from that of earlier marxist critiques of bourgeois economists. In the light of this, I concluded, it made no sense for marxist economists to treat Keynes simply as another apologist for capitalism, because this did not address his main role.

My book explained and justified at some length this thesis, then went on to lay out the Keynesian theory of income-level determination, with an emphasis on the novel idea of the possibility of protracted states of underemployment equilibrium. I did not take issue with this theory, but instead tried to translate it into marxist terms and put it in the framework of Marx's schemata for expanded reproduction. As a matter of fact, despite his devastating critique of capitalism, Marx had not foreseen the possibility of underemployment equilibrium. He wrote repeatedly and in great detail about the unemployment, waste, and underutilization of productive capacities that prevailed during the periodic depressions of the economic cycle, but he always viewed these as swings of the pendulum inherent in the spontaneous mechanism through which economic equilibrium imposes itself, never as a possible state of equilibrium in itself. In other words, I argued that the notion of underemployment equilibrium was new to marxist economists and should become part of their critique of capitalism. Finally, I examined the Keynesian remedies and showed how they were supposed to work, stressing their limitations and the temporary nature of the relief they could bring.

I finished the book in the fall of 1957. By that time, the thaw that had started in 1955 was turning into a freeze; nevertheless, there still was enough uncertainty about the "correct" ideological line and the exact boundaries of what was and was not permissible in terms of intellectual debate, that I saw a chance—not more than a chance—to have the book published. But if that was to happen, the publisher had to have some political clout, since there was some risk in the undertaking. Thus, I submitted my manuscript to Editura Politica, the publishing house closest to the party. I knew the editor who would be in charge of having my book refereed; he was a young, bright, marxist economist, who had great respect for me and was sufficiently enterprising to try to go ahead with the publication.

One of the reviewers was Ion Rachmuth, the head of the Political Economy Department at the party school, and one of the most revered marxist theorists of the country. In many ways he had long been "Mr. Party Line" in matters of economic theory, but I knew that his views had been changing. He was deeply shaken by the revelations of the twentieth congress and started doubting many things, although he would not speak to anyone about his thoughts. I "knew" this because we were living in the same apartment house and occasionally spoke to one another; he lived on the first floor with his wife and two children, whereas we lived on the fifth floor. Once I met him in the park with his family while I was walking with mine; our groups joined and I had the chance to have a longer discussion with him. I knew him as somebody who had been utterly dogmatic, but who was also very bright and, unlike the other champions of the ideological front, clean and honest. So I opened a discussion on the political situation and frankly stated my opinion on conditions in Romania, taking it more or less for granted that, even if he disagreed with me, he would not report me. He listened and did not comment, except that at the very end he said, "You are not the only one who thinks this way; but conditions don't seem to be ripe yet for a change." Rachmuth was given my book by Editura Politica for reviewing. When he finished, he told me that he had found the book extremely interesting, that he himself had not been familiar with Keynes's theories but now he felt he understood them. Then he said, "But why do you want to publish it? More likely than not, it will lead to trouble for you." I answered that I was not oblivious to the risks and dangers of having the book published, but I felt that I had a stake in the direction in which things were developing in the country, and as an intellectual, I wanted to make a contribution toward changing the climate for the better. He shook his head, said that he would write a basically positive appraisal of the book, but was privately advising me not to publish it. I do not recall who else refereed the book, but it was accepted for publication and went to print at the end of April 1958.

At first, the book was well received. It was reviewed favorably during the early summer in *Scinteia*, the party daily, and in some other publications. The clouds started gathering in late summer, and by the fall there was serious trouble. Several viciously hostile reviews branded the book as alien to marxist thinking, reflecting a rotten, bourgeois mentality and an attitude of subservience to capitalist ideology. One of them appeared in the August 1958 issue of *Probleme Economice*, the economic journal that had published my three articles in 1955–57, and was signed by a person who had neither the knowledge nor the interest in the subject to write such a devastating review on his own initiative: he obviously had been ordered to do so, and he complied. Another devastating review appeared later in *Scinteia*. This time the writer of the reviewer warned of the danger of relaxing one's vigilance and being taken in by the tricks and subterfuges of the enemy, who often hides behind seeming theoretical sophistication and the pretense of scientific "objectivity"—as if such a thing existed—as had regrettably happened in the pages of that very newspaper, when a favorable review of this abomination had been published a few months earlier. Finally, a few weeks later, the book was withdrawn from circulation: all existing copies were removed from the bookstores, public libraries, and reading clubs. Its contents had been clearly branded as heresy.

Shortly after my book was attacked in the press, I had an opportunity to visit Budapest for the first time since the forties, and there I discussed my book with two of the leading Hungarian economists at the time, Tamás Nagy and Péter Erdös (no relation to the famous mathematician, Paul Erdös, whom I came to know later). I knew their names from the Hungarian economics journal and had a degree of respect for both, which I did not have for any Romanian or, for that matter, Soviet economist. They knew about my book, and became interested in it the minute they learned that it had been lambasted in the Romanian party press. They had ordered a translation, which they showed to me and which they could not understand. The translator knew Romanian, but understood neither economics nor Keynesian terminology. Neither Nagy nor Erdös knew much about Keynes, nor, I suspect, about Western economic thought in general. They were both marxist economists, but not dogmatic ones; they wished to overcome the limitations of marxist doctrine and to some extent were open to critical ideas. Their problem was that instead of studying Western economists, whose work they judged largely irrelevant to the command economy of our countries, they were trying to build the economics of socialism from scratch. Both showed themselves eager to learn about Keynes and what I had to say about his theories. I started to explain the contents of my book, but they had so many questions at literally every step that after a discussion of more than two hours we had managed to cover only a small part of the subject. They then proposed to resume our discussion in the evening at Erdös's home, where we could continue late into the night if necessary.

It was indeed necessary, and we finished around two o'clock in the morning. Erdös and his wife served some snacks and there was wine, which Nagy seemed to enjoy very much. Finally, in the early morning hours, Nagy said: "I think I now understand what you mean by under-employment equilibrium, and your reasoning about how this may happen and how it may be affected by government policies. Of all that you wrote, I like most your explanation of this phenomenon in the marxist framework. I think I have had enough wine by now so that I won't offend you if I say that you are a fool. You should have written what you had to say without ever mentioning Keynes. You are explaining a new phenomenon of the capitalist economy not known to, and even less understood by, marxist economists. You should have given your expla-nation of this phenomenon as your own, and your book would have been a great success." I do not remember what I answered, but I did not regret then or later that I had not proceeded along the lines suggested (perhaps not entirely in earnest) by Tamás Nagy. Anyway, I was very flattered by the keen interest that these two people, whom I held in very high regard, showed for my work. Their reaction was a much needed balm for my soul and consolation for my ego after the roughing up and kicking around that I had been subjected to back home.

Even before the negative reviews of my book appeared, I lost my teaching job at the ISE. This happened in September 1958, as part of a tightening of the political strings attached to teaching positions in ideological fields, of which economics was one. I cannot resist the temptation to reproduce here one of the ironic details of my sacking from that distinguished institution. Upon termination I received a standard document giving my job history at the ISE (formerly ISEP), including my salary and the reason for my termination. For the reason, some standard article of the Labor Act was invoked, the same as for others who were being terminated. The history of my employment went like this: 1949–50, assistant professor, salary . . . ; 1950–52, associate professor, salary . . . ; September 1952–December 1954, associate professor without salary; 1955–58, associate professor, salary. . . . So, from being a guest of the noble house of Malmezon, I had now been promoted to "associate professor without salary"—a nice leave of absence, one might say.

In the meantime, several changes had occurred at my main workplace, the Institute of Economic Research. Some time during the winter of 1957–58, Gogu Rădulescu, the director, had been called to the Central Committee and offered a position in the government: he was to become minister or deputy minister of commerce, I don't remember which. He had several days to think about the offer, and he asked for my advice. I knew how he felt about the current situation; indeed, I knew that our views were very similar. He asked me whether he should accept. I answered without hesitation that I saw no reason not to: a ministerial position was a position of influence and he might be able to have a positive effect on what was happening in the country. As long as the offer was not tied to conditions that were contrary to his views, why not? Should he be asked to do something that ran counter to his conscience, then he could and should resign. His answer was that he saw it slightly differently. He saw no chance of imposing his views on the leaders, nor of influencing them, and since he did not want to ruin his life by getting into a conflict with the leadership, he did not view it as a viable alternative to resign when he disagreed with something. He was not, nor did he intend to become, a hero. Still, he thought that from a position in the government he might be able to do some good, if not for the general cause, which he felt unable to affect, at least for certain individuals: he might be able to give somebody a job, or a better job, than he or she had, and that might be a sufficient reason to "become corrupt," as he put it. He clearly viewed joining the government as a form of corruption, and he was weighing the merits of going along with that. He finally decided to accept, and so left the institute.

A few months earlier there had been a significant incident involving Gogu Rădulescu. Gogu had an old friend in Moscow, Ilya Konstantinovsky, a fellow communist from his days in the student movement before the war. Unlike Gogu, Konstantinovsky was Jewish, and in 1940, when Bessarabia was incorporated into the Soviet Union and there was a ten-day period of choice, he went over to the Soviet side. After the war, Konstantinovsky did not return to Romania, but became a Soviet citizen, and in the fifties he was working in Moscow as a journalist. Gogu had talked to me about him several times with great admiration, saying he was by far the smartest in their group when they were comrades in Bucharest, very much the intellectual leader. They had not been in correspondence over the years, but there had been sporadic contacts through third parties and each knew of the other's fate. At some time in late 1956 Gogu told me that Ilya was coming to Bucharest for a short visit. He was very much looking forward to meeting him again, and I had the impression that he expected to get answers to many of the basic questions that were preoccupying both of us.

Konstantinovsky's visit lasted only three days. Gogu apparently had one or two long conversations with him, and was very much put off by him. For a few days he just grumbled and did not want to talk about it, but finally he confided to me that Ilya had essentially told him the following: The ideals of their youth were gone forever; the Soviet Union no longer had anything to do with them. Everything was a big lie; it was impossible to change and therefore futile to try. There was nothing to do about it, except to forget one's ideals and learn to live with the ugly reality. His main concern was, and had been for many years now, to take care of his own personal life and family, to protect himself against the dangers of his profession, and to avoid traps and provocations. He advised Gogu to do the same, not in the interest of the cause—there was no such thing any longer—but for the simple purpose of survival in our ugly and dangerous world. Gogu said that he had also talked to Ilya about me, describing briefly my imprisonment and my current views as a reform communist dedicated to changing the system, and mentioned the book I had written. Konstantinovsky's reaction, Gogu told me, was, "It sounds like your friend is a brave and honest man, but it is naive of him or of you to think that anything can be accomplished along these lines. It is hopeless, and you should look out for yourselves." Although I did not know Konstantinovsky, I had heard enough about him from Gogu to prevent me from dismissing his opinions as those of a self-centered individual who at some point in his life had turned sour. In fact, his remarks to Gogu upset me almost as much as they had upset him. They became one of the nails in the coffin of my ideals.

After Gogu left the institute, Miron Constantinescu, the former member of the politburo and president of the State Planning Commission, was appointed his successor. Constantinescu had been ousted from the politburo and the government shortly before his appointment. The circumstances under which this had come about have important ramifications and are worth sketching here.

Ever since 1955, and especially after the twentieth congress of the Soviet Communist Party, Khrushchev had been exerting pressure on the "fraternal" parties to embark upon the same path of de-Stalinization that he was following in the Soviet Union. In Hungary, Poland, and Czechoslovakia this had led to genuine changes in the leadership of those parties; but Gheorghiu-Dej had restricted the de-Stalinization process in Romania to regurgitating some of the information about Stalin's crimes—balanced with reflections on the great leader's merits—and to paying lip service to the condemnation of any kind of personality cult, a disease from which, we were reassured, Romania had never suffered. In the wake of the Hungarian uprising, during which Gheorghiu-Dej had a chance to see for himself on a visit to Budapest the widespread and violent hatred against the Russians, he apparently decided to switch gears in his relations to the Soviet Union and to distance himself from Moscow. In my opinion, this decision was dictated to a large extent by his fear of a Soviet attempt to have him ousted as a former Stalinist. Anyway, he went about it with sufficient shrewdness to manage in the summer of 1958 to obtain the withdrawal of Soviet troops from Romania.

In the following year or two, Gheorghiu-Dej started taking an independent stand in the Comecon, the Council for Economic Cooperation of the socialist countries, where he refused to go along with some Soviet recommendations that, in the name of the international division of labor, would have slowed down Romania's plans for developing its own heavy industry. In a short time, this initially muted and sporadic friction with the Soviets developed into a full scale, more or less open policy conflict. Thus the party leader who for the first decade after the war had been the most obedient servant of his Soviet masters discovered his patriotism when he felt threatened by these same masters, and started "defending Romania's interests" from the Soviet Union. By the way, it was suggested in the Western press at the time that the schism with the Soviet leadership was just a pretense to facilitate Romania's contacts with the West. This was a misjudgment of the situation. The conflict with the Soviets, and the mutual suspicion of the two leaderships, became so significant at one point that all those with close Soviet connections (such as having spent the war in the Soviet Union, or having studied in the Soviet Union, having married a Russian woman, etc.) became ineligible for jobs in the higher echelons of the Nomenklatura.* Furthermore, all those persons in this category who held responsible positions in the Securitate or in the interior or defense ministries were sacked during the late fifties and early sixties.

It was in this context that Gheorghiu-Dej turned against Miron Constantinescu, who after the twentieth congress either felt genuine remorse or simply wanted to endear himself with the new Soviet leadership, that is, Khrushchev. Whatever Constantinescu's motives, he apparently had tentatively raised the issue of de-Stalinization in Romania. He did not get beyond a few remarks, however, as his attempt was instantly foiled by an already alert and suspicious Gheorghiu-Dej, who lost no time in ousting him from the party leadership. This is how Constantinescu came to be appointed director of our institute. Constantinescu took his job utterly seriously. He did not behave in the least like the offended prince who had been unjustly kicked in the buttocks, but held meeting after meeting with the various groups of the institute, working to learn what they were doing, how things were go-

---

*This specifically Soviet term, also used for the satellite countries, can be loosely equated with "the party brass" or simply the communist elite. More precisely, it denotes the list of positions (whether political, administrative, or military) whose holders could only be appointed by the central organs of the party.

ing, what kinds of difficulties they were encountering, and so on. He tried to be friendly to everybody and create a good atmosphere around himself. In his references to the party leadership he always used a tone of utmost respect, and in general he followed the party line and the rules of behavior set by it. I knew in a general way the antecedents of his demotion and watched him with interest: had he somehow managed to start a reform movement in the party, I would have joined him in spite of my reservations about his past behavior (he had been a staunch supporter of Gheorghiu-Dej and Chişinevschi, and of the purges and show trials they had organized). But nothing of the kind happened. Instead, his tenure at the institute was rather short-lived, mainly because of Costin Murgescu, the deputy director.

Murgescu was an ambitious young man, smart and well informed enough to size up the situation. He knew that once Gheorghiu-Dej classified somebody as his enemy, that person's political career was finished—and he would be lucky to get off so lightly. Therefore to Murgescu, Miron Constantinescu was a leper, and since they were supposed to work together, he had to protect himself against contagion. I was bemused at the skillful way in which, from the very start, Murgescu manufactured a conflict between himself and the new director. This was not easy to do, since Constantinescu went out of his way to get along with him and even to please him. But every day Murgescu would raise a different point on which he happened to disagree with the new director. No matter what the latter said, Murgescu was always able to find something to object to. Being a sophisticated and capable man, Constantinescu soon understood what was going on, but was unable to do anything about it. He could not simply say every time that Murgescu was right and back off from what he had said—no matter how insignificant the "issue" at hand was, without completely losing face. The minute he started arguing with Murgescu and defending what he had said, the latter would respond with a full-blown position paper rebutting the new director, a copy of which was always sent to the party.

Thus, in a few weeks everybody knew that there was a very serious conflict between the new director of the institute and his deputy, and in about two months Murgescu thought the situation ripe for a frontal attack. He sent a memo to the Central Committee of the party stating, in effect, that he had done everything in his power to work in a disciplined manner with the new director, but found it impossible. He therefore had to ask the party to relieve him of his job as deputy director as long as the current director remained in his position. Murgescu got some help from Malinschi, the vice president of the Academy in charge of the Social Sciences, who was an old foe of Constantinescu with many scores to settle. He testified before the party that Murgescu was a nice, cooperative fellow who could work easily with anybody, and that he had had no similar conflicts with anybody in the past. Gogu Rădulescu, the former director of the institute, who had also suffered plenty of blows and humiliations at the hands of Constantinescu when the latter had been president of the State Planning Commission, testified that Murgescu was pleasant and easy to work with, and it could not possibly be his fault if the new director did not get along with him.

In the end, Miron Constantinescu was ousted as director in the fall of 1958, and Murgescu was appointed editor-in-chief of a new economic magazine, *Viaţa Economică*, while also maintaining his position as head of the Section on the History of the National Economy (but not the one of deputy director). A new director was appointed in the person of Roman Moldovan, the head of some government agency, who would therefore work only part time; and a new full-time deputy director was appointed in the person of Ion Rachmuth, the economist from the party school who had advised me against the publication of my book.

My account of the brief episode in Miron Constantinescu's career when he was the director of the Institute of Economic Research would be incomplete without my mentioning the terrible tragedy that befell him not long after he left our institute. Constantinescu was married to a party activist called Sulamita. They had two or three teenage children and Sulamita had a reputation as a very strict mother. One day one of the Constantinescu daughters was invited to a party. Sulamita said no. The girl very much wanted to go; she insisted, but her mother was adamant. The girl took a hammer or an icepick and hit her mother in the head, killing her.

During these years, an important development occurred in my private life, which may sound trivial to a Western reader but which throws a sharp light on conditions in the Romania of those days. As I mentioned, our fifth-floor penthouse apartment at 72 Bulevardul Stalin was in a beautiful part of Bucharest and had a wonderful view over Stalin Square and Stalin Park. After Khrushchev's report to the twentieth party congress, the names of the square, the park, and the boulevard were all changed, and our address became 72 Bulevardul Aviatorilor. Although our apartment was very attractive, it was small for a family with two children; it had one large, elegant living-and-dining room, one small bedroom, a kitchen, and a bath. But while its indoor floor space was quite limited, the apartment had two huge balconies, and soon after we moved back into it Edith and I started thinking about transforming one of the balconies into two additional rooms. It could be done nicely, without changing the appearance of the building; that is, the new outside walls could be made to blend with the old ones without being noticeable from the street. So there should have been no problem with zoning regulations. The main difficulty was that the house was state property, and I had no right to make any modifications to it. The only way our project could have been carried out would have been to get the housing office of the District Council (Sfatul Raional) to include it in its construction plan and then act on it. Unfortunately, as in every district, the housing office had a miserable record for maintaining the district's housing. In fact, nothing was done by way of maintenance and repair, and a building, or at least a wing of it, had to crumble before anybody would touch it. The idea of getting the housing office to build us two rooms on our balcony seemed absurd. All my friends to whom I mentioned it laughed at me and were surprised, because they did not think of me in general as a naïve person. Yet the legal framework did not rule out something like this, so I set out to implement our plan.

First of all I needed some connection to the District Council. I inquired and found out that the engineer who was the director of the housing office was a man of good intentions, who had been trying to overcome the mess that the housing office had been for many years. He was not corrupt, and it was not advisable to try to bribe him. I asked to see him, and after repeated attempts managed to get an appointment. I then put my plan to him in the following context: the party had lately been stressing that increased attention had to be paid to the citizens' needs, and more strenuous efforts had to be made toward improving their living standards, including their housing conditions. It so happened, I said, that I had discovered a place where two rooms could be built at less than half the cost of building them elsewhere, because by making intelligent use of existing structures one could transform the floor and walls of a balcony into a floor and walls for two rooms. One only had to add the outside walls, one relatively small interior wall, and the ceiling with an extension of the existing roof over it. My preliminary calculations showed that the cost to the district would be less than half the normal cost of two rooms. Although the rooms would become part of my apartment, they would also become part of the district's housing patrimony and would be of equal use to whoever occupied the apartment in the future.

The director was torn between the appealing aspects of this project, especially its low cost, and the avalanche of pressing problems that he was struggling with, mostly in vain. He said he would think it over, but anyway in order to be included in the plan for next year, the proposal would have to be submitted to the District Council, which was most unlikely to approve it, as it did not serve any urgent need. I said that I would like to try my luck, and he finally agreed to submit the proposal to the District Council. Now I set out to investigate the workings of that illustrious body, and found a connection to its secretary, Ilonka Néni (Aunt Ilonka), a middle-aged woman who spoke Hungarian and whom my friend Köves knew. Köves told me that Ilonka Néni, though not corrupt, would not refuse a small present, but there was a more important condition attached to obtaining a favor from her: one had to listen to her stories. I listened to a number of them and, to make my own story short, found out who on the committee might be favorable and who might not, and managed to arrange with Ilonka Néni that our proposal would come up for discussion when the member most likely to be hostile was away. This meant waiting for a few weeks or perhaps longer, but there was no better way. After several months, Ilonka Néni finally succeeded in piloting our project through the committee, which included it in the plan.

This was an important step, but just a first step. It was a necessary but far from sufficient condition for having the district undertake the project. The district plan had numerous projects that had been accepted many years earlier but whose turn to be implemented had never come. At the beginning of every three-month period there was a discussion followed by a selection of the projects for that period. At this point the input of the director of the housing office was important. I tried various maneuvers to influence him, such as seeking connections to his superiors in the hierarchy, obtaining a letter of support from the City Council, and so forth. I cannot remember all the stages that we went through with this project during the two years from the date I started it, but one number sticks in my mind. After the first few weeks, realizing that I was spending an enormous amount of time making telephone calls connected to the project, it occurred to me that if I wanted to keep track of my efforts, the best way was to count the calls I was making. So I started a log. In the end, I made close to two thousand telephone calls over a period of about twenty-two months.

When work finally started on our balcony, we could not believe our luck. Up to that point, I had spent an enormous amount of energy and time, but very little money—there was no major bribe involved. From then on, however, I needed plenty of money. The building group wanted to use the cheapest, lowest-quality materials, so I had to pay to have them upgraded to a higher quality. The workmen would show up one day, then not show up for two. I instituted a premium, paid by me, for finishing certain tasks by certain dates, and that worked. I could afford these expenses because I had already received the royalties for my book, which amounted to the equivalent of more than six months' salary. In addition, Edith's parents were earning well above the average through Klara's artificial flower shop, and they regularly helped us. Finally, toward the end of 1958, the two new rooms were finished. One of them became our bedroom, the other my study. Our former bedroom became the girls' room. That still left a small but very nice balcony (an unconverted portion of the huge former balcony) adjacent to our new bedroom, as well as the second, large balcony adjacent to the living room.

With our newly enlarged, attractive apartment we now often felt that life had to be enjoyed in spite of political adversity. I resumed playing tennis after a break of about eighteen years. Edith and I would sometimes go out for dinner and dancing with friends. We tried not to miss any good plays—of which there were few—and from time to time we went to the opera. We had an opportunity to see a couple of Fellini movies: *La Dolce Vita* and *8½*.

The apartment building where we lived had been the property of a certain Mr. Marinescu, one of the owners of Romania's only airplane factory, located in Braşov. When Marinescu was expropriated like the rest of the bourgeoisie, he left the country and moved to Paris. Although our building was very well conceived and executed, its maintenance was no better than that of other state-owned apartment buildings. There was a maintenance man in his fifties, Nea Marin (Uncle Marin), the same as under Mr. Marinescu. He was allegedly a mechanic and was in charge of running the heating in the winter and the hot water throughout the year, as well as keeping the elevator working. I used to have conversations with Nea Marin, who—at least when nobody else besides me could hear him—expressed great admiration for his former boss. Mr. Marinescu was now living in the United States and, at least according to Nea Marin, visited his friends in Paris by crossing the Atlantic in his own, self-piloted airplane.

I did not expect at that time ever to hear this story from anyone else; nevertheless, that is exactly what happened about thirteen years later in the summer of 1969 when, having emigrated to the West, I was attending a week-long conference on mathematical programming held on the island of Bandol in the south of France. As the conference was sponsored by NATO, a French admiral based in nearby Toulon served as honorary chairman, and at one point he gave a luncheon to which some of the speakers were invited. As I was the only French-speaking American at the luncheon, the admiral made me his main conversational partner. When, he noticed that I was not a native American, and when I told him about my background, he said: "I know one of your countrymen who now lives in the West; actually he is a friend of mine. He lived in Paris for a while—that's when we became friends—then moved to America. However, he is rich and has many French friends, so he comes to Paris quite often." By this time I had already had three or four glasses of a strong burgundy. In front of my eyes was Nea Marin, telling me about a Romanian in America who was a frequent visitor to Paris. I said, "And he comes in his own plane piloted by himself."

The admiral looked at me in astonishment. "That's exactly true. How do you know?"

"His name is Marinescu," I continued.

"Yes," he said, even more amazed, "but how do you know?"

"I know because in Bucharest I happened to live in the house that had once been his. It's a small world."

But this was at another time, in another place. To come back to the Bucharest of the mid-to-late fifties, the maintenance of our building was rather shaky. It was extremely difficult to get anything replaced, so not having hot water or a working elevator for several hours was not an unusual event. Since we lived on the top floor, we were especially vulnerable to elevator breakdowns, and I gave frequent tips to Nea Marin to make sure he would keep the elevator in working condition (there were other tenants to worry about the heating and the hot water). Once we had a major problem with the elevator and the electric motor had to be replaced. Although the house was state property, if we wanted the replacement within, say, a week, as opposed to within a year, we had to buy the new motor ourselves. We did, it was installed, and the elevator went back to work—except that every few weeks it would break down and the motor would need repair. When this happened the third or fourth time, I took Nea Marin to task. "A motor needs periodic repair," he said. "There is nothing surprising in that." "But the old motor never needed repair during the three years I've been living here," I objected. He looked at me with reproach in his eyes and said, "But Mr. Balaş, how can you compare our socialist motors to that old capitalist motor?" He clearly won the argument; his healthy proletarian instinct saw the deeper truth that had eluded me.

The two balconies of our apartment overlooked the former Stalin Square, a huge circular space that, on its northwestern side, at the entrance to the park, had an enormous statue of Stalin. After the twentieth congress of the Soviet party, Stalin's statues started being taken down throughout the Soviet Union and some of the satellite countries. In others, they were torn down by the people. Thus, in Budapest, early in the 1956 uprising, the demonstrators set out to tear down the gigantic bronze statue in one of the city's central squares. But this was no easy task, since this particular piece of art was exceptionally solid and heavy. The demonstrators produced a team of metalworkers and welders who, after sizing up the task, decided to cut the metal where it was thinnest, between the knees and the rims of the boots. Everything above the knees fell down and was carried away, but the pedestal of the statue, with the boots, remained for many months, as nobody had time to take care of it. Thus the square came to be known as *Csizma Tér*—Boot Square. In Bucharest, when the party finally gave orders for Stalin's statue to be taken down, the first step was to surround it with a high, massive fence, so that nobody could see what was happening to it. Apparently, and with good reason, the party leaders figured that the sight of Stalin's statue being torn down was not likely to enhance their authority, so it had to be done out of sight. However, from our penthouse balcony we could see very well what was happening behind the fence. And what did we see? That no matter how reactionary the Hungarian uprising—officially called a counterrevolution—had been, a good revolutionary could still learn something from it: Stalin's statue in Bucharest was demolished by the same method that the workers of Budapest had used a few months

Egon with Anna and Vera in the late fifties

earlier. The statue was chopped off right beneath the knees, leaving only the pedestal with the boots, while the rest was taken away. However, the "boot phase" of the Romanian statue was not seen by anybody besides ourselves; it was blasted with dynamite during the night, and the square did not get the corresponding name.

A few lines about our children during this period. From the spring of 1955 till the fall of 1957, when Anna reached school age (which was seven), our daughters usually had a maid as babysitter. The maids were Hungarian peasant women from Transylvania, and they varied widely in quality. Anna and Vera were also taking daily German lessons from an elderly woman who would take them for walks in the park. During the summer, both girls stayed in Cluj in their grandparents' garden, which they liked very much. There the German lessons were replaced with singing and a great deal of free time. Also, the girls would join us every summer for two or three weeks at one of the Black Sea resorts, Mamaia, Eforie, or Carmen Silva.

When Anna reached school age, she went to the neighborhood elementary school—the best one in town—named after Ion Luca Caragiale, a famous nineteenth-century playwright and satirist of Romanian society. Anna did well in school from the beginning; we never heard anything but praise from her teachers. She did well in all subjects, particularly mathematics, and was among the two best students in her class. She also started taking piano lessons and the following year we bought a piano. She continued her piano lessons until about 1961, when she stopped and started taking French lessons.

As for Vera, I remember a typical episode from her preschool days. On Sunday mornings we would usually go for a walk in the park, the whole family together, and I would tell the girls some improvised story. Edith noticed that whenever we approached a militiaman (policeman), Vera would hide behind my coat or Edith's. For a while we could not understand her behavior, which she refused to explain, and I jokingly told Edith, "She has healthy instincts." It turned out, though, that Vera was in the habit of leaving the house surreptitiously with a pair of scissors tied by a string to her neck, going into the park, and returning with a beautiful bouquet of roses. Cutting roses in the park was, of course, forbidden, and her fear of the militia man arose from her bad conscience. When Vera reached school age, she went to the same school as Anna and did quite well, although she had to live up to the expectations of teachers who had taught her sister.

The period beginning in 1958 brought some changes in Edith's situation at work. In the aftermath of the Hungarian events, the Romanian party embarked, among other things, upon a campaign of "improving the national composition" of the educational and cultural institutions. After earlier campaigns aimed at the class composition, the focus was now on the ethnic composition. This meant reducing the number of Hungarians and Jews—in Bucharest, mainly Jews. In 1958, as part of this campaign, Edith lost her position in the Department of Philosophy of Parhon University. After a while, she managed to find a similar job in another, politically less exposed, Department of Philosophy in an institute for postgraduate studies for physicians. Here she taught the same subjects as before to doctors rather than students.

In the summer of 1958, the chairman of her department, a certain Dr. Dumitriu, was attacked in a party meeting and accused of deviations from the party line. The district party secretary came in person to lead the attack, which was obviously aimed at totally discrediting Dumitriu before firing him. Although Edith had not been close to the director and did not know much about his activities, the accusations sounded so artificial and lacking in any foundation that she could not bring herself to join the crowd in asking for his punishment. After almost everybody had duly spoken up against the culprit and had painted him with the ugliest colors available to his or her imagination, it was proposed that he be given a "reprimand with last warning." This was the maximum punishment short of expulsion from the party. A vote was taken and all but one of the participants favored the proposal. Nobody voted against it, but there was one abstention: Edith Balaş. This was so unusual that all present turned their heads to see who the maverick was. This adventure might have resulted in Edith's losing her job again, had things not subsequently taken a different turn: Dumitriu turned out to be well connected to circles above the district secretary, so the latter did not manage to have him fired. The reprimand with last warning remained in force, but Dumitriu kept his job. He never discussed the events of that meeting with Edith, but at the end of the month, out of the blue, without any obvious connection to her work, Edith received a big bonus, equivalent to about half her monthly salary. Sometimes—but unfortunately not too often—it pays to have courage.

But this job did not last very long either. The hostile wind was getting stronger, and after my expulsion from the party in the spring of 1959, to be discussed below, Edith had to leave higher education and the teaching of philosophy altogether. In the fall of 1959 she became a history teacher at one of the largest and best-known high schools of Bucharest, Liceul Matei Basarab. She taught ancient history, in particular that of Egypt, Assyria, Babylonia, Persia, Greece, and Rome. After some fighting with an obnoxious headmaster who would sit in her classes to gather material against her, the dust settled and Edith had a more or less quiet, if difficult, life at the school.

The new, nationalistic party line had many far-reaching political consequences. At one point the party decided to abolish the Hungarian university in Cluj. The means chosen to do this was a merger of the two universities of Cluj, the Romanian—called Babeş—and the Hungarian—called Bólyai—into a single university, called Babeş-Bólyai. This sounds rather democratic; but the language of instruction in the new university was to be Romanian, except for specifically Hungarian subjects such as Hungarian language and literature. The merger did not go easily, because the Hungarian teaching personnel tried to resist. Nevertheless, in the end the party prevailed, of course. The joint faculty of the two universities voted unanimously in a plenary meeting in favor of the merger, but not before the vice president of the Hungarian university, a statistician called Csendes, and two of the professors, Molnár and Szabédi, had committed suicide. Csendes took an overdose of sleeping pills; Molnár jumped to his death from the fifth floor of a building. The press celebrated the general enthusiasm stirred by the merger.

Another personal tragedy that unfolded in the same year, though unrelated to the events in Cluj, was that of the economist Pavel (Paul) Dan. A highly talented, extremely bright, young Jewish intellectual (his original surname had been Davidovici), one or two years younger than myself, Pavel Dan started out in the party's propaganda section in Cluj during the period from 1945 to 1947, when I was there. At the same time he studied for a degree in economics, which he completed around 1948. He was later moved to the propaganda section of the Central Committee in Bucharest, and from there to the chamber of commerce, while also holding a teaching position in political economy at the ISEP. Unlike myself, he had a "clean" Party record, untainted by any deviation. I had great respect for his intellectual capacities, but was never close to him. For a while, I viewed him as being on the other side of the fence from me, where all the party people belonged. But around 1957 we became closer and, in a couple of conversations, he revealed himself to me as a person utterly disillusioned. He had a wife who taught philosophy, a son, and a daughter, Marika, who later became a friend of our Anna's. After 1956 Pavel sympathized with the ideas of reform communism, though not publicly. He told me that when my book came out he was asked to demolish it in a review for the party's theoretical monthly, *Lupta de Clasă*. Though he did not have the strength to refuse, he did not write it in the end, claiming that he had no time. (Somebody else "reviewed" the book in that journal.)

Pavel Dan was one of the few intellectuals who were occasionally allowed to travel to the West. He had been sent to a meeting of a United Nations agency in Geneva, and he told me about a waiter who would serve him at the restaurant and then get into his car and drive away— which for somebody in 1950s Bucharest was like a fairy tale. So much, he implied, for "wicked capitalist exploitation." When I last saw him around November 1958 he said that he felt deeply depressed by the political situation and saw no hope for improvement; on the contrary, things were likely to get worse. On New Year's Eve he went into the bathroom of the family's apartment, got into the bathtub, and shot himself through the heart. In a suicide note he made clear that nobody was to blame but himself; he "just couldn't take it any longer." He had not yet been buried when the party began spreading rumors to the effect that he may have been recruited by a Western espionage service while in Geneva and killed himself to avoid being caught.

In the spring of 1959 I was finally expelled from the party and kicked out of my job at the Institute of Economic Research. The meeting for my expulsion—my second public political execution—was no less stormy than the first in 1952, but it was emotionally much less trying, since I was no longer a believer. The director of the institute, Roman Moldovan, called the meeting jointly with the party secretary of the institute, a young economist named Părăluță. The atmosphere was heavy, especially after it had been announced that the decision to expel me came from the highest party forum, the politburo. The reason given was that I was a bourgeois element alien to the party and the working class, as demonstrated by many aspects of my activity, of which the writing of a harmful, poisonous book was merely the latest. My *Korunk* article was also dignified with the epithet "subversive." After the reading of the party decision, everybody had to take turns in the ritual of criticizing me, demolishing my book, and—for those working directly with me—exercising self-criticism for not having recognized the devil earlier for what he was. Rachmuth, the deputy director, who had reviewed the book for the publishing house and had recommended acceptance, talked mainly of his own shortcomings in not recognizing the harmful nature of the book and having recommended its publication. I had no reason to blame him for what he said; after all, he had warned me against publishing it. None of my colleagues in the section that I had headed until the day before said anything that went beyond the generic accusations that were part of the ritual. But others used the occasion to obtain some brownie points with the party by attacking me ferociously. My most "enthusiastic" critic was Părăluță, the party secretary, who volunteered numerous personal contributions. When I was asked to speak, I regretted the harm that my book might possibly have done, and assured the party that it was unintended. I did not repent and humiliate myself, but neither did I play Don Quixote. After the meeting a colleague, Finca Mohr, said to me in private, "I envy you for your ability to always keep your head up. What is your secret?" I thanked her for her kindness without answering her question. In retrospect, I guess, my "secret" was that my conscience was clear, that I had done nothing I was ashamed of, and that it was simply not in my character to humiliate myself in an attempt to buy favors. I was fired from the Institute of Economic Research as of April 15, 1959. The reason given in the official notification of the termination of my job was the ominous paragraph d of article 20 of the Labor Act, defined as "(politically) unsuitable for the job." No great help in trying to find my next job!

My expulsion from the party sealed a process of political evolution that was going on within me. Partly by coincidence, it more or less marked that point of my inner development at which I gave up on reform communism. From roughly that time on, or perhaps a few months later, I ceased to believe that the system could be redeemed through reform. By that time I knew enough about conditions in Yugoslavia, where the economic system was based on the ideas of market socialism, to conclude that that version of socialism was, economically at least, not significantly more successful than ours. Also, I knew enough about the West to not only to question, but to regard as out-and-out wrong, the marxist evaluation of capitalism. This raises the valid question of why I had not seen this during the year that I had spent in London in 1948 and 1949. The answer is, at that time I had my intellectual and emotional blinders on: I was a believer. But it is interesting to remark, as an insight into how psychological transformations work their way in the human soul and mind, that for a long time, at least a couple of years before I had completely abandoned my earlier "creed," I started having, along with the occasional nightmares that I have described, pleasant, soothing dreams: I was in a new environment, where I felt free (or rather, FREE). The concrete circumstances varied, but the underlying atmosphere was that of freedom, and the recurring theme that marked these scenes was my standing on the escalator of the London subway, going down slowly and watching the people coming up on the opposite side. Apparently, without my being conscious of it, the London subway had become the symbol of freedom for me, back in 1948.

On a different plane, it was one thing to understand that something was deeply wrong with the system I was living in, and quite another to understand what exactly it was. The people who had become communists under the oppressive regimes of the past were often of exemplary character, willing to risk their freedom and sometimes their lives for what they perceived as the common good. While it is true that after coming to power some of them underwent a sometimes radical change of character—power corrupts, as they say, and absolute power corrupts absolutely—still, the anomalies of the regime that they instituted could not be simply attributed to flaws in their characters. There was a factor here at play, which one may call the power of the system or of the institutions, which was recognized as far back as ancient Rome, where the saying was coined: *Senatori boni viri, Senatus autem bestia* (the senators are good men, but the Senate is a beast). The system develops its own momentum and acquires a power uncontrollable by any individual.

Coming back to 1959, putting together all the information I had about both worlds left no doubt in my mind that the socialist economic system, in any of its forms that had been tried, was far inferior to modern capitalism. More importantly, the political system that accompanied the building of socialism in all the countries where the Communist Party had come to power was marked by brutal repression and a complete, universal lack of freedom. When abuses of power were revealed and steps were taken to prevent their repetition, that process was also arbitrary, depending upon the mood of the actors in the political drama. There was no objective analysis of what had happened and consequently there could be no real drawing of conclusions or drastic institutional reforms. The accepted dogma of the dictatorship of the proletariat as the political system of the transition to socialism remained in force. I concluded that this world bore no resemblance to that of my dreams, and I finally gave up on trying to change it. In other words, not long after my exclusion from the party I concluded that, in a way, it had been justified. I no longer belonged there.

Once I came to this conclusion, I had a twofold reaction. On the one hand, I felt a kind of emptiness in my soul. For almost two decades I had lived as a communist, as a person dedicated to an ideal in the service of which, at least for a while, I was willing to sacrifice almost everything. But from now on I would have to live without such an ideal, without a commitment to a "noble cause." On the other hand, along with the emptiness I also felt a strange kind of relief, as if a burden had been lifted from my shoulders. I could breathe more freely than before. I was no longer in the service of a cause; I was free to look out for myself and my family.

In retrospect, I can see that the chapter of my life that ended in the spring of 1959 was but one particular incarnation of the common fate of an entire generation of people like myself. Some of the best people of my generation, some of the most decent and respected young intellectuals in the central and eastern Europe of the late thirties and early forties, especially if they were Jewish, turned toward the political left. Those among them who had the courage of their convictions joined the Communist Party and opposed the nazi war effort with the means at their disposal. In so doing, they risked their lives in the service of a cause they believed in. To be sure, at the same time countless others around the world were fighting the nazis on the battlefront; however, unlike most of those others, the ones I am talking about were volunteers. The members of this generation who were lucky enough to survive the war were caught up in an immense tragedy that engulfed their entire lives: The society of their dreams, the paradise of justice and equality that they had hoped to build, turned out to be a nightmare. The revolution they helped to bring about sacrificed them to its whims, ate them alive, and from its heroes turned them into its villains.

■ ■ ■

CHAPTER 14

From Economics to Mathematics

Intellectually, the five-year period that started in the spring of 1959 was perhaps the most difficult and adventurous of my life. At the age of thirty-seven I embarked upon transforming myself into a mathematician. Few people had pulled that off, or so I was told. According to the accepted wisdom, mathematics can be, and has to be, learned early in life because the capacity for abstract thinking does not seem to develop after a certain age. I did not know whether this was always true, true to some extent, true in certain cases, or outright false—a prejudice like so many others. I did have my doubts at the time, but they were overcome by a very strong feeling that this was the only course I could chart for myself that I could pursue with the enthusiasm and energy needed for at least a chance of success.

All I knew was that my life had reached a turning point. I was considered a talented man by my former teachers, my professional colleagues, and my friends; yet everything I had accomplished professionally had gone down the drain. True, I had a certain reputation as an economist. But that reputation had now become practically meaningless: Not only had I been thrown out of the Institute of Economic Research, but I was categorically forbidden to publish in any economic journal. More important, that reputation had become meaningless in my own eyes. My earlier motivation—to help develop the science of economic planning in order to build a better society—had disappeared, and in the process I had lost my respect for marxist economics, the only kind of economics I knew really well. In short, I was facing complete professional failure.

On the other hand, I felt strongly attracted to the new field of applied mathematics called operations research. Its development started during World War II and grew out of the need for optimizing certain military activities. After the war the field underwent a spectacular development and crystallized into a number of subdisciplines, the most important of which became known as linear programming. I had known about the existence of operations research since around 1956 and was keenly interested in it, but because of other preoccupations I did not find out more about it until late 1958, when I came across a newly published book by Dorfman, Samuelson, and Solow, *Linear Programming and Economic Analysis*. Its contents caught my imagination. The subject had both intrinsic appeal and enormous potential for applications; moreover, I felt confident that I could learn and master it in a relatively short time. Of course, I realized that if I wanted to change fields and become an expert, a researcher, in linear programming and optimization theory, as opposed to an interested reader of the literature, I would have to do a lot of hard learning; but I was keenly interested and strongly motivated. I figured that if I put together a systematic study plan and applied myself to it for several hours a day, in a year or so I would be able to attack a specific research topic and obtain some results. I set this as my goal.

This sounds nice in retrospect, but when I made this decision, it would have seemed outright crazy to anyone to whom I would have confided it (which I did not). I was without a job, freshly kicked out onto the street. Naturally, the first order of the day was to get a job and earn a living, and at first I devoted all my energies to that task. But in order to gather the strength needed to confront my difficulties, I had to have a clear picture of where I was heading. Now I had it. I thought about the kind of job that I should be looking for, and it seemed to me that with my reputation as an economist and my knowledge of six languages, it should not be too difficult to get a low level job as an economic analyst in some study group. As it turned out, I had underestimated the stigma attached to my expulsion from the party and the institute. I placed several phone calls to the heads of such study groups, but was told that there were no openings.

Then I remembered that the State Bank had a study group for world economic trends, where I could certainly make myself useful, and that the director of the group was Imre Deutsch, a communist intellectual from Arad, whom I knew to be a decent, straightforward, bright person.

So I called him, explained my situation—which he already knew—and asked whether he thought he could find a position for me at the lowest level in his group. He replied that he would love to have somebody with my qualifications and that finding a position would not be a problem, given the many ways in which I could help his group. The only difficulty was my political situation, which prevented him from acting on his own; but if I asked the Central Committee of the party to call him and authorize him to hire me, he would gladly do so. I did not tell him what I thought—that even my worst enemy would have to hire me if the Central Committee told him to do so. Instead, I said that it had never crossed my mind that I could be hired without the approval of the appropriate party forum, but I thought that maybe he could call his party connection, report that I had applied for a job in his group, and ask for instructions. He declined to take such an initiative. Since Deutsch was in general a man of good faith, certainly no worse than the average, this conversation of ours was a good measure of what a dangerous individual I had become. There was, of course, no use in my turning to the party. Just to make sure, I had called party officials right after my expulsion and firing to ask whether they could advise me as to what kind of employment I should seek. Their answer was that the party was not an employment agency and that the country was large and full of jobs for anyone who wanted to work.

Two months passed without my being able to find employment, two months during which, in spite of the daily frustrations of the job hunt, I was able to make some progress with my mathematical studies. Then in June, Finca Mohr, the colleague at my former institute who had spoken kind words to me, called to tell me that her husband's workplace, IPROCIL, the Design and Research Institute for the Timber Industry, was having a competition for the position of design engineer in charge of the economic evaluation of projects. I looked up the job announcement, then talked to Finca's husband, Gogu Mohr, chief engineer at IPROCIL. Mohr said that the opening was in fact for an engineer; but there would be a written competition, and he thought that if there were few candidates and I did well on the test, the committee might overlook the fact that I was not an engineer. However, there was also the matter of my political situation. Here everything depended on the institute's party secretary. The director, a certain engineer named Naftali, was a decent man who would certainly not oppose my hiring; however, the party secretary would have to give the green light. Mohr described this person as a reasonable man, who understood the importance of knowledge and expertise in the work of an institution like IPROCIL, and gave me his name.

The next day I asked to see the party secretary and got an appointment. I introduced myself and told him that I was interested in the job for which IPROCIL had announced a competition. I felt qualified for the job, but I had a political problem and did not want to apply before asking for his opinion. Then I told him bluntly that I had just been expelled from the party and from the Institute of Economic Research for serious ideological deviations. I said that if the job was one involving state secrets, confidential data, or decisions that required an ideologically reliable individual, then he should tell me so right away and not consider me at all. But if the job lacked those aspects and instead required somebody with good economic judgment, who knew how to distinguish an efficient solution from a waste of resources and was willing to learn the technological facts needed to make such judgments in the context of the timber industry, then he should consider letting me take the test. He asked what my ideological deviations had been, and I told him they were many, but mainly a book whose ideas had been found harmful. He wanted to know who had published the book, and was surprised that the Editura Politica had not seen the harmful ideas before publication. He seemed favorably impressed by the fact that I answered all his questions promptly and openly, without trying to defend what I had done. In the end, he said that he saw no reason why I could not compete for the position, which was strictly practical rather than ideological.

The competition took place about a week later. There were eleven candidates: myself and ten engineers. Knowing how professionally self-centered engineers tend to be, I did not think I stood a chance. But I turned out to be wrong. The test consisted of a list of questions that had to do with methods of evaluating investment projects in general and industrial designs in particular, plus an essay on a well-defined subject. My paper carried the day and the committee chose it as best. Before giving his approval, the party secretary asked the party's District Committee whether it had any objection to my being hired, but he was told that the committee had not heard of me, had no particular instructions about me, and could neither approve nor disapprove my hiring: the secretary should act within his own sphere of responsibility. Thus, the secretary gave his approval, as he said in his written note on my application, because he thought that it was in the institute's interest to hire well-qualified people. I do not think he ever came to regret his decision: after a year or so, he began getting praise from the district party organization for the results we had obtained using my linear programming approach to planning the distribution and transportation of firewood throughout the country. Director Naftali hired me at a starting salary that was about 60 percent of the pay in my last job, and I started working on July 15, 1959.

Eager though I was to continue my mathematical studies, I realized that learning my new job had to take precedence. So the first two months passed without much mathematics, but with plenty of engineering concepts and manuals; basic facts about woodworking, the timber industry, and the utilities needed by an industrial plant; principles of industrial design; and so on. Most of my knowledge came from examining designs that had been approved a year or so earlier and were at the stage of execution.

In Romania, as in the other socialist countries, the design of industrial plants and facilities was carried out in a centralized manner by specialized design institutes, one for each industry. These institutes were enormous: the design division of the institute for forestry and the timber industry—of central importance in a country one-third of whose area was covered by forests—had about a thousand employees, of whom more than six hundred were engineers. The rest were draftsmen, technicians, secretaries, and so forth. The research division, at a different location, was largely separate and had its own personnel—another three hundred or so engineers.

The director of the institute, Naftali, had prewar experience with the timber industry and communist sympathies during the war, which was the reason for his being director. He was not only knowledgeable, but a very decent man and a relatively good, though demanding, boss. His deputy, Necşulescu, was a bright young engineer with less practical experience. Gogu Mohr was chief engineer and played an important role in the decision-making process. The three of them formed the team that led the institute. Every design, when completed, had to be submitted first to the State Planning Commission, which usually went into a detailed analysis of the project, had long lists of questions for us to answer, and often requested changes in the design before submitting it to the Ministry of Forestry and the timber industry. When the design was finally submitted to the ministry, it was studied there; rarely were there any questions at that stage. Then it had to be defended in a plenary meeting at which all the major directorates of the ministry were present. Our institute was represented by one member of the leading triumvirate described above, plus the engineer who headed the design team for the project, accompanied by four or five of the design engineers who had worked on the project, always including the engineer in charge of the economic evaluation.

The institute's workload was many times greater than that of most comparable institutions in the West: In a single year, in addition to enlarging several existing facilities, it was not unusual to design one or two dozen completely new plants, from furniture factories to vast woodworking complexes. The latter, which dealt with the processing of raw timber, included beam-producing facilities, sawmills, plywood and veneer factories, and so on. Each design involved possible locational and technological alternatives, and variants for implementing this or that aspect. My task was to prepare a detailed economic analysis of each design, to evaluate the various alternatives and compare them economically, and to compare the efficiency forecast for the new facility to that of existing ones. I was part of a group of six or seven engineers in charge of the economic evaluation of all the designs. Learning on the fly was not easy, but after about two months I got to the stage where I only needed to ask a couple of questions a day.

■   ■   ■

At that point I resumed my mathematical studies. Originally, I had started out by reviewing calculus, a subject I had once learned and then forgotten. Besides some standard introductory texts in use at the time in Romania, I looked at books dealing with applications of calculus, such as R. G. D. Allen's *Mathematical Economics*. I got hold of the 1951 Cowles Commission monograph, *Activity Analysis of Production and Allocation* and managed to read the paper by Koopmans. When I tried to read the one by Dantzig, though, the going got tough. Then I realized that I needed algebra more than calculus and turned to the Romanian translation of *Linear Algebra* by the Russian mathematician Kurosh. I worked my way through several books on matrices. As to linear programming itself, besides the book by Dorfman, Samuelson, and Solow, my introduction came mainly from the 1953 book by Charnes, Cooper, and Henderson, *An Introduction to Linear Programming*.

A linear program is an optimization problem in which a linear function is to be maximized or minimized subject to linear inequalities. This is the simplest, most straightforward representation of a large variety of practical situations in which some activity is to be optimized while still made to satisfy certain requirements. The discovery of the fact that so many important problems can be formulated in this way, and that these problems can be solved by an efficient algorithm (procedure)—the so-called simplex method, discovered by George Dantzig in 1947—once the algorithm is implemented into a computer program, has opened the way to myriads of everyday applications in all fields of economic and other activity.

While still at the Institute of Economic Research, in early 1959 I had established contact with Grigore Moisil, a famous Romanian algebraist and member of the Academy whose work in the theory of automata had interested him in the development of computers and their applications. There was some research in computers, both hardware and software, going on at the Institute of Nuclear Physics, and Moisil had a commanding influence on that group. Moisil was interested not only in computers, but in all the new applications of mathematics, among them operations research, and he was eager to develop ties to economists and the Institute of Economic Research. At my first meeting with him we had hit it off very well: he had sized me up and had obviously liked me.

Moisil, in his early fifties, at the peak of his career and perhaps the best-known scientist of the country to the general public, was both a very influential and a very active person, well known for his independent mind and often strong-headed opinions. Therefore, I did not rule out the possibility that he might still be willing to talk to me after my political disgrace, and I felt that establishing some kind—*any* kind—of connection with him and his group at the Institute of Mathematics of the Academy would facilitate my work and the transition into my newly chosen field. Also, if I intended to do research with practical applications, I needed access to computers and computer programmers. For all these reasons, I contacted Moisil again soon after my dismissal, told him what had happened, and said that I was studying mathematics and planning to work in the area of mathematical programming. As soon as I was in a position

to do so, I hoped to use this knowledge to research optimization problems in the economy. I asked whether he was still interested in having
anything to do with me. His reaction was that what had happened to me
was certainly bad, but that it did not affect his interest in seeing mathematics applied to economic problems, nor did it change his estimate
that I might be the right person to help bring this about. Once Moisil
held a view, he had the courage to stand up for it; and so, luckily for me,
he was not deterred by my party status. He said he liked my determination and was interested in what I was trying to accomplish. He wished
me good luck with my job search and invited me to come and see him
periodically to discuss what I was doing.

Grigore Moisil was more than a great mathematician; he was a great
man. He affected my life in an important way, in that he made my
transition to mathematics much easier than it might have been without
him. He was an *unusual* individual in the noblest sense of the word.
Early on, mathematics became the passion of his life. His doctoral disser-
tation at the University of Bucharest stirred sufficient interest abroad to
enable him to spend some time in Paris. There he became immersed in
the world of mathematics at its best, and came to know and be known
by Hadamard, Lebesgue, Borel, and other great mathematicians. Later he
spent a year in Rome.

Back in Romania, he became a professor at the University of Iaşi (Yassi)
and later at the University of Bucharest, where the war found him. He
contributed to many areas of mathematics, primarily algebra, set theory,
and logic, but was perhaps best known for his work on the theory of
automata. Throughout the thirties and the war years, when right-wing,
fascist politics held sway among many if not most Romanian intellectuals, he kept aloof from those currents and remained faithful to the ideals
of enlightened humanism that he had absorbed as a young man through
his contacts with French culture. In particular, he was never tainted by
anti-Semitism: throughout his career he had many Jewish friends, students, and collaborators. At the end of the war he joined the Communist
party and served for a while as Romania's ambassador to Turkey. When
he returned, he was elected a member of the Academy, the supreme
honor for a scientist. He worked as a professor at the University of
Bucharest, but his real scientific home was the academy's Institute of
Mathematics.

The Institute of Mathematics, a research establishment of worldwide repute, had as its first director the well-known functional analyst Stoilow. An ethnic Bulgarian, Stoilow had been an outstanding mathematician of a generation older than Moisil's. Because he was world famous and had been a wartime communist, he had sufficient political clout to keep the Institute of Mathematics clear of those troubles that were ruining the other research institutes, such as appointments based on social origin rather than merit, and evaluations based on class criteria and hours of attendance rather than on scientific results. Thus, in the early fifties the Institute of Mathematics became an island of science and research in an ocean of politically troubled waters. After Stoilow died—he suffered a heart attack during a dispute at the party Central Committee, where he was defending the institute's regime—Moisil could have succeeded him as director, but he declined.

Throughout his life Moisil shunned administrative positions of any kind, not because he was immune to the temptations of power, but because he understood how to wield power indirectly. Although he was only head of the Algebra Section, everybody knew that he was the *éminence grise* at the institute. The director, a distinguished geometer named Vrănceanu, did not mind this, and they got along well. Vrănceanu was known as the director, whereas Moisil was "the professor," and it was understood that, although the director signed the papers, the professor made the decisions. Moisil's great merit with respect to the institute was that he kept Stoilow's regime intact: he rejected all the politically desirable and socially "healthy" young cadres whom the party tried to foist upon the institute every year, and held every candidate's feet to the fire of scientific merit. Nothing else counted, be it class background, ethnic origin, or whatever. There was only one notable exception: He would not tolerate informers in his environment, even if they were scientifically meritorious. He felt an organic revulsion against them. To run the institute along these lines was not made easier by the fact that Moisil was not the director; nevertheless, he managed to do it— Vrănceanu always did what he recommended. When there was trouble, it was Moisil who would go to the party to discuss matters, as he was a party member while Vrănceanu was not. Vrănceanu was a world-class geometer, a bundle of raw geometric talent; however, he knew only three things in life and nothing else—geometry, geometry, and more geometry. Outside his field, he was at the level of a moderately schooled peasant. The way Stoilow died may also have helped Moisil indirectly: nobody in the politburo wanted to see another leading scientist struck down by a heart attack at the Central Committee.

Moisil was a short, stocky, bald, jovial man, with a great sense of humor, straightforward and informal in the extreme. He did most of his research at home, in his relatively modest three-room apartment on Strada Armenească in the center of Bucharest, where he lived with his wife, Viorica. They had no children. The apartment was always filled with Moisil's papers, folders, notes, and books; they spread from his desk all over the living room table, the sofa, and the floor. According to his wife, this mess was drastically reduced every once in a while, when Grigri—the name by which she and his parents called him—would put his papers in order, but I never had the occasion to visit him at those times. You could usually find him at home; he left home only to attend to business at the institute (never for more than a couple of hours), exchange some books at the library, or sometimes to take a walk. People who wanted to see him had to visit him there, after a telephone call. You were free to call him at any time between ten in the morning and ten in the evening, and if you asked to see him, he would say, "Come now," or "I have somebody here, come in forty-five minutes." Often he would receive you in a dressing gown or even, on warm summer days, pajamas. He would be invariably friendly and direct, with a matter-of-fact style, and he expected his visitors to be concise and to the point. Despite being a scientist preoccupied by his research problems, Moisil was never a loner. He enjoyed the company of his friends, collaborators, and students. He was the center of a large circle of "fans of Moisil," whose average age was below thirty and who would sometimes all be invited for a party. He enjoyed good food and liked good wines a little too much.

Moisil had great respect for talent of any kind and detested fools. He did not hide his displeasure at displays of foolishness. The great love of his life, the subject he most enjoyed talking about, was mathematics. In Romanian the word is used in the singular, but Moisil would often use it in the plural when he wanted to stress the multiplicity of its aspects. He liked to emphasize that in the twentieth century mathematics, once a science of quantitative relations, had become the science of structure, of all kinds of relations between things, not just quantitative. His favorite activity was, as he used to say, "to do mathematics." A journalist once asked him how he could so easily agree to give an impromptu talk on a mathematical subject before a television audience: didn't he need time to prepare, to think about the subject? Moisil replied, "Sure. But you forget that I have been thinking about this for twenty-five years." He would often say, "Mathematics is not necessarily done at your desk. Mathematics is done when you wake up in the morning and do not immediately get out of bed; it's done in the bathtub; it's done while sitting on the toilet; it's done while you are dressing; and it is done when you are taking a walk."

Although he was keen to see mathematics applied to more and more new fields—in a way, he was an enthusiast for the mathematization of everything—Moisil strongly opposed demands for making mathematics more "relevant," meaning more applied. "I know that mathematics is useful," he once wrote, "but I do mathematics because I like it. This is the great luck of mathematicians: They can be useful to society while pursuing what pleases them most." He argued that pressuring mathematicians to do "useful" mathematics would lead to a weakening of the discipline, ultimately diminishing its usefulness. In his view, the usefulness of mathematics *has to be* indirect; otherwise, its results become less general and therefore less widely applicable.

Moisil had strong views on many things in life and did not hide them. He also had a rather striking way of expressing them. In one of his early course introductions, in urging his students to go beyond learning mathematics and to try to take in human culture as a whole, he said, "Don't leave your soul with a single window!" He loved paradoxes of all kinds. Talking about a presentation by the great Polish logician Sierpinski, he said, "He brought ideas that were not hard to understand, but were very hard to accept." This is how he explained Bertrand Russell's aphorism that "mathematics is the science in which you don't know what you are talking about." There is this mathematical theorem, says Moisil, with applications to electrical engineering, astronomy, and medicine. The electrical engineer encounters it in a form specific to his field and uses it in that form; the astronomer works with a rather different form of it, in which certain parameters disappear whereas others acquire an increased significance; finally, the doctor needs a third incarnation of the theorem, which at first sight bears only a vague resemblance to the other two. But all three are forms of the same theorem. The strength of the mathematical result comes from its generality, which comes from its being abstract.

The mathematician who proves it knows nothing about its application to this or that field. He does not know or care that he is in fact talking about electrical engineering or astronomy or medicine. In short, the strength of his method lies precisely in the fact that he does not know what he is talking about. This is the meaning of Bertrand Russell's aphorism, says Moisil.

During the summer or early fall of 1959 Moisil told me that he had an exceptionally bright young researcher at the Institute of Mathematics, a former student of his, who was also interested in working in the area of operations research. He suggested that I team up with his young collaborator and try to do joint research, but he had one condition: the research had to be on something practical and applicable. This needs some explanation after what I have said about Moisil's views on mathematics and its applications. Mathematical economics—the application of mathematics to economic theory, as in marginal analysis and various equilibrium models—was an ideologically suspect field, vigorously attacked by marxist ideologues as "bourgeois apologetics." However, operations research— the application of mathematics to formulating and solving various problems of the real economy, as opposed to economic theory—was accepted as useful and had no stigma attached to it. What Moisil meant was that we should concentrate on operations research as opposed to mathematical economics, and, even within that delimitation, start with something practical that would demonstrate the usefulness of what we were doing, thereby earning ourselves some "goodwill." It was a perfectly reasonable requirement and I accepted it without hesitation. I then met the young researcher, Ladislau (Laci) Peter Hammer, and we began a collaboration that lasted for three fruitful years, until the end of 1962.

Laci Hammer was twenty-three years old when I met him. He had graduated from the faculty of mathematics of the University of Bucharest less than a year before and was working as a researcher in Moisil's section at the Institute of Mathematics. He was exceptionally bright and mature far beyond his years. I soon befriended him and, despite the fourteen-year difference in our ages, I was able to relate to him and discuss issues of daily life and politics with him as I would with my older friends. Laci came from a family of Hungarian Jews in Timişoara. Early in his childhood he had contracted polio, and that terrible disease had left him with partial paralysis of his legs. He could walk only with crutches and with great difficulty. As if to compensate for this weakness, nature had endowed him with unlimited resources of energy: rarely if ever in my life have I encountered a person with such stamina. He lived alone in a studio in a downtown apartment building. We started our work by meeting every few days, usually—because of the difficulty Laci had in moving around—at his apartment.

We decided to begin by solving a practical problem that I found at the ministry to which my institute belonged: an optimal transportation plan for a category of lumber that had to be shipped regularly throughout the year in fairly large quantities from thirty-six production sites to seven different consumption centers. We had to determine which production sites should supply which consumption centers so that the total cost of transportation would be as small as possible. We collected data from the ministry and read up on the theory. We studied several existing meth- ods, then selected a combination of two of them to be implemented. At first we did not have access either to a computer or, more important, to a programmer who could implement the procedure we selected, so we put together a team of students to carry out by hand and by calculator the computations needed for every iteration of the procedure. Each suc- cessive tableau was calculated by two independent teams; the results were compared and the discrepancies eliminated by repeating the calcu- lations where needed. Once a tableau was correct, we chose the change to be made for the next iteration by a well-known analytic criterion, and the calculations of the team resumed for the next iteration. It was a very time-consuming operation, and today, when computers do calculations a million times more complex in a fraction of a second, it seems ridicu- lous. But we had no other means at our disposal (we were to acquire them soon) and solving this particular problem was meant to demon- strate something important: the solution that we obtained for the month of December 1959 was about 8 percent cheaper than the plan actually being used. We presented our results in January 1960 at a conference and managed to get our paper published in the July 1960 issue of *Revista de Statisitică* (*Review of Statistics*).

The news about the 8 percent cost reduction that Laci and I were able to obtain in our lumber shipment plan made the rounds of my institute and ministry. These were not yet actual savings, because the plan was developed post factum and thus could not be used; the quantities changed from month to month, and our plan was meant for comparison with the actual plan used in a specific month. Nevertheless, the results clearly indicated the method's potential. Furthermore, the differences between our optimal transportation plan and the one that had been developed by the economists at the ministry suggested improvements that could be applied without actually solving the problem optimally for a new data set. The ministry took advantage of this information, obtained a degree of permanent improvement, and gave us the credit for it. Moisil was very pleased and saw to it that we had access to the one (Romanian-built) computer available at the time, which was at the Institute of Nuclear Physics. We also got in touch with a computer programmer who would help us implement some of the algorithms we needed.

As a result of the publicity received by our efficient transportation plan, we soon became involved with a second application, of a more complex but also economically more interesting nature. In the summer of 1960 we were approached by the State Planning Commission. Some of its members had read about linear programming and were interested in exploring what could be done in the way of optimizing the development plan of an industry over a period of several years. To avoid problems with confidential data and state secrets, they chose the textile industry, which was considered relatively innocuous and unimportant. We agreed to study the problem, and formulated it as a parametric linear program which we then solved for various parameter values. In the matter of calculation, we made one small advance over our first project: we were able to use a computer for the most time-consuming step of the computation, which had to be frequently repeated. The remaining calculations were done by hand and by calculator, as before. The solutions we found for various parameter values yielded some insights that the planners found interesting, especially in terms of the relative merits of installing new equipment as opposed to upgrading existing equipment. We presented our results at the Conference on Theoretical and Practical Issues of Industrial Automation, held in October 1960, and published them in the proceedings of the conference.

Along with the practical applications that we were working on, we also started doing research into solution methods for new variants and generalizations of the transportation problem. Between the spring of 1960 and the winter of 1961-62, we wrote a sequence of five papers, developing new solution methods for various problems in this area. They were published in *Studii si Cercetari Matematice*, the mainstream Romanian mathematics journal, between mid–1960 and early 1962, as well as in the

Revue de Mathématiques Pures et Appliquées of the Romanian academy, where they appeared in English. Finally, we collected our results into a longer English-language study in two parts, which appeared in 1962 in *Cahiers du Centre de Recherche Opérationnelle*, a journal published in Brussels, under the title "On the Transportation Problem, Part I–Part II." Our most important result was an efficient method for solving parametric transportation problems, a special case of parametric linear programs. The publication of our paper in a Western journal "put us on the map," as they say. We started getting reactions, both through the mail and in the pages of the Belgian journal, from American researchers.

It did not go unnoticed that within two years of my expulsion from the party, my firing from the Institute of Economic Research, and my banishment from the pages of economic journals, I was back on the scientific scene as a mathematical programmer, with articles in mathematical and statistical journals and mentions of my practical results in the press. I heard that a party hack, who was certainly no friend of mine, had expressed a kind of grudging respect for me: "You kick him in the stomach, push him under the water, and think that you are done with him for good. But you turn around and there he is again, riding high as if nothing had happened." Dr. Farchi, with whom I had had the fatal conversation about Korea in early 1952, and who became our family doctor after 1955, remarked to a mutual friend that Balaş "survives even in chlorine." I admit that I enjoyed that reputation.

Laci Hammer and I wrote our last joint paper in 1962, under the title "On the Generalized Transportation Problem," and submitted it to an American journal, *Management Science.* The model treated in this paper was considerably more general than the transportation problem and its variations that we had worked on earlier. It later became known as minimum-cost flows in networks with gains, and entered the literature under that name.

An interesting episode related to this paper throws some light on the difficulties one used to encounter when trying to publish in the West from behind the Iron Curtain. We received two referees' reports. The first said that the paper contained a new characterization of basic solutions resulting in an efficient algorithm, but that some of our results overlapped with those of Dantzig, whose book on linear programming was in the process of publication at the time. The referee attached to his report the galley proofs of one of Dantzig's book chapters, and recommended accepting our paper for publication, leaving it to us to work out the connections with Dantzig's research and show how we differed. We were rather pleased with this aspect of the refereeing process. After all, Dantzig was the founder—often called the father—of linear programming, and the fact that some of our results overlapped with his was nothing to be ashamed of. In our revision of the paper we readily acknowledged the help of the referee who had sent us the galley proofs. We pointed out the connection of our work to that of Dantzig and the partial overlap of our results with his, as well as the significance of those remaining results that were not covered by Dantzig.

The second report, however, was a different story. Here the referee claimed that a computer program written by two individuals, which had neither been published nor made available to us, was based on a method that relied on results (also unpublished) essentially similar to ours. On the basis of this assertion, he expected us to recognize the priority of these two individuals in solving the problem. We diplomatically rejected this demand by inserting a footnote in which we related what the referee had told us and added, "That unpublished paper is not available to us, but we seize this opportunity to give due credit to the above-mentioned authors for all the results contained in that paper, which of course are prior to ours." Our paper was accepted and the footnote appeared exactly as we wrote it. Years later, when I came to the West, some colleagues told me they had a hilarious time reading it.

After 1962, although Laci and I pursued our separate interests, our research and career trajectories evolved along somewhat similar lines and later crossed each other many times. Laci embarked upon a major project with a fellow researcher at the Institute of Mathematics, Sergiu Rudeanu. Together they wrote a book on Boolean methods in operations research, which was published in 1968.

Toward the end of 1960 or the beginning of 1961 Laci married Anca Ivănescu, a very bright, lovely Romanian girl whom he had been tutoring in mathematics. He took her family name, as permitted by Romanian law. The reason? Although officially there was no anti-semitism in Romania and Jews enjoyed full equality before the law, the campaign to "improve" the ethnic composition of educational and cultural institutions was primarily directed against Jews. Thus, as far as a young professional's career prospects were concerned, Ivănescu, a typical Romanian name, was preferable to Hammer, a name that only Jews and

Germans had. As a result of this change, all our joint papers published during or after 1961 appeared under the authorship of E. Balaş and P. L. Ivănescu. Seven or eight years later, when Laci and Anca defected, going first to Israel, then to Canada, he changed his family name back to Hammer. In the late sixties, a colleague at Carnegie Mellon University asked me what had happened to my former collaborator, Ivănescu. I told him that Ivănescu was the same as Peter L. Hammer, and explained the double name change. My colleague's reaction was, "What a pity!" "Why?" I asked. "Well, Ivănescu was so exotic, so romantic. Hammer? There are thousands of them." There may have been thousands, but few were like this one, as it soon became clear to everybody.

While still working with Laci Hammer, I had also engaged in some research on my own. An early topic had to do with my old hobby, Leontieff's input-output tables, and the result was a piece titled "On the Uses of Input-Output Analysis," published in *Revista de Statistică* in December 1960. It dealt with the mechanics of recalculating the so-called Leontieff inverse—a basic planning tool—in case of price changes, and with related problems. A second paper, about a year later, dealt with dominance relations in linear programming and was published in the same journal in early 1962.

A major, longer-term project that I embarked upon in 1961 was inspired by my job environment. It was a mathematical model of the entire woodworking industry to be used as a tool for analyzing questions related to the optimal use of timber resources. With forests covering almost one-third of Romania's area timber and timber products represented about 15 percent of all Romanian exports. Most types of timber have alternative uses. For example, a certain kind of wood is traditionally used for lumber, which in turn is used in construction, cabinetmaking, and so on. However, this same kind of wood can also be used to produce plywood and veneer, products of much higher value but more expensive to make. How much of the material in question should be used one way, and how much the other? Issues of this type abound, and they are all tied together. Thus, it seemed that valuable insights might be gained from a mathematical model that would tie together all these questions and many others, and examine them in their mutual interdependence.

The proposed study was approved in the fall of 1961 and from that time on, I worked on it full time, interviewing scores of forestry and timber experts. The insights that I gained from these interviews led to a large linear programming model incorporating all the major decision problems concerning the possible alternative uses of wood resources. Completed in July 1962, the study resulted in a two hundred–page mimeographed report which was made available to the various directorates of the ministry, as well as to the State Planning Commission. It was discussed, based on a presentation I was asked to make, and approved by the ministry's Technico-Scientific Council. Although the study was never published in its entirety (it was treated as a confidential internal document), I was able to publish an article on it in the May 1963 issue of *Revista de Statistică*. When I received several requests from other socialist countries for copies of the full-scale study, I told the inquirers to ask my ministry through official channels. At least one person followed through with the process; about two years later I saw details of my unpublished study quoted in a Czech economic journal.

After completing this nine-month study, I was appointed head of a new mathematical programming group, whose task was to work on applications of mathematical techniques to the timber industry. In the spring of 1962 I started a project with Corban, a researcher at the academy's Center of Mathematical Statistics, for regularly developing optimal quarterly transportation plans for the entire supply of firewood produced in the country. For this purpose, we obtained access to the (Romanian-built) computer CIFA II belonging to the Institute of Nuclear Physics, and used it every three months to obtain the optimal plan for the updated supply and demand data of that period. In 1964 Corban and I published an article summarizing our experience: we reported annual savings of 14 million ton-kilometers as calculated by the users of our results at the ministry.

Some time in 1962 or 1963 I had a disturbing conversation with Grigore Moisil. I was discussing my career plans with him, and he expressed strong reservations about my intention to become a mathematician. In his view, it was all right, even necessary, for an economist who wanted to keep in touch with modern developments to study mathematics and learn to use it in his work. It was also all right, even highly desirable, for an economist to team up with a mathematician to solve problems in operations research. But Moisil believed there had to be a clear demarcation of tasks and responsibilities. It was the economist's job to recognize a situation that had an underlying mathematical structure, to formulate the problem mathematically ("put it in equation," as Moisil would say), and, after a method of solution had been devised and the problem solved, to interpret the results, verify them in practice, and see to their application. However, the intermediate links in the chain—identifying the best available solution method, implementing it on a computer, and solving the problem in as many versions as needed—were the task of the mathematician: a routine task if a reasonably good method could be found in the literature, a difficult task requiring creative research if no satisfactory method existed and one had to be invented. It was a mistake, according to Moisil, for a mathematician interested in these kinds of problems to try to become an economist, or for an economist interested in this area to try to become a mathematician. As no single person could possibly master two such huge fields as mathematics and economics, problems involving both had to be solved by teamwork.

It was hard to take issue with this well thought-out and largely reasonable view, although, like all generalizations of this type, it was a little simplistic. All I said was that for reasons known to the professor, and for other, personal reasons, I was no longer interested in pursuing a career as an economist. As late in life as it may be, I said, I wanted to change my profession and become a mathematician. To which he replied, "Look, you have proven to me beyond any reasonable doubt that you have considerable mathematical talent, and you have learned an enormous amount in these two years. But you are forty, and you can't be so foolish as to base your career on what you have learned in the last two years!"

This sentence—"You can't be so foolish as to" do exactly the thing I wanted to do—stuck in my mind (and heart?) forever. It haunted me as I pursued precisely the foolish path that Moisil had warned me against. The reason his words had such a strong impact on me was the respect I had for Moisil and his wisdom. Was I indeed committing a foolish, fatal error? This conversation gave me more psychological trouble than all the abuse I had received from the minions of the apparatus. I tried to allay my renewed doubts with the adage, "You don't really have a choice, my fellow."

A major accomplishment of my new research career occurred in the fall of 1963. I had started reading about the new field of integer programming, where the first results had been obtained only in the previous five years. The problem is one in which a linear function is to be optimized subject to linear constraints, as in linear programming, but with the additional condition that some of the variables can only take integer values. At first this sort of problem seemed contrived to me. For instance, if some of the variables in a problem were such that fractional values would make no sense—say, the number of people assigned to a task—it seemed to me that one could always solve the problem as a linear program, then round off the numbers obtained in whatever way seemed reasonable: The result should be a satisfactory approximation. But then I found out that the most important kinds of integer programs are those in which the variables, or some of them, are either 0 or 1. These problems arise when modeling situations in which either-or choices play a role: You either embark upon some activity *or* you do not; you either place a facility in some location *or* you do not; you either join two points by a cable, a pipe, or a road, *or* you do not. Furthermore, many other seemingly different situations—such as, "if you do this, you must also do that," or "this action, if undertaken, must precede (or follow) that action in time"—are also reducible to binary choices. Logical conditions like these, as well as many others, can be introduced into an otherwise linear program by means of binary, or 0–1, variables; however, if such a problem is solved as a linear program, there is usually no easy way of obtaining a reasonable solution by rounding the fractional numbers to 0 or 1: hence the importance of solving integer programs, in particular 0–1 programs. This particular class serves as a mathematical model for problems in fields as diverse as capital budgeting, project selection, pipeline or communication network design, structural design, switching network design, fault detection, clustering, facility location, truck dispatching, tanker routing, crew scheduling, machine sequencing, and in a host of other problems involving logical alternatives.

I learned about the importance of integer programming partly from the literature and partly through my own experience in trying to apply linear programming to forestry problems. One of the topics included in the 1963 annual plan for my newly instituted mathematical programming group was the application of mathematical methods to forest management. Here we were interested in an optimal harvesting plan for a specified area covered with forests over a certain time period. We knew the age composition of the various forest plots, the quality of their timber, the cost of harvesting the timber from each plot, and the price at which that timber could be sold. We could set up this problem nicely as a linear program. Most of the harvesting costs, as well as the sales value of the harvested products, were proportional to the amounts harvested;

that is, the problem was linear in the variables representing these amounts. But one crucial element, the cost of building roads through the forests in order to haul away the harvested timber, was not proportional to the quantities harvested. No matter how much timber was harvested from a plot, whether all of it or only a quarter, a road had to be built to reach it; it was only if nothing was cut from a plot that we could forego building a road. Thus, we needed 0–1, yes-or-no variables to represent either building or not building each separate road segment. Furthermore, the decisions concerning individual road segments were connected to each other by logical constraints: we could not build a given segment without also building at least one other segment to connect it to the road network, and so on. The problem was therefore a so-called mixed integer program (mixed in the sense that not all variables had to be integers), more specifically a mixed 0–1 program.

Integer programs, pure or mixed, are much more difficult to solve than linear programs. The main reason for this is that the solutions to the constraints of a linear program form a convex set, which simply means that if you take any two solutions, then their weighted average is also a solution. Integer programs do not have this property; their solution set is nonconvex. The pioneering work of Ralph Gomory, published between 1958 and 1963, consisted of an attempt to convexify this nonconvex solution set by finding its "convex hull," that is, the smallest convex set containing it. As the finding of the convex hull turned out to be an elusive, often an almost impossible task, Gomory had proposed a method for approximating it gradually through so-called cutting planes. In spite of its mathematical elegance, his method had not caught on, because attempts made at the time to implement and test it had resulted in poor computational performance. Only very small problems, and only some of those, could be solved in a reasonable length of time. Another approach, proposed in 1960 by Land and Doig, solved the linear program obtained by removing the integrality conditions, then replaced the original problem by several new problems in which some variables were forced to integer values, and applied the same procedure recursively to each of the new problems. This approach was subsequently modified and amended by other researchers, and it became known as "branch and bound." At the time when I was working on the forest management problem, there had been no computational experience with the algorithm of Land and Doig.

None of these procedures was available to me at the time in the form of a computer program. Besides, both of them were meant for solving integer programming problems in general, not 0–1 programs in particular, and I felt that the binary property of the variables had to be exploited. So I tried to invent my own method. The approach that I developed for solving 0–1 programming problems did not require one to solve the associated linear program; instead, it was based on systematically assigning the value 0 or 1 to certain subsets of variables and exploring the implications of these assignments through a sequence of logical tests. This exploration involved only additions and comparisons; therefore I called the algorithm additive. A little later, when it became known to more experienced researchers in the West, it came to be called "implicit enumeration"—a better name that reflects the essence of the procedure, which is to find the best among all 0–1 solutions by enumerating and examining only a small subset. The algorithm would discard (that is, exclude from consideration) large numbers of 0–1 value assignments that could be proved to lead to no better solution than the best one currently at hand. This was done by a sequence of logical tests. The proof of validity for the algorithm consisted in showing that the logical tests were correct and exhaustive, in the sense of covering all possible cases. One of the advantages of the procedure was that it lent itself easily to computer implementation.

My algorithm seemed more efficient than anything available at the time in the literature. Apart from a variety of small problems, meaning about a dozen variables, we succeeded in solving and obtaining meaningful answers to a forest management problem at my institute, involving alternative road networks, that I formulated as a 0–1 programming problem with forty variables and twenty-two constraints. I did not know it at the time, but later I discovered that this method was particularly well suited for solving problems that were either very loosely or very tightly constrained.

I was extremely excited by my discovery, which I presented at the Third Scientific Conference on Statistics held between November 29 and December 1, 1963, in Bucharest. I wanted to have my result published in the Western literature as soon as possible. The fastest way to do this was to have it published as a short communication in the Bulletin of the French Academy of Sciences, the *Comptes Rendus de l'Académie des Sciences, Paris*, where the time between submission and publication was usually about two or three months.* But the communication had to be submitted by a member of the academy in Paris. I knew that Moisil was in contact with Robert Fortet, a French mathematician who, though not himself a member of the academy, had in the past arranged for the publication of communications by Moisil or his collaborators by asking Jean Leray, an algebraist and a member of the academy, to present them. Fortet himself had published a paper in 1960 that had some connection with my topic, in that it gave a procedure for linearizing nonlinear functions of 0–1 variables; so he might even have taken some interest in my results; I was actually planning to use Fortet's procedure for extending my method to nonlinear programs with 0–1 variables, and said so in my paper.

I went to see Moisil, explained to him the significance of what I had found, gave him a concise presentation of the algorithm in French on four typed pages, and asked whether he would be willing to send it to Fortet for an opinion and possible submission through Leray to the *Comptes Rendus*. Moisil seemed very interested. He said that he needed a few days to consider the matter and wanted the long version of my paper, containing all the proofs of the theorems and propositions in my French note. (As was the habit at the *Comptes Rendus*, the paper itself did not contain proofs: The academician who presented it served as guarantor for the correctness of the claimed results.) I gave Moisil the long version, which was in English, and less than two weeks later he let me know that he was sending my note and the long English version for Fortet's perusal. In his letter to Fortet, he wrote that the attached paper was the work of one of his collaborators and asked Fortet, in case he felt the result deserved it, to arrange for my communication to be submitted to the *Comptes Rendus*. This must have happened in December 1963 or January 1964. My communication, "Un algorithme additif pour la resolution des programmes linéaires en variables bivalentes," was presented by Jean Leray at the session of March 9, 1964, and appeared in the April

---

*Although most scientific journals rely on the opinions of outside experts (referees) in their judgment of papers submitted for publication, the *Competes Rendus* considers only papers recommended ("communicated") by a member of the *Académie des Sciences,* and the recommendation of the member serves as the basis of judgment. This on the one hand restricts access to the journal; on the other it reduces the time span between submission and publication.

13, 1964, issue of the *Comptes Rendus*, volume 258. I was as happy as a lark. A few weeks later, also at Moisil's request, Fortet arranged, again through Jean Leray, for the same journal to publish another communication of mine on an extension of the additive algorithm to the nonlinear case, using the above mentioned result of Fortet. From then on, with Moisil's permission, I addressed my communications directly to Fortet, asking him to arrange for their presentation, and he did so every time, always through Leray.

My next step was to submit the full version in English to the leading journal of my new profession, *Operations Research*, published in the United States. I did this in February 1964, when I also submitted the paper to the International Symposium on Mathematical Programming to be held in London in July 1964. I had no chance of being allowed to attend that symposium; but a month before its scheduled date, I sent the organizing committee fifty mimeographed copies of the paper for distribution in the session where it was supposed to be presented. As I learned later, the paper was indeed distributed. Several months after I sent my article to *Operations Research*, I received a letter from the associate editor, William W. Cooper, along with two mostly favorable referees' reports. After a minor revision, the paper was accepted and appeared as "An Additive Algorithm for Solving Linear Programs with Zero-One Variables" in the July–August 1965 issue of *Operations Research*.

In the years ahead, this article became a so-called citation classic. According to the Institute for Scientific Information, the publisher of *Current Contents*, this was the most frequently cited article of *Operations Research* between 1954 (when the journal had first appeared) and 1982 (the year of this finding). According to the July 20, 1982, issue of *Current Contents,* "the *Science Citation Index* and the *Social Sciences Citation Index* indicate that this paper has been cited in over 220 publications since 1965." When I got this information, I would have liked to show it to Moisil, who certainly would have enjoyed reading it. But Moisil was no longer around. He died in 1973 at the age of sixty-seven in Montreal. Two days after his death he and his wife were scheduled to fly to Pittsburgh to visit us and deliver a lecture at Carnegie Mellon University. Edith had invited friends to our house to have a party in the Moisils' honor. Instead of their visit, we got a sad phone call from Viorica Moisil, who was in the process of arranging to take home her husband's remains.

This is a brief outline of how I made the transition from marxist economics to mathematical programming and operations research. This was just the beginning: I continued to learn mathematics for many years to come, both before and after 1968, when I obtained a doctoral degree in that field from the University of Paris, with Robert Fortet as my thesis advisor. The process of learning has never stopped. I sharpened my tools, made exciting discoveries, and in the process published about 180 papers over the years. I also enjoyed seeing some of my methods implemented into software packages and applied to solving everyday decision problems in production, distribution, and finance. As a recognition of my mathematical accomplishments, in 1995 I was honored with my profession's most important award, the John von Neumann Theory Prize of INFORMS (the Institute for Operations Research and the Management Sciences).

CHAPTER 15

■ ■ ■

Would-Be Emigrant

While I was experiencing this major transition in my professional life, there were changes in my private life as well. Some time after the Hungarian revolution, alongside the policy of "improving" the ethnic composition at various institutions, there was a loosening of restrictions on Jewish emigration from Romania. In the late forties, right after the formation of the independent state of Israel (which the Soviet Union had at first embraced as a blow against British imperialism), Romanian Jews were permitted to emigrate to Israel, and more than fifty thousand Jews went. This, however, came to an end in 1951, when the policy changed and emigration was stopped. Around 1958, the policy was reversed once again, and emigration to Israel became possible under certain conditions, which were never explicitly stated.

It was simply made known by word of mouth that it was possible to apply for emigration to Israel. The processing of applications was arbitrary and haphazard. When applying for emigration, you sometimes had to give a reason, such as having a relative in Israel; at other times, no reason was required. Approval could take two months, six months, a year, or forever. Cases of official refusal were rare; typically, a rejected applicant was simply allowed to languish for years without receiving an answer. In other words, applying for emigration meant living in uncertainty for an unspecified length of time. This uncertainty was not only psychological: once it became known that you had applied for emigration, you were regarded as an alien at best or a traitor at worst, depending on your job, your place of employment, and your political situation.

397

The closer you had been to the Communist Party before applying for emigration, the more of a traitor you were considered afterwards.

On the other hand, an application to emigrate did not invariably become public: the passport office where one had to apply—a branch of the Ministry of the Interior that was closely connected to the Securitate— would sometimes, but not always, notify an applicant's employer, and whether or not this would happen was anybody's guess. There were no firm rules, but typically applicants who were employed by politically significant organizations (government ministries, universities, institutes of the academy, and the media) or who held high-ranking positions in less significant institutions could expect their employers to be notified. When this happened, the applicant was either fired or demoted, and if he was a party member he would be expelled. Firings and demotions were left up to the head of the institution, but in one way or another he was supposed to retaliate against the sinner. Applicants whose requests were not granted could be left waiting for years without an answer, regardless of whether their employers had been notified or not. In the sixties I came to know a good many people who had applied for emigration in 1948 and had parents or other close relatives in Israel, yet had still not received answers to their applications. Although the reasons for refusal were not stated, it was believed that younger people with technical training had poorer chances of being allowed to emigrate than older people without technical education. Those lucky applicants whose requests were approved had to renounce their Romanian citizenship before leaving the country. Then they would get, not a passport, but an emigration document.

Some time in 1960 I decided that I wanted to emigrate, to go to what had by now become for me, as for everybody not blinded by ideology, the free world. America was my chosen destination, but the main thing was to get out of Romania and anywhere into the free world. When I raised the question with Edith, she was surprised at first: she knew that my outlook had changed, but had not yet realized how far removed I had become from my earlier self-image as a communist. I told her that I had not wanted to complicate her life with my doubts as long as they had been only doubts, but now that my views had become more crystallized I needed to discuss them with her. It did not take much effort to get Edith to agree. We decided to keep our decision to ourselves and not tell the children for the time being; there was no point in disrupting their lives, friendships, and loyalties when we knew we might have to wait for years, and might not be allowed to leave at all. We also decided not to apply for emigration directly. Because I had been involved in the underground movement, served as a diplomat in London, and held a directorship at the Foreign Ministry, it was most unlikely that my application would be granted. There were no precedents for this. Instead, we decided to try other means. The first of these was ransom—but this requires some explanation.

Although thousands of people were involved in the emigration process at any given time, and tens of thousands of others were following what was happening with keen interest, no information about any aspect of it was publicly available. One had to rely for every bit of information on personal connections, friends, and friends of friends; accordingly, one had to cultivate connections with informed circles. I started doing this in early 1960, and soon had regular encounters with several people who were actively trying to emigrate and were very well informed on all aspects of the problem.

At some time in 1958 or 1959, my uncle and friend Tibor Rényi, who had been living miserably in Bucharest with his family, had applied for emigration. He had lost his job some time earlier because he was a former capitalist. It did not matter that he had become a communist during the war, participated in the underground movement, and raised funds for the communist inmates at the Vapniarca concentration camp. His and his family's application was approved in 1959 and they left Romania, settling in Brazil. There they were just barely able to eke out a modest living, and he soon became ill with emphysema, which put serious limits on what he could do. His wife, Bözsi (a Hungarian nickname for Elisabeth), gave language lessons; she spoke flawless French and reasonably good English. Their children were in their mid- to late teens. We kept in touch through regular correspondence and communicated through code words about matters we did not want the censor to understand.

Around 1960 it became known that there was a channel through which Romanian Jews could be ransomed. An elderly businessman in London named Jakober, a Hungarian Jew from Transylvania who was ostensibly involved in export-import operations between his country and Romania, was undertaking to obtain emigration permits for Jews in exchange for money. The price was about $10,000 for a family. Jakober insisted that he was not making a profit, that this was a purely humanitarian effort on his part, and that all the money went to his Romanian negotiating partner. I never heard any evidence cited either for or against this claim. When I first heard about these deals from a reliable source, I assumed that this was a rogue operation run by somebody at the Securitate. However, I soon realized that it could not have been done without the knowledge and approval of the party leadership. For one thing, the Securitate's operatives were the highest paid employees in Romania: the salary of the lowest-ranking Securitate officer was at one time equal to that of a deputy minister in the government. For another, any Securitate officer who took bribes faced a life sentence, if not death. Since the communists had come to power, I had not heard of a single case in which somebody managed to bribe a Securitate officer, let alone a decision maker in a high position. Moreover, as no single person could decide to issue an emigration permit for a Jewish family, the ransom money would have had to be spread among a number of people, making it even more unlikely that it could be kept secret. I had my sources of information, but the Securitate had better ones. Whatever I had heard, they must have heard, too. And they certainly knew who was dealing with Jakober on his frequent trips to Bucharest. So I concluded that whoever was acting as Jakober's business partner on the Romanian side was in fact acting on behalf of the Securitate and with the full knowledge and approval of that august body, the politburo of the Communist Party.

I decided to explore this channel and let Rényi know that I was trying to raise the money to allow my family to emigrate. Although Rényi was fond of me and willing to do whatever he could to get us out of Romania, he simply did not have $10,000, nor could he, as a new immigrant to Brazil, take out a loan for such an amount. He started contacting mutual friends, people who had emigrated somewhat earlier, in the hope of raising some money, but his attempts were not successful. I did several things: I sent messages to a couple of old friends, longtime emigrants who were living in the West, asking them to get in touch with Rényi and help him in his fund-raising efforts. I also sought connections to people in Romania who had well-to-do relatives in the West who were willing to help them. I would pay such people a certain amount in Romanian currency, and the relative in the West would send Rényi the equivalent amount in dollars. All told, by one means or another, I managed to get

$7,000 to Rényi, enough to allow him to open the negotiations with Jakober and get him started on our case. This involved depositing several thousand dollars into an account.

Jakober visited Bucharest every three or four months with a list of people to be ransomed. He would submit the list on one visit and get his Romanian partner's answer on the next. Sometimes he would phone people on his list before coming to Bucharest and let them know when he would arrive. Although he never called me, I was able on several occasions to find out when he was in Bucharest and where he was staying. I would then call him at his hotel and ask him to confirm whether he had me on his list. I knew that these conversations were being taped by the Securitate, but I was willing to risk yet another negative entry in my file. The first time I reached him he said no, and he did not seem to remember my name; the second time he confirmed that he had me on his list and said that he was waiting for an answer; the third time he said he was still waiting. But the fourth time, as soon as he heard my name, he said, "Yes, of course, I know about you. Well, what is the problem with you, my son?" To which I replied that I just wanted to leave with my family and knew of no other problem. "Well, there must be *some* problem with you, because your name was rejected. I cannot do anything on your behalf." Upon his return to London he released the deposit to Rényi, saying he could do nothing for me. That was the end of Rényi's attempt to ransom us. In the meantime, he had done several other things on our behalf: in November 1961 Brazilian entry visas for our family were sent to the Brazilian embassy in Vienna, and about the same time we received a letter from France-Voyage, a travel agency in Paris, informing us that it was holding tickets in our names for a ship leaving Genoa for Santos. This was nice to know, but of no practical use in our situation.

As soon as it became clear that the ransom attempt had failed, I decided that the time had come to act openly. Although our chances of being allowed to emigrate on the basis of a straightforward application were slim indeed after the ransom offer had been rejected, I knew enough about the moody, fluctuating nature of the party's emigration policies not to give up hope. Besides, I had reached the point where I was willing to take great risks for even the smallest chance of success. So in the spring of 1962 Edith and I lined up at five in the morning in front of the

passport office in Strada Grădina cu Cai (I remember that ironically picturesque name of the street housing this somber office, the object of so
many people's anguish: It was "the Garden with Horses," and its origin
is a mystery to me to this day.) Fortunately, there was nobody among the
two hundred or three hundred people there who knew either of us, so
our filling out and handing in the application went unnoticed. Our
employers were not notified of our application, and for the time being
we suffered no consequences.

We thus joined the ranks of those people, usually a few thousand at
any given time, who had applied for emigration and were waiting for
approval. The waiting time among my acquaintances varied from six
months to fourteen years. The process was entirely unpredictable. Various jokes circulated about it. One of them went like this: "I've finally
found out how the applications to be decided upon on any given day are
selected." "How?" "It depends on the height of the officer on duty: if he's
tall, he picks folders from the upper shelves; if he's short, he picks them
from the lower shelves."

We still refrained from involving our children in our decision: it would
have disturbed their relationship to their whole environment, and possibly for nothing, as there was no guarantee we would ever be allowed to
emigrate. In 1962, however, I started teaching Anna English. Vera was
supposed to start a little later. We did let Edith's parents know about our
application. Edith's father suggested they should also apply, but we
advised against this. Being elderly people without technical qualifications
(Klara's artisanry did not count as such), they were not likely to encounter any difficulties in obtaining a permit. Once they obtained it, they
would have to leave, and we might not be able to follow them for a long
time, if ever. Thus, we might become separated from each other for an
indefinite period. Unless they were willing to face such a situation, it was
better for them to apply only if our application was approved.

More than a year earlier, in September 1960, Edith and I had made a
trip to Budapest. This was to be our last trip abroad for a long time. After
we applied for emigration in 1962, we were no longer allowed to leave
the country. The visit to Budapest turned out to be a major event in our
lives. I met a number of new and interesting people: mathematical economists like András Bródy, János Kornai, and others. My lengthy conversations with them were both enlightening and uplifting. But beyond these
personal contacts, the cultural life of Budapest, which at that time was

incomparably more colorful and freer than that of Bucharest, was a boon hard to overestimate. It is difficult for anyone unfamiliar with the gray, depressing intellectual atmosphere of the Romania of those days to appreciate the uplifting feeling of suddenly having the windows flung open, even if only in a limited way. For that is what the Budapest of September 1960 meant to us, although it was only Budapest, not the West.

To start with, we saw a superb performance of Friedrich Dürrenmatt's play *The Visit of the Old Lady* (its English version is titled *The Visit*) at one of Budapest's best theaters. A Westerner who has not lived under either fascism or communism cannot grasp what Dürrenmatt's play meant to me. It is a fantastic, symbolic story of corruption in the broadest, most fundamental sense of the word: the corruption of an entire society, under the pressure of a temptation too great to resist. Very briefly, a small town in postwar Germany, Güllen, which has been ruined economically, is visited by a former resident, Clara, who had gone to America and married a multibillionaire whose fortune she has recently inherited. When she had lived in Güllen, Clara had had an affair with Ill, now one of the town's most respected merchants, who got her pregnant but denied having fathered her child. On her return, Clara promises to donate a fabulous amount of money, half of it to the city, the other half to be distributed equally among its citizens. It would suffice to cover amply everybody's existential needs for a lifetime. But Clara has one condition: Somebody must kill Ill, her former lover who had left her in the lurch. We learn all this in the first ten minutes; the rest of the play portrays the psychological transformation of the citizens of Güllen during the weeks following Clara's announcement.

At first everybody is outraged by the brazen arrogance of the offer ("Madam, this is Europe!" the Latin teacher protests). They reject it and assure Ill of their support. "I can wait," says Clara, as she rents a room at the hotel for several weeks. Then people who had been swimming in debt, unable to buy even the barest necessities of life, suddenly start making purchases on credit. First a pair of shoes, then a new skirt, next a tennis racket and so on. Many of them buy at Ill's shop, and he wonders how they plan to pay. Little by little, he realizes that everybody is counting on Clara's promised money. Nobody wants to kill Ill, or to know who will kill him, but it gradually enters their consciousness that someday he *will* be killed. And they gradually convince themselves that, after all, he deserves it. Poor Clara, it was not nice what he did to her.

When Ill realizes what is going on in people's minds—including his own son's and daughter's, who buy a car on credit—he tries one night to leave town. But it turns out that he is being watched: people surround him with kind and reassuring words; they accompany him to the railway station, all the time expressing their regret that he wants to leave. The train arrives, but when Ill tries to board it he is surrounded by friends who hug him and prevent him from taking the train; it leaves without him. At this point Ill understands that he is lost and no longer resists; he tells the mayor that he is willing to submit to the wish of the majority. A vote is taken and the decision is unanimous: Ill has to die; this is his punishment for what he did to Clara. The verdict is carried out collectively: all the male citizens of the town put their hands on the knife as it pierces Ill's heart. The scene of the killing is then followed by one of prayer, in which the citizens of Güllen ask God to allow them to enjoy their newfound wealth and happy lives "in good conscience."

I could not resist the temptation of telling this story here, because it had a disproportionately huge effect on me. As Ill was being prepared for execution I relived my own two public "executions," where the atmosphere had been very similar. True, in my case the underlying force was not temptation, but pressure and threats; however, *mutatis mutandis*, the phenomenon was the same. An otherwise decent community of ordinary people agree to do a horrible thing under pressure or temptation too strong to resist. I felt that Dürrenmatt had caught wonderfully the spirit of something that is typical of our times: typical under nazism, typical under communism, perhaps typical of our century. After having seen the play, I bought the book and read it more than once. The play is a classic piece of literature, Shakespearean in its conciseness: every half-sentence has its significance and adds a nuance to the picture being drawn.

Dürrenmatt's play was the strongest, but not the only, entertainment that we had in Budapest. We saw a few other good plays and some highly enjoyable musicals. We returned home refreshed and with more open minds, more determined than ever to leave Romania. In fact, shortly after this trip we formally applied to move to Hungary for good. This type of emigration request, from one socialist country to another, was handled on an entirely different basis than a request to leave for a capitalist country, and did not carry the same stigma or trigger the same retaliation. But we were immediately and explicitly turned down—needless to say, without being given a reason.

. . .

In 1962 a scandal with political dimensions shook the institute where I was working. One of the draftswomen, an articulate, pleasant woman in her fifties, widely read and knowledgeable about the world, was known to be descended from a famous Romanian aristocratic family: that was why she held a low-level, low-salary job. One day she told her friends at the office, out of the blue, that she would probably be fired the next day. Why? For twelve years she had been working as one of the Securitate's informers in the Institute; she had to report on her colleagues, reproduce conversations she had taken part in or heard, occasionally ask people provocative questions, and report their answers. She had been black-mailed into doing this, at first because of her family background, then by the threat that what she had already reported would be revealed. Over the years she got in deeper and deeper, and now she felt that she had had enough and, whatever the consequences, could no longer go on with the deal. The Securitate asked that she be fired instantly. Naftali said he would discuss the issue with the party. He told the party (and let this be known to his colleagues) that the woman in question was one of his best draft artists, skillful and conscientious, and that the institute needed her services. He also argued that the Securitate should not be allowed to use the institute to settle its scores. But it was all in vain, and he was forced to fire her. He finally did it, but not before calling a friend and finding a low-paying job for her at another institute.

The political atmosphere among most of the engineers and other employees of the institute was one of apathy, coupled with an absolute disbelief in everything reported in the newspapers. It was this politically hostile or, at best, indifferent, bored mass of people that was dragged out three or four times every year, on the various anniversaries that served as national holidays—May Day, August 23, November 7—as well as on the occasions of visits by friendly foreign statesmen, to demonstrate enthusiastically, chanting slogans, waving flags, and applauding. On Liberation Day (August 23) in 1952, ten days after my arrest, Edith was required, as a newly hired employee of the Scientific Publishing House, to demonstrate, chanting and waving Lenin's book. So much for the demonstrators' "spontaneous enthusiasm," often reported by gullible Western press correspondents. At our demonstrations in the early sixties we would march in wide columns, ten people in a line, with an agitator at the end of each line. I vividly remember Orădeanu, a highly capable engineer in his mid-forties, who always had a memory lapse when he talked to party people in that he forgot the word "No." He was appointed our agitator. There he marched to the right of our line and half a step ahead of us so he could see our faces, screaming wildly as he read from a piece of paper the slogan that we were supposed to "spontaneously" chant. He always avoided my eyes, not because he knew what I thought—everybody, including himself, thought the same thing—but because I would make a grimace or do something else to make him laugh and fall out of his role.

Sometimes these marches and demonstrations had their comical side. Around 1960 the president of Indonesia, Sukarno, who claimed to be a socialist of marxist vintage, came on a state visit. All of Bucharest was ordered into a huge parade and we marched into the largest square of the capital, filling it with half a million wildly enthusiastic demonstrators. Sukarno must have been very impressed by how many people knew about Indonesia, although nine out of ten people had no idea where his country was. When Sukarno's convoy arrived, that exceedingly elegant old man was riding in the company of his four young, sexy, though somewhat flashy concubines. ("Probably his daughters," suggested a party agitator, but somebody made a sarcastic remark that froze this explanation to his lips.) Then the great leader, having been warmly greeted by our prime minister as a comrade, a fellow socialist who was pursuing the same goal as we were, although sometimes leading his nation on a slightly different path, stepped to the rostrum and opened his mouth to speak. But he was unable to begin; the roaring of the crowd forced him, as is usual on such occasions, to wait until the enthusiasm settled down a little. Then he said: "I am a disciple of Marx and Engels, and an admirer of those same great revolutionary leaders who are your standard-bearers: Lenin, Trotsky, and Stalin." A Westerner cannot imagine the magnitude of the sacrilege that he committed by putting the name of the traitor Trotsky alongside those of Lenin and Stalin. It was as if someone were to stand up in St. Peter's Church in Rome and describe a scene of passionate lovemaking between the devil and the Virgin Mary. I laughed loudly for minutes. The leaders on the tribune tried to keep straight faces while fighting off their revulsion. The next day's newspapers naturally omitted the undesirable name from the speech.

Disbelief in everything that came through official channels of information, and the cynicism born from it, were so rampant that many people, even educated ones like my engineer colleagues, lost much of their ability to distinguish truth from falsehood. When the Soviets launched the first manned spacecraft in 1961, carrying on board Yuri Gagarin, I was very impressed and tried to discuss the event with my colleagues. I had always been intrigued by the contrast between the generally low quality of Soviet life and peacetime industrial products, and the superb feats they were able to accomplish in matters of military significance. But it was very hard to have a reasonable discussion because my colleagues simply refused to believe the Gagarin story. They dismissed it as "propaganda like the rest." I argued in vain that I was not naive in believing this story, that it had to be true because it could be verified, and that if the Soviets were lying about it, they would be found out in no time.

Skepticism was so strong among the people that they would not believe even the truth. Skepticism and political apathy had even squeezed out those nationalistic feelings that typically lurked beneath the surface of most Eastern European intellectuals' minds. Nobody really cared any longer for the Fatherland. Most ordinary people—though not the officials, of course—had ceased to regard wanting to get out of the "fatherland" as a betrayal of anything. Some of the Jewish engineers at the institute were known to have applied for emigration, because the institute had been notified. They had been demoted one step on the ladder (this was Naftali's policy, to satisfy the requirement for punishment in the mildest possible way) and were otherwise doing the same work as before. When, after years of waiting, one of them was notified that his application had been approved, he celebrated the event with his colleagues and friends, mostly Gentile, who all wished him good luck in his new life and new homeland.

It was typical of the atmosphere that every unpleasant activity had to be undertaken "voluntarily," with enthusiasm. One day at work I received a written notification that I had been "appointed a volunteer firefighter." Just to see their reaction, I showed the letter to several colleagues and asked what they thought. Nobody laughed. They simply did not understand what I found unnatural or surprising in the letter.

One day in 1963 I was urgently summoned by Naftali. He told me to drop everything I was doing; he needed me full time for three weeks.

I tried to argue that I was in the middle of solving an important problem, but he cut me off by saying, "Listen, when you needed me, I was
there; now I need you. Are you willing to do what I ask or not?" There
could be only one answer to that and I gave it without hesitation: "Of
course."

He then explained that the day before he had been called to the party's
District Committee, where the party secretary told him the following:
"You have a maverick at your institute, an economist or mathematician
or whatever, who did those fancy transportation plans for your ministry
that brought big savings. I want you to lend him to us for three weeks."

"Sure," said Naftali, "but may I ask for what purpose?"

The secretary replied, "The most important plant in our District is
Electronica, which as you know produces television sets and radios. It is
the only one in the country and the largest in southeast Europe, and the
guys at the Central Committee have their eyes on it all the time. Now for
the third time in three consecutive quarters, Electronica has vastly
underfulfilled its plan. We tried to do something about it when it happened the first time; the State Planning Commission also got involved,
but nobody knows what the trouble is. Are they lazy? Is somebody bent
on sabotaging the plan? All we know is there's trouble and it keeps
getting worse instead of better.

"Now, you were boasting at our review meetings about those mathematical transportation plans that brought your ministry big savings. I
want you to lend us your man who developed them for three weeks:
maybe he has a mathematical method to cure the problem at Electronica.
I want him to go there, study the situation, and write a report about what
should be done."

Naftali added, "I could not refuse. I realize that you cannot do anything in terms of mathematical methods in three weeks, and maybe not
even beyond that. But you have common sense and a keen eye; you may
be able to see something the others did not. Also, you now have this aura
created by the successful transportation plans. They will listen to you.
There is no obligation on your part to do anything beyond trying to help.
Give it your best for three weeks; put your mind and all your energies
to it; and after that you can return to the work you like."

I had little choice but to say "OK. I have no idea whether I will be able
to even begin to understand what is going on, but I will do my best not
to let you down." I put everything aside and the next morning showed

up at Electronica, where people were already expecting me—and expecting me in considerable fear, as I was the man sent by the District Committee of the party.

Had I not been agonizing about what, if anything, I would be able to do, I would have been amused by the irony of the situation: imagine *me* as the guy from the party who spreads fear all around, whose every step is followed in anguish, whose every question is answered eagerly by three people speaking at the same time, whose favors everybody is obviously eager to win! The word *sabotage* had been in the air for a couple of weeks, and everyone in a position of responsibility was a little scared. Although the days when people were routinely jailed for acts of alleged sabotage had passed, their memory was still sufficiently alive to make people quite uncomfortable. I decided upon an initial plan of action. I would first try to gather the basic facts, get a picture of the production process, and look at all the relevant statistics; then I would see what I could do. I did not expect to find the necessary statistics readily available, so I asked for help: an accountant or an economic planner who knew where to look for the information that I needed, and who would be armed with a calculator and a written order from the director requiring everybody to respond immediately to our requests. I asked for one man and got two, with two calculators. I was given an office and a tour of the plant.

The factory manager was an electronics engineer. He struck me as bright, competent, and lively; the only fault I could see in the way he related to the situation was that he was always mired down in details and seemed to lack a vision of the whole. He was unable to answer the basic question of why the plant had systematically fallen behind the plan; he kept saying that he and his collaborators had done and were doing their best. I asked whether the plan had been imposed upon them from above without their consent. He said no, the plan had been worked out on the basis of their own proposals. Some of the tasks had been incremented according to the wishes of the State Planning Commission, but not in unreasonable ways. I asked for a breakdown of the planned monthly production volume by individual production units, and checked it against the capacities of those units. I found that the tasks were well within production capacities.

I then asked my two aides to put together a detailed flowchart of production over the previous twelve months, day by day for each shop of the plant—and the picture started to fall into place. Instead of steady lines of constant output, the charts showed zigzagging, fluctuating lines for most of the plant's shops. Output was steady for a while, then dropped sharply or stopped completely, then returned to the earlier level, then dropped again, and so on. When I asked for an explanation, I got several, a different explanation for each drop in production. Shop A's drop on March 7, for instance, was due to shop B's not delivering the parts that were due the previous day, without which the parts that shop A was producing could not be assembled. When I looked up the chart for shop B, I found that it had indeed missed its production target on March 5 and 6, partly because some of its personnel went on sick leave. When I asked why that had happened and what attempts had been made to replace the missing persons, I found out that the sick leave was actually fake, and the head of the shop had agreed to it because the shop had no work to do. Although the staff had fallen behind their plan, they could not catch up on those two days because the screws they needed from a factory in Brasov had not arrived.

Little by little, step by step, I discovered that, almost without exception, the ultimate cause of each breakdown or slowdown was some outside delivery that was supposed to arrive but did not. All the other reasons given for the zigzags in the production charts could usually be traced to this. The reason the people at the plant, including the manager, were unaware of this was that the phenomenon was masked by the complexity of the production process. Electronica handled some ten thousand different parts. The most important of these were produced by the factory itself, so when one of them was missing and production fell behind, people would blame the shop that produced that part. In reality, the shop had been held back by a delay in the delivery of another part from another shop at Electronica; but when I pursued the matter far enough, I inevitably found that the culprit was one of about sixty essential items that came from outside the plant and were systematically not being delivered on time.

Two factors helped me diagnose the trouble for what it was. First, my interest in input-output analysis inspired me not to stop at the first step when an input item coming from another shop was not delivered for some reason, but to follow the chain to the end. Second, I was aware of the basic shortcoming of a socialist economy; namely, that it was an economy of supply shortages, one in which the market—to the extent that one can use this inappropriate term—was never a buyer's market, but always a seller's market.

I reached my conclusion after about ten days at the factory and used the rest of my time to document it. I took the most important production slowdowns or stoppages during the past nine months and traced them back to delays in the deliveries of materials or parts by outside suppliers. I talked to the plant manager and showed him the outcome of my analysis. His reaction was that there was nothing he could do about the problem; it was beyond his reach. I asked whether he had a system by which he was alerted when a delivery would not arrive on time. He said there could be no such system, since the deliveries would *never* arrive on time. He was not moved when I told him that his problem was not unique, yet other plants were managing to meet their production goals. Perhaps other plants were less dependent on outside suppliers, he retorted.

Since my basic evaluation of the plant manager was positive, I did not want to antagonize him. I told him that I was convinced that he knew a thousand times more about his plant than I was able to learn in two weeks, and that I was just trying to share with him the observations of an outsider, which might prompt him to take a fresh look at some aspects of the situation. I assured him that my goal was not to find fault, but to help him solve his problem. My impression was that the plant was very well run internally, that from top down, starting with the manager, the technical personnel seemed well qualified and in control of the situation. The trouble was with the supply chain, and the weakness of the plant management was its apparent inability to cope with this trouble.

I made several recommendations. First, I suggested that he think about getting another buyer and moving the current buyer to some other job. The engineer currently responsible for buying supplies was a competent, knowledgeable person who had been given the task because of his thorough familiarity with the parts and materials that had to be purchased and with their quality requirements. But the buyer had to be much more than a technical expert: he had to be a resourceful, agile person and an indomitable fighter. He had to know how to court, cajole, or threaten the suppliers, and he had to view the supply plan as his own, for the execution of which he was just as responsible as was the head of a shop for his own production plan. The buyer had to be both able and willing to accept responsibility for the execution of the supply plan. He had to be well connected to the rest of the industry, and have contacts at the ministry and the State Planning Commission whom he could occasionally call upon for help in the form of a phone call to a supplier. It was even desirable for him to use his connections to solve a problem for a supplier, in order to obtain prompt delivery of the materials in exchange. In other words, delivery contracts were not simply to be signed with the expectation that they would be executed; on the contrary, the expectation had to be that the contract would not be executed in a timely fashion unless special efforts were made to that effect. I asked the plant manager whether he knew his main suppliers personally. He did not. I suggested that he start getting to know and cultivate them. He should visit them and invite them to visit, so that when there was trouble with a delivery he could pick up the phone and talk to a friendly person rather than to a stranger.

I asked the manager whether Electronica was producing television sets and radios for the military. He said yes, of course (I suspected as much, since it was the only factory of its kind in the country). I then proposed that he establish a contact in the Ministry of National Defense, whom he could warn when a delay in supplies threatened the timely delivery of products to the army. This way, the person from the defense ministry could call the supplier himself. It was well known that plant managers were allergic to calls from the party, the Securitate, and the defense establishment: Complaints by any of these institutions could easily raise the specter of sabotage. In my letter to the District Committee accompanying my report, I also proposed that if Electronica's fulfillment of its production plan was such a high priority, it would help to institute a monitoring system which would, in the case of certain critical delays in deliveries, trigger a phone call to the party organization of the delinquent supplier, asking for help.

The manager and leading personnel at Electronica said they were very grateful both for the appraisal I gave them in my report and for my advice and recommendations. As to the District Committee, I tried to avoid personal contacts with the members and managed not to meet anybody. Naftali said they seemed to be satisfied. He had also read my report and liked it. So, to my great relief, after the three weeks I was indeed allowed to return to my work.

■ ■ ■

Soon after I started working in mathematical programming, I developed ties to some people working at the Central Directorate of Statistics, or DCS, its Romanian acronym. My friends at the DCS were Vladimir Trebici, a former colleague from the ISEP and now director of demographic studies at the DCS, and Petre Năvodaru, who became deputy head of DCS in the early sixties. Năvodaru was a wartime communist and a well-known economist-statistician, brother of Luiza Năvodaru who had been a friend of mine in the late forties. The DCS organized scientific meetings, starting with weekly seminars on various subjects centered around mathematical statistics. Partly at my initiative, these seminars increasingly included operations research and mathematical programming. The scientific activities were directed by Octav Onicescu, the famous probabilist and member of the academy, then already in his seventies, but invariably active and interested in new developments. Onicescu and his former student Gheorghe Mihoc, another well-known probabilist and member of the academy, regularly invited me to present my research to the weekly seminar at the DCS. Mihoc was the director of the Center of Mathematical Statistics of the academy, a research institute that had split off recently from the Institute of Mathematics and was considered a kind of sister institute of the latter. Thus by 1963, along with my connections to the Institute of Mathematics, I had developed a second set of connections to the group of probabilists and statisticians around Onicescu, Mihoc, and the Center of Mathematical Statistics. I let both groups know that I was interested in joining one of the two research institutes of the academy as an investigator.

These two groups were, of course, in contact; in particular, Mihoc regularly consulted Grigore Moisil on matters concerning the center's development as an academic research institute. After the publication of my first paper in the *Comptes Rendus,* Moisil and Mihoc decided together that it was time to invite me to join one of their institutes. Moisil broke the news to me, along with the following details. He personally would have liked to bring me to the Institute of Mathematics, but it had no positions open at a rank that would provide a decent salary. On the other hand, the Center of Mathematical Statistics, which was more recent and still growing, had funds and research slots for a new Sector of

Mathematical Programming, and Mihoc was planning to appoint me head of that sector, at a salary comparable to, or even slightly better than, the one I was earning in my current job. Moisil advised me to accept Mihoc's offer, adding that if for any reason I did not like it at the center, we could always try to get me transferred later to the Institute of Mathematics.

I accepted Mihoc's offer and in the spring of 1964 moved to the Center of Mathematical Statistics of the academy, taking leave of my colleagues at the Institute of Forestry Studies and Design. Naftali understood the reason for my change of jobs and congratulated me on my appointment. The regime at the center was still the one inherited from the Institute of Mathematics. There had not been enough time for it to deteriorate, as it was bound to do sooner or later, since Mihoc was anything but a fighter and could not resist the party pressures that would develop in time. Upon joining the center, I immediately got two young collaborators in my Sector of Mathematical Programming, the two strongest graduates of the mathematics faculty in that year: Cristian Bergthaller and Mihail Dragomirescu. They were both very talented, but in different ways. Dragomirescu had a very strong geometric intuition, which he used in examining any problem, but which he also needed for understanding a proof: when no geometric interpretation was available or possible, he would have difficulty following the reasoning. Bergthaller, on the other hand, thought in purely algebraic terms and was indifferent to geometric interpretations; they did not help his thinking about the problem. Dragomirescu soon became interested in nonlinear programming and started working in that direction. Bergthaller's interests were more on the discrete side, meaning integer programming. Soon after he had joined our group he published his first paper. Later, after I had emigrated and joined Carnegie Mellon University, he visited me for a semester and we wrote a joint paper titled "Benders's Method Revisited."

In 1965 Dragomirescu was accused of being a homosexual, and there was some pressure from the District Committee of the party to fire him. It was not very strong, however, and when I talked to the head of the section to which we belonged and argued that we had to resist the pressure, he went along. Although Dragomirescu was in the end not fired, he became depressed by the onus that had fallen on him. When I tried to broach the subject in order to allay his feelings of humiliation and isolation, he said that the accusations were false: a single homosexual encounter in his youth was being dragged out of his past and inflated. I knew from the section head that the situation was quite different, but I did not want to intrude on his privacy by discussing the details of the case against him. Instead, I said I did not know what was true and what was not, and was not really interested in finding out, because I regarded this as his private business. The only thing I knew was that, even if he was a homosexual, he had no reason to be ashamed or depressed; it was not something he had chosen, but something that nature had given him, over which he had no control. Rather than being downcast about it, he should face up to the situation and come to terms with himself about it. Different people have different crosses to bear in their lives; they bear them and life goes on, I said; there is nothing to be ashamed of. Several months later, when he seemed to have overcome his depression, he told me, "You have no idea how much that conversation has meant to me."

The time I spent with the Center of Mathematical Statistics was professionally fruitful. I wrote a paper with Mihoc which appeared in 1965 as "The Problem of Optimal Timetables." In 1963 I had developed a fast, iterative method for very large-scale transportation problems based on a new approach called aggregation, and this was published in January 1965 in *Operations Research*. In 1964 I published in Romanian a paper with V. Sachelarescu on the application of mathematical programming to the operation of a saw mill. At some point I became interested in decomposition theory, an approach to solving large linear programs with a certain structure by decomposing them into smaller ones. Thus, in the fall of 1964 I developed two versions of a new decomposition method and sent two communications on them to Robert Fortet in Paris, who got them published in the *Comptes Rendus* in early 1965. I submitted a longer and more detailed English version to the First World Congress of Econometrics held in Rome in September 1965, which of course I was not allowed to attend as I could not get a passport to go abroad. I saw to it that copies of the full-length English version were distributed at the congress, and I submitted it for publication to *Operations Research*, where it appeared a year later. Also, during the winter of 1964–65 I worked out a new method for solving generalized transportation problems that extended the ideas of my joint paper with Laci Hammer on the parametric transportation problem to this more general case. I submitted the resulting paper to *Management Science* and it was published in early 1966. Finally, in the fall of 1965 I worked out a new version of my additive algorithm for 0–1 programming that made explicit use of the linear programming structure and extended the method to the mixed case, where only part of the variables are integer-constrained. I sent two notes on it to Fortet, who had them published in early 1966, and submitted the complete English version to *Operations Research,* where it appeared in 1967.

My research job at the Center of Mathematical Statistics allowed me to do some consulting, and when interesting opportunities arose that introduced me to new problems, I followed them up. Thus, I became a consultant to the Institute of Research for the Construction Industry (INCERC), where I helped put together a procedure for solving critical path problems in so-called PERT networks. I also worked for a while as a consultant to the Energy Research Institute on a study of "Mathematical Models for Optimizing the Development Plan of the Electric Power–Generating Industry."

As I made some extra money, in the fall of 1964 we decided to buy a car. This was a major undertaking; there was a long waiting period and the cost of a car was the equivalent of about three years' salary. It was mainly Edith's wish; I was not enthusiastic about the idea—not that I would not have liked to have a car, but I wanted to concentrate all of our efforts on trying to leave. Besides, in spite of my somewhat improved earnings, we were far from having the required savings, and car loans were an unknown concept. Edith put up for sale a Persian rug as well as her fur coat, and her parents contributed almost half the amount we needed. We signed up for the car in the fall and our turn came in late January 1965. By February we had the car, a Fiat 1100, which soon became the source of much joy. We used it for weekend excursions to the mountains—Sinaia, Predeal, Brasov—as well as short trips to Lake Snagov and in town. Acquiring a car was a major leap in our living standards.

One day in August 1964 Sanyi Jakab was released from jail under a general amnesty. He came to our home and stayed with us for a couple of months. He was barely recognizable after twelve and a half years of imprisonment. And what imprisonment! For all but the last six months he had been kept in solitary confinement, with no reading or writing materials, literally held incommunicado. *Twelve years* of solitary confinement! He was two inches shorter than at the time of his arrest and had lost all his teeth; his skin had a greenish color, and in general he seemed to be in terrible physical condition. His mental alertness and capacities also seemed to have been affected, although he had not gone insane as so many others in his situation had.

He told me bits and pieces of the story of his interrogation between March 1952, when he had been arrested, and October 1954, when his group's trial took place and he was sentenced to twenty years. He was questioned day and night without sleep for weeks on end, then was cruelly beaten until he fainted. When he came to, the beatings resumed. The Securitate officer in charge of the Luca group, in which Sanyi was the major figure after Luca himself, was none other than Ferenc Butyka, a former party activist of the Regional Committee of Cluj in 1946 and 1947, now a Securitate colonel. Both Sanyi and I had known Butyka well, and Sanyi said the fact that Butyka would often personally direct the beatings was an additional torture for him. He told me that after a while he could no longer bear the beatings and would sign anything the interrogator wanted. At the next interrogation he would then retract his statement. But signing statements was not enough. He was forced to invent criminal acts he had allegedly committed; at one point he invented an espionage story. His only concern was, he said, not to involve any friends and make the story such that it could easily be proven false. But in the end these invented criminal stories were discarded, and he was tried for his activities as deputy finance minister, which were described as a sequence of acts of sabotage meant to harm the party and the country. By this time Sanyi had a very low opinion of Luca, who chose early on to fully cooperate with the Securitate in his own political destruction and character assassination, as well as that of his collaborators. Among other things, Luca declared himself to have been an agent and informer of the Siguranța, the old Romanian security agency. When confronted with Sanyi about some alleged act of sabotage that Sanyi was denying, he would maintain that Sanyi had indeed engaged in such activities. He smoked cigarettes all the time, appeared well fed, and did not show any signs of lack of sleep. Luca was sentenced to life in prison at the same trial at which Sanyi got twenty years. As the two of them, along with others, were being driven to jail in the same truck, he mumbled to Sanyi, "They have betrayed me, they lied to me, this is not what they promised."

Edith and I did what we could to ease Sanyi's way back to normal life. We tried to entertain him, brought friends to talk to him, and had long conversations to fill him in on what had happened in the world during the past twelve and a half years. It was not easy. After a while, he was medically examined and his heart and lungs were found to be in order. He got some medication for stomach complaints, and a few months later had his teeth replaced with implants by a dentist friend from Arad, Ferkó Halász, the only one in the country who was familiar with this new technology. He charged Sanyi nothing. Soon after he was released, Sanyi found a job as an economic planner at a medium-sized state company in Bucharest. He moved into his own small apartment, but continued to be a frequent guest at our house. His wife, Magda, who had been at the mental hospital in Cluj for several years, had been taken by her sister in 1960 to France and from there to Israel, where she had been under medical care ever since, at times in a mental institution, at other times under private supervision. Much later, in the seventies, Sanyi had a chance to go to Israel and visit Magda, but she did not recognize him.

My daughter Anna was very moved and shocked by what had happened to Sanyi. She was fourteen at the time, and had not been exposed to any of the shadowy aspects of our political life. She knew very little about the circumstances of my arrest when she had been a small child, or about my expulsion from the party. Nor did she learn (at that time) the details of Sanyi's horror story. But she did find out that he had just spent many years in jail, although he was a close friend of mine and so clearly could not be a "bad" man. Anna had some other negative political experiences about the same time. The Pioneer (communist youth) organization at her school had to elect a leader of her class, and the vast majority of the class wanted a boy who, while a very good student, was not the teacher's recommended choice. The teacher wanted the son of a party big shot to be elected. But the class stood up for its choice and elected him with a huge majority—whereupon the teacher canceled the vote, calling it invalid for some ridiculous reason, then postponed the election indefinitely and appointed the big shot's son on a temporary basis. Anna was beside herself with indignation.

In early 1965 I learned about several defections that had taken place through Yugoslavia. People would go to Yugoslavia for a vacation and, once there, take advantage of the rather lax border controls to cross into Italy. It was an undertaking not without risks: in addition to a few successful escapes, there had been cases in which the Yugoslav guards on the Italian border had turned back people without proper visas. I discussed the pros and cons with Edith, and we decided to try to get a passport for a family vacation on the Dalmatian coast. Once there, we would decide on the basis of information gathered on the spot whether to try crossing into Italy. In March we went once more to the passport office in the street with the fancy name (the Garden with Horses) and applied for a passport for a three-week vacation in Yugoslavia.

Nothing happened for about two months, then some time in May I was summoned to the same office, presumably for an answer. I arrived at the specified hour and, after a short wait, two civilians escorted me from the waiting room to an office. They had me sit down in front of a table, then sat themselves at another one, facing me from some distance, and carefully closed the window. I sensed as soon as I met them that they were not passport officers or clerks but Securitate operatives—there was something unpleasantly familiar about them—and when they closed the window, that gesture seemed to confirm my suspicion: if our conversation was going to be taped, the noise from the outside had to be excluded.

The older of the two men asked me why I had applied for a passport to Yugoslavia. For the reason stated in my application, I said: to vacation on the Dalmatian coast with my family. But didn't Romania have a nice seacoast? Why wasn't that good enough for me? The Adriatic was different from the Black Sea, I said, and we wanted to broaden our experience. At that point the man said the he and his colleague were from the Securitate, and they knew that a few years earlier my wife and I had applied for emigration. Therefore, they strongly suspected that we wanted to go to Yugoslavia in order to defect to the West. But whatever my intentions, he continued, he was a little surprised at my naïveté in applying for a passport to visit Yugoslavia. Didn't I know that you can't ask to leave the country for good, then request permission for a short trip? Didn't I see the contradiction in that? I said that I saw no contradiction in my actions: three years earlier we had indeed applied for emigration, but that application had not been granted and we had to return to our normal lives. A vacation was part of normal life, and now that it had become possible to visit the Adriatic coast, I saw no reason why we should not be allowed to take advantage of that opportunity. As to the allegation concerning my intentions, I had not entertained the idea of an illegal border crossing, and there was nothing in my record to justify such a suspicion.

The man then said that, whether I found it fair or not, the rule was that once you applied for emigration you could not get a visiting passport.

This was the general rule, he added, but there were exceptions. If I had a strong desire to visit Yugoslavia *for whatever reason* (he stressed this last part), well, that was not impossible: they could help me. They were in a position to arrange such a trip for me. But they wanted some reciprocity, some evidence on my part that, even though I had wanted to emigrate and perhaps still intended to, I had not completely thrown away my loyalty to the country where I was born and grew up, and still knew my duty as a citizen. If I were willing to help them as a good citizen, we might be able to strike a deal.

I thought for a moment and then said, "Yes, you may be right. I may be able to help you. Over the last few years I have developed solution methods for optimization problems that occur in every area of human activity. I am sure you also have scheduling problems, transportation problems, or other optimization problems. I would be happy to help you formulate them and solve them."

There was a moment of silence. Then the man said, "Well, that's not what we meant by help."

"It may not be exactly what you meant," I said, "but this is my area of expertise, my profession. This is where I could be useful to you."

"We want a different kind of help from you," he went on. "You are an intelligent man with a lot of experience. We want you to help us discover enemies of our regime, enemies of our people. You don't have to be in open contact with us. You will have a telephone number that you call whenever you have something to report, and nobody will know about it."

I was trying to think fast. These two had summoned me here with the intent of recruiting me as an informer for the Securitate. Was that all? It could not be. They knew my past, and they knew I was the most unlikely person to become an informer. So why were they asking me? Because the bribe they were offering me was enormous: they were saying, though not in so many words, "If you agree to work for us, we will help you get a passport to Yugoslavia. There you can defect to the West. You will have impeccable political credentials and you will be working for us. Get it?" I got it.

For a moment I tried to think through the consequences of accepting the offer. We would go to Yugoslavia, defect, and as soon as we crossed the border to Italy, I would get in touch with the U.S. embassy and report that I had defected after having agreed to work for the Securitate but without ever intending to carry out the agreement. There had been precedents for this in the past. On the other hand, I could not believe that the Securitate would allow me to leave the country on the basis of a mere promise to work for them. They must be after a more tangible commitment on my part, which would in all likelihood be unpalatable to me. So I said, "Help you discover enemies of the people? But for this you don't have to give me anything in return. I know my duty as a citizen very well. Rest assured, as soon as I come across an enemy, I will alert the authorities, without any special arrangement for this."

Now the man changed his tone and, in a businesslike manner, asked whether I knew a certain person for whom I will use the pseudonym Landman. Yes, I said, he had been a friend of mine for more than a decade; I knew him quite well. What did I think of him? Would I describe him, sort of give a characterization of him? Sure, I said, and I described his professional qualifications, his skills, everything that I knew they could also find in his vita, and added a few words about his work habits, reliability, and seriousness. Could I imagine him telling reactionary jokes, the man asked, or making hostile remarks about our party, about our regime? I thought for a moment; then I laughed heartily and said, "Well, that's a surprise. I thought you were hunting for lions and tigers, not for rabbits."

"What do you mean?" the man asked.

"I mean I thought that you intend to catch spies, enemies of the people, not occasional gossips who are afraid of their own shadows when they see them." I had no idea, I explained, whether Landman had ever told a reactionary joke; he certainly had not told one to me. But I could vouch for the fact that Landman was not a dangerous man. "He is a man of many qualities," I said, "honest, hardworking, capable. But courage or daring is not one of the assets that nature has endowed him with, and therefore he can never become a danger to the regime. I would advise you not to waste your time with him. If you are worried about the jokes he might tell, you have only to give him the mildest warning and I guarantee that for the next five years he will not tell a single joke, even in the middle of the night under his pillow." The picture I painted of Landman was not entirely correct, or at least it was vastly exaggerated, but I wanted to get the Securitate off his back.

Next the man asked whether I saw Landman often and when I had seen him last. I said I didn't see him at regular intervals, but I would sometimes come across him in a library or in the street. On such occasions we would often talk for a while. The last time that I saw him must have been three or four months before. Did we ever call each other to arrange a meeting? Yes, I said, we must have done that, though I couldn't recall any specific occasion. Would I be willing to give Landman a phone call and ask him to meet me? Sure, I said, why not, if I had a reason; but just then I didn't have one. "Well," the man said, "here is the reason. We want you to meet him at a place we will agree upon, ask him a couple of questions that we will specify for you, and report his answers back to us." So this is it, I said to myself. We would start with a couple of provocative questions, the answers to which I would have to report. I would have no way of deceiving them, since I would not know whether the specified meeting place—perhaps a particular bench in the park— was bugged, nor whether Landman himself had not also been recruited to report on our conversation. It would be a small step, making it easy for me to cross the threshold. Perhaps the questions would not even be particularly provocative; perhaps the sole purpose of the exercise was just to have me take a first step in their direction, tiny though it might be. The next step was sure to be bigger and also harder to refuse. After all, a precedent would have been set: I would have executed a task received from the Securitate and have informed on a friend, even if the information contained in the first report was completely innocuous. A big red stop sign appeared in front of my inner eyes.

"No," I said. "I cannot do that."

"But why not?" the man asked. "You don't even know the questions we want you to ask Landman; maybe they are completely innocent. Why are you so hostile to us? Earlier you said you would be willing to help us."

"I still say it, and I'll repeat it: I am willing to help you in the way in which I am most effective, in modeling optimization problems you might have and solving them for you. This is my profession, this is what I know how to do. The thing you are asking me to do is something that I am very bad at. Let others do it, who are more apt at it. I am not at all good at role-playing. I would give myself away immediately."

"Don't worry about that, leave that worry to us. We can help you with advice and teach you not to give yourself away. We have vast experience and you are good at learning new things, we know that."

At that point I became a little irritated. "Maybe so, but this is something I do not wish to learn."

"Why?"

I would have liked to say, "Because I find it repugnant, because I hate your system of spying on everybody, and I would hate myself if I were to do it." But it made no sense to antagonize my interlocutors and make them more my enemies than my rejection of their offer already had. Instead, I said, "Because I have a profession that I like; I do not wish to change it. What you are proposing is that I learn a new profession that I know I am very bad at. No, thanks."

"Is that your last word?"

"Yes, that is my last word."

"Sorry. In that case you will have to change your vacation plans." And that was the end of our vacation on the Dalmatian coast.

My first reaction after this episode was an urge to warn Landman that the Securitate was interested in him. But upon thinking over the situation, I concluded that the proposed meeting with Landman most likely would have served the sole purpose of testing the sincerity of my engagement, which would have meant that Landman was supposed to report to the Securitate on our conversation. I could find no explanation for why the Securitate would want to use me—who must have been a much bigger fish in their eyes than Landman—in a petty attempt to entrap that poor soul into making some stupid statement. The proposed conversation with Landman only made sense as a way to check on *my* reliability, not Landman's, and that would involve having Landman report on the meeting. Thus, not being quite certain whether or not Landman worked for the Securitate—and there were many honest but intimidated people who did—I resisted the temptation to warn him.

CHAPTER 16

• • •

Exodus

In March 1965 Gheorghiu-Dej died. The new party leader, Nicolae Ceauşescu, had been his disciple at Doftana, the prison where they served time during the war years. He was, to put it mildly, a less imposing figure than Gheorghiu-Dej, less intelligent but equally shrewd and, if possible, even more ambitious. There was no reason to expect any improvement in the general situation, except for hope that change can only be for the better. Soon after this event Edith and I decided to intensify our attempts to leave the country. After our plan to go on vacation to the Dalmatian coast fell through, we decided to repeat our formal application for emigration. In October 1965 Edith and I again went to the passport office, spent several early-morning hours waiting in line, and finally filled out our application forms. This time I told several of my friends that I had applied for emigration, since I expected the fact to become known and did not want them to find out from others. Most of those who knew my history, my involvement in the underground communist movement, and my role as a diplomat in London and a director in the Foreign Ministry, thought that I was crazy or naïve to imagine I would be allowed to leave. I remember the reaction of Petre Năvodaru, a friend and the deputy head of the Central Directorate of Statistics. He quoted the famous saying attributed to the nineteenth-century French diplomat Talleyrand: *"C'est pire qu'un crime; c'est une faute!"* ("This is worse than a crime; this is a mistake!"). When I asked why, he said, "Because it is futile. With your past record, there is no way you can emigrate."

Two months after we filed our application, in late December, the passport office notified the academy of my request to emigrate and I was promptly fired from my job at the Center of Mathematical Statistics. I had the honor of being fired through a letter signed by the president of the academy, Ilie Murgulescu himself. The letter reached me on December 30 or 31, and I said to Edith that we had got a nice New Year's present. The news that I was fired rather than demoted to a lower rank, and thus left without a job, produced some consternation among mathematicians and others in somewhat broader circles. Full employment and the alleged absence of unemployment was one of the regime's most cherished "accomplishments" whereby it proved its superiority over the capitalist system. Leaving somebody without employment was considered scandalous. Mihoc, the director of the center where I had worked, was very apologetic and assured me he had nothing to do with the decision; it had been made by higher-ups and there was nothing he could do about it. He was obviously telling the truth.

I remember a conversation from this period which turned out to have a strange echo in some later developments in my life. The conversation was with Mrs. Bǎlescu, a lady in her late forties who usually typed my mathematical papers. She was intelligent, with a broad culture, and she took an interest in her clients' lives: She would ask questions about how their papers came about, their families and so on, and talk about events in her own life, such as taking a vacation, or seeing a great movie or play. She asked me many questions about how I had turned to mathematics and what method I used to learn it. Naturally, when I was thrown out of my job I told her about it, and she was very upset. The fact that I had applied for emigration with my family was new to her, and I told her frankly that we had actually applied a few years earlier, and our more recent application had been a renewed attempt. She remarked how odd it was that Jews, who had been traditionally discriminated against, now had an enormous privilege and advantage over non-Jews in that they could apply to emigrate.

Then she said, "I understand how badly you must feel, Mr. Balaş, to have been frustrated for so long in your attempt to emigrate. But let me give you something to think about. Life is so complicated, with so many unforeseen twists and turns, that it is hard to predict whether something that happens will turn out to be good or bad for us in the long run. I had a very good friend who wanted to emigrate with her husband to Canada after the war. They were unable to leave then, and she was very upset. A few years later they obtained permission to leave, and my friend was a very happy woman. After she and her husband left, we corresponded occasionally. Five years after she arrived in Canada, she got breast cancer and soon after that she died."

I did not think at the time that I would remember this story. But in the spring of 1972, exactly five years after Edith and I arrived in the United States, Edith was diagnosed with breast cancer. She was operated on, and fifteen months later she had a regional recurrence for which the literature put the probability of survival for five years or longer at only 4 percent. I shuddered when I recalled Mrs. Bălescu's story, which sprang to my mind immediately with extraordinary clarity. Fortunately for us, the unexpected blow that fate delivered to us in 1972 ended on a happy note: Edith recovered and has gone on to live a happy and productive life. But it was a very close call.

When I was fired from my job, we decided that it was time to inform Anna and involve her in our plans; we told Vera a little later. Anna was now fifteen and a half; she had led a rather sheltered life and knew little if anything about our political problems. She had some apprehensions about the system, but was far from contemplating emigration. When she found out that we had taken steps to emigrate, she was surprised, if not shocked. It took quite some effort to explain to her our personal motives and the general situation; but once she understood, she gradually internalized our point of view. Nevertheless, she retained some lingering doubts without voicing them to us, as it turned out. A few years later, when she went on a trip to Israel after graduating from college, she adventurously visited Romania without telling us beforehand and spent a week in Bucharest. After her return, she told us about her visit, adding that she had been cured of all her remaining doubts and felt deeply grateful to us for having taken her out of communist Romania.

To return to our story, in early January 1966: Ceauşescu had taken over nine months earlier. There were some weak, tentative political winds in the air in the direction of stricter "socialist legality," a code phrase signifying more respect for human rights, better relations with the West, more civilized discourse in the press, and so forth. I decided not to seek employment for two months but instead to use my status as an unemployed scientist to vigorously argue in support of my request to emigrate. Edith's place of work had not been notified about our application, so she still had her job. We had a small cash reserve and could also count on Edith's parents. In a few days I wrote nine memoranda, one to every party and government forum that might conceivably have been involved in the decision concerning my request. I argued that (1) all the members of my family who had survived the war (meaning the Rényis) were living abroad, and (2) I was not being allowed to work in my profession and actually had no job, so I was no longer useful to anyone. In conclusion, I respectfully asked to be permitted to leave the country with my wife and children.

I found out that there was a Governmental Commission on Passports and Visas that handled certain emigration applications. Most cases were handled on a routine basis, but those that raised questions were taken up by this commission. I also found out that the head of the commission was Alexandru Bârlădeanu, deputy prime minister, and that among the commission's members was Gogu Rădulescu, minister of Commerce, who had been the director of the Institute of Economic Research when I had joined it in 1956, and who had been a close friend at the time. I had not talked to Gogu for eight years, since his elevation to the rank of a minister, but I decided to seek him out now.

Instead of calling his secretary and asking for an appointment, I went to his house unannounced at a time when I knew he would be at home. Dorina, his wife, opened the door and invited me in, half-happy to see me after many years, half-embarrassed and uncomfortable. I said I had come to see Gogu, and she went upstairs to fetch him. Through the open door, I inadvertently overheard the first part of their conversation. "Gogu, Egon is here and wants to talk to you." "Egon? Which Egon?" "Don't be silly. . . ." The door closed and I did not hear the rest. But what I heard was enough to kill my hopes concerning the outcome of this interview. Egon was not a common name in Bucharest, and Gogu knew no other person by that name, so his reaction was clearly one of spontaneous self-defense, an attempt to keep the unpleasant visitor at arm's length. It crossed my mind to leave the house immediately, but I forced myself to stay until Gogu appeared a few minutes later. Originally, when I had decided to see him, I had been planning to remind him of our last conversation a decade earlier, in which he said he was accepting a position in the government in order to occasionally help his friends and other decent people. But after the scrap of conversation I had just overheard, I decided to forego hinting at our one-time friendship. I simply described my situation and informed him of the contents of my letter to the governmental commission of which he was a member, leaving it to his sense of fairness whether he wished to support it or not. It must have been a very awkward conversation, because I do not remember any of it. I only have a vague recollection of telling Edith afterwards that I might as well not have bothered visiting him.

■ ■ ■

The head of the governmental commission, Alexandru Bârlădeanu, was also someone who knew me. I was confident that he still remembered the occasion around 1950 when he had been summoned to Gheorghiu-Dej, and I had substituted for him on very short notice in giving a lecture at the party school, for which at the time he seemed genuinely grateful. I asked his secretary for an appointment and got a vaguely positive answer to the effect that he was extremely busy (besides his role on the commission, his main function was that of deputy prime minister overseeing all economic affairs), but that he intended to give me an appointment later. I was asked for my telephone number and the secretary said she would call.

I received an appointment with the foreign minister, Corneliu Mănescu, about three weeks after my request. The foreign minister was no relative of Manea Mănescu, with whom I had had a conflict in 1949 at the ISEP. Corneliu Mănescu lived on our street, a few houses down from ours. His daughter was a classmate of Anna. The girls used to see each other and occasionally we, the parents, exchanged a few words when we met in the street. Mănescu was a nice man with a relatively good reputation. However, he was not very powerful or influential. He received me in a friendly and polite manner in his office at the Foreign Ministry, whose threshold I now crossed for the first time since my ejection in 1952. He listened to what I had to say, then explained that he did not have much input into problems of the kind I was describing, which were handled by a special governmental commission. All the same, he would look into the matter, and if he could do anything to help me, he would let me know. I thanked him and came away with the feeling that I had been treated well but had not accomplished anything.

After some deliberation I decided upon an unusual step: I asked for an audience with the head of the Securitate, General Negrea, whom I had never met in person. His secretary asked the reason for my request. I said the reason was confidential and I would give it only to General Negrea himself. She asked me to call back in a couple of days and when I did, she said the general was very busy, but his deputy would see me. I told her I could wait until General Negrea had time, but I was not willing to talk to anybody else about the matter that I wanted to bring to the general's attention. The next day I got an appointment with Negrea for the following week. When I showed up for my appointment, I was seated in a waiting room alone; clearly my audience was not one in a sequence of standard audiences. After a brief wait I was led by a Securitate officer through some long corridors, and on our way I imagined myself traversing those same corridors blindfolded and being led by the arm. Finally we reached the boss's office.

I was ushered in and seated in front of a desk facing General Negrea. He looked at me with curiosity and expectation in his eyes, and as I started talking and he realized why I wanted to see him, his expression turned into one of disappointment. I then understood that the reason for my having been granted this audience was the expectation that I would be bringing some information about somebody, some antiparty group, or some hostile activity. Or perhaps he hoped that I was coming to offer myself as a spy. Anyway, the general was disappointed. I briefly explained my situation; then I stated the reason for my wanting to see the general about this issue. I spoke very politely and respectfully, but at the same time firmly and directly. I said that the reason I had not been granted permission to leave in spite of my repeated applications could only be opposition to my departure on the part of the Securitate. I had come to clarify the situation in this respect, I said, and I had insisted on seeing the general in person, because I wanted to entrust my case to his personal judgment and sense of fairness. The truth of the matter was that, although I had worked as a diplomat at the London legation and then as a director in the Foreign Ministry, the first had taken place eighteen years ago and the second had come to an end fourteen years ago. Nothing that I had been involved with at that time could still be a secret today. Therefore, I said, I considered the vetoing of my emigration request by the Securitate unwarranted by any justifiable concern for the confidentiality of information that I might still be in the possession of. I was respectfully asking the general to weigh these facts and lift the ban on my emigration.

Negrea was apparently taken aback by the direct way in which I put the issue to him, and he, the mighty general, arbiter of the fate of so many people, became defensive. He had looked at my file before I came to see him, he said, and he could assure me that it was not the Securitate that had vetoed my emigration request. In fact, he said, the Securitate had no objection to my leaving. He thought that I was a capable man and could still be a useful citizen, but it seemed to him that I had "gotten it into my head" that I had to leave. It was not within his purview to help me solve my problem, but he wanted me to know that the Securitate was not blocking my exit. I thanked him for the audience and for his understanding. My evaluation of this interview was on the whole positive. Although I obtained no promise of help in solving my problem—in fact, I had been told the exact opposite—Negrea had clearly stated that the Securitate was not blocking and would not block my emigration. If Negrea meant what he said, then one of the main obstacles, perhaps the primary one, to my being permitted to leave had vanished. Of course, I could not be certain that he did mean it; my past experience with his institution did not inspire trust.

Another person whose office I called was Avram Bunaciu, the chairman of the Commission of the National Assembly for the Application of the Constitution. This strange-sounding name was an oxymoron: the role of the recently instituted Commission of the National Assembly was purportedly to act as a watchdog over the executive branch and oversee the government's activities from the point of view of how it observed the provisions of the constitution. To a Western ear this may sound like an innocuous or even a reasonable task, but to somebody familiar with Soviet-style societies it sounds hilarious. It is on a par with similar names in George Orwell's *1984*, where the Thought Police is the Ministry of Love and the Propaganda Office is the Ministry of Truth. The Romanian constitution, like the Soviet constitution, was among the most democratic in the world; you would be hard put to define a freedom not guaranteed by it. The only problem was that nobody paid any attention to it; it was merely a piece of paper with no connection whatsoever to Romanian realities. To ask whether the constitution was being applied properly was to ask whether, in a swimming contest held in a river, the rule that the water had to remain motionless during the contest was being faithfully observed. The commission had absolutely no power, it had the same "right" to observe and report the truth as everybody else, and nobody had yet heard of any issue raised by it. But my case certainly fell within the purview of the commission, since the procedure of firing me and leaving me without a job was a violation of my most elementary constitutional right, the right to work.

Avram Bunaciu had been a communist intellectual during the war, and shortly thereafter had held several high positions, mostly in the Ministry of Justice. For a brief period he served as minister or deputy minister of justice. In early 1952 he had been appointed deputy minister of foreign affairs, a few months before the right-wing deviation was "discovered" and I was fired. So he knew me from those days and, although we had not worked together, he had heard enough about me to have an opinion. I did not know him well, but the little that I knew about him was positive: He was a decent man, who had never been tainted by anti-Semitism, intelligent, not overly courageous, but one who tried to keep his integrity and did not get caught up in the general power struggle and the corruption that went with it. This partly explains why he was chosen for the position of chairman of the new commission: to lend it some credibility.

I called Bunaciu's office one afternoon and had this conversation with his secretary: "I am so-and-so and would like an appointment with Dr. Bunaciu."

"Certainly. When would you like to come?"

"Well, whenever his schedule allows. I have no particular date in mind, but the sooner the better."

"How about tomorrow morning at nine?"

"That's just perfect."

I had surmised that Bunaciu's job could not keep him very busy, but I never imagined that he had absolutely nothing to do. Yet this seemed to be the case, judging not only from my conversation with his secretary, but also from the fact that I was the only visitor to his office the following morning, that I found him reading the newspaper, that he engaged me in a long conversation with no concern for the time.

Bunaciu did not ask why I had come. He greeted me like an old acquaintance whom he had not seen for years but of whom he had pleasant memories. He had heard about my "mishaps," he said, about my having been kept in jail for two years, and was very happy when he learned that I was innocent and had been released. He had then followed my career as an economist, he said, and was saddened when he heard about the "mishap" with the book I had written. Maybe I should have thought more carefully before publishing it: sometimes we inadvertently make mistakes that later we regret. But anyway, he went on, he was again happy to hear how quickly and fully I had recovered and become a mathematician; he admired me for that. Then he told me a few things about his own career during those same years: His brief stint in the Foreign Ministry, where he actually felt outside his expertise, then his years in the Justice Department where he knew his business but had problems of a different nature.

Bunaciu had not heard about my having applied for emigration and, as a result, having been ousted from my job. He was taken aback when I told him. He agreed that my status flatly defied the constitution, and that therefore my problem was of legitimate concern to him in his official capacity. But he could not get over his surprise and misgivings about the fact that I had reached the point of wanting to emigrate. How was it possible that such a capable and valuable man like myself should decide to leave the country? That was a shame, a major failure "for us," meaning the party, the regime. "We need people like you," he said. Then he started arguing at length that in my—partly legitimate—reaction to the unfair manner in which I had been treated, I had drawn the wrong conclusion when I took the extreme measure of applying for emigration. This had been a rash decision on my part, he said, one with grave consequences, but not fatal. I must reconsider this decision. It would be absurd for the country to lose a man like me; there must be a way to accommodate me and provide me with the right working environment. "We need people like you," he kept repeating. Then he went on to say that he was going to raise the issue with the party and he was sure he would find some acceptable solution for me; he was not hoping to obtain a reversal of the decision by Murgulescu to fire me, but he was confident the party would provide a working environment where I could "fully exercise my talents," as he put it.

The discussion was becoming increasingly unpleasant for me, because I was sitting in front of an apparently decent person (or at least one who was responding decently to my situation) and I had to disappoint him by making it clear that I did not want him to find me another job. How could I make him understand that I had crossed my Rubicon quite some time ago? That his ideals—once my own ideals—were no longer shared by me? That I no longer cared for, and no longer wished to be useful in, the construction of the communist society? I did not quite know what to say; but I knew that I had to stop him from acting along the lines he was proposing, for he might succeed in convincing somebody at the party to offer me an acceptable job on the condition that I give up my emigration plans, which I was not prepared to do. Then if I refused the party's "generous" offer, that would be interpreted as a blatantly hostile act, certainly not one to be rewarded with an emigration certificate.

This is roughly what I said to Bunaciu: "I am very touched by your genuine concern and willingness to help. Yet I must turn down your offer. Let me explain. You see, you may be quite right when you say that it was a mistake on my part to ask to leave the country. But it is a mistake I have already committed—and once I have committed it, there is no turning back: *alea jacta est.* Let's not fool ourselves in this respect. You know as well as I do that once the stigma of a would-be emigrant has been affixed to you, you are a traitor in the eyes of the party, and no amount of self-criticism, no achievement in your work, can ever wash that off. You are a pariah for the rest of your days. So there is really no way back for me; having said A, I *must* say B. I therefore have to ask you not to do anything along the lines you propose. Do not try to persuade people to find an accommodating job for me. I do not know whether you want to help me leave, since you consider that a mistake, and if you wanted to, I don't know whether you could. If you do, I will be forever grateful to you. If you say no for any reason, I will fully understand and will not hold it against you. But please do not try to convince anybody to attempt to keep me here by offering me a job."

There was silence for a while. Then he said, "I am saddened by what you say, but I have to accept it. I have no idea whether I will be able to help you obtain an emigration permit, but I will try. I want you to know, though, that in my eyes you are the same Egon Balaş that I have known for many years. I don't know how your life will evolve if you manage to leave. But one thing I am sure of: we will hear great things about you, wherever you go." I came away from this audience with the uplifting feeling you get when you suddenly run into unexpected decency. I did not expect any results from our conversation, simply because Bunaciu did not seem to carry much weight in leading circles. Nevertheless, I felt good about it. I never found out whether he did anything on my behalf, or whether he had any role in my finally getting permission to leave.

Of all the people whom I wanted to see, only Bârlădeanu was now left. But he was one of the central actors in my drama, as the head of the Governmental Commission on Passports and Visas. Also, I was counting on him because, on the one hand, he had had a very pleasant experience with me many years earlier that I was confident he had not forgotten; on the other, he was not a friend or former friend of mine, like Gogu, who might have felt he had to go out of his way to avoid being seen to favor me. Bârlădeanu's secretary had asked for my telephone number so she could call me when her boss had a free moment, but such a moment never seemed to come. After a while, I called the secretary again, and she explained that I was on a short list of people whom the minister wanted to see, but that he was being drawn in so many directions at once that it was impossible to predict when he would be able to see me. I sensed that she was not lying or just trying to get me off her back. She spoke to me in a very considerate and respectful tone, which—given the fact that she had never met me—could only reflect her boss's attitude toward me. Because of this, I opened up to her and told her what my problem was, and that I wanted to see Bârlădeanu not in his capacity of deputy prime minister, but in that of chairman of the Governmental Commission on Passports and Visas. I added that I had sent Bârlădeanu a letter that described my case in detail, and gave her the registration number of the letter. Soon after, in early March, she told me that her boss had received my letter and was aware of my problem. "He has still not found a way to fit you in his schedule," she said, "but he knows about your case and I can tell you that he is or will shortly be dealing with it, because your file is on his desk." This was excellent news and I felt very encouraged.

In March 1966 I started looking for a job. By then I felt that I had made the maximum use of my status as an unemployed scientist in arguing for permission to emigrate. I had written nine letters, including, beside the ones I have mentioned, letters to Ceaușescu, the first secretary of the Communist Party; Ion Gheorghe Maurer, the president of the republic; Chivu Stoica, the prime minister; and Gheorghe Apostol, the secretary general of the Trade Union Council. Unemployment was now hurting me financially, and the sacrifice of prolonging it was becoming too costly. My first thought was to try to return to my former workplace, which had in the meantime become the Institute for Forestry Studies and Design (ISPF). Naftali, the director of that institute, had been very good to me. Had I been fired for any other reason than attempting to emigrate, I could have turned to him and he would have helped me, I am sure, even at some risk to himself. But he was Jewish and, like any Jew in a position of responsibility, had to prove his loyalty to the regime against accusations of Israeli sympathies. So I immediately dropped this idea as unworkable. Next I thought of the Institute of Forestry Research (INCEF), which had split off the Designing Institute in the early sixties. I contacted V. Sachelarescu, the engineer with whom I had written a joint paper in 1963 on mathematical programming in the sawmill. He was a researcher at INCEF, without rank or influence, but he had worked with me, knew my qualifications, and could talk about me to the others. In particular, I asked him to contact on my behalf Iacovlev, one of the section heads about whom I had heard that he had the courage of his opinions. In two days I got a phone call from Iacovlev, and after a couple of interviews I was hired starting April 1, 1966, as a member of his section.

During the relatively short period that I spent with the INCEF, I enjoyed full freedom in pursuing my research interests. It was during this period that I received the galley proof of my decomposition paper to be published in *Operations Research*. I changed my affiliation to INCEF (also mentioning my former affiliation), and thus the name of my new institute appeared for the first time in a nonforestry journal with worldwide circulation. Also while at the INCEF, I did some new work on a graph-theoretical model for machine sequencing, which I wrote up under the title "Finding a Minimaximal Path in a Disjunctive PERT Network" and submitted to an upcoming conference, Théorie des Graphes: Journées Internationales d'Étude, to be held in Rome in July 1966. The chairman of the conference's program committee, the French graph theorist Claude Berge, confirmed the acceptance of my paper. As in earlier such cases, I duplicated my paper and sent a number of copies to Rome for distribution at the conference, explaining that I was unable to participate in person.

Some time in mid-April Edith called me at work. She could not find me; I was new at the institute, people did not know my extension, and I was in somebody else's office when the call came. Unable to get through, she left a message which reached me a couple of hours later. When I called her back, she said that Bârlădeanu's secretary urgently wanted to get in touch with me. I phoned the secretary, who told me there had been three people on Bârlădeanu's list of audiences for that morning and, as one of them could not make it, she thought she would substitute me for that person, since I was also close to the top of the list. However, by the time I called back, Bârlădeanu had been called to the prime minister's office and the audiences for that day were over. She promised to call me as soon as there was another opening. I felt terribly frustrated: Here was the opportunity for which I had been waiting almost three months, and when it finally materialized I had the bad luck to lose it for who knows how long. But I kept in touch with Bârlădeanu's secretary, calling her every three days, and she was very encouraging. She told me, for instance, that the boss had gone to a meeting of the governmental commission, and she thought that my case was among those to be discussed.

About this time I received a phone call from Edith, asking whether I could come home because I had a foreign visitor. I went home and met a young Bulgarian mathematician called Marinov who was studying for his doctorate in Trondheim, Norway. He told me that some Norwegian colleagues were following my work with interest and were familiar with my additive algorithm and the developments that it had triggered in the literature. As he was going home to Bulgaria for a month's vacation, they had asked him to stop for a day or two in Bucharest and convey a message to me. He had arrived the previous night; in the morning he went to the Center of Mathematical Statistics and was told that I had left that institution. Nobody was able to tell him where I was working, so after trying in vain to get help in locating me, he left. But somebody from the Center (who obviously had not wanted to do this in the presence of others) came out of the building, caught up with him on the street, and gave him my home address. This was how he found me. The message from the Norwegians was that they knew I wanted to leave Romania and was not allowed to; they also knew that there were unorthodox ways of getting people out of Romania, through high-level intervention, money, or other means. They wanted to know what, specifically, they could do to help me get out.

I thought about the meaning of this message. First, I needed to check out Marinov's credentials, so I drew him into a conversation about life in Trondheim, got him on some pretext to show me his passport, and talked a little about Bulgaria. I was soon convinced that what he was telling me about himself was by and large true, and that he had not been sent by the Securitate. Next, I tried to find out as much as I could about the colleagues in Trondheim who had sent the message. I wrote down their names but decided that I was not going to ask for anything specific through Marinov. For one thing, he was going to spend a month in Bulgaria and could not take back a message for several weeks anyway. For another, although he made an excellent impression on me, I was not sure how trustworthy he was. Now that I had name and address, I could find other means to send a message if I had anything concrete to suggest. I asked Marinov to take back the following oral message: I was most impressed with and grateful for their offer to help, but I had recently renewed my application to emigrate and it was currently being considered by the competent authorities. I did not want to do anything that might interfere with the process; however, should my application again be rejected, I would let them know and perhaps ask for their help. Apart from the message, I had a long conversation with Marinov on technical matters, mostly for the purpose of making his stopover worth the effort he had put into it. I took him to dinner, we did some sight-seeing, and he left the next day satisfied that his mission was successful.

Throughout the second half of April I continued to call Bârlădeanu's secretary every three or four days. It was from her that I got the first sign that the ice had finally broken. During one of my calls toward the end of April, when I had not spoken to her for a week because I could not find her, she asked, "Haven't you heard from anybody yet?"

"No," I said. "What should I have heard?"

She was somewhat hesitant: "As far as I know, your case has been settled."

"Settled in what sense? Favorable or unfavorable?"

"Your application has been approved, as far as I know," she replied. "You should be notified soon of the favorable decision."

It sounded wonderful. I called Edith immediately to tell her, but cautioned her about the "as far as I know" part of the sentence. Nothing happened for a few days, and I called Bârlădeanu's secretary again. I told her that I had not yet been notified of anything. Could she tell me where to inquire so that I need not disturb her any longer? And was she *sure* that my application had been approved? She said yes, she was sure; she had checked after our last conversation. There was no need for me to call anybody, she said; I would soon be notified. These things took their normal course, she added. I asked her to convey my heartfelt thanks to her boss.

A week, perhaps ten days, passed without anything happening. I was sitting on pins and needles. One morning in early May, Edith called me again at the institute. "They came to see the apartment," she said. A huge weight fell off my shoulders. The first sign indicating that a would-be emigrant's application had been approved was not an official announcement or a call from the passport office or anything like that, but an innocuous visit from employees of the city housing office, who would ask, without stating a reason, to inspect his or her apartment. Because there was a long line of people waiting to move into vacant housing, the city housing office was notified as soon as an emigration request was approved, so that they could quickly decide who would get the apartment when it became free. That is what happened to us. Edith told me later in the day that two well-dressed gentlemen showed up at the apartment and introduced themselves as being from the city housing office. Edith, of course, realized the significance of their visit. She invited them in and asked, "Is this in connection with our application to emigrate?" "No," said one of them. "We don't know anything about that; we are not involved. This is just a routine inspection." They sized up the apartment, took some notes, exchanged some observations, and, before leaving, said to Edith politely: "Madam, you have a truly beautiful apartment."

We were, of course, very excited. Edith wondered whether we should start liquidating our belongings, but we decided not to do anything until we knew for certain, then to take care of everything as quickly as possible, so as not to waste a single day. Last-minute hitches were not at all uncommon. Often, the authorities changed their minds at the last minute owing to a denunciation or some alleged discovery by the Securitate. There had been cases of people receiving their emigration papers only to have them revoked three days before their scheduled departures. People had been removed from airplanes they had boarded with perfectly valid emigration documents. I even knew of a case in which a man, allowed to emigrate, sold all his things, said goodbye to his friends, and boarded a plane to Vienna, which at that time was the transit point to Israel. He arrived safely at the Vienna airport, left the plane, and was standing in line at the passport control point when the loudspeaker called his name, saying "Mr. so-and-so has left something on the airplane. Will he please return to the plane to pick it up." He walked back to the plane, boarded it to pick up whatever he had allegedly had left behind—and woke up five hours later in Bucharest, where the Securitate started to investigate him in connection with some last-minute information they had received about him.

There were further visits from housing officials, accompanied by various individuals who looked like candidates for the apartment. These were positive signs that our application had been approved, but a positive sign is less than a certainty. There was another sign one could look for. The emigration document was a travel certificate printed on a single sheet of paper. On the front it had the emigrant's photograph, name, birth date, birthplace, address, plus the date of issue; on the back it had the Romanian exit visa, as well as an Israeli immigration visa and an Italian transit visa. All emigrants, no matter where they intended to go, had to leave with an Israeli immigration visa. Those who intended to go elsewhere had to change their destination in Naples, which was the transit point to Israel. In order to minimize the would-be emigrants' contacts with foreign embassies, the Romanian Foreign Ministry obtained the necessary Israeli and Italian visas on their behalf, and gave them their travel certificates with the visas already stamped in. Thus, one way of finding out whether one's emigration had been approved was to ask the Israeli legation in Bucharest whether it had received a travel certificate in a certain name from the Foreign Ministry, with a request for an immigration visa. The Israeli legation kept track of the immigration visas it issued, and provided this information upon request. Although going to the Israeli legation meant being photographed at the entrance by the Securitate, at this stage of the game I did not care: I had a good reason to go there, to inquire about the status of my visa. I went toward the middle of May and was told that my travel certificate had not yet arrived. They gave me a telephone number I could call to find out, so that I would not have to keep coming in person, and I called the number every few days. Finally, in the first days of June, I was told that an Israeli immigration visa had been stamped onto our travel certificates on May 31. Now we had hard evidence that approved and signed travel documents actually existed. This was it.

At that point we began preparing for the trip. As one could take out of the country only twenty-five kilograms (fifty-five pounds) of personal belongings per head, almost everything we owned had to be sold. The money could not, of course, be taken out legally, but we left it with Edith's parents and they found ways to forward it to us. I did not mind leaving behind such things as boots, coats, and suits, but I did not want to lose my books. One could send books abroad through the mail, but in order to guarantee that no secret or subversive materials were being sent with them, the sender had to sign every book. We selected a couple of hundred of our favorite volumes, and put Anna in charge of making them up into packs of the allowed weight and mailing them at the central post office. Vera helped her with this. Every day for about two weeks they took twenty or thirty books to the post office and sent them by surface mail to Edith's uncle in Israel, Károly Lébi, who in turn would send them on to us in the United States after we arrived there.

During the first week of July we were finally summoned to the passport office to be given our travel certificates. There were three of them, one for Edith and Vera (children under fourteen appeared on their mother's certificate), one for Anna, and one for myself. They were dated May 14, 1966; they had Romanian exit visas with the same date, Israeli immigration visas dated May 31, and Italian transit visas dated June 10. (I did not remember those dates, but we have the certificates to this day.)* I immediately went to the office of TAROM, the Romanian airline, to get tickets for the next available flight to Naples. There was no charge for the tickets—Israel had a deal with the Romanian government that paid for every emigrant's airline ticket—but there were various taxes to be paid. There were two flights a week to Naples, carrying only emigrants, on relatively slow, propeller-driven airplanes. The first flight with available seats was on July 26. That became our flight.

We now placed a newspaper ad for the sale of our belongings. The car was the easiest to sell, as there were long waiting lists for cars of all types, and our Fiat 1100 was relatively new and in excellent condition. As soon as our ad appeared several people came to see the car, and it was sold that very morning at the price we paid for it. The other things took a few more days.

There was a long, complicated procedure for passing the permitted fifty-five pounds each through customs; it took several days, and there was considerable uncertainty about when the bags or cases would be accepted for processing and how long it would take. Rather than risk

---

*These travel certificates were documents issued by the Ministry of Interior on a single sheet of paper, with the name, birthdate, birthplace and photograph of the owner; the date of issue and term of validity (one year); and the warning: "Can not be changed into a passport—can not be extended."

missing the July 26 flight, we decided to "travel light," if I can use a term which usually has a pleasant connotation to describe a situation in which we had to leave behind essentially everything we owned. We decided to avoid the procedure, and take only standard luggage of up to ten kilograms (twenty-two pounds) each. This luggage could be passed through customs and actually checked in for the flight the day before departure.

We also spent a good deal of time memorizing addresses and phone numbers. Not only was it forbidden to take any amount of currency out of the country, as well as gold, silver, and platinum objects in any form (including wedding rings and other jewelry); it was also forbidden to take along any kind of written material, including notebooks and address books. So we had to learn by heart any addresses and telephone numbers that we wanted to keep or thought we might need. We made sure that at least two members of the family knew every telephone number and address, so that if one forgot, the other would remember.

Our flight was scheduled to leave in late afternoon. Edith's parents, Bandi and Juci Klein, as well as Sanyi Jakab accompanied us to the airport and kept waving until the plane took off. Most of them were to follow us soon: my in-laws applied for emigration as soon as we left and joined us in a little over a year. The Kleins emigrated in the late sixties to West Germany. Sanyi remained in Bucharest until the eighties, when he went to Sweden.

■ ■ ■

The six-year-long struggle to get out of Romania has apparently left a deep mark on my consciousness. For many years after we had left, I had periodic dreams with the following recurring theme: I am walking the streets of Bucharest, one of the main boulevards. There is sunshine and the weather is pleasant. I enjoy the walk and am in a relaxed, comfortable mood when it suddenly dawns on me that I have been trapped. I had let myself be lured into coming back for a visit, and I would never be allowed to leave again. It is hard to adequately describe the sudden transition from the pleasant feeling of the walk on the sunny Bucharest boulevard to the nightmarish sensation of suddenly realizing that I have been had and the situation is beyond repair. I would wake up in cold sweat and it would take me minutes to convince myself that the nightmare was just that. This theme would recur in many variations, the common thread being the chilling transition from a pleasant, relaxed mood somewhere in Bucharest to the sudden realization that I had again become a prisoner and all escape routes were blocked.

■ ■ ■

When the plane took off on that sunny late afternoon of July 26, 1966, all four of us looked back at the waning landscape of Bucharest. As far as I was concerned, I was saying a most happy farewell: I felt few regrets and had the uplifting feeling of being on my way to freedom. It was already dark when we saw the lights of Trieste through the windows of the plane. Their brightness made a stark contrast to the pallid illumination of Bucharest and other Romanian cities at night. As the plane crossed the Adriatic and then the Italian peninsula, my thoughts were focused on the immediate problems facing us upon landing in Naples. The more distant future was veiled by a thick curtain. Could I have lifted a corner of that curtain, I might have seen myself conquering the peaks of my profession over the next three decades. Or I might have seen Edith embark upon a daring new path, turning her one-time hobby into her new profession and becoming a famous art historian. Or I might have seen Anna as a psychoanalyst and Vera as a physics and math teacher, both happy mothers. Finally, I might have seen the arrival in the early to mid-eighties of our Three Musketeers, as I like to call our three grandsons. All of this was in the cards, but I could foresee none of it at the time.

Shortly after midnight, our plane landed on Italian soil, and we were led to an airline terminal in Naples. I felt great. As I learned later, the rest of my family had mixed emotions, but they felt the contagion of my enthusiasm and did not resist it too much. On this early morning of July 27, 1966, I felt as though I had wings and was ready to fly, to organize our new life.

Epilogue

On a summer evening in 1996, thirty years after our memorable exit from the communist paradise, I was reflecting on my career. For the last three decades I had been living the happy, creative life of a successful scientist. Every new result had been a thrill. I had spent my days, and a good part of my nights, mostly doing what I like: investigating—and often solving—problems that intrigued me, working with talented students, teaching subjects that I like. I was enjoying the respect of my colleagues, publishing at a high rate, presenting invited papers at international conferences all over the world, and serving on the editorial boards of eight or nine professional journals. I had just been named the Thomas Lord Professor of Operations Research, an honor bestowed upon me by Carnegie Mellon, in addition to the university professorship that I had been given a few years earlier. During the previous year I had been awarded the John von Neumann Theory Prize, the highest honor of my profession.

Thus, on the thirtieth anniversary of our emigration from Romania I had every reason to be satisfied and to look back with pride on the accomplishments of those three decades. However, there was a question on my mind to which I had no answer. How was all this connected to my earlier life? The span of my life seemed to be clearly divided into two distinct parts, the only link between them provided by the person of the protagonist. To use a mathematical metaphor, the space of my life was not only split into two subspaces, but the two seemed to be orthogonal. The preoccupations, pursuits, events, joys, and sorrows of my current life seemed to be radically different from those of the days before the exodus. To be more precise, there was a bridge: the years between 1959, when I embarked upon retraining myself as a mathematical programmer, and my emigration in 1966, can be viewed as a prelude to what followed afterwards. But apart from this period of transition, the past seemed to be completely absent from my new life. Occasionally I would tell stories to friends about this or that episode from my earlier life—I liked doing this mostly with young people, as if I felt that I had something useful to convey to them from my past—but that was all. Otherwise the past might never had taken place, or so it seemed. Did it have to be like that? Were the first decades of my life irrevocably wasted, lost forever? On the thirtieth anniversary of our emigration, a chain of thoughts started in my mind that soon led to the decision to write this book. There must be a way, I felt, to salvage that experience from oblivion, to make it widely known, so that people could understand the motivations and lives of individuals in my category, and maybe learn something from them. Also, there seemed to be some merit to the point of view that a person who has been through the things that I have should bear witness. And so I started writing.

■　■　■

What follows is a brief outline of what happened in my life after my family and I left Romania. In the summer of 1966, when I finally managed to leave behind the Iron Curtain with my family, I crossed a watershed in every sense of the word. Fate started treating me in a radically different way: before, I had had to fight bitterly and conquer a thousand obstacles for everything that I accomplished; once in the free world everything seemed to go my way and whatever I wished seemed within reach. Soon after our arrival in Italy, a sequence of lucky things happened to us. I got an ideal job for the time we had to wait for an entry visa to the United States: a research fellowship at the International Computing Center in Rome (whose director was Claude Berge). We were able to get Anna and Vera accepted as students at the American School in Rome, with fellowships that covered tuition for both of them. Moreover, I managed to enroll in a doctoral program at the University of Brussels and one at the University of Paris, which subsequently led to my earning doctoral degrees in economics and mathematics. The only difficulty I encountered was that, in view of my communist past, I had to undergo a more thorough scrutiny for the U.S. immigration visa than most other applicants, and so the procedure of approval took eight months instead of the usual three or four. Everything else went smoothly.

While still in Italy, I got job offers for visiting positions from Stanford University and the Carnegie Institute of Technology, two leading centers in my profession. After a short stint at the University of Toronto, in the spring of 1967 we got our immigration visas to the United States and moved to Stanford. There I spent five exciting months with George Dantzig's group, considered at the time the strongest operations research department in the world. I was thrilled by the experience and learned a great deal. I slept little, worked hard, and did everything I could to fill the gaping holes in my mathematical education as fast as I could.

In the fall of 1967 we moved to Pittsburgh and I joined the Graduate School of Industrial Administration (better known as GSIA) of the Carnegie Institute of Technology, which had just merged with the Mellon Institute to become Carnegie Mellon University. This school turned out to be ideally suited to my professional needs and goals. In the fifties it had been the scene of the first industrial applications of operations research. It was a place where research unfettered by disciplinary boundaries was strongly encouraged; where unconventional approaches, if they showed promise, were enthusiastically supported. A light teaching load allowed me to spend the bulk of my time on research. The professional latitude that I enjoyed was part of the general atmosphere of freedom that struck me as the dominant feature of my new life. On my first visit to GSIA (whose faculty had of course been informed of my background) one of my new colleagues gave me a brochure listing my rights in case of arrest: It said that I did not have to answer any question before speaking to my lawyer. I imagined myself telling my interrogator at the Malmezon that before answering his questions, I wanted to see my lawyer; he would certainly not have believed his ears.

Professionally, my first seven or eight years at GSIA were probably the most fruitful period of my life. In the late sixties and early seventies, I became well known in the area of integer programming. Besides being asked to give talks and seminars, I was also hired by companies like Control Data and others to give one-day seminars on integer programming in the major capitals of the world. On the other hand, although my additive algorithm was highly popular—years later it was identified as the most frequently cited article of the journal *Operations Research* between 1954 and 1982—I felt an urge to dig deeper into the structure of the problem I was studying. Thus, during the period from 1969 to 1974 I developed a new approach based on a branch of mathematics called convex analysis, which led to what became known as disjunctive programming. My approach was not immediately embraced by the research community. In fact, my most important paper on the subject was not published at the time, because I refused to rewrite it according to the taste of a referee. But when sixteen years later two colleagues and I resumed the same approach from a different perspective under the name of lift and project, and implemented it into an efficient computer code, it got wide recognition as one of the most fruitful ways of dealing with the problem. As a result, my unpublished 1974 paper was published twenty-five years later as an invited paper, with a foreword by two distinguished colleagues discussing its significance for the profession.

Back in 1976, when the United States was struggling with the consequences of the Arab oil embargo, I volunteered to spend a semester with the Federal Energy Administration (FEA) in Washington as a visiting scientist "on loan" from Carnegie Mellon. The U.S. Congress had just legislated the setting up of a strategic petroleum reserve (SPR) to avoid future crises of the type that we were going through, and the FEA was trying to determine the optimum size of the SPR. I was asked for my input. I found that all of the studies meant to answer that question shared a basic assumption that I disagreed with: they took as a given some probability of a future embargo, and tried to minimize the cost of such an event to the nation. I was of the opinion that the probability of a future embargo should not be taken as given, i.e., assumed to be independent of the existence and size of the SPR. On the contrary, one of the missions of the SPR had to be deterrence: to send a clear message to any potential embargoer that the United States was not vulnerable to that weapon. So I set up a game theoretic model in which the event of a future embargo was not a given, but was one of the strategies available to a potential adversary or coalition of adversaries capable of wielding that threat, whereas the SPRs of varying sizes were part of the strategies available to the United States. I also implemented a solution method for the resulting bimatrix game and was thus able to come up with specific recommendations concerning the desirable reserve size. My study helped tip the balance in the debate in favor of a larger reserve size than had

Egon in 1985

been contemplated, and a memo summarizing it was entered in the *Congressional Record*.

After 1976 I continued my research on various aspects of integer and combinatorial optimization, focusing on efficient solution methods for problems with practical applications, but also on theoretical efforts to better understand the structures we were dealing with. In 1980 I was given a Senior U.S. Scientist Award of the Humboldt Foundation, which took me for a year to the University of Cologne in Germany. It was during my tenure there that a Canadian colleague and I developed the approach that became known as extended formulation and projection. Later, throughout the decade starting at the end of the eighties, I worked with an Italian colleague on the theory of optimal ordering of objects known in the profession as the traveling salesman problem, which had become the classical test bed for new ideas and approaches to combinatorial optimization.

Occasionally I would also consult for industry, and sometimes such activities would lead to new scientific discoveries. In the eighties I became interested in scheduling problems of various kinds and developed efficient procedures for several of them. One of these, the result of joint work with a former doctoral student of mine, was a scheduling system for steel rolling mills, introduced in early 1991 at the Cleveland Works of LTV Steel and still in daily use seven years later.

I have published about 180 papers in technical journals. Roughly half of these papers have joint authorship, with about fifty distinct coauthors, half of them former students of mine. My coauthors are from the United States, Canada, Britain, Germany, Switzerland, Italy, Holland, Denmark, Sweden, Hungary, Romania, Czechslovakia, Greece, China, Taiwan, Australia, Argentina, and Peru.

Apart from my research, I was also steadily involved in teaching. Over the years, I taught a variety of courses, mostly at the doctoral level, but also in the master's and occasionally in the undergraduate program. I enjoy teaching and interacting with students. A few years ago I took the initiative of starting an interdisciplinary doctoral program in algorithms, combinatorics, and optimization (ACO), offered jointly by GSIA and the mathematics and computer science departments. This program filled an essential need and stirred a highly enthusiastic response. While the ACO program was the first of its kind worldwide, it is no longer unique: In the mid-nineties two similar programs were started, one in the US and one in Germany.

■　■　■

And now a few words about my family.

Edith had a remarkable professional career in America. Soon after we moved to Pittsburgh, she decided to use the opportunities offered by our new environment to change her profession and to pursue what had been her lifetime hobby: she became an art historian, with a Ph.D. from the

Edith, Egon, and Anna in 1998

University of Pittsburgh. True, our good luck did not extend over all aspects of life: in the spring of 1972 Edith developed breast cancer. Soon she had a recurrence; at that point the outlook was pretty gloomy and the odds were strongly against us. But the disease was successfully treated, and in spite of a few subsequent episodes, Edith is leading a happy and highly active professional and private life. In time she became a professor of art history at Carnegie Mellon University and published more than two dozen papers in art journals. She continued to be an active swimmer and tennis player and we traveled the world together. In 1978 she published a book on the sculpture of Brancusi, pointing out and documenting the roots of his art in his Romanian heritage. Later she turned to the study of Renaissance art. Her book of 1995 on Michelangelo and the Medici Chapel offers a new interpretation of that masterpiece on which hundreds of scholars had tried their hands before. A third book deals with the art of Joseph Csaky, a Hungarian-born French sculptor of the early twentieth century.

Edith, Anna, and Vera in 1998

Our daughters also fared well, although not without the kind of personal difficulties that are the standard share of life. Anna went to Brandeis University and the Albert Einstein College of Medicine. After earning her M.D., she specialized in psychiatry and became a psychoanalyst. She lives in New York with her husband, Sherwood Waldron, also a psychoanalyst, and their son, Alex, born in 1986. She has a private practice and also teaches at the Psychoanalytic Institute.

Vera went to a school of visual arts, but quit before finishing. She married Vaios Koutsoyannis, a Greek immigrant. They moved to Florida and had two children, John in 1981 and Robert in 1985. In the early nineties the marriage broke up. Vera went back to school, first to junior college—where she was the valedictorian at her graduation—then to Florida Atlantic University, and became a successful high school teacher of physics and mathematics. She and her two sons are living in Coral Springs, Florida.

Egon with his three grandsons in 1998

■   ■   ■

Finally, returning to the question I asked before: Is there any connection between my life in the free world during the last three decades, which essentially amounts to a sequence of victories interrupted on rare occasions by minor setbacks, and my earlier life in Eastern Europe, with its dizzying sequence of ups and downs, its terrible blows, and its pattern of an obstacle race? Overcoming those obstacles required certain personal traits. Did these same traits play any role in the successes of my later life? Also, did any part of my earlier life experience contribute in any way to the accomplishments of my new life? I can only attempt a tentative and fragmentary answer to these questions.

The above sketch of my research career may have conveyed the wrong impression that the life of a scientist is a sequence of pleasant ventures with happy endings. Nothing could be further from the truth. My life as a researcher was and is characterized by frequent periods of tension:

whenever a new discovery is on the horizon, a tremendous amount of effort and concentration is needed in order to snatch the secret from nature by digging deeper and deeper. One day the new result seems at hand; you just have to write it down. Next day it all seems to have been an illusion; nothing seems to work when you want to put it together. When you finally manage to crystallize your findings into a theorem that you think you have proved, upon going the third or fourth time through the logical steps of your proof you suddenly discover a minor, insignificant-looking crack. But when you set out to repair it, the crack widens into a gaping hole. It turns out that what you thought was true is only true under certain circumstances. Maybe there is something of the same flavor that is true under more general conditions; but it is not what you had originally thought it was. So now you nail down your result for the more limited situation for which it is true, and you go on groping for a more general result that holds beyond those specific circumstances. And so on. . . . This is the flavor of mathematical discovery. It is an uneven process that often becomes hectic, with periods of sleepless or half-sleepless nights. It requires the kind of passionate concentration in the grip of which you forget about everything else for a while. To be successful at it, you must have "fire in your belly." And it certainly helps if your basic inclination is to persist and not give up in the face of difficulties, not to become dejected in case of setbacks, but to try again and again until you manage to find the right way.

How did the events of my earlier life affect my subsequent career? I have, of course, no way of knowing what kind of a man I would have been without those experiences. They certainly toughened me: made me stronger and more resilient, less likely to be deterred by difficulties or discouraged by setbacks. After all, I could always make the comparison between a current unpleasantness, mishap, or defeat, and the terrible events of my past, to make me feel that what was happening now was nothing in comparison with what I had been through before. My past experiences also made me a better judge of people—having had the opportunity to observe human nature under extreme circumstances is an asset hard to match in this respect. They definitely influenced my system of values.

I am known among my peers and students as one who stands up for his convictions and is not easily intimidated. No threat is ever likely to match what I have been through. I am rarely neutral about what is happening around me, and people who are wronged in one way or another know they can count on my active support. When it comes to evaluating people, I try to put their accomplishments in perspective: What obstacles did they have to overcome? In choosing my friends, I put a high price on character, independence of mind, and courage. As the popular saying has it, "A friend in need is a friend indeed," and I sometimes try to imagine how this or that person might behave if I came under attack for some reason (although my two public political executions in the fifties— at the Foreign Ministry and the Institute of Economic Research—are unlikely to ever be repeated).

A word is in order on my political views: How did they evolve in the West? First of all, I never lost my interest in what was happening in the world at large. I like to be well informed and follow world events through the printed press rather than through television. Needless to say, I was a strong opponent of the communist regimes of Eastern Europe—and not only those of Eastern Europe—before they were overthrown, and jubilated when the Soviet empire fell apart. I remain allergic to totalitarianism in any form, whether fascist or communist, and my supreme political value is freedom. I hate injustice and would like to see as much social justice as can be brought about without a threat to basic freedoms. But when it comes to choosing between freedom and equality, my bias is in favor of freedom: I am convinced that equality gained at the cost of freedom ends up being ephemeral and unenjoyable. I also support a strong international role for the United States, which I consider the main guarantor of freedom in the world at large. I sometimes find our leaders naïve in matters of international politics, and I have the feeling that they do not always know how to distinguish friend from foe, what is good from what is bad for the country and the world. But then, I am not a politician, just a mathematician.

Index